The Third Republic in France
1870–1940

This book is an essential introduction to the major political problems, debates and conflicts which are central to the history of the Third Republic in France, from the Franco-Prussian War of 1870–1 to the fall of France in June 1940.

Illuminating the contemporary issues of the day through a wealth of primary sources including memoir literature, personal correspondence, parliamentary debates, public speeches, contemporary newspapers, and government documents, *The Third Republic in France 1870–1940* provides an engrossing first-hand account of life in this defining period of French history.

This book provides original sources, detailed commentary and helpful chronologies and bibliographies on:

- the emergence of the regime and the Paris Commune of 1871
- Franco-German relations
- the character of the Third Republic and the nature of French Republicanism and Socialism
- Church–state relations
- anti-Semitism and the Dreyfus Affair
- the role of women and the importance of the national birth rate
- the character of the French Right and of French fascism

William Fortescue is Senior Lecturer in History at the University of Kent.

ROUTLEDGE SOURCES IN HISTORY
Series Editor
David Welch, University of Kent

OTHER TITLES IN THE SERIES
The Suez Crisis
Anthony Gorst and Lewis Johnman

Hitler
Martyn Housden

Resistance and Conformity in the Third Reich
Martyn Housden

The Fascist Experience in Italy
John Pollard

The Russian Revolution 1917–1921
Ronald Kowalski

The Rise and Fall of the Soviet Union
Richard Sakwa

FORTHCOMING
The German Experience
Anthony McElligott

The Stalin Era
Philip Boobbyer

The Third Republic in France 1870–1940

Conflicts and Continuities

William Fortescue

London and New York

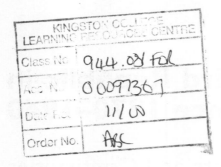

First published 2000
by Routledge
11 New Fetter Lane, London EC4P 4EE

Simultaneously published in the USA and Canada
by Routledge
29 West 35th Street, New York, NY 10001

Routledge is an imprint of the Taylor & Francis Group

Typeset in Galliard and Gill by Keystroke, Jacaranda Lodge, Wolverhampton
Printed and bound in Great Britain by MPG Books Ltd, Bodmin, Cornwall

British Library Cataloguing in Publication Data
A catalogue record for this book is available from the British Library

Library of Congress Cataloging in Publication Data
Fortescue, William, 1945–
    The Third Republic in France, 1870–1940 : conflicts and continuities / William Fortescue.
      p.   cm. — (Routledge sources in history)
    Includes bibliographical references and index.
    1. France—History—Third Republic, 1870–1940. 2. France—Politics and
government—1870–1940. I. Title: 3rd Republic in France. II. Series.
DC340.F64 2000
944.081—dc21   00–024849

ISBN 0–415–16944–5 (hbk)
ISBN 0–415–16945–3 (pbk)

Contents

Series editor's preface

Sources in History is a new series responding to the continued shift of emphasis in the teaching of history in schools and universities towards the use of primary sources and the testing of historical skills. By using documentary evidence, the series is intended to reflect the skills historians have to master when challenged by problems of evidence, interpretation and presentation.

A distinctive feature of *Sources in History* will be the manner in which the content, style and significance of documents is analysed. The commentary and the sources are not discrete, but rather merge to become part of a continuous and integrated narrative. After reading each volume a student should be well versed in the historiographical problems which sources present. In short, the series aims to provide texts which will allow students to achieve facility in 'thinking historically' and place them in a stronger position to test their historical skills. Wherever possible the intention has been to retain the integrity of a document and not simply to present a 'gobbet', which can be misleading. Documentary evidence thus forces the student to confront a series of questions with which professional historians also have to grapple. Such questions can be summarized as follows:

1 *What* type of source is the document?
- Is it a written source or an oral or visual source?
- What, in your estimation, is its importance?
- Did it, for example, have an effect on events or the decision-making process?
2 *Who* wrote the document?
- A person, a group, or a government?
- If it was a person, what was their position?
- What basic attitudes might have affected the nature of the information and language used?
3 *When* was the document written?
- The date, and even the time, might be significant.
- You may need to understand when the document was written in order to understand its context.
- Are there any special problems in understanding the document as contemporaries would have understood it?
4 *Why* was the document written?
- For what purpose(s) did the document come into existence, and for *whom* was it intended?

- Was the document 'author-initiated' or was it commissioned for somebody? If the document was ordered by someone, the author could possibly have 'tailored' his piece.
5 *What* was written?
- This is the obvious question, but never be afraid to state the obvious.
- Remember, it may prove more revealing to ask the question: what was *not* written?
- That is, read between the lines. In order to do this you will need to ask what other references (to persons, events, other documents, etc.) need to be explained before the document can be fully understood.

Sources in History is intended to reflect the individual voice of the volume author(s) with the aim of bringing the central themes of specific topics into sharper focus. Each volume will consist of an authoritative introduction to the topic and chapters will discuss the historical significance of the sources. Authors will also provide an annotated bibliography and suggestions for further reading. These books will become contributions to the historical debate in their own right.

In *The Third Republic in France, 1870–1940: Conflicts and Continuities*, William Fortescue has produced an introduction to the history of the Third Republic from the German invasion of 1870 to the German invasion of 1940. Set within a chronological framework, Dr Fortescue's emphasis on major political and social themes provides a revealing overview of French history during a period of troubled national identity. This work also offers trenchant insights into the historiographical debates on numerous aspects of the Third Republic. Dr Fortescue's penetrating analysis of a rich variety of sources (including many translated into English for the first time) presents a cogent exposition of events and developments and of contemporary attitudes and mentalities. He reveals a society divided by conflict over a range of key issues, conflicts which often continued throughout (and beyond) the life of the Third Republic. This study will be widely welcomed by students and teachers of French and European history.

Preface

The aim of this book is to introduce readers, through texts from primary sources and accompanying commentaries, to eight topics that are central to the history of the Third Republic in France. Each section covering a topic is designed to be self-contained, with its individual chronology and bibliography, so that it can be used as the reading for a seminar or an essay. The book does not attempt to provide a comprehensive treatment of the history of the Third Republic – there is little, for instance, on economic or cultural history or on the French peasantry. Instead, the focus is on the major political problems, debates and conflicts, particularly those related to Franco-German relations, the defence of France against Germany, the character of the French Republic and of French Republicanism, Church–state relations, the role of the French army, anti-Semitism, Anglo-French relations, the role of women and the importance of the national birth rate, and the character of the French Right and of French fascism. The Third Republic was not just a regime; it formed a distinct period in French history. Apart from a brief experiment during the Second Republic (1848–50), it was the first parliamentary regime in France based on manhood suffrage. It was also a regime characterized by continuing political conflicts, which contribute much to the regime's lasting fascination and to its enduring significance.

Acknowledgements

I would like to thank Professor David Welch for commissioning this book, Mr David Ward for his encouragement at an early stage of my academic career, Mr Antony Copley for his loyal support, Trish Hatton for her unfailingly cheerful and helpful assistance with my computer, Dr Julian Jackson for allowing me to use his flat in Paris, Dr Graham Thomas for advice on sources and for the loan of books, and my wife Clare for her continuing efforts to improve my literary style.
Unless otherwise indicated, translations are my own.

The emergence of the Third Republic, 1870–1

The Third Republic in France emerged in the most unfavourable circumstances – military defeat, revolution, further military defeats, civil war and a humiliating peace treaty. These circumstances profoundly influenced nearly all aspects of French life, particularly during the first decades of the Third Republic.

During the 1860s the diplomatic situation in Europe was transformed by the rise of Prussia under Otto von Bismarck and the policies that he successfully pursued to create a united Germany. After military victories against Denmark (1864) and Austria (1866), Bismarck had in 1866 formed the North German Confederation, dominated by a greatly extended Prussia, but excluding the South German States. Bismarck then decided to persuade the South German States to join a united Germany by provoking a confrontation with France. His first attempt, the Luxembourg Affair (1867), failed, but his second, the Hohenzollern candidacy to the Spanish throne, succeeded. After the Spanish throne had become vacant in September 1868, Bismarck pressed the candidacy of Prince Leopold of Hohenzollern-Sigmaringen (a junior member of the Prussian royal family) and, on 2 July 1870, several Parisian newspapers reported that the Spanish crown had been offered to a Hohenzollern prince. Napoleon III and his government reacted to this news in a belligerent manner for several reasons.

Throughout the 1860s the Second Empire had been losing popularity, particularly among the French urban working class. In response, a series of liberal reforms had been introduced, but these had done more to help the opposition than to win popular support for the imperial regime. In a national plebiscite held in May 1870 a significant majority voted in favour of accepting a new constitution, but this probably indicated support for liberal reform rather than for Napoleon III, and in any case it made the regime more susceptible to public opinion.

Foreign policy reverses had also contributed to Napoleon III's unpopularity. French military intervention in Italy (1859) had alienated Catholics because it led to the absorption of the Papal States into a new Kingdom of Italy, while republicans considered that Napoleon III had betrayed the cause of the Risorgimento by not fighting on until Venetia had been liberated from Austrian rule and by maintaining a French garrison in Rome to defend what remained of the Papal States. During the 1860s, while the balance of power in Europe was increasingly threatened by the aggrandizement of Prussia and the prospect of a united Germany, Napoleon III in various ways alienated the other main European powers and wasted French resources on a costly and disastrous military intervention in Mexico (1861–7).

Faced with these weaknesses and failures, the Emperor, along with the Duc de Gramont (the Foreign Minister) and Emile Ollivier (the Prime Minister), decided to restore his fortunes by threatening the use of force unless the Hohenzollern candidacy was withdrawn. Initially, this policy succeeded: as a result of pressure from the French government on King William of Prussia, the Hohenzollern candidature was withdrawn on 12 July 1870. However, Gramont instructed Benedetti, the French ambassador in Berlin, to extract from William, as King of Prussia, an assurance that the candidacy would never again be authorized. In response, William refused to make what he regarded as a humiliating and unnecessary declaration, and from Bad Ems informed Bismarck of his decision. The famous Ems Telegram (13 July 1870) was not edited but completely redrafted by Bismarck so as to give the misleading impression that Bismarck had dismissed the French ambassador. In order to influence public opinion, Bismarck's version was communicated to the press (Carr, 1991, pp. 196–8).

Egged on by an outburst of chauvinism in Paris, by the bellicose enthusiasm of the Empress Eugénie (who was Spanish by origin), by unfounded confidence in the French army, and by equally unfounded hopes of support from Italy and Austria-Hungary, the French government decided to declare war on 15 July (although Bismarck did not formally receive the French declaration of war until 19 July). Hopelessly unprepared for the magnitude of the task confronting it, the French army lost a series of engagements at Wissembourg (4 August), Forbach and Froeschwiller (6 August). Marshal MacMahon, the senior French commander, decided to concentrate most of his forces, known as the Army of Châlons, in and around the small town of Sedan, where almost immediately on 31 August they were encircled by superior German forces. Outnumbered, lacking adequate supplies of ammunition and food, burdened with large numbers of wounded, and almost entirely within range of German artillery fire, the French position was hopeless. After a day's fighting, Napoleon III, who had unwisely left Saint Cloud to join his army on 28 July, decided to surrender.

Document 1.1 The French Defeat at Sedan (1 September 1870)

The interior of Sedan and the approaches to the town were in an indescribable state: the gates of the town were obstructed with carts, waggons, cannon and all the 'impedimenta' and débris of a routed army. Bands of soldiers, without rifles or equipment, constantly rushed forward, throwing themselves into the town. At the drawbridges the congestion was terrible, with some unfortunate soldiers being crushed to death. Cavalrymen were dragged by their horses through the crowd with their stomachs on the ground. Ammunition carts passed by at the gallop, cutting a path through the panic-stricken masses. The few soldiers who had retained some reserve of energy seemed to use it only to accuse and to curse: 'We have been betrayed!', they cried: 'We have been sold out by traitors and cowards!'

Source: E.F. de Wimpffen, La Bataille de Sedan. *Paris: A. Le Chevalier. 1872, p. 57*

General de Wimpffen had been recalled from Algeria, where he had been serving as governor of Oran, to replace the general commanding the French troops defeated at Froeschwiller. He joined the Army of Châlons on 30 August with instructions from the Minister of War in Paris to take command if Marshal MacMahon should be incapacitated. Around six in the morning of 1 September MacMahon was severely wounded, but he passed his command to General Ducrot, and it was not until approximately four hours later that Wimpffen was confirmed in his command. He tried to organize break-outs without success, and then offered his resignation to Napoleon III. The Emperor declined it and instead insisted that Wimpffen should negotiate the surrender of the army to the Germans.

In the passage quoted, Wimpffen was obviously anxious to confirm that the situation at Sedan was hopeless. He was also anxious to attribute blame for the disaster, and he pointed the finger at Napoleon III as 'le grand coupable' (Wimpffen, 1872, p. 44). As active head of the regime, as ultimately responsible for the French declaration of war and as an interfering presence on the battlefield at Sedan, Napoleon III must bear a heavy responsibility for the catastrophe. However, the Franco-Prussian War also revealed major deficiencies in the French army.

The art of warfare had recently been revolutionized by the development of breech-loading rifles and artillery and by the possibilities provided by railways for the rapid concentration and supply of mass armies. Prussia had already demonstrated this in the war against Austria of 1866. The French army had benefited from reforms and improvements: a law of January 1868 introduced a five-year term of military service, followed by a further five years in the reserve; plans were drawn up for a new militia (garde mobile), but were not implemented outside the Paris region for political and financial reasons; and new weapons were brought into service, the chassepot (a breech-loading rifle) and the mitrailleuse (an early form of machine-gun). However, the French had not mastered the military use of railways and their mobilization was a shambles; the standard of education and training of most officers and men was well below that of their German counterparts; the German artillery and supply services were better than those of the French; and, unlike the Prussians, the French had no general staff to keep commanders in the field supplied with a regular flow of information and advice. The failure at Sedan was not just that of an army, but of a whole system.

Document 1.2 The French Surrender at Sedan (2 September 1870)

General de Wimpffen began by presenting to General von Moltke the Emperor's letter which empowered him to negotiate the terms of the surrender. General Moltke spoke first and, while acknowledging the bravery with which the French army had fought during the day, he stated that, since the war threatened to continue, the King of Prussia had considered it necessary to reduce as much as possible the forces with which France could oppose him. Consequently, he insisted as a condition for the surrender that the French troops should hand over their arms, and that the entire army should become prisoners of war, with only the officers being allowed to retain their swords, horses and personal possessions. General de Wimpffen observed that these terms seemed very severe, that they would humiliate the army and France, and that, instead of leading towards the peace treaty which everyone wanted signed as soon as possible, they could result only in prolonging the war and in pushing France towards more obstinate resistance. He requested that the French army should be allowed to leave Sedan with its weapons and equipment, and that the officers, non-commissioned officers and soldiers should be free to return to France while promising on their word of honour not to bear arms against Germany again as long as the war lasted.

Count von Bismarck then intervened. He said that the King of Prussia had too much esteem for the French nation to think of humiliating the French army; that there was nothing humiliating in the terms presented; that French ill-will towards Germany had been known for a long time and that it had erupted in the present circumstances in the most unfortunate manner for his country; that Germany had been provoked in this war; that it had unsuccessfully attempted to avoid the war by making all the concessions consistent with the maintenance of its dignity; that for two centuries the aggressive character of the French had disturbed the peace of Europe; that Germany had to protect herself against similar aggression in the future; that, in order to sustain the current war, Germany had had to shoulder the heaviest sacrifices, which it would be impossible for Germany to repeat often, and that, consequently, it was necessary for Germany to acquire material guarantees for peace in the future; that these guarantees would be found by making it impossible for France to start the war again easily; that he did not doubt that all the officers would faithfully observe any engagement which they might make, but that he could not have the same confidence in the word of non-commissioned officers and soldiers; that once they had returned home, their promises would be circumvented; that it would be said that they had been disposed of without their consent; that they were not obliged to keep a promise which they had not given, which they certainly would not have given, etc.; and that even if the French government had the scruples not to reintegrate them in the army, they could not remain inactive in the midst of a movement of national defence, and that they would form an excellent nucleus or at least instructors for the organization of the military forces of the country.

General de Wimpffen replied. He said that he had the highest opinion of the French soldier's respect for an engagement taken either by himself, or on his behalf by his commanders; that no nation was more appreciative than the French of noble sentiments and distinguished conduct; that Prussia, in showing herself to be generous in the present situation where it was the stronger, would do more for the maintenance of peace in the future, for the appeasing of old grudges and the establishment of a genuine regard for two neighbours which were made to respect each other, than in being excessively preoccupied in searching for material guarantees. He then based his argument on the past, maintaining that France had always treated Prussia generously, and that France had a right to expect a certain reciprocity of goodwill.

Source: 'Sedan et Wilhelmshöhe', La Revue de Paris, 15 October 1929, pp. 857–9

This is a record made of the exchanges between General de Wimpffen (the French army commander), General von Moltke (the German army commander) and Count von Bismarck (Chancellor of the North German Confederation) when they first met late in the evening of 1 September 1870 to begin negotiations for a French surrender. One of the French negotiators, General de Castelnau, recorded what was said.

The exchanges are interesting for what they reveal about French and German attitudes at this crucial moment and, in particular, about Bismarck's intentions towards France. The German terms of surrender were no less severe than might reasonably have been expected, and, indeed, for Napoleon III (honourable confinement in the German palace of Wilhelmshöhe for six and a half months) and for French officers (allowed to retain their personal weapons, horses and possessions), they were arguably quite generous. In contrast, the French proposal, that the French forces in Sedan should be allowed to leave with their weapons and equipment and just a promise not to rejoin the war against Germany, was quite unrealistic and unacceptable. As Moltke pointed out, the conditions of surrender had been set by the King of Prussia, not by Bismarck or himself, and the French were not in a position to bargain – 82,000 exhausted, demoralized and ill-equipped French troops were trapped in Sedan by a formidable German army approximately 230,000 strong. In arguing that generous treatment of defeated France by Germany was the best long-term basis for peaceful and cordial relations between the two countries, Wimpffen was on firmer ground. However, as this text illustrates, Bismarck regarded France as an inherently aggressive power from which Germany would need protection in the future. Hence his insistence on material guarantees, which would soon be translated into demands for territorial concessions.

Sedan was a watershed. It represented a colossal military defeat for France. For the loss of 9,000 officers and men, the Germans captured 104,000 French soldiers, 419 cannon and all the equipment of an army after just one day's serious fighting (Howard, 1968, pp. 222–3). This confirmed Germany as the dominant military power in Europe. With the German capture of Napoleon III, Sedan also meant the end of the Second Empire. However, Napoleon III surrendered on behalf of himself and his army, not of France, so the Franco-Prussian War continued.

Document 1.3 The Proclamation of the Third Republic (4 September 1870)

Leaving the Chamber [the Legislative Body, the lower house of the French parliament], we went at once to the Hôtel de Ville. The number of people assembled there was enormous, and we found the same fraternization existing between them and the National Guard as elsewhere. The building had been invaded by the people, and all the windows fronting on the square were filled with rough and dirty-looking men and boys. Soon we heard a terrific shout go up. Rochefort was being pulled in a cab through the crowd by a multitude. He was ghastly pale; he stood up in the vehicle, covered with sashes of red, white and blue, waving his hat in answer to the acclamations. As he was slowly hauled through the crowd to the main door of the Hôtel de Ville, the delirium seemed to have reached its height, and it is impossible to describe the frantic acclamations which were heard. At precisely four o'clock and forty-five minutes in the afternoon, as I marked it by the great clock in the tower of the Hôtel de Ville, at one of the windows appeared Gambetta; a little behind him stood Jules Favre and Emmanuel Arago; and then and there, on that historic spot, I heard Gambetta proclaim the Republic of France. That proclamation was received with every possible demonstration of enthusiasm. Lists were thrown out of the window, containing the names of the members of the provisional government. Ten minutes afterwards, Raspail and Rochefort appeared at another window and embraced each other, while the crowd loudly applauded them.

During this time the public were occupying the Tuileries, from which the Empress had just escaped. Sixty thousand human beings had rolled toward the palace, completely levelling all obstacles; the vestibule was invaded, and in the court-yard, on the other side of the Place du Carrousel, were to be seen soldiers of every arm, who, in the presence of the people, removed the cartridges from their guns, and who were greeted by the cries, 'Long live the nation!' 'Down with the Bonapartes!' 'To Berlin!' etc. During all of this time there was no pillage, no havoc, no destruction of property, and the crowd soon retired, leaving the palace under the protection of the National Guard.

Source: E.B.Washburne, Recollections of a Minister to France, 1869–1877. *New York: Charles Scribner's Sons. 1887, I, pp. 107–9*

The news of the surrender at Sedan reached Paris during the night of 3–4 September 1870. Large crowds began to gather, particularly around the Palais Bourbon where the Legislative Body met. During the morning of 4 September Adolphe Thiers, an opposition Paris deputy, proposed that the Legislative Body should declare the throne vacant, dismiss the existing government, form a new government commission, attempt to secure an armistice from the Germans, and convoke a new national parliament. However, a crowd invasion of the Palais Bourbon suspended parliamentary debates, whereupon a group of republican deputies headed by Jules Favre and Jules Simon led the crowd to the Hôtel de Ville (the Paris town hall), where in the afternoon of Sunday, 4 September the Third Republic was proclaimed. At the same time, a crowd invaded the Tuileries Palace, compelling the Empress Eugénie (Napoleon III's wife, who was acting as regent) to flee to England.

Washburne was the American Minister at Paris, representing both a republic and an administration which had recently won a civil war. With an American friend, he personally and favourably observed the events he described. The huge size of the crowds was an indication of the unpopularity of the Second Empire among most Parisians, which the results of the general parliamentary election of May 1869 had already demonstrated. This hostile attitude to the Empire was shared by most members of the Paris National Guard, a part-time civilian militia responsible for maintaining order in Paris. This helps to explain why the 'revolution' of 4 September was achieved with virtually no violence to life or property.

After the demise of the Second Republic (1848–52), republicanism had gradually re-emerged in France from the late 1850s, and by 1870 approximately thirty republicans sat in the Legislative Body, representing Paris and other large cities. This group of republican deputies, particularly those representing Paris, seized the initiative in proclaiming the Third Republic.

The republican deputies, though, were divided: some belonged to the 1848 generation (Emmanuel Arago, Jules Favre, François Raspail), while Léon Gambetta and Henri Rochefort (just released from prison by the crowd, hence his pallor) were younger and, together with Raspail, more radical. In the Government of National Defence, which was formed late in the afternoon of 4 September, Gambetta became Minister of the Interior, but moderate republicans predominated – Jules Favre (Foreign Affairs), Adolphe Crémieux (Justice), Ernest Picard (Finance) and Jules Simon (Education and Religion) – and another moderate republican, Etienne Arago, was appointed mayor of Paris.

Document 1.4 Gambetta and National Defence

PROCLAMATION TO THE ARMY

Tours, 9 October 1870

Soldiers,

I have left Paris to be your Minister of War. In the circumstances in which we find ourselves, I have decided to abandon usual procedures. I want to give you army commanders who are young, active, capable, intelligent and vigorous, so as to repeat the prodigious achievements of 1792. To achieve this, I unhesitatingly break with customary administrative traditions.

On your part, soldiers, I have an imperious duty to demand of you. There is no need to ask the sons of France to be courageous and determined; but if you are the bravest soldiers in the world, you must also be the most disciplined! This is the price of victory! It is therefore for the salvation of everybody that I order corps commanders to punish with the utmost rigour all infractions of regulations. You will know, I am sure, how to spare the councils of war their painful duties.

Soldiers, national guardsmen, irregular forces, and all of you who have taken up arms for the honour of France, forget the diversity of your origins and the differences in your status which tend to undermine your solidarity. You belong to one and the same army, the army of France, and you will march in step towards victory together!

Firmly banish the weaknesses which have been able, at certain moments, to affect your spirits, and loudly repeat that, defended by your heroism, the Republic is invincible!

Member of the Government of National Defence and Minister of War, Léon Gambetta

Source: J. Reinach (ed.), Dépêches, circulaires, décrets, proclamations et discours de Léon Gambetta. *Paris: G. Charpentier. 1886 and 1891, I, pp. 45–6*

After Sedan, German forces advanced on Paris, encountering little resistance, and by 20 September they had encircled the French capital. Meanwhile, on 18 September Jules Favre had met Bismarck in the hope of securing at least an armistice, if not a peace treaty, only to discover the material guarantees on which Bismarck was now insisting – the surrender of several fortresses in return for an armistice and the surrender of the provinces of Alsace and German Lorraine in return for peace. Instead of attempting to negotiate, Favre rejected these terms outright, so the siege of Paris began. The Government of National Defence now found itself trapped in Paris with the tasks of defending the capital, maintaining its authority and directing the war effort in the provinces.

The son of an immigrant from Genoa, Léon Gambetta had become a radical lawyer and in the general parliamentary elections of May 1869 had been elected in constituencies in both Paris and Marseilles. As Minister of the Interior in the Government of National Defence he quickly emerged as one of the most determined proponents of continuing the war against the Germans. On 7 October he escaped from Paris in a balloon and managed to reach Tours, then the government's provincial headquarters, where he assumed the additional powers of Minister of Defence. Appealing to the precedent of 1792–3, when a vigorous attempt had been made to mobilize the entire human and material resources of the nation for the revolutionary war effort, Gambetta hoped to win the Franco-Prussian War through a movement of popular and national resistance rather than through the exclusive efforts of France's professional army, which had become tainted by its record of incompetence and defeat and by its allegiance to Napoleon III. Such a policy, however, required massive and sustained popular support for the war effort, which was not forthcoming.

Document 1.5 Bazaine and the Capitulation of Metz (27 October 1870)

Ban-Saint-Martin, 7 October 1870

The time approaches when the Army of the Rhine will find itself in a position more difficult perhaps than that which any French army has had to suffer. The serious military and political events, which have occurred far away from us and which have painful consequences for us, have shaken neither our morale nor our courage as an army. But you are not unaware that complications of another order add daily to those which external developments create for us.

Food supplies are beginning to run out, and, within only too short a period, they will be absolutely exhausted. Fodder for our cavalry and draught horses has become a problem, which as every day passes becomes more difficult to solve; once our resources are exhausted, our horses will wither away and die.

In these serious circumstances, I have summoned you to explain the situation and to share with you my feelings. The duty of a commanding officer, in such circumstances, is not to leave the corps commanders placed under his orders in ignorance of anything, but rather to benefit from their opinions and advice.

Source: F.-A. Bazaine, Capitulation de Metz: rapport officiel du maréchal Bazaine. *Lyon: Lapierre-Brille. 1871, pp. 19–20*

A veteran of campaigns in North Africa, the Crimea, Italy and Mexico, Marshal Bazaine was appointed Commander-in-Chief of the Army of the Rhine on 12 August 1870, by which time German armies had successfully invaded France. Aiming for the fortified city of Verdun, Bazaine was checked in the engagements of Rezonville (16 August) and Saint-Privat (18 August), compelling him to withdraw to the less well-fortified city of Metz (19 August), where he was rapidly besieged by German forces. Attempts to effect a break-out were not pursued effectively by Bazaine. The surrender at Sedan ended any hope of the siege being relieved, while the capitulation of Strasbourg (28 September) came as another blow. Cut off from orders and supplies, the Army of the Rhine was soon reduced to eating their own horses. The overthrow of the Empire and the proclamation of the Third Republic further demoralized Bazaine, who considered that he owed his allegiance to Napoleon III.

In these circumstances, on 7 October Bazaine ordered his corps commanders and commanders of special forces to attend a council of war on 10 October. The tone of the letter was defeatist, and the council of war duly concluded that the Army of the Rhine could not last much beyond 20 October. In finally surrendering on 27 October, Bazaine arguably was simply acknowledging the reality of his situation. On the other hand, he surrendered approximately 155,000 men, many of whom had scarcely fought, together with large supplies of ammunition and equipment; and Bazaine never showed much determination to fight.

Document 1.6 Gambetta and the Capitulation at Metz

Tours, 30 October 1870

Metz capitulated on 27 October. For a long time Bazaine was involved in intrigues, as the missions of General Boyer to Bismarck and to the Empress in England testify. Bazaine concluded these intrigues with betrayal. He has given away everything. His capitulation is as shameful as that of Sedan, and the consequences are even more terrible than those of Sedan. All the army are now prisoners of war; all the equipment has been abandoned. This appalling catastrophe has produced in France feelings of rage and exasperation, but also of resolution and energy. The country wants vengeance at any price. The country today feels itself to be liberated from traitors; it wants to go forward. I believe that it will be difficult to keep control of the situation if satisfaction is not given to this patriotic fever.

At this moment our country is sublime with grief and courage.

Source: J. Reinach (ed.), Dépêches, circulaires, décrets, proclamations et discours de Léon Gambetta. *Paris: G. Charpentier. 1886 and 1891, 1886, I, pp. 103–4*

In this letter to Jules Favre, Gambetta expressed what became the conventional wisdom, namely that, in surrendering Metz, Bazaine had betrayed France and was therefore a traitor. A military tribunal confirmed this view in 1873 by finding Bazaine guilty of treason and by sentencing him to death and to the loss of all military ranks and honours (a sentence commuted to twenty years' imprisonment, though Bazaine managed to escape in 1874, to live out the rest of his life in exile until his death in Madrid in 1888).

In contrast, Colonel Denfert-Rochereau, who refused to surrender the fortress-city of Belfort, became one of the few French national heroes of the war of 1870–1. While Bazaine had shown both a reluctance and an inability to fight the enemy effectively, and had, on his own initiative, opened negotiations through General Boyer with Bismarck and the Empress (negotiations which turned out to be fruitless), by the end of October the only alternative to capitulation for himself and his army was mass starvation.

Bazaine, therefore, was arguably a realist rather than a traitor and had the misfortune to become a convenient scapegoat. Gambetta's policy of national resistance may have been heroic and the stuff of myth and legend, but it failed at enormous cost. The provincial armies raised by the Government of National Defence were defeated, destroyed and immobilized; Paris was not relieved and eventually capitulated on 28 January 1871; the mood of provincial France became over-whelmingly anti-war and anti-republican; and the peace terms accepted by France in the Treaty of Frankfurt (10 May 1871) were probably worse than those which could have been achieved in September 1870.

Gambetta may have been wrong, but he was consistent and honest – he resigned from the Government of National Defence on 6 February 1871 in protest at the armistice terms.

Document 1.7 The Peace Terms

I trembled to broach the question of the conditions of peace; however, it must be done.

'Let us come now to the great question,' said I to the Count [Bismarck].

'I have already told you my mind on the matter,' he replied. (At these words I hoped he would not ask much more than in November.) 'I do not wish to jockey you, it would be unbecoming. I might speak of Europe, as they do on your side, and demand in her name that you should give back Savoy and Nice to their rightful owners. I will do nothing of this kind, and will only speak to you of Germany and France. I already asked you for Alsace and certain parts of Lorraine. I will give you back Nancy, though the Minister for War wants to keep it; but we shall keep Metz for our own security. All the rest of French Lorraine will remain yours.'

Count Bismarck looked at me to guess what I was thinking. Mastering my emotion, I answered coldly:

'You had only spoken of the German portion of Lorraine.'

'Certainly, but we must have Metz; we must have it for our own safety.'

'Go on,' I said, waiting to know the whole extent of his exactions before I should answer.

Count Bismarck then opened the question of money.

'When I saw you in November,' he said, 'I mentioned a sum to you. That cannot now be the same figure, for since then we have suffered and spent enormously. I had asked you for four milliards: today we must have six.'

Source: Memoirs of M. Thiers, 1870–1873. *London: Allen & Unwin. 1915, pp. 106–7*

Adolphe Thiers, whose long political career had begun in the 1820s and who, as an opposition Paris deputy, had played a role in the formation of the Government of National Defence on 4 September, was invited by Jules Favre to serve as the government's envoy to London on 9 September. Convinced that the Franco-Prussian War should be ended as soon as possible to avoid further useless suffering and the possibility of revolution, Thiers persuaded the government to authorize him to tour the capitals of Europe so as to secure international support for the negotiation of an immediate armistice. During September and October Thiers visited London, St Petersburg, Vienna and Florence, duly securing the international backing he requested. However, Favre had already discovered at his meeting with Bismarck at Ferrières on 18 September that the price of an armistice would be the cession of Alsace and German Lorraine, terms which Favre had indignantly rejected, refusing to concede 'a stone of our fortresses or an inch of our territory'; and the military situation had continued to deteriorate from France's point of view. Thiers nevertheless had a series of meetings with Bismarck at Versailles between 1 and 4 November 1870. Bismarck repeated his demands and insisted that, if Paris were to be resupplied during an armistice (as the French requested), one of the forts defending Paris would have to be surrendered. This was rejected and the siege continued.

The exhaustion of food supplies in Paris, the collapse of serious provincial resistance, the beginning of a German bombardment on 5 January and the failure of a final *sortie* on 19 January all finally convinced the Government of National Defence that they had to accept an armistice on Bismarck's terms. The armistice, signed on 28 January, provided for national parliamentary elections. Rapidly held on 8 February, these elections produced a National Assembly with an overwhelmingly conservative and pro-peace majority. On 17 February the National Assembly, meeting at Bordeaux, chose Thiers as head of the executive. Having formed his government, Thiers met Bismarck on 21 February to discuss the peace terms. In the exchanges recorded by Thiers, Bismarck repeated his territorial demands and claimed an indemnity of six milliard francs. He also revealed his irritation at references Thiers made to 'Europe', and reminded Thiers that after the Italian campaign of 1859 the French had had no scruples in annexing Nice and Savoy.

Thiers was in no position to bargain, though he managed to retain Belfort in return for a token German military occupation of central Paris (until the National Assembly had ratified the peace preliminaries) and to reduce the indemnity from six to five milliards. The peace terms, known as the Treaty of Frankfurt, were finally signed on 10 May 1871. As early as 1873 the indemnity had been paid off, resulting in the withdrawal of the last German troops from French territory, but the loss of Alsace and much of Lorraine prevented any permanent reconciliation between France and the German Empire formed by Bismarck in 1871.

Document 1.8 The Proclamation of the Paris Commune (28 March 1871)

The proclamation of the Commune was splendid; it was not the celebration of power but the pomp of sacrifice: one felt that those who had been elected were ready for death.

The afternoon of 28 March, in clear sunlight recalling the dawn of 18 March, on 7 Germinal Year 79 [according to the revolutionary calendar of 1793], the people of Paris inaugurated the entry into the Hôtel de Ville of their Commune, which they had elected on 26 March.

A human ocean under arms, bayonets as thick as the ears of corn in a field, brass bands rending the air, the sound of muffled drums, and among it all the unmistakable beat of the two great drums of Montmartre. These were the self-same drums which, the night of the entry of the Prussians [into Paris on 1 March] and the morning of 18 March, had awoken Parisians from their meagre breakfasts, with strange sounds produced by steel drumsticks.

This time the bells were silent. At regular intervals, the deep rumbling of cannon saluted the revolution.

The bayonets were dipped in front of the red flags, which draped the statue of the Republic.

Above the statue there was an immense red flag. The National Guard battalions of Montmartre, Belleville and La Chapelle had their flags surmounted with a Phrygian cap [a traditional revolutionary emblem, symbolizing a freed slave], recalling the sections [Paris administrative districts] of 1793.

There were ranks of soldiers representing all the elements of the army which had remained in Paris, regiments of the line, the marines, the artillery and *zouaves* [colonial troops]. The ever-thickening mass of bayonets spread into neighbouring streets as the square in front of the Hôtel de Ville filled up. It was just like a field of corn. What will be the harvest?

The whole of Paris was there, with the cannon thundering at intervals.

The members of the central committee [of the Paris National Guard] were on a dais, with the members of the Council of the Commune, each wearing a red sash, in front of them.

There were few speeches in the intervals between the artillery salutes. The central committee declared that its mandate had expired and that it was transferring its powers to the Commune.

A roll call of names was held and then a great shout went up: 'Vive la Commune!' The drums sounded a general salute, the artillery shook the ground.

'In the name of the people,' declared Ranvier [Gabriel Ranvier, mayor of Belleville and member of the central committee of the Paris National Guard and of the Council of the Commune], 'the Commune is proclaimed.'

Every aspect was imposing of this inauguration of the Commune, the climax of which was to be death.

No speeches, just one immense shout: 'Vive la Commune!'

All the bands played 'La Marseillaise' and the 'Chant du départ'. A multitude of voices took up the words of the songs.

Source: L. Michel, La Commune. *Paris: P.V. Stock. 1898, pp. 163–4.*

Since 1789, Paris had had a revolutionary tradition, which had resurfaced in 1830 and 1848. The military suppression of a workers' rising in Paris in June 1848, the subsequent repression of the Left, and the military *coup d'état* of December 1851 which led to the authoritarian and imperialistic regime of the Second Empire, all represented severe setbacks for the Left. However, the lack of effective democracy and of civil and trade union rights, the expansion of the urban working class, due partly to Napoleon III's policies of economic modernization, and the rebuilding of Paris to the advantage of the wealthy rather than the poor all helped to produce a resurgence of working-class consciousness and militancy when the regime liberalized during the 1860s, especially in Paris. Hence the spontaneous popular revolutionary movement which swept away the Second Empire and proclaimed the Third Republic in Paris on 4 September. However, apart from Gambetta, the Government of National Defence was composed essentially of middle-class moderate republicans who were unenthusiastic about continuing the war and who wanted to avoid a social revolution.

In opposition, during the siege of Paris a radical popular movement developed demanding a vigorous prosecution of the war, reliance on mass conscription rather than on the regular army and elected Paris municipal councillors and National Guard officers. With the founding of numerous popular clubs and left-wing newspapers, and with the establishment of central committees for both the National Guard and the twenty *arrondissements* (Paris administrative districts), this radical popular movement acquired influence and organization.

However, the Government of National Defence retained power, overcoming attempted radical coups on 31 October and 22 January, refusing to introduce radical measures (even the introduction of bread-rationing was delayed until 18 January), and agreeing to an armistice on 28 January. One of the conditions of the armistice was the holding of elections for a National Assembly. The elections, which took place on 8 February, resulted in a massive right-wing victory, except in Paris and a few other cities. Consequently, a National Assembly with a large conservative majority and a new government headed by Thiers faced a militantly radicalized Paris with a greatly expanded and radicalized National Guard that had not been disarmed. In various ways the National Assembly and the Thiers government, both based in Versailles, alienated the radical popular movement of Paris, the final straw being an attempt to remove cannon parked in the working-class strongholds of Belleville and Montmartre on 18 March. This provoked spontaneous popular resistance and the lynching of two generals, whereupon Thiers ordered all military and civilian personnel of the Versailles government to withdraw from Paris.

The power vacuum thus created was quickly filled by the central committee of the National Guard, which assumed all official responsibilities and organized elections on 26 March for an independent municipal administration or Commune in Paris. The central committee of the National Guard formally handed over its powers to the elected members of this Commune at a ceremony in front of the Hôtel de Ville on 28 March.

Louise Michel, the author of this passage, was the illegitimate daughter of an aristocrat and a servant girl. By the end of the 1860s she had become a teacher in a private school and a left-wing activist in Paris. During the siege she continued with her teaching, joined left-wing clubs, and, dressed as a National Guardsman, took part in the attack on the Hôtel de Ville on 22 January 1871. Under the Commune she combined the activities of teacher, ambulance-worker, left-wing propagandist and National Guard. After the fall of the Commune, she was captured and sentenced to deportation to a French Pacific penal colony in New Caledonia. From her return to France in 1880 until her death in 1904 she was a propagandist for left-wing ideas and became a legend of the Left. Her description of the proclamation of the Commune captures the ceremony's popular militarism, republican symbolism, enormous enthusiasm and impending doom.

Document 1.9 The Paris Commune and Popular Democracy

21 March 1871

Paris, since 18 March, has had no government other than that of the people, which is the best form of government.

Never has a revolution been achieved in a situation comparable to ours.

Paris has become a free city.

The centralization of power no longer exists.

The monarchy died through this admission of impotence.

In this free city, everyone has the right to freedom of speech, without claiming any influence whatsoever on the destinies of France.

However, Paris demands:

1   The election of the mayor of Paris;
2   The election of mayors, assistant mayors and municipal councillors of the twenty *arrondissements* of the city of Paris;
3   The election of all officers of the National Guard, from the most junior to the most senior;
4   Paris has no intention of separating herself from the rest of France, far from it; for France, Paris has endured the Empire, the Government of National Defence, and all their acts of treason and cowardice. The intention now is definitely not to abandon France, but only to say to her, as an elder sister: defend yourselves as I am defending myself; oppose oppression as I am opposing oppression!

The delegated commander at the former Prefecture of Police,
E. Duval

Source: Réimpression du Journal officiel de la République française sous la Commune, *pp. 14–15*

Emile Duval, the proclamation's author, is a representative figure of the Paris radical left at this time. He emerged at the end of the Second Empire as a strike leader among Paris metal-workers and as a member of the Socialist International. After 4 September 1870 he became a colonel in the Paris National Guard and an advocate of vigorous and radical measures. He participated in the occupation of the Paris Hôtel de Ville on 31 October and in the anti-government demonstration of 22 January 1871. The central committee of the National Guard, of which he was a member, appointed him on 18 March to take over the Prefecture of Police. He subsequently became one of the three main military commanders of the Commune and an elected member of the Council of the Commune. An advocate of taking the offensive against Versailles, he was captured while leading a *sortie* and executed (4 April 1871). His proclamation emphasizes his commitment to direct popular democracy and his hope that the Paris Commune would inspire the rest of France.

In fact, the need for an effective and centralized command structure led the Commune to form a Committee of Public Safety at the beginning of May, and, despite short-lived communes in Marseilles and some other French cities, the Paris Commune did not serve as an example or inspiration for the rest of France. Nevertheless, a commitment to decentralized power and to popular democracy was one of the most striking early features of the Commune; and only in 1977 was the demand for an elected mayor of Paris finally realized.

Document 1.10 The Paris Commune and Socialism

The Commune of Paris,

Considering that a number of workshops have been abandoned by those who ran them in order to escape their civic obligations, and without any regard for the interests of the workers;

Considering that as a result of this cowardly desertion, numerous activities essential to civic life have been interrupted and the livelihoods of workers compromised,

DECREES:

The workers' federations are summoned to set up a committee of inquiry which will:

1   Draw up a list of abandoned workshops, as well as a precise description of their condition and of the tools and equipment which they contain;
2   Present a report establishing the practical possibilities of immediately putting these workshops into operation, not by those who have abandoned them, but by co-operative associations of the workers who were formerly employed there;
3   Draft a constitution for these workers' co-operative associations;
4   Appoint an arbitration panel which will determine, on the return of the owners of abandoned workshops, the terms whereby the workshops will be permanently ceded to the workers' co-operative associations and the amount of compensation to be paid by the associations to the former owners.

This committee of inquiry will submit its report to the Commune's trade and industry committee, which will be required to present to the Commune as soon as possible a draft decree satisfying the interests of the Commune and of the workers.

Paris, 16 April 1871

Source: Réimpression du Journal officiel de la République française sous la Commune, *p. 286*

The extent to which the Paris Commune was socialist has been a matter of controversy. In the decree on abandoned workshops of 16 April, the Council of the Commune indicated the limits of its socialism. The decree applied just to abandoned workshops, so the taking of all workshops into public ownership was not envisaged. It was planned that such workshops should be handed over to a co-operative association of the workers who had formerly worked there. It was also envisaged that compensation would be paid to the owners of abandoned workshops. In other words, private property rights were being infringed only to a degree and out of necessity, and co-operative associations of workers, rather then publicly owned and directed units of production, were to be the new economic model. Capitalism as such was not targeted, with even the Bank of France being allowed to retain its gold reserves.

Many strands of the Left were represented in the Commune, but the dominant influences seem to have been patriotism, republicanism, anti-clericalism and a commitment both to the working class and to direct popular democracy, rather than to socialism (however defined). Intellectual influences on the Commune ranged from the anarchism of Auguste Blanqui to the communism of Karl Marx, but such influences are difficult to determine precisely, and even Pierre-Joseph Proudhon, who advocated artisan and peasant co-operatives, may not have been as influential as has been supposed (Fitzpatrick, 1985). Instead, the Commune can more convincingly be seen as a reaction to the authoritarianism, centralization, clericalism and bourgeois domination of the Second Empire, and to the reluctance of the Government of National Defence to prosecute the war in a vigorous and radical manner. Hence the Commune adopted many radical measures in order to defend Paris and to establish a municipal administration with a working-class character which tried to meet the needs of ordinary Parisians. However, the Commune was at its most radical in its attacks on the Roman Catholic Church, not in its attacks on private property.

Document 1.11 Art and the Paris Commune

As standing President of the Federation of Artists, I have been asked by several of them to offer some general suggestions about the future organization of the arts, so that in the general meeting we can proceed immediately to the study of the by-laws and avoid too much confusion. In response to that request I have prepared the following outline, which corresponds to the spirit of the Commune.

As Paris has finally won itself freedom of action and independence, I call upon artists to assume control of the museums and art collections which, though the property of the nation, are primarily theirs, from the intellectual as well as the material point of view.

As I see it, in order to attain that goal, the artists from the twenty-two *arrondissements* of the Seine shall appoint two delegates per *arrondissement*, who are to assemble in the Louvre, in a special room, with the purpose of forming a new committee and determining its ad hoc jurisdiction.

That assembly alone shall be able to appoint museum directors and curators of art collections, as well as the necessary personnel.

It shall also have the right to advise on annual exhibitions, their opening date, duration, and the appointment of an administrative board, while leaving to the exhibitors, following hallowed usage, the responsibility for choosing the admission jury – in sum, adoption of the measures that are in everyone's greatest interests.

In accordance with the principles established above, the fine arts section of the Institute shall be abolished and shall no longer have a *raison d'être* except as a private association.

The Ecole de Rome shall also be abolished and so shall the Ecole des Beaux-Arts; but the Parisian building shall be left at the disposal of students so as to cultivate the development of their studies by allowing them totally free choice among their professors. This shall not prevent the city of Paris from allocating a certain sum every year for a contest which shall provide the winners with the means of studying the arts of other nations.

The authority of the city of Paris over the provinces shall be abolished as well.

The drawing teachers of the parochial schools of Paris shall be appointed by representative delegates on the basis of a competitive examination.

For any commission for art works with a recognized purpose a competition shall be organized by the same delegates. Through their efforts a newspaper shall be published which might be entitled the *Arts Monitor*.

Artists who feel the need to separate themselves from the majority shall be allowed to exhibit together in one of the rooms of the common exhibition area.

The general assembly, together with the jury, shall preside over the distribution of the prizes, which shall be awarded by way of an official report listing every exhibitor.

Decorations and medals of all kinds shall be entirely abolished.

Gustave Courbet

Source: Le Cri du peuple, *10 April 1871; cited in P. ten-Doesschate Chu,* Letters of Gustave Courbet. *Chicago: University of Chicago Press. 1992, pp. 410–11*

Traditionally, French regimes had taken an interest in art and architecture as expressions of prestige and as forms of propaganda. The French state influenced artistic education and training through its control of the Ecole des Beaux-Arts and the Ecole de Rome, artistic production through its control of official commissions and patronage, and artistic recognition through its control of the Salons (the annual prestigious Paris art exhibition) and of official honours and decorations. France also, though, had a revolutionary tradition in the arts. The revolutionary movement of the 1790s had its artistic and cultural, as well as political and social, dimensions; and art, and artists of the stature of Jacques-Louis David, had been enlisted to serve the revolutionary cause. The French Revolution of 1848 witnessed a revival of 'republican' art and an attempt to democratize the French art world, with the establishment of a General Assembly of Artists which attempted to take control of government art policy and patronage.

Influenced by this revolutionary artistic tradition and by socialist ideas, Gustave Courbet became a prominent dissident painter through the subject-matter of some of his most important paintings and through his rejection of the official art establishment of the Second Empire. Therefore, when an art commission was formed after 4 September 1870 to record and preserve works of art threatened by the Franco-Prussian War, Courbet was appointed its president. He extended the scope of this commission and began to plan a complete overhaul of the French art establishment, and after the outbreak of the Commune he promoted the formation of an Artists' Federation representing all the artists in Paris. As the elected president of this federation, Courbet in the letter cited outlined his programme: control by artists themselves, through their elected representatives, of museums, art galleries, art schools, art education, artistic patronage and art exhibitions.

The defeat of the Commune meant the end of such plans and of the Artists' Federation, and Courbet himself was arrested by the Versaillais on 12 June 1871 and charged with the destruction of the Vendôme Column (commemorating Napoleon I's military victories) and the illegitimate usurpation of public functions. In a letter to the Government of National Defence of 14 September 1870, Courbet had advocated the demolition of the Vendôme Column; he had closely associated himself with the Commune through the Artists' Federation, election to the Council of the Commune on 16 April and appointment as mayor of the sixth *arrondissement* on 23 April; and he was partly responsible for the dismissal of the curators of the Louvre and Luxembourg museums. On the other hand, Courbet was not directly responsible for the destruction of the Vendôme Column, which he subsequently offered to restore at his own expense; and he helped to preserve the collections of the Louvre and even the private art collection of Thiers, whose Paris house the Commune demolished. Nevertheless, Courbet was sentenced to one year's imprisonment and, denied state patronage, he lived the rest of his life in impoverished exile in Switzerland. Under the Third Republic, state control and patronage of art were resumed, to the benefit of religious art and ecclesiastical architecture in the 1870s and to the sculptors of 'republican' statues thereafter. The Impressionists, notoriously, suffered from official neglect.

Document 1.12 The Defeat of the Paris Commune

Monday, 29 May [1871]
From a member of our congregation living in the Rue de la Victoire we have received the following communication: May 26, – They fought all round our house from Monday morning to Tuesday evening. Our quarter was surrounded with barricades, one at least in each of the following streets: Rue de la Victoire, near the Faubourg Montmartre, Chaussée d'Antin, Rue Joubert, Rue Caumartin, Rue de Provence, Rue St Georges, Rue Laffitte, Rue Lafayette. The barricade in the Chaussée d'Antin was large and strong, as may well be supposed from the fact that, although the soldiers began to fire upon it on Monday evening, it was not carried till Tuesday evening. You cannot imagine what it is to hear the cannon, *mitrailleuses*, and guns almost at one's door. The cannon of the troops were placed in the Square of the *Trinité*, near the church; those of the insurgents behind the barricade at the corner of the Boulevards. The noise was frightful. Our house has been injured by the shells; but, thank God, no lives have been lost. Several houses in the Chaussée d'Antin have been seriously damaged, the Church of the *Trinité* is injured both outside and inside. Numbers of insurgents who were taken were summarily shot in front of the church. I cannot tell you what joy we all felt when we saw the real French flag

[the Tricolore, as opposed to the red flag of the Commune]. The army was greatly applauded throughout our quarter; cigars, wine and money were distributed to the soldiers; and oranges and flowers thrown out of the windows. It was a horrible sight to see men and horses lying dead in almost every street. . . . The army lost no men in our quarter; but as they advanced they had much more to suffer, as many of the people in the faubourgs were on the side of the Commune. Even the women fired from the windows, and threw paving-stones on the soldiers' heads; and some, dressed in men's clothes, fought behind the barricades. The army has been obliged to take Paris almost street by street, the insurgents leaving one barricade to run to the next. To-day they are fighting at Belleville, the Buttes Chaumont, and the Faubourg St. Antoine; and we hope that in a day or two all will be finished. A great number of the chiefs are already taken and shot. Thousands of the insurgents have been killed, and ten thousand taken prisoners. The wives of the insurgents, seeing that their husbands are lost, are revenging themselves by poisoning our poor soldiers, giving them wine in which they put poison. We saw a woman in the Chaussée d'Antin yesterday, who has poisoned forty soldiers, taken to her home to be shot at the door of her house as an example. Fourteen women were shot this morning at the end of our street for the same cause. Six hundred women were taken prisoners yesterday, some of whom had been throwing petroleum into the cellars by the air-holes.

Children behind them were throwing matches to light it. Thus several streets have been burnt. The insurgents have set fire to most of the principal monuments of the city. Some are burnt down; others are still burning.

Source: W. Gibson, Paris during the Commune. *London: Whittaker. 1872 pp. 291–3*

The defeat of the Paris Commune was not at first a foregone conclusion. The Versailles government had to rely on troops who had been defeated and disorganized, and who suffered from low morale and uncertain political loyalties; other communes might have gained control of major provincial cities; and the Germans, still surrounding the eastern half of Paris, might not have co-operated with Thiers. However, the prompt withdrawal of government troops from central Paris after 18 March ended fraternization and permitted a revival of morale and discipline. At the same time, the insurrections that had occurred in some provincial cities were quickly suppressed, and the Germans released large numbers of captured French soldiers so that they could fight against the Commune.

At the beginning of April the Commune did attempt to mount a *sortie* against Versailles, but this failed, and the Versaillais went on the offensive, capturing the forts of Issy (9 May) and Vanves (14 May) and eventually entering the wealthy western districts of Paris on 21 May. The Communards nevertheless maintained a fighting retreat for a week, defending themselves behind street barricades and attacking the Versaillais from the cover of buildings. The last resistance, in the working-class districts of Belleville and Montmartre, collapsed on 28 May.

The report recorded by William Gibson, an English Methodist minister in Paris, illustrates the views of residents of one of the wealthiest disricts of Paris. The Versaillais were welcomed as liberators; the Communards were regarded as insurgents, if not as destructive savages; and the women who fought on the side of the Commune were portrayed as poisoners of the Versaillais and as *pétroleuses*, who deliberately set buildings alight with paraffin. Intense hatred and widespread violence characterized the suppression of the Commune. Communards killed hostages (including the Archbishop of Paris), while the Versaillais systematically executed large numbers of prisoners. In their last days of fighting, Communards burnt several public buildings, including the Tuileries Palace, the Hôtel de Ville, the Palais de Justice and the Ministry of Finance, though artillery was probably responsible for starting some fires and the alleged role of the *pétroleuses* was almost certainly exaggerated. The number of those killed in the suppression of the Commune may have been approximately 15,000, while about 38,000 were taken prisoner to Versailles. Of the latter, nearly 5,000 were transported to penal colonies in New Caledonia and over 1,000 were deported to Africa (Tombs, 1981, p. 191).

The hatred and violence on both sides, and the severity of the repression, helped to scar the French political psyche and to turn the Paris Commune and its defeat into a heroic left-wing legend.

CHRONOLOGY

1870

8 May	Liberal constitution approved in French national plebiscite
12 July	Withdrawal of Hohenzollern candidacy to the Spanish throne
13 July	Ems Telegram
19 July	French declaration of war
19 August	Beginning of siege of Metz
2 September	Surrender of Napoleon III and Army of Châlons at Sedan
4 September	Overthrow of the Second Empire and proclamation of the Third Republic in Paris
18 September	Abortive peace discussions between Jules Favre and Bismarck at Ferrières
20 September	Paris encircled by German army
27 October	Capitulation of Bazaine at Metz
31 October	Temporary radical occupation of the Paris Hôtel de Ville
1–4 November	Meetings between Thiers and Bismarck at Versailles

1871

5 January	Beginning of German bombardment of Paris
18 January	Introduction of bread rationing in Paris
19 January	Unsuccessful *sortie* from Paris
22 January	Paris Hôtel de Ville attacked by radical elements of National Guard

28 January	Armistice signed by Favre and Bismarck: capitulation of Paris
8 February	Conservative majority in National Assembly elections
26 February	Preliminary peace terms signed by Thiers and Bismarck
1–3 March	German occupation of central Paris
17–18 March	Unsuccessful attempt to remove cannon from Belleville and Montmartre
20 March	Opening session of National Assembly at Versailles
26 March	Municipal elections for Paris Commune
28 March	Proclamation of Paris Commune
2 April	Fighting between Versaillais and Paris Commune
3–4 April	Unsuccessful *sortie* by Communards
16 April	By-elections to fill 31 vacancies on Council of Commune
1 May	Committee of Public Safety replaced Council of the Commune
10 May	Signing of Treaty of Frankfurt
21 May	Entry of Versaillais into Paris
28 May	Defeat of the Paris Commune

BIBLIOGRAPHY

Bernstein, S., 'The Paris Commune', *Essays in Political and Intellectual History*. New York: Paine-Whitman. 1955.

Bury, J.P.T., *Gambetta and the National Defence: a republican dictatorship in France*. New York: Howard Fertig. 1970.

Bury, J.P.T. and Tombs, R.P., *Thiers, 1797–1877: a political life*. London: Allen & Unwin. 1986.

Carr, W., *The Origins of the Wars of German Unification*. London and New York: Longman. 1991.

Edwards, S., *The Paris Commune, 1871*. London: Eyre & Spottiswoode. 1971.

Fitzpatrick, M., 'Proudhon and the French Labour Movement: the problem of Proudhon's prominence', *European History Quaterly*, 15 (1985), 407–30.

Giesberg, R.I., *The Treaty of Frankfurt: a study in diplomatic history, September 1870–September 1873*. Philadelphia: University of Philadelphia Press. 1966.

Greenberg, L.M., 'The Commune of 1871 as a Decentralist Reaction', *Journal of Modern History*, 41 (1969), 304–18.

—— *Sisters of Liberty: Marseille, Lyon, Paris and the reaction to a centralized state, 1868–1871*. Cambridge, Mass.: Harvard University Press. 1971.

Horne, A., *The Fall of Paris: the siege and the Commune, 1870–1871*. London: Macmillan. 1965.

Howard, M., *The Franco-Prussian War: the German invasion of France, 1870–1871*. London: Rupert Hart-Davis. 1968.

Jellinek, F., *The Paris Commune of 1871*. London: Victor Gollancz. 1971.

Johnson, M.P., 'Citizenship and Gender: the Légion des Fédérées in the Paris Commune of 1871', *French History*, 8 (1994), 276–95.

—— *The Paradise of Association: political culture and popular organizations in the Paris Commune of 1871*. Ann Arbor: University of Michigan Press. 1996.

—— 'Enlightening the 'Misguided Brothers of the Countryside': republican fraternalism in the Paris Commune of 1871', *French History*, 11 (1997), 411–37.

Katzenback, E.L., 'Liberals at War: the economic policies of the Government of National Defence, 1870–1871', *American Historical Review*, 56 (1951), pp. 803–23.

Leith, J.A. (ed.), *Images of the Commune*. Montreal and London: McGill-Queen's University Press. 1978.

Marx, K., *The Civil War in France*. Various editions.

Sánchez, G.Z., *Organizing Independence: the Artists' Federation of the Paris Commune and its legacy, 1871–1889*. Lincoln, Nebr., and London: University of Nebraska Press. 1997.

Schulkind, E.W., 'The Activity of Popular Organizations during the Paris Commune of 1871', *French Historical Studies*, 1 (1960), 394–415.

—— 'Socialist Women during the 1871 Paris Commune', *Past and Present*, 106 (1985), 124–63.

Shafer, D.A., '*Plus que des Ambulancières*: women in articulation and defence of their ideals during the Paris Commune (1871)', *French History*, 7 (1993), 85–101.

Tombs, R., 'The Thiers Government and the Outbreak of Civil War in France', February–April 1871', *Historical Journal*, 23 (1980), 813–31.

—— *The War against Paris*, 1871. Cambridge: Cambridge University Press. 1981.

—— 'Harbingers or Entrepreneurs? A workers' cooperative during the Paris Commune', *Historical Journal*, 27 (1984), 969–77.

—— 'Paris and the Rural Hordes: an exploration of myth and reality in the French civil war of 1871', *Historical Journal*, 29 (1986), 795–808.

—— *The Paris Commune, 1871*. London and New York: Longman. 1999.

Williams, R.L., *The French Revolution of 1870–1871*. London: Weidenfeld & Nicolson. 1969.

Wolfe, R., 'The Parisian *Club de la Révolution*, 1870–1871', *Past and Present*, 39 (1968), 81–119.

Wright, G., 'The Anti-Commune: Paris, 1871', *French Historical Studies*, 10 (1977), 149–72.

2 | The political Right and Left in the early Third Republic

The political opposition to the Second Empire which developed during the 1860s was, to a considerable extent, an urban, and particularly a Parisian, phenomenon. In contrast, rural and provincial France tended to accept the imperial regime. The experience of the Franco-Prussian War and of the siege of Paris accentuated this political divide. Paris, and to a lesser extent other major urban centres, became more left wing, whereas the conservatism of rural provincial France was reinforced by a widespread association of left-wing republicanism with Gambetta's policies of national resistance. The national parliamentary elections of 8 February 1871 illustrated the political polarization of France. Of the 645 candidates elected, approximately 200 were Legitimists or supporters of the senior line of the Bourbon dynasty which had been overthrown in the revolution of 1830, while a further 150 to 200 were Orleanists or supporters of the junior line of the Bourbon monarchy (which had ruled France in the person of Louis-Philippe between 1830 and 1848), including the younger sons of Louis-Philippe, the Prince de Joinville and the Duc D'Aumale. Moreover, no less than 106 members of the National Assembly of 1871 possessed titles of nobility, of which 44 were pre-1600 (Locke, 1974, p. 58).

The strength of the parliamentary Right in 1871, and its monarchical character, can be explained in a number of ways. The surrender at Sedan and the proclamation of the Third Republic had thrown Bonapartists into disarray. In contrast, Legitimists, galvanized by the prospect of social upheaval, had begun active electoral preparations after the Government of National Defence had announced the convocation of a National Assembly on 8 September 1870. They were therefore generally well prepared when on 29 January 1871 the elections were announced for the following 8 February. The elections themselves were held on the basis of *scrutin de liste*, whereby each voter voted for a list of candidates to represent his department, which tended to accentuate electoral swings. Legitimists stood, not as campaigners for a monarchical restoration, but as conservatives who would bring peace to France.

The 350–400 monarchists in the National Assembly of 1871 constituted a clear majority over approximately a dozen Bonapartists and 250 republicans. A monarchical restoration therefore seemed possible, particularly after 8 June 1871, when the National Assembly overwhelmingly voted for the lifting of the 1832 and 1848 laws banning the Bourbons from France and for the validation of the elections of Joinville and Aumale. Moreover, Thiers, the head of the government, was not seen as a convinced republican: he had served the July Monarchy as Prime Minister under Louis-

Philippe; he had just appointed royalist aristocrats to key diplomatic posts (Gontaut-Biron to Berlin and the Duc de Broglie to London); and on 1 July 1871 he had even hosted a dinner party for the Orleanist princes, the Comte de Paris and the Duc de Chartres. It also seemed possible that the problem of having two competing Bourbon pretenders to the French throne, Henri, Duc de Bordeaux and Comte de Chambord (Legitimist), and Louis-Philippe, Comte de Paris (Orleanist), could be resolved by a process of 'fusion': the Orleanists would recognize as king the childless Comte de Chambord, who in turn would recognize the Comte de Paris as his heir. However, on 2 July 1871 in by-elections, caused by multiple elections and resignations, republicans won about a hundred seats while just twelve were won by royalists. This was an early indication that 8 February had been a freak election result. A further devastating blow to royalist hopes soon followed.

Document 2.1 Manifesto of the Comte de Chambord (5 July 1871)

Frenchmen! I am ready to do anything to help my country rise from its ruins and take again its proper place in the world. I am prepared to sacrifice everything for my country, except my honour.

I am, and I wish to be, a man of my time. I render sincere homage to all of France's grandeurs. Whatever the colour of the flag under which our soldiers marched, I have always admired their heroism and given thanks to God for everything that their bravery has added to the treasury of the glories of France.

Between you and me, there should be no misunderstandings and nothing hidden.

Just because there has been ignorant and credulous talk of privileges, absolutism or intolerance – and what else? – of tithes and feudal rights, phantoms which the most audacious dishonesty attempts to revive before your eyes, I will not allow the standard of Henri IV, Francis I and Joan of Arc to be snatched from my hands.

It was with this standard that national unity was achieved, it was with this standard that your ancestors, led by my ancestors, conquered Alsace and Lorraine, whose loyalty will be the consolation of our misfortunes.

This standard conquered barbarism in Africa and witnessed the first feats of arms of the princes of my family, and this standard will conquer the new barbarism which threatens the world!

I will entrust this standard to the valour of our army, which knows that the standard has followed only the path of honour.

I received this standard as a sacred trust from the old king, my grandfather, dying in exile. For me, the standard has always been inseparable from the absent fatherland; it flew over my cradle, and I want it to cover my tomb.

In the glorious folds of this standard without stain, I will bring you order and liberty.

Frenchmen! Henri V cannot abandon the white flag of Henri IV.
Henri
Chambord, 5 July 1871.

Source: A.F.P., Comte de Falloux, Mémoires d'un royaliste. Paris: Perrin et Cie. 1888, II, pp. 481–2

The Comte de Chambord, grandson of Charles X, lived most of his life in exile in the Austrian village of Frohsdorf and, during the winter months, in Venice. Believing that the monarchy might be restored, he made a rare and brief visit to France in the summer of 1871. From Chambord, the Loire château from which he derived one of his titles, he issued this manifesto, published by the Paris evening newspapers on 6 July. In his manifesto he promised to respect manhood suffrage, parliamentary government and administrative decentralization, and he also dissociated his cause from aristocratic privilege, absolute monarchy, religious intolerance, tithes and feudal rights (all of which had characterized the Bourbon monarchy up to 1789 and which, to some extent, continued to do so in the popular imagination). However, he refused to abandon the standard of the absolute monarchy (gold fleurs-de-lys on a white background) for the blue, white and red Tricolore, which had been France's national flag since 1792 (except during the Restoration Monarchy, 1814/15–1830). A compromise, retaining the Tricolore as France's national flag and adopting the Bourbon fleurs-de-lys as the royal standard, does not seem to have occurred to anyone at the time.

The manifesto effectively ended the chances of a restoration of the monarchy, since the overwhelming majority of the French population would not have accepted the replacement of the Tricolore with the old Bourbon flag. Thiers, in conversation with Falloux on 6 July 1871, ironically described Chambord as 'the founder of the Republic in France', whom posterity would name the French Washington (Falloux, 1888, II, p. 494).

The manifesto also split the French royalists: about eighty Legitimist deputies (known as the Chevaux-légers, from the street in which they met) remained loyal to Chambord ('Henri V'), while another eighty royalists agreed on a public statement affirming their commitment both to monarchy and to the Tricolore.

Relations between Legitimists and Orleanists also deteriorated until the summer of 1873, when a 'fusion' compromise was finally agreed. However, Chambord then restated his position on the national flag in a letter (27 October 1873) published in a conservative French newspaper, *L'Union*. Only, though, with the passing of the Wallon amendment on 30 January 1875 by one vote did the National Assembly finally confirm that France would remain a republic.

Document 2.2 Adolphe Thiers and the Conservative Republic (13 November 1872)

The Republic exists, it is the legal government of the country: to want anything else would involve a new revolution and the most fearsome of all revolutions.

Do not waste our time in proclaiming such a revolution; instead, let us employ our time in giving the Republic its necessary and desirable characteristics. A few months ago, a committee appointed by you called itself the Conservative Republic. We should appropriate this title and above all ensure that it is merited.

All government should be conservative, and no society can live under a government which is not. The Republic will be conservative, or it will cease to exist.

France cannot live in a state of continual alarms: France wants to be able to live peacefully, so as to work to feed itself and to face up to its immense responsibilities. Any government that fails to provide France with peace and calm, which are so absolutely essential for her, will not be tolerated for long! Let us not be under any illusions! You might believe that, thanks to manhood suffrage, with the support of the masses it might be possible to establish a republic which would be the republic of one political party! That Republic would last only a day.

The masses themselves need peace, security and work. They can live an agitated life for a few days, but not for long. Having made others afraid, they become afraid themselves; they throw themselves into the arms of an adventurer, and pay with twenty years of slavery for a few days of disastrous licence.

This has often happened, as you know, and do not believe that it cannot happen again. This sad and humiliating progress from anarchy to despotism, and from despotism to anarchy, will be repeated a hundred times, with its humiliations and its calamities, whereby France has suffered the loss of two provinces, the tripling of her public debt, the burning of her capital, the ruin of her monuments, and this massacre of hostages that one would never have imagined to have witnessed again!

Source: Thiers in the Chamber of Deputies, 13 November 1872: Journal officiel de la République française, *14 November 1872, pp. 6981–2*

At first, Adolphe Thiers enjoyed an unassailable political position: he was triumphantly elected on 8 February 1871 in twenty-six departments as the opponent of war and the negotiator of the armistice; he was appointed head of the executive with the almost unanimous support of the National Assembly; he successfully defeated the Paris Commune and concluded the Treaty of Frankfurt; and his government presided over national economic recovery, army reforms (including the introduction of a five-year term of military service in July 1872), and the successful raising of loans to secure the rapid payment of the indemnity to Germany and the consequent liberation of the national territory.

However, by the summer of 1872 the national consensus which had hitherto generally backed Thiers was beginning to disintegrate. Royalists were becoming more restive at the refusal of Thiers to support a monarchical restoration or to condemn with sufficient vigour the radicalism of some republicans. Orleanists and moderate royalists acquired a skilful parliamentary leader in May 1872, when the Duc de Broglie resigned his post as French ambassador in London and returned to France to play a more active political role. However, the royalists remained divided between Legitimists and Orleanists, and the results of by-elections and local government elections regularly confirmed their limited electoral appeal. Bonapartists, on the other hand, were beginning to win some elections and to commemorate publicly Napoleonic anniversaries. More serious, though, was the potential threat from radical republicanism. By the summer of 1872 a coherent radical republican programme had been developed, including an amnesty for the Communards, an end to martial law, the introduction of free, compulsory and secular education, and the dissolution of the National Assembly and the election of a new parliament. This programme was effectively publicized in newly founded radical newspapers and in the speeches of Léon Gambetta, who made a series of provincial speaking tours from November 1871. Newspapers and pamphlets published the texts of these speeches, which often had a considerable impact. In particular, Gambetta succeeded in outraging the right in a speech delivered at Grenoble on 26 September 1872, when he referred to the working world to whom the future belongs making its entry into politics and to a new social class ('*nouvelle couche sociale*') coming to power in France.

In his presidential address at the opening of the new parliamentary session on 13 November 1872 Thiers was attempting to achieve a political balancing act. On practical grounds he had become convinced that France had to have a republican regime, but he did not want to lose the support of the moderate royalists, seeing in them useful allies against the radical republicans. The latter he saw as irresponsible rabble-rousers who might stir up political and social conflict within France and upset the nation's delicate relations with Germany. Hence his renewed commitment to republicanism, his appeal for national peace and calm, and his attempt to resurrect the spectres of left-wing anarchy and right-wing dictatorship. While the Left applauded the speech, the Right regarded it as an act of betrayal. But the Right at this time could not unseat Thiers or prevent the National Aseembly from assuming the task of drawing up a new constitution for France.

Document 2.3 The Constitution of 1875

1   The legislative power is exercised by two assemblies, the Chamber of Deputies and the Senate. The Chamber of Deputies is elected by manhood suffrage, according to the terms determined by the electoral law. The composition, the form of election and appointment and the powers of the Senate will be regulated by a special law.

2   The President of the Republic is elected by an absolute majority of the votes cast by members of the Senate and the Chamber of Deputies voting together in a national assembly.

     The President is elected for seven years and he is eligible for re-election.

3   The President of the Republic shares the right to legislate with the members of parliament. He promulgates the laws when they have been voted by the two chambers; he oversees them and ensures their execution.

He has the right to grant pardons; amnesties can be granted only by a law. He is ultimately responsible for the armed forces. He makes all civil and military appointments. He presides over solemn national occasions. The envoys and ambassadors of foreign powers are accredited to him.

A minister must counter-sign every act of the President of the Republic . . .

5   The President of the Republic can, in accordance with the recommendation of the Senate, dissolve the Chamber of Deputies before the legal expiry of its mandate. If this situation arises, the electoral colleges must be summoned for new elections within a period of three months.

6   The ministers are jointly responsible to parliament for the general policies of the government and individually for their personal ministerial performance. The President of the Republic is responsible only in a case of high treason . . .

[8   Parliament and the President will have the power to revise the Constitution.]

9   Versailles is the seat of government and the seat of parliament.

Source: Loi relative à l'organisation des pouvoirs publics, *15–28 February 1875; J.P.T. Bury,* France, 1814–1940. *London: Methuen. 1969, pp. 328–9*

The ambition of Thiers to preside over the consolidation of a conservative republic unravelled in 1873, as French politics became more polarized between radical republicans and conservatives. Finally, on 24 May 1873 a combination of the Right and some moderate republicans defeated Thiers in a vote of confidence, and Thiers resigned the presidency. In his place the National Assembly elected Marshal MacMahon, the army commander responsible for the suppression of the Paris Commune and a monarchist, who appointed the Duc de Broglie to head a conservative administration. A restoration of the monarchy once again seemed possible, but for the obstinacy of the Comte de Chambord over the flag issue. However, on 30 January 1875 the National Assembly accepted by one vote (353 to 352) an amendment proposed by a deputy called Henri Wallon that parliament should consist of two houses, a Chamber of Deputies and a Senate, whose members meeting together should elect the President of the Republic. In this anticlimactic manner, the republican regime in France was confirmed.

Yet, on points of detail, the Right gained many victories: two parliamentary chambers, whereas left-wing Radicals such as Louis Blanc and Edgar Quinet would have preferred one; a Senate of 300 members, 225 elected by the French departments and colonies, 75 elected for life by the National Assembly and subsequently by the Senate; a forty-year age qualification for senators, who were to be elected for nine years, with one-third of the elected senators standing for election every three years; elections by *scrutin d'arrondissement* in the main administrative unit (*arrondissement*) of each department, rather than by *scrutin de liste*, whereby the department, not the *arrondissement*, constituted the constituency; election of the President by parliament, not the electorate, for a seven-year term, and the granting to the President of extensive executive powers, including the right to appoint government ministers (who were nevertheless responsible to parliament) and, with the approval of the Senate, to dissolve the Chamber of Deputies and hold new parliamentary elections within three months; and the continued location of parliament and government at Versailles, rather than their return to Paris (as the Radicals wanted).

Altogether, the Constitution of 1875, or series of constitutional laws passed in 1875 (there was no single constitutional document and no bill or declaration of rights) had a strong conservative character; and this conservatism was reinforced in other ways; for instance, the provision that mayors of communes should be appointed, not elected. Moderate republicans such as Thiers, and even many Radicals such as Gambetta, were prepared to accept all this (at least for the time being) because, as they saw it, they had won on the two most important points – the maintenance of the Republic and of manhood suffrage as the basis of parliamentary elections.

Document 2.4 Republicanism and National Reconciliation

I say finally that the true manner of giving confidence to those whom you want to reassure is above all to succeed in the enterprise which you have begun in founding the republican regime in France; and if you succeed in this task, as I hope you will and as I am sure you will, the ruling classes, the people whom you are afraid of alarming, will be sufficiently reassured if you tell them that there is nothing to be alarmed about in the amnesty [for the Communards]. But if your policies are hesitant and uncertain, if you are only half successful, when you present yourselves before the electors in 1880, the year to which the monarchists will postpone the elections, your opponents will not lack political ammunition to use against you even if you have refused the amnesty a hundred times.

I ask you to have confidence in the country, I ask you to have confidence in yourselves; and you cannot give more striking proof of confidence in yourselves and in your stature than in voting for the amnesty. You urge your prefects to pursue policies of peace and reconciliation; in our turn, we urge you to pursue the same policies. You tell the prefects that the Republic can be founded only by putting an end to our divisions. I fear that in pronouncing these words you have had in mind above all the so-called upper classes, whom you understandably want to rally to the Republic.

I ask you to take account at the same time of the so-called lower classes, who must also be reconciled and conciliated. I tell you that it is only through the reconciliation of all classes and all citizens that you will achieve the social peace which we all want.

I ask you to proclaim the amnesty while it is a proof of strength, and not wait until public opinion demands an amnesty, when the granting of the amnesty will be a sign of weakness. Do not give up, as you have been advised to do. Act.

What are you afraid of? You will always be strong if you govern with the country; you will always be weak if you govern against it.

Source: Georges Clemenceau in the Chamber of Deputies, 16 May 1876: Journal officiel de la République française, *17 May 1876, p. 3341*

The Paris Commune of 1871 cast a long shadow on French politics. Many on the Right could not forgive or forget the resort to armed insurrection, the shooting of hostages and the destruction by fire of so many of the capital's prominent buildings. Many on the Left could not forgive or forget government policies towards Paris and the Franco-Prussian War, and the systematic brutality with which the Communards were suppressed. There were also those who tried to obliterate the memory of the Commune, an exercise assisted by the reconstruction of destroyed buildings exactly as they had been, except for the Tuileries Palace (the burnt-out remains of which were finally demolished in 1882).

In his parliamentary speech of 16 May 1876 supporting a bill by François Raspail to grant an amnesty to the Communards, Georges Clemenceau was tackling a very sensitive subject in a courageous manner. Having been appointed mayor of the eighteenth *arrondissement* of Paris on 5 September 1870 by the newly formed Government of National Defence, Clemenceau had played a role in both the siege of Paris and the Commune. During the siege he had urged a policy of patriotic defence, which had helped secure his election in Paris to the National Assembly on 8 February 1871. Yet, while sympathizing with the Communards, he did not support their recourse to violence against a democratically elected republican government, and he tried, with little success, to mediate between the Communards and Versailles. In so doing, he attracted criticism from the Right for not having prevented the lynching of General Thomas and General Lecomte in Montmartre (in the eighteenth *arrondissement*) on 18 March, and from the Left for not backing the Commune in the manner of some more radical Paris mayors.

Clemenceau resigned from the National Assembly on 27 March 1871 in protest over its policies towards the Commune, but he rebuilt his political career in Paris local government, finally gaining election as chairman of the Paris city council on 29 November 1875. The following year (20 February 1876), Montmartre returned him to the Chamber of Deputies on a radical programme which included an amnesty for the Communards. Raspail's bill was rejected by 392 votes to 50 with 58 abstentions, and no complete amnesty was granted until July 1880. Nevertheless, Clemenceau's speech of 16 May 1876 established his reputation as an orator.

Document 2.5 Republicanism and Anti-clericalism

How is it, gentlemen, that we could have arrived at this situation? How have we reached this degree of weakness and powerlessness such that we see the Pope directly addressing people in France, both individually and collectively, without recourse to the intermediary of the civil authority, without communicating his briefs, or his bulls, or his allocutions, or his acts, which, in contempt of the secular laws of this country, are often publicized and executed without any intervention on the part of the government administration?

How is it that bishops, leaving their churches, their role and their mission, directly address themselves to the country's civil servants, mayors, justices of the peace, prefects and sub-prefects, and talk to them about orders and injunctions which they have received from Rome?

How can this happen if it is not due to a weakness and a powerlessness which are the result of the mistakes accumulated since 1870 in this country? . . .

The evil of clericalism – and that is one of the aspects of the question which we are concerned with today – the evil of clericalism has profoundly infiltrated into what is called the ruling class of this country. Those who spread and promote the evil of clericalism have for twenty years taken such good care, whether in the schools which prepare candidates for careers in public administration or in the spheres of government and administration themselves, to advance both their views and their followers that now they nearly always have, if not the complicity, at least the acquiescence, of a large number of public officials.

Source: Léon Gambetta in the Chamber of Deputies, 4 May 1877: Journal officiel de la République française, *5 May 1877, pp. 3281–2*

For centuries, there had been a conflict in France between the supporters of papal authority (known as Ultramontanes) and their opponents (known as Gallicans). The revolutionary decade of 1789–99 added another dimension to this conflict by creating a gulf between Catholicism and republicanism. During the Revolution the Roman Catholic Church in France lost most of its wealth, privileges and independence, and suffered periods of violent persecution, so that the Church and its adherents tended to become hostile to the Revolution and to republicanism. For their part, republicans invariably associated the Roman Catholic Church with the Old Regime and with the Counter-Revolution. Thereafter, the Roman Catholic Church tended to be identified with conservative regimes, such as the Restoration Monarchy and the Second Empire, while anti-clericalism surfaced at times of revolutionary upheaval, particularly during the Paris Commune of 1871. From 1871 the traditional alliance between the Roman Catholic Church and conservatism in France was renewed, with, for instance, the public financing of the construction of a large Catholic basilica on the heights of Montmartre in Paris, and the law of 12 July 1875 allowing Catholic institutions of higher education to award university degrees.

As a Radical republican, Gambetta was almost inevitably anti-clerical, and the separation of Church and state featured in the political programme which he outlined in a speech at Bordeaux on 13 February 1876. The specific prompting for his parliamentary speech of 4 May 1877 came from an allocution issued by Pope Pius IX on 12 March 1877 to all Catholic clergy, urging them to exert Catholic pressure on governments to support the Holy See in its quarrels with the Italian state. In France Catholic Action Committees organized a petition to the President of the Republic, to which the government headed by Jules Simon responded by dissolving the committees and by instructing the prefects to stop the petitions. This provoked a belligerent response from some bishops, notably the Bishop of Nevers, who sent President MacMahon a letter of protest which he circulated to all mayors and justices of the peace in his diocese.

Apart from this particular dispute, Gambetta objected to the Catholic Church because it allegedly undermined French sovereignty, because it was associated with anti-republicanism, and because it exercised too much influence. He concluded his speech with a phrase which became notorious: 'Clericalism? There is the enemy' ('*Le cléricalisme? Voilà l'ennemi!*') (*Journal officiel*, 5 May 1877, p. 3284). Gambetta's opponents in the debate, such as the Bonapartist Paul de Cassagnac, argued that Gambetta had insulted French Catholics by suggesting that it was impossible to be a French Catholic and a French patriot. The majority of deputies, however, agreed with Gambetta and voted for a motion which urged the government to repress the 'anti-patriotic' agitation of the Ultramontanes.

Document 2.6 The Crisis of 16 May 1877

A cabinet, which never lost its majority in any vote, has been dismissed without debate. Our first thought is to turn ourselves towards you and say to you, like the republicans of the National Assembly after 24 May 1873 [when the conservative MacMahon replaced Thiers as President of the Republic], that the men who take up power today will once again be politically powerless. France wants the Republic, she said that on 20 February 1876 [the first round of elections to the Chamber of Deputies], she will say it again . . . We, your representatives . . . , we appeal to you to choose between the policies of reaction and adventure, which suddenly call into question everything which has been painfully achieved over the last six years, and the wise, firm, pacific and progressive policies which you have already endorsed. Within five months, France will be able to express her opinion; she will not betray herself. The Republic will emerge stronger than ever from the electoral ballot boxes.

Source: Spuller's Manifesto, 18 May 1877; M. Reclus, Le Seize mai. Paris: Hachette. 1931, p. 50

Weakened by its handling of relations between the French Republic and the Roman Catholic Church, Jules Simon's administration suffered another reverse when, against its wishes, an overwhelming majority of deputies voted to abolish a press law of 29 December 1875, which had excluded some press offences from trial by jury. The next day (16 May 1877) President MacMahon angrily reacted by virtually demanding the resignation of Jules Simon, who duly resigned. The Constitution of 1875 had conferred on the President the right to appoint and dismiss government ministers, but it was widely understood that a governement should not be dismissed by the President unless it had been defeated in a vote of confidence in the Chamber of Deputies. Therefore, a major political and constitutional crisis rapidly developed, with parallels being drawn with the appointment of the Polignac ministry and the Address of the 221 which had led to the revolution of July 1830.

The crisis of 16 May 1877 was an episode in the long-drawn-out conflict between Left and Right for control of the Third Republic. In the first elections for the Chamber of Deputies, which had been held in two rounds on 20 February and 5 March 1876, approximately 350 republicans had been elected against approximately 150 conservatives (royalists and Bonapartists), though the conservative Marshal MacMahon remained President with his seven-year term of office not due to expire until 1880. A clash between the Chamber of Deputies with its substantial republican majority and the conservative MacMahon with his extensive presidential powers thus became highly likely, though the suddenness and intensity of the crisis which began on 16 May were unexpected. Left-wing deputies at once began to meet to co-ordinate their opposition, while Gambetta on 17 May declared in the Chamber of Deputies that the dismissal of Jules Simon had been unconstitutional. MacMahon nevertheless soldiered on, the following day appointing a reactionary government headed by the Duc de Broglie and issuing a presidential message that parliament had been adjourned for a month. Left-wing deputies then assembled in the Hôtel des Réservoirs in Versailles, where a personal friend and political ally of Gambetta, Eugène Spuller, drafted a manifesto which was eventually signed by 348 deputies. Opposition also continued in the Chamber of Deputies, which on 19 June passed a vote of no confidence in the Broglie government by a crushing majority of 363 to 158. However, conservative supporters remained in a small majority in the Senate, and on 22 June it voted by 149 to 130 to dissolve the Chamber of Deputies. During the months of electioneering that followed, the government dismissed numerous officials suspected of left-wing sympathies, harassed republican newspapers, and generally exerted every effort to oppose the re-election of the 363 who had voted for the no-confidence motion. The Left, though, were unusually united, and fought a vigorous and well-funded election campaign, so that in the elections held on 14 and 28 October 1877 they won 315 seats against 199 for the conservatives. This represented not just another electoral victory for the Left, but a blow to presidential power (and, to a lesser extent, to the authority of the Senate). More immediately, the election result led to the resignations of de Broglie (20 November 1877) and MacMahon (30 January 1879).

Document 2.7 The Programme of the Parti Ouvrier Français (1879–82)

A – Political Section

1   Abolition of all legal restrictions on the press, public meetings and associations, particularly the law against the Workers' International. Suppression of the *livret*, that identity card of the working class, and of all articles of the Civil Code making workers inferior to employers and women inferior to men;

2   Suppression of public financial subsidies for the Roman Catholic Church and return to the nation of all inalienable ecclesiastical property (decree of the Commune of 2 April 1871);
3   Suppression of the national debt;
4   Abolition of standing armies and the general arming of the population;
5   The communes to be in charge of their own administration and their own police force.

B – Economic Section

1   Rest day one day a week or legal prohibition on employers from making people work more than six days out of seven. Reduction of the legal working day to eight hours for adults. Prohibition on the employment of children under fourteen years of age in private workshops; and reduction in the working day for those aged between fourteen and eighteen to six hours;
2   Protective supervision of apprentices by workers' corporations;
3   Legal minimum wage, determined every year according to the local price of essential food items by a workers' statistical committee;
4   Legal prohibition on employers from employing foreign workers on wages lower than those earned by French workers;
5   Equal wages for equal work for workers of both sexes;
6   Society, represented by the state and the commune, to provide without charge scientific and professional education for all children;
7   Old people and those injured in work to be cared for by society;
8   Suppression of all interference by employers in the administration of workers' mutual savings banks and similar institutions, which should be exclusively controlled by workers;
9   Responsibility of employers for accidents at work . . .
10 Involvement of workers in the special regulations of different workshops; suppression of the right usurped by employers to penalize workers in the form of fines or deductions from their wages (decree of the Commune of 27 April 1871);
11 Annulment of all contracts that have privatized public property (banks, railways, mines, etc.), and the operation of all state-owned workshops by the workers employed there;
12 Abolition of all indirect taxes and transformation of all direct taxes into a progressive income tax on incomes over 3,000 francs per year. Suppression of all collateral inheritance rights and of all direct inheritance rights above a limit of 20,000 francs.

Source: J. Guesde and P. Lafargue, Le Programme du Parti Ouvrier: son histoire, ses considérants, ses articles. *Paris: Henry Oriol. 1883, pp. 3–5*

As a result of the repression that followed the defeat of the Paris Commune, most of the prominent French socialists who had survived were either imprisoned or exiled, and socialist political activity in France was largely driven underground. However, gradually socialist and working-class political activity revived. For instance, the first workers' congresses under the Third Republic were held in Paris in October 1876 and in Lyons in January–February 1878; a number of socialist newspapers began to appear, including *L'Egalité*, edited by Jules Guesde and first issued on 18 November 1877; and during 1879 and 1880 Jules Guesde and Paul Lafargue founded a French Marxist political party, the Parti Ouvrier Français or POF.

Like Georges Clemenceau, Jules Guesde and Paul Lafargue had emerged at the end of the Second Empire as left-wing journalists hostile to the imperial regime. However, unlike Clemenceau, Guesde and Lafargue publicly supported the Paris Commune, suffered imprisonment and exile under the Third Republic, and became converts to Marxism.

Lafargue had married Karl Marx's daughter Laura in April 1868, and he encouraged Guesde to adopt Marxist ideas. The programme of the POF was developed and confirmed at a series of conferences held between October 1879 and October 1882. It included some elements of the radical republican programme (repeal of restrictive legislation on the press, public meetings and associations, separation of Church and state, provision of free, secular and compulsory education), but in other respects went much further. Politically, the POF campaigned for the substitution of the nation in arms for France's standing army and the devolution of power to the level of the commune (the smallest French administrative unit); and economically and socially the POF proposed a whole raft of measures (eight-hour working day, six-day working week, legal minimum wage, provision for the care of the infirm and elderly, introduction of a progressive income tax and of strict inheritance laws) that would, if implemented, have changed the balance of wealth and power in French society. It is striking, too, that two items were based on decrees of the Paris Commune, and that the legal and employment rights of women were addressed.

Guesde, Lafargue and the POF helped to make the French socialist and workers' movement much more militant and left wing (the French workers' congress of October 1876 had condemned revolution and even strikes). However, the extremism and Marxist dogmatism of the POF alienated many socialists, including the followers of Pierre-Joseph Proudhon (who believed in workers' and peasants' co-operatives), Auguste Blanqui (who were anarchists) and Paul Brousse (who opposed Marxist materialism and were known as Possibilists).

Document 2.8 The Republicanism of Jules Ferry: Education

This system of national education which connects primary school education in a simultaneously powerful and flexible structure to the most sophisticated fields of human knowledge; this system of national education which has been courageously prefaced with the assertion that education is a right for citizens, that society owes access to practical knowledge to everybody and to the successive levels of intellectual culture to all those who are capable of assimilating it . . . , this recognition of the value of the nation's intellectual capital, of all the latent abilities, of all the talents that can be misunderstood or stifled, in a great and creative democracy, that, gentlemen, was the dream of our fathers; and we have the right to declare that insofar as it is possible to claim that something has been accomplished, thanks to you and thanks to the country, your principal partner in this great enterprise, the dream has become a reality . . .

Certainly, the means have not yet been found to achieve great things with limited resources – a system of national education is expensive, and it is for this reason that it is attacked today; it is on financial grounds that the system of national education is put on trial in front of these enfranchised masses who are both attracted to notions of economy and very reluctant to pay taxes. The opposition hopes to mobilize against this supremely popular achievement the tide of discontent and weariness with the better things in life. These are often referred to and oppositions excel in exploiting boredom with governments that have been in power for eighteen or twenty years. This polemic must not be scorned, gentlemen, doubt and uncertainty must not be allowed to spread in the country on the basis of false statistics. We must not allow people to think that our system of higher education is just a luxurious decoration behind which there are only over-paid professors and imaginary students, that our academic education is just a factory for the socially inferior, just a vast business, just an architectural disaster . . .

I have not been surprised by the lively attack which has been directed against our institutions, our laws, our organization of primary education; it is a long and ancient quarrel. But I admit that I do not understand and I cannot understand how the spirit of party politics blinds intelligent, perceptive and sincere people so that they fail to appreciate the grandeur of the achievement undertaken and accomplished in the field of higher education.

Source: Jules Ferry in the Chamber of Deputies, 6 June 1889: Journal officiel de la République française, *7 June 1889, pp. 1280–1*

Traditionally, the Roman Catholic Church had controlled and provided education in France. During the revolutionary decade of the 1790s, this control and provision had been destroyed, and plans had been developed for the creation instead of a national system of education that was secular and, at the primary level, universal. For financial and political reasons, these plans remained largely unfulfilled, and from the Napoleonic period onwards the Church regained much of its previous educational role, particularly under Napoleon III and during the early years of the Third Republic, when conservatives were in power. The association of the Catholic Church with conservatism and anti-republicanism meant that republicans distrusted the Church's influence, especially in education. Republicans also believed that the young should be exposed to republican values at school and that the interests of social justice required that all children should receive primary education. It was also argued that one of the reasons for France's defeat in 1870–1 was the superiority of German over French education, and that national survival required a modern educational system, staffed by properly trained and qualified teachers and offering a modern academic curriculum.

The achievement of a national system of education that was secular and, at the primary level, free and compulsory, was largely the work of Jules Ferry. Having served as Prefect of the Seine during the siege of Paris (which earned him the title 'Ferry-Famine') and having won successive elections to the National Assembly and the Chamber of Deputies, he was appointed Minister of Education on 4 February 1879 and remained in government for much of the period until March 1885. On most issues, Ferry could be described as a moderate or even as a conservative republican, but he was a determined and energetic educational reformer: he was responsible for a whole series of educational laws, including those which introduced gymnastics in schools (27 January 1880), a secular system of higher education (27 February and 18 March 1880), secondary education for girls (21 December 1880), military training in *lycées* (21 April 1881), professional qualifications for teachers (10 June 1881) and compulsory primary education (28 March 1882). These laws were part of a wider assault on the Catholic Church, which included such measures as the repeal of the 1814 law forbidding work on Sundays, the suppression of unauthorized religious congregations, the introduction of non-denominational cemeteries and secular funerals, and the establishment of lay control over hospitals. Inevitably, many conservatives and Catholics were alienated; and equally inevitably, as Ferry observed in his parliamentary speech of 6 June 1889, a good state educational system was expensive, and taxes were always electorally unpopular.

Document 2.9 The Republicanism of Jules Ferry: Colonialism

It is not true that France is weak. It was weak until 1875–1876, before the war-wounded country had reformed her army and restored her finances. At that time she could imagine herself to be at the mercy of a sudden vigorous ambush or attack. Even then, as has been so justly remarked, France remained one of the most important moral powers in the world; her revival, after her fall, caught the admiration of Europe, and her moral grandeur served her as a shield.

But today France is strong, and she has an invincible ability to defend herself. It is because she is strong that she is respected. It is because she is strong that injury is done to her by the argument, carelessly thrown to the four winds in debate, an argument which fortunately nobody abroad takes seriously, that this great military state cannot maintain, without danger, ten thousand men in Indo-China! It is because France is strong that she should not abdicate her role and her rights as a great power either in the Mediterranean or in the Indian Ocean.

It is impossible to be a great power by hiding away in one's own territory . . .

Without compromising the security of the country, without abandoning any of its hopes or memories, the republicans in less than ten years have given France four kingdoms in Asia and Africa. Three of these kingdoms are united to the national patrimony by legal contracts and by tradition. The fourth represents our contribution to the conquest of civilization in the heart of Africa by peaceful and persuasive means. If the Republic had claimed, with the doctrinaire thinkers of the Radical school, that French territory ended at Marseilles, in whose hands would Tunisia, Indo-China, Madagascar and the Congo now be?

Source: J. Ferry, Le Tonkin et la mère-patrie. *Paris: Victor Havard. 1890, pp. 47–8*

In the eighteenth century France was one of the great colonial powers of Europe. However, in a series of wars with Britain, France lost most of her colonial empire, which by 1815 consisted of a handful of islands (Saint-Pierre and Miquelon in the Gulf of the St Lawrence, Guadeloupe and Martinique in the West Indies, Réunion in the Indian Ocean), French Guiana in South America, and trading posts in Senegal and India. In 1830 the French conquest of Algeria began, an enterprise with which the July Monarchy was closely associated; and Napoleon III expanded French interests in the Far East, annexing Cochin-China in 1862 and imposing a protectorate on Cambodia in 1863. By a treaty of 1874, the Vietnamese king recognized French possession of all six provinces in Cochin-China and gave the French government the right to station consular officials and maintain small military garrisons in three treaty ports in Tonkin. Having suppressed a revolt with Chinese help, the Vietnamese king in 1879 tried to repudiate the 1874 treaty, to which the French responded with military action. Meanwhile, in 1880 territories in the Congo were ceded to France; in 1881 a French military force invaded Tunisia, which became a French protectorate; and in 1883 France claimed northern Madagascar and occupied the island's ports (France did not formally annexe the whole of Madagascar until 6 August 1896).

This phase of French colonial expansion, which accelerated around 1880 and continued until 1914, was due to a complex combination of pressures from both the centre (government ministers and politicians such as Jules Ferry, certain generals and admirals, a number of newspapers and journals, geographical and colonial societies, business groups and chambers of commerce with colonial interests) and the periphery (army and naval officers, colonial officials, explorers, missionaries and adventurers of all kinds), as well as advances in medicine, technology and weaponry, which reduced the costs of colonial conquests, and the competition engendered by the 'scramble for Africa', in which several European states participated. It is striking that Ferry, a republican rather than a right-wing politician, became perhaps the politician most closely associated with French colonial expansion in this period, on the grounds that France as a colonizer had a civilizing mission to play, that France needed colonies to maintain her position as a great power, and that France's rivals would annexe territories that France did not annexe.

Critics of Ferry, such as Clemenceau, argued that colonial expansion distracted French attention from the lost provinces and Germany, wasted precious resources of money and manpower, and, by promoting colonial conflicts, threatened to alienate potential allies such as Britain and Italy. There were also complaints that parliament was not adequately informed or consulted over colonial policies and decisions. Public opinion in France condemned the government of the day both for not intervening in Egypt in 1882 and for a relatively minor military reverse in Tonkin in 1885, which contributed to the fall of the Ferry government on 30 March. In *Le Tonkin et la mère-patrie* Ferry was defending himself and his policies of colonial expansion against his critics, but the value of France's colonial empire to the country as a whole remains a matter of dispute.

Document 2.10 Socialism and Strikes

The coal miners of Decazeville [a mining town in the Aveyron in southern France] – whose 'general misery' can alone explain their tragic entry on to the public stage, according to M. Jules Garnier, a colleague of Watrin [deputy director of the mine, killed by the miners in January 1886] – have nothing to hope for from the government of the bourgeois Republic. Nothing except condemnations, arrests and martial law.

In response to the miners' complaints communicated to the Chamber of Deputies by Basly, and supported by Boyer and Camélinat, the Minister of Public Works initially and then later the President of the Council of Ministers [the equivalent of Prime Minister] have replied with a formal refusal.

Refused, the eight-hour day!

Refused, a minimum wage or a minimum old-age pension, while minimum profits are, in the name of 'guaranteed interests', assured to the extent of 100 million francs this year for the Rothschilds [a Jewish bank] and for the mini-Rothschilds of our railways!

Refused, even the ending of that triple theft represented by the retention by employers of workers' wages for the first month of employment, the obligation to shop in the company store, and the reduction of fines imposed for disciplinary reasons!

Apart from payment on a fortnightly rather than a monthly basis, which the Company of Léon Say [the Compagnie du Nord, a railway company, of which Léon Say was the director] has agreed to consider, the serfs of the Aveyron have been sent back empty-handed.

In contrast, thanks to government intervention, the mining company emerges from the present crisis with considerably reduced transport charges and with a new order from the Orleans Railway Company for 130,000 tons of coal a year for ten years.

It was starvation labour which cried for help from members of the government.

It is to the aid of capitalism and dividends that government members have in a republican manner gone!

But it is not this thousand and one bankruptcy inflicted on our working class by the bourgeois state which will characterize yesterday's debate in the Chamber of Deputies, any more than the reasoned order of the day which crowned the debate in such a dignified manner.

In confirming its confidence in the 'concern' and 'zeal' of the ruling classes, which are expressed, under Freycinet as under Ferry, under Ferry as under Bonaparte, by the same bayonets defending the interests of the same employers, the Chamber of the *scrutin de liste* has simply continued the Chambers of the *scrutin d'arrondissement*.

What makes the parliamentary session of 11 February 1886 unforgettable is the unanimity and spontaneity with which all the bourgeois political parties joined together and found themselves united against the leading spokesmen of the working class, who are themselves working class.

Source: Le Cri du peuple, *February 1886; J. Guesde,* Le Socialisme au jour le jour. *Paris: V. Giard et E. Brière. 1899, pp. 96–7*

From 1877 the republicans had gradually acquired control of the Third Republic, with republican gains in a series of local and parliamentary elections and with the election of a republican, Jules Grévy, as President of the Republic (30 January 1879 – he was re-elected to a second seven-year term of office on 28 December 1885). Republican governments, such as those headed by Charles de Freycinet (29 December 1879–19 September 1880, 30 January–29 July 1882, 7 January–3 December 1886) and Jules Ferry (23 September 1880–10 November 1881, 21 February 1883–30 March 1885), inevitably pursued republican policies in areas such as education, Church–state relations, legislation on the press and public meetings, local government (the introduction of elected mayors), and reform of the Senate (abolition of life senators). Although all this amounted to a radical republican programme, it did not do much to improve the lives of the working classes; and government intervention in the economy, for instance to promote the construction of railways and other infrastructure projects, seemed to favour the interests of capitalists rather than workers. This apparent marriage of capitalism to republicanism was personified by Léon Say – director of railway companies, friend of the Rothschilds, long-serving parliamentarian, four times Minister of Finance between 1872 and 1882, firm supporter of free trade and the market economy, and equally firm opponent of socialism. At the same time, republican governments, like their predecessors, failed to improve working conditions for the proletariat and responded to industrial violence by arrests, legal proceedings and the deployment of troops.

With the founding of the POF and the Anzin coal miners' strike of 1880, the Third Republic began to experience socialist politics and serious industrial unrest. Candidates who stood solely as POF candidates in the general parliamentary elections of 4 and 18 October 1885 attracted just 7,700 votes in the six departments they contested (Willard, 1965, p. 41), but a number of deputies from working-class backgrounds who were sympathetic to the workers were elected in urban constituencies such as Paris and Marseilles, including Emile-Joseph Basly, Antide Boyer and Zéphirin Camélinat. One of the leaders of the Anzin miners' strike of 1880 and founder in 1883 of the miners' trade union (of which he became Secretary and President), Basly defended the murder of the engineer Watrin as an 'execution' and 'act of popular justice'. A little less provocatively, Boyer and Camélinat, both ex-Communards, also supported the miners in parliament. However, as Jules Guesde complained, at the end of the debate on 11 February 1886 the overwhelming majority of deputies voted for an order of the day confirming 'the confidence of the Chamber in the government's concern for the interests of the workers and in the government's zeal in maintaining public order'.

Document 2.11 Anti-Semitism

The source of Jewish wealth is usury, in all its forms: dealing, secondhand trading, market speculation, businesses with misleading prospectuses, all the ways of ensuring that the products of labour go to the unproductive. Work is the source of public wealth. In this immense vessel that sustains work, the Jews have made a crack through which all the liquid constantly runs into the barrels of their cellars.

This great crack is usury, it is the interest on money, the interest on capital, which the Church has always condemned.

It is a puerile objection to respond that not all financiers or speculators on the stock exchange are Jewish. I agree.

I am even prepared to admit that, as has been very well understood in Spain, the Judaicized, those affiliated to the Jewish system, are even more grasping and less scrupulous than the Jews, if that is possible. The Jew likes to fleece people without attracting attention. He likes to asset strip with a velvet glove, except in cases like the Union Générale when he felt his monopoly was threatened and when he became ferocious. When Jewish ideas enter a Christian consciousness they produce a complete perversion of all sense of morality. Certain financiers, who have houses in all the quarters of the capital and a chapel in their châteaux in the outskirts of Paris, exceed the rapacity of Shylock in the way they treat their poor tenants. I know of examples of unbelievable behaviour by them.

What is certain is that the system is Jewish and that Jewish civilization has replaced Christian civilization.

Source: E. Drumont, La France juive devant l'opinion. *Paris: C. Marpan et E. Flammarion. 1886, pp. 127–8*

Jews had been expelled from the kingdom of France in 1394, and the French Jewish community was still quite small, and mostly resident in Alsace, by 1789. The Revolution emancipated the Jews, which encouraged some Catholics and royalists to interpret it as an anti-Catholic and anti-monarchical conspiracy organized by Protestants,

Freemasons and Jews. During the nineteenth century, the French Jewish community slowly increased in size: in 1872, according to official figures, about 50,000 Jews lived in France, nearly half of them in or around Paris; and by 1900 France probably had approximately 80,000 Jewish residents (50,000 in or near Paris), with a further 45,000 Jews in Algeria (Marrus, 1980, pp. 30–1). In comparison with Austria-Hungary, Germany or Russia, France still had comparatively few Jews. Anti-Semitism, nevertheless, existed in France as elsewhere in Europe, and for the same reasons: traditional Catholic hostility, the age-old association of Jews with usury and money-lending (as in Shakespeare's Shylock), and Jewish 'strangeness', exclusivity, limited integration into the wider community, and the relatively low level of intermarriage between Jews and non-Jews. However, French anti-Semitism was not really significant except in years of political and social crisis, such as 1830 and 1848, and even then it remained a marginal phenomenon.

This situation changed in 1886 with the publication and reception of *La France juive* by a minor journalist, author and playwright, Edouard Drumont. The book instantly became a sensational success: it appeared in numerous editions; it was serialized in a popular newspaper, *Le Petit Journal*; and it released a flood of anti-Semitic literature, including further publications from Drumont. Anti-Semitic publications had appeared before in nineteenth-century France, such as Alphonse Toussenel's *Les Juifs, rois de l'époque* (1845), but not with the same consequences, so new factors seem to have been at work. The Jew, frequently personified by the Rothschilds, was often seen in both the socialist and popular imagination as the symbol of an industrial capitalism that was destroying traditional France. The disasters of 1870–1 had undermined national self-confidence and made anybody with a German-sounding name (which many Jews had) automatically suspect. The German annexation of Alsace was followed by the migration of many Alsatian Jews to France, mostly to Paris, where they were joined from about 1880 by Jewish refugees from Russia, Poland and Romania, fleeing pogroms and persecution. In the expanding and increasingly cosmopolitan Jewish community in Paris, Jews became more prominent in banking, business, politics and the professions. Inevitably, this caused resentment and fears of a Jewish takeover of Catholic France.

Such fears surfaced in 1882 when the Union Générale, a Catholic bank founded in 1878 by a former employee of the Rothschilds, suddenly collapsed, causing its largely Catholic clientele to lose their savings. This financial disaster, due to maladministration and unwise speculation, was widely blamed on a Jewish conspiracy. Hence Drumont, in scapegoating the Jews and those allegedly imbued with 'Jewish values', in associating the Jews with ruthless capitalist exploitation and financial corruption, and in portraying Jews as the enemies within, contributing to and revelling in France's misfortunes, struck a powerful and dangerous chord.

Document 2.12 Boulangism

The trembling hypocrites who have oppressed us for too long struggle hard to pretend that General Boulanger has no programme and that nobody knows what he wants, what he thinks or what he can do.

To those critics, we reply: Do you want to know what Boulanger stands for?
Boulanger stands for EMPLOYMENT!
Boulanger stands for LIBERTY!
Boulanger stands for HONESTY!
Boulanger stands for JUSTICE!
Boulanger stands for the PEOPLE!
Boulanger stands for PEACE!

BOULANGER STANDS FOR WORK!

Workers, what do you want?
To live by working!
What do you lack?
Employment and the means of subsistence!
Who has caused you unemployment, ruin and misery?
Those who have given precedence to their needs, appetites and unhealthy ambitions before your interests which they should have defended, and who observe, with a dry eye and a light heart, as the workers suffer and die of hunger!
To them positions, honours, luxury and power!
To you misery!
It is time that this stopped!
Give way to the avenger!
Give way to the person who will rid you of this horde of parasites, living off your suffering and betraying your trust, who have done nothing for you apart from sending your sons to die far away, without any benefit to France which is left disarmed!
Give way to the person who will revive national employment!
Give way to the General who, making us strong, will give us security, without which no enterprise is possible!
Give way to the Reformer who, protecting industry, commerce and agriculture, will enable you to raise your children and to turn them into good and sturdy workers!
Boulanger will defend you against foreign competition!
Boulanger, whose hands are untainted by any corruption, will be motivated only by your interests . . .

BOULANGER STANDS FOR PEACE!

Yes, peace, but an honourable peace!
That is what we want!
That is what he will give us!
It is in vain that his disloyal opponents are not afraid of writing that his name is synonymous with the next war . . .
All of you workers, crushed by the dreadful consequences of disastrous policies, which reduce national employment!

All of you peasants, who want to keep your ancestral acres and not be demeaned and made landless!

You, bourgeois and employers, whose interests are harmed by the chaos at the bottom of which swarm members of parliament!

You also, the intellectual élite of the nation, humiliated by the insolent wealth of shameless mediocrities!

Support General Boulanger!

His hand on the hilt of the sword of France, the General will make it understood to those who threaten us that the time of timid submissions is past, and that, in the balance of the destinies of Europe, this sword, reforged by his efforts, can carry a great weight.

Confident in her mission of progress and civilization, seeing an era of justice, calm, order and liberty open before her, France, freed from those who enslave her, will wait, serene and impassive, for Justice, formerly misunderstood and violated, to gain a devastating revenge over Force!

This is the programme of General Boulanger.

It is up to you, Frenchmen, to enable him to accomplish it.

LONG LIVE FRANCE!

LONG LIVE THE REPUBLIC!

April 1888

Source: Bibliothèque nationale Fol. Lb 57.9588; O. Wieviorka and C. Prochasson (eds), La France du XXe siècle: documents d'histoire. Paris: Editions du Seuil. 1994, pp. 91–4

The political formula which had served the Right and Louis-Napoleon Bonaparte (Napoleon III) so well during the Second Republic – defence of private property, law and order and the interests of the Roman Catholic Church, combined with repression of the Left – failed to work in the 1870s, so that republicans had come to power in France by the end of the decade. Electoral defeats and consequent exclusion from power, and the introduction of a series of republican measures, encouraged some elements of the Right to seek a new political formula in a heady mixture of populist nationalism, anti-parliamentarianism and the unscrupulous exploitation of scandals, grievances and all forms of discontent, as well as xenophobia and anti-Semitism. Boulangism was in part one of the earliest significant manifestations of this new and dangerous phenomenon.

On 7 January 1886 General Boulanger was appointed Minister of War (a post then reserved for serving officers, not civilian politicians) on the grounds of his action-packed military career and his reputation as a republican (unusual at that time for so senior an officer). As Minister of War, Boulanger tried to reform and modernize the French army, but he also presented himself as 'General Revenge' (for 1870–1), notably during the Paris military review of 14 July 1886. This anti-German posturing eventually led to a serious crisis in Franco-German relations, the Schnaebelé Affair of April 1887. Considered a liability by the government, Boulanger was dismissed from the Ministry of War on 30 May 1887 and posted to a provincial command at Clermont-Ferrand.

Extraordinary demonstrations of popular support accompanied his rail journey to Clermont-Ferrand (28 June 1887), which encouraged him to pursue his political ambitions. Having been dismissed from the army for his political activities in March 1888, Boulanger immediately plunged into electoral politics, winning by-elections in the Dordogne and the Nord the following month. He went on to win three more by-elections in August; and 245,000 voters in the Seine triumphantly returned him to the Chamber of Deputies on 27 January 1889. As rumours of an impending coup d'état circulated, judicial proceedings apparently threatened him, so he fled into exile. This ended Boulanger's political career in France. On 30 September 1891 he killed himself over the grave of his mistress in a Belgian cemetery.

Boulanger's electoral manifesto of April 1888 illustrates his attempt to exploit poverty, unemployment, Ferry's unpopular colonial policies, the widespread distrust of politicians, and France's recent humiliation by Germany, as well as his attempt to appeal to all classes of the population. The attractiveness of this programme to the French electorate was clearly remarkable, but what is not so clear is the precise political character of Boulangism. It has been argued that Boulangism was a form of non-Marxist or anti-Marxist socialism (Sternhell, 1978, pp. 35, 49 and 55; Hutton, 1996), though the links between Boulangism and conservatism, and even royalism, have also been stressed (Irvine, 1988 and 1989). It is difficult to categorize Boulangism as belonging purely to the right or to the left as it drew ideologically from the patriotic nationalism of Jacobinism and from the anti-parliamentarianism of anarchism; and it was supported by republicans such as Henri Rochefort and Alfred Naquet, by the radical republican and militant nationalist Paul Déroulède and his Ligue des Patriotes (Patriotic League), and by working-class voters in the Nord and the Seine. On the other hand, Boulanger received media support from royalist newspapers and financial support from wealthy royalists such as the Duchesse d'Uzès; conservatives and royalists voted for Boulanger in a series of elections in 1888 and 1889; Boulanger himself was in secret contact with the royalist pretender, the Comte de Paris; and Boulangism attracted anti-republicans and anti-Semites such as Maurice Barrès and the Marquis de Morès, who later became anti-Dreyfusards and whose political heirs were fascists.

CHRONOLOGY

1871
8 February   National Assembly elections
5 July   Manifesto of the Comte de Chambord

1872
14 March   Law against the Socialist International
27 July   Law introducing five-year term of military service

1873
24 May   Resignation of Thiers; MacMahon President of the Republic

| 16 September | Liberation of French territory |

1875

30 January	Wallon amendment
24 February	Law on the Senate
12 July	Law allowing Catholic institutions of higher education to award university degrees

1876

30 January	Senate elections
20 February–5 March	Elections to the Chamber of Deputies
2–10 October	First French Workers' Congress, held in Paris

1877

16 May	Dismissal of Jules Simon by President MacMahon
17 May	Broglie government
18 May	Manifesto of the 363
25 June	Dissolution of parliament
14–28 October	Parliamentary elections
20 November	Resignation of Broglie

1878

| 28 January–8 February | Second French Workers' Congress, held in Lyon |

1879

4 January	Senate elections
30 January	Resignation of MacMahon; Grévy President of the Republic
4 February	Ferry appointed Minister of Education
21 June	Return of parliament to Paris
20 October	Socialist Workers' Congress, held at Marseilles

1880

29 March	Decrees against unauthorized religious orders
23 May	Public commemoration of the Commune at the Mur des Fédérés
21 June	Amnesty for Communards voted by Chamber of Deputies
14 July	Official celebration of the national holiday
21 December	Law on the secondary education of girls

1881

12 May	French protectorate proclaimed over Tunis
16 June	Law on free primary education
29 July	Liberal press law
21 August–4 September	Parliamentary elections

1882

| 19 January | Failure of the Union Générale Bank |

28 March	Law on compulsory and secular primary education
18 May	Foundation of the Ligue des Patriotes (Patriotic League)

1884

5 April	Law on municipal government

1885

30 March	Fall of Ferry
4–18 October	Parliamentary elections

1886

7 January	General Boulanger appointed Minister of War
14 July	Longchamps military review

1887

20–3 April	Schnaebelé Affair
30 May	Dismissal of Boulanger
2 December	Resignation of Grévy after Wilson honours scandal

1888

14 March	Boulanger retired from army
8 April	Boulanger elected in the Dordogne
15 April	Boulanger elected in the Nord
19 August	Boulanger re-elected in the Nord, and elected in the Somme and Charante-Inférieure

1889

27 January	Boulanger elected in the Seine
13 February	Electoral law changed from *scrutin de liste* to *scrutin d'arrondissement*
1 April	Flight of Boulanger to Brussels
14–21 July	Founding congress of the Second International, held in Paris
15 July	Three-year compulsory military service
22 September–6 October	Parliamentary elections

BIBLIOGRAPHY

Andrew, C.M., 'The French Colonialist Movement during the Third Republic: the unofficial mind of imperialism', *Transactions of the Royal Historical Society*, fifth series, 26 (1976), 143–66.

Auspitz, K., *The Radical Bourgeoisie: the Ligue de l'Enseignement and the origins of the Third Republic, 1866–1885.* Cambridge: Cambridge University Press. 1982.

Bury, J.P.T., *Gambetta and the Making of the Third Republic.* London: Longman. 1973.

Bury, J.P.T. and Tombs, R.P., *Thiers, 1797–1877: a political life.* London: Allen & Unwin. 1986.

Cooke, J.J., *New French Imperialism, 1880–1910: the Third French Republic and colonial expansion.* Newton Abbot: David and Charles. 1973.

Dallas, G., *At the Heart of a Tiger: Clemenceau and his world, 1841–1929*. London: Macmillan. 1993.

Duroselle, J.-B., *Clemenceau*. Paris: Fayard. 1988.

Elwitt, S., *The Making of the Third Republic: class and politics in France, 1868–1884*. Baton Rouge: Louisiana State University Press. 1975.

—— *The Third Republic Defended: bourgeois reform in France, 1880–1914*. Baton Rouge and London: Louisiana State University Press. 1986.

Fulton, B., 'The Boulanger Affair Revisited: the preservation of the Third Republic, 1889', *French Historical Studies*, 17 (1991), 310–29.

Grévy, J., *La République des opportunistes, 1870–1885*. Paris: Perrin. 1998.

Grubb, A., *The Politics of Pessimism: Albert de Broglie and conservative politics in the early Third Republic*. Newark and London: University of Delaware Press. 1996.

Guiral, P., *Adolphe Thiers*. Paris: Fayard. 1986.

Hazareesingh, S., 'The Société d'Instruction Républicaine and the Propagation of Civic Republicanism in Provincial and Rural France, 1870–1877', *Journal of Modern History*, 71 (1999), 271–307.

Hutton, P.H., 'Popular Boulangism and the Advent of Mass Politics in France, 1886–90', *Journal of Contemporary History*, 11 (1976), 85–106.

—— *The Cult of the Revolutionary Tradition: the Blanquists in French politics, 1864–1893*. Berkeley: University of California Press. 1981.

Irvine, W.D., 'French Royalists and Boulangism', *French Historical Studies*, 15 (1988), 395–406.

—— *The Boulanger Affair Reconsidered: royalism, Boulangism, and the origins of the radical right in France*. New York and Oxford: Oxford University Press. 1989.

Locke, R.R., 'A New Look at Conservative Preparations for the French Elections of 1871', *French Historical Studies*, 5 (1968), 351–8.

—— *French Legitimists and the Politics of Moral Order in the Early Third Republic*. Princeton: Princeton University Press. 1974.

Marrus, M.R., *The Politics of Assimilation: the French Jewish community at the time of the Dreyfus Affair*. Oxford: Oxford University Press. 1980.

Marseille, J., 'Les Relations commerciales entre la France et son empire colonial de 1880 à 1913', *Revue d'histoire moderne et contemporaine*, 31 (1994), 286–307.

Mazgaj, P., 'The Origins of the French Radical Right: a historiographical essay', *French Historical Studies*, 15 (1987), 287–315.

Millman, R., 'Jewish Anticlericalism and the Rise of Modern Antisemitism', *History*, 77 (1992), 220–36.

Munholland, K., 'Admiral Jauréguiberry and the French Scramble for Tonkin, 1879–83', *French Historical Studies*, 11 (1979), 81–107.

Rothney, J., *Bonapartism after Sedan*. Ithaca, NY: Cornell University Press. 1969.

Sternhell, Z., *La Droite Révolutionnaire, 1885–1914: les origines françaises du fascisme*. Paris: Seuil. 1978.

Watson, D.R., *Georges Clemenceau: a political biography*. London: Eyre Methuen. 1974.

Willard, C., *Les Guesdistes: le mouvement socialiste en France, 1893–1905*. Paris: Editions Sociales. 1965.

3 | The Dreyfus Affair and its aftermath

Historians have attached enormous importance to the Dreyfus Affair and its aftermath for the history of the Third Republic and even of modern Europe. 'The Affair bears comparison with the greatest crises that French society has experienced' (Mayeur and Rebérioux, 1984, p. 179); and it has been described as 'a matter of life and death for the Third Republic' (Snyder, 1973, p. xxii), as 'the conflict that helped shape the political landscape of modern France' (Burns, 1992, p. xiii), and even as 'a kind of dress rehearsal' for the twentieth-century anti-Semitism that climaxed with the Holocaust (Arendt, 1967, p. 10).

At one level it is surprising that the Dreyfus Affair was so significant. Initially, the Affair involved the apparent sale of military intelligence by a French army officer to a German diplomat. Such acts of treachery are not uncommon in the history of most modern states. The Affair then became a case of an alleged miscarriage of justice, again, regrettably, a common phenomenon in the history of most modern states. However, the Dreyfus Affair was so significant and had such a profound impact because it raised so many sensitive issues – military espionage, the competence and honour of the French army, and Franco-German relations initially, and then, because Captain Alfred Dreyfus was Jewish, anti-Semitism. Second, the Dreyfus Affair from its inception received widespread and sensational coverage in the French press, so that it captured public attention and later the interest of politicians and intellectuals. Third, the Dreyfus Affair became, in effect, a battleground between elements of the French Right and their opponents over the fundamental question of the definition of France's national identity and of the character of the French Republic.

The eventual defeat of the opponents of Dreyfus involved a major swing to the Left in French national politics with the coming to power of the Waldeck-Rousseau government in June 1899. The consequences for the French army and for the Catholic Church in France were traumatic. The prestige of the French army was gravely compromised by the Affair; a number of senior army officers were personally disgraced; an attempt was made to 'republicanize' the officer corps; and the term of compulsory military service was reduced to two years in March 1905. In the course of the Dreyfus Affair elements within the Catholic Church displayed a virulent anti-Semitism and opposition to Dreyfus, and as a consequence the whole Catholic Church in France suffered: 'unauthorized' religious orders were expelled; many

Catholic schools were closed; the French Republic broke off diplomatic relations with the Vatican (July 1904); and the Catholic Church in France was disestablished (December 1905).

Document 3.1 The Toast of Algiers (12 November 1890)

Gentlemen, permit me, before we separate, to propose a toast to the French navy, represented today with such distinction in our midst.

Our navy recalls glorious and cherished memories for Algeria: from the beginning it has contributed to the conquest of Algeria, and the name of the current distinguished commander of the Mediterranean squadron is a reminder of this conquest like the distant echo of the first songs of victory.

I am therefore happy, Admiral, in the absence of our Governor General who is detained far from us, to have been able to create here, as it were, a crown of honour of all those who represent the authority of France in Algeria: the commanders of our brave army, the heads of our administration, and our senior magistrats. What touches me above all is that they have all come to this table, on the invitation of the old Archbishop, who, like them, has made Africa his second country in order to serve France better.

May it please God that the same spectacle is reproduced in our France, and that the unity which is displayed here among us, in the presence of the foreigner who surrounds us, will soon reign among the sons of the Mother-Country!

Unity, in the presence of a still painful past and an always threatening future, is, in effect, what at this time we need most. Unity is also, let me assure you, the first wish of the Church and of all ranks of its clergy.

The Church certainly does not ask you to renounce either the memory of past glories or the sentiments of loyalty and gratitude which honour all men. But when the popular will has been clearly expressed, when the form of a government in no way contradicts, as Pope Leo XIII recently proclaimed, the principles according to which Christian and civilized nations alone can live, when it is necessary to protect one's country from the dangers that threaten it by unreservedly supporting that form of government, the moment finally comes to declare that the test has been made, and, to end our divisions, to sacrifice everything which conscience and honour permit and require each of us to sacrifice for the national interest.

Source: X. de Montclos, Le Toast d'Alger: documents, 1890–1891. *Paris: E. de Boccard. 1966, pp. 68–9*

On 12 November 1890 in his official residence, Cardinal Lavigerie, the most senior figure in Algiers after the Governor General, received forty officers of the Mediterranean squadron of the French fleet, then paying a visit to the port of Algiers. Also present at the reception were leading figures of the French community in Algiers. At the end of the banquet, Cardinal Lavigerie gave a short speech that ended with a toast to the French navy. In his toast he referred specifically to the squadron's commander, Admiral Charles-Marie Duperré, a descendant of Admiral Guy Victor Duperré, Minister of the Navy 1834–6 and 1839–40. This flattering reference, and the whole thrust of the cardinal's speech, were designed to state publicly that the Catholic Church now accepted and supported the Third Republic and that all patriotic Frenchmen, whatever their personal loyalties and convictions, should do the same.

The policy known as the *Ralliement* was, as Cardinal Lavigerie implied in his speech, inspired by Pope Leo XIII. The Pope had become convinced that a monarchical restoration was no longer a practicable possibility in France and that the interests of the Catholic Chuch in France would benefit from better relations with the French Republic. Also, the Pope hoped that France might be an ally in his conflict with the Kingdom of Italy over the lost Papal States, particularly as Franco-Italian relations were then at a low ebb. When Cardinal Lavigerie had an audience with the Pope in Rome in October 1890, he was told that he had been chosen to publicize a policy of reconciliation between the Catholic Church and the French state. In Algeria and Tunisia Lavigerie had vigorously promoted the spread of Catholicism and of French influence, thereby demonstrating that the intereststs of the Catholic Church and the French state could coincide; and in his role as the founder of the religious order of the White Fathers and as an active opponent of the African slave-trade, he had acquired distinction and prominence. So, despite past Legitimist sympathies, Lavigerie was an obvious spokesman and propagandist for the *Ralliement*.

Most French Catholics did not welcome the *Ralliement*. Admiral Duperré and his fellow-officers allegedly listened to the cardinal's speech 'in icy silence' (Brogan, 1967, p. 262). Only two French bishops openly supported Lavigerie, while several publicly opposed him. The Catholic press also tended to be hostile, with the combative journalist and parliamentary deputy Paul de Cassagnac being positively abusive. Eventually, five French cardinals published a long letter to Catholics in January 1892, accepting the Republic but attacking freedom of conscience, secular education, and civil marriage and divorce; and, after failing to defend Lavigerie, Leo XIII did finally confirm that the *Ralliement* was official papal policy with his encyclical, *Au milieu des sollicitudes* (16 February 1892). The latter encouraged a number of royalist leaders to rally to the Republic, such as Albert, Comte de Mun in May 1892 and Armand, Baron de Mackau in October 1892; and in parliamentary terms the *Ralliement* for a time enjoyed some success since in the mid-1890s moderate republicans were prepared to combine with Catholic Ralliés to keep left-wing republicans and socialists out of office. In the longer term, fear of the Left and of anti-clerical legislation might have won over more French Catholics to the *Ralliement*, had it not been for the Dreyfus Affair.

Document 3.2 The *Bordereau*

Without any news indicating to me that you want to see me, I am nevertheless, sir, sending you some interesting information.

1   A note on the hydraulic brake of the 120 and the manner in which this gun behaves.
2   A note on the covering troops (some modifications will be made under the new plan).
3   A note on a modification to the artillery formations.
4   A note about Madagascar.
5   The draft Firing Manual of the Field Artillery (14 March 1894).

The last document is extremely difficult to obtain and I can have it at my disposal only for a very few days. The Ministry of War has sent a specific number to the Corps and the Corps are responsible for them. Each officer holding one must return it after manoeuvres. If, therefore, you wish to take from it whatever interests you, and then keep the original for me, I will secure an example of the Manual, unless you would just like me to have it copied *in extenso* and send you the copy.

I am about to leave on manoeuvres.

Source: B. Lazare, Une Erreur judiciaire: l'affaire Dreyfus. *Paris: P.V. Stock. 1897, p. 40*

This memorandum, usually known by the French word *bordereau*, is the key document in the Dreyfus Affair. It lists five topics of military significance that, with one exception, were not particularly secret or important, and the list is imprecise and inaccurate. The French army then had in service two 120-millimetre guns, of which only the older siege-gun had a hydraulic brake. The function of this hydraulic brake was to absorb the recoil, removing the need to re-aim after every discharge and so permitting much more rapid fire. Particularly when applied to the 75-millimetre gun, it gave France 'a tremendous lead over Germany in field artillery' (Kaplan, 1999, p. 501). However, the other matters constituted relatively low-grade military intelligence. The references to covering troops and artillery formations are very vague but probably refer to revised military plans which were being introduced following the agreement of a Franco-Russian military convention (December 1893–January 1894). Aspects of these plans had already been publicly discussed in the French parliament. Plans were also in hand for a French military expedition to Madagascar, which might have potentially threatened German East Africa, but these plans were then very much at a preliminary stage. Finally, the *Firing Manual of Artillery in the Field* was a printed pamphlet, of which approximately 3,000 copies had been distributed to army formations. This manual had not been classified as confidential or restricted, and some copies had even been put on sale.

The *bordereau* was written on onion-skin semi-transparent paper and had been torn across twice. There was no signature, date or envelope. The author of the *bordereau* was Major Count Walsin-Esterhazy, then the commander of a battalion of the 74th Infantry Regiment, stationed at Rouen. In financial difficulties, he had made a series of visits from 20 July 1894 to the German military attaché, Lieutenant-Colonel Maximilian von Schwartzkoppen, at the German Embassy, offering to sell confidential military information. Probably at the end of August he left the *bordereau*, listing the information he intended to sell, with the concierge at the German Embassy. The *bordereau* was then retrieved from the German Embassy, possibly from Schwartzkoppen's waste-paper basket by a cleaner called Mme Bastian, who doubled as a French agent. On 26 September the *bordereau* was passed on to Major Henry, responsible for receiving and (if necessary) reconstituting documents brought in by agents to the French army's counter-espionage bureau, officially known as the Statistical Section. Major Henry and his colleagues in the Statistical Section immediately assumed that a French army officer was selling military secrets to the Germans, and the hunt began to find the traitor.

Document 3.3 The Arrest of Captain Alfred Dreyfus (15 October 1894)

HE IS NOT A FRENCHMAN

Misfortunes frequently follow each other. At the very moment when we lost the Emperor Alexander III, we learnt that a captain of our Army General Staff had been accused of communicating military intelligence with our enemies.

Public opinion has been grievously affected by this infamous act, the most abominable of all.

The arrest for the crime of high treason of a man who wore the uniform of an officer and who had communicated national defence secrets to a foreign power has dismayed the army. Neither the army nor the country will admit that a Frenchman could forget his duties and his honour to the extent of betraying his country.

It has to be recognized that Captain Dreyfus was attached to the first department of the General Staff, that his rank, that his position, that the very important matters for which he was responsible, that the documents and the files to which he had access, meant that he could give the enemy invaluable service and inflict on France irreparable harm.

But how can one explain the monstrous aberration that led the accused to exploit his responsible position to reveal the secrets of our military mobilization to the agents of the Triple Alliance?

Alas!, we fear an impassioned response! The people disown Dreyfus as a compatriot; officers protest against the usurpation of a military rank, conferred on a colleague who had insinuated himself into their intimacy.

It is a great misfortune for Jews that Captain Dreyfus is Jewish.

Rightly or wrongly, the avenging indignation of whoever is proud to call himself French by origin will be soothed only by denying the legitimacy of the accused officer's claims to the insignia of his rank; this indignation will be directed against his irresponsible admission into the ranks of the army, polluted by the presence of a traitor.

We are far from sharing the fanatical feelings of those who condemn the wealth of the Jews, who denounce the source of their extraordinary success as suspicious, who fulminate against their financial intrigues and their universal influence.

We are even less supportive of the association made between religious quarrels and commercial competition: we do not anathematize anybody and we deplore the intemperate character of certain polemics that mix up all sorts of questions and attack people wholesale. We detest social hatreds, the accursed ferment of civil war.

We are nevertheless forced to recognize that many Jews have retained from their traditional customs over the centuries a sort of tenacious internationalism: it is only a small minority of them, since the majority have become French; it is still painful to note sometimes differences of opinion, divergences of conscience, contrasts of custom which make these minority Jews appear to be foreigners.

Source: Le Petit Journal, *3 November 1894; B. Lazare,* Une Erreur judiciaire: l'affaire Dreyfus. *Paris: P.V. Stock. 1897, pp. 18–20*

Captain Alfred Dreyfus was arrested in Paris on 15 October 1894 as the presumed author of the *bordereau* and therefore as a traitor responsible for communicating secret military information to a German agent. The Statistical Section assumed that the *bordereau* could have been written only by an artillery officer attached to the General Staff, even though the vagueness and phraseology of the *bordereau* might have suggested otherwise. Captain Dreyfus was rapidly selected as the most likely culprit because he was an artillery officer attached to the General Staff, had served in four departments of the Ministry of War, allegedly was unpopular with his fellow-officers and behaved in a suspicious manner, and because his handwriting was thought by some to resemble that of the *bordereau*. On the other hand, Dreyfus was not about to go on manoeuvres during the summer or autumn of 1894.

The arrest of Dreyfus can partly be explained by the context in which it occurred. Military defeat in 1870–1, the role of the army in the suppression of the Paris Commune and the loss of Alsace and Lorraine to the German Empire meant that military affairs and Franco-German relations were always likely to be sensitive issues. The introduction of compulsory military conscription, the Boulanger phenomenon, a continuing obsession with military espionage, the occasional use of soldiers in industrial disputes, and republican perceptions of the army officer corps as being characterized by upper-class conservatives who had been educated at private Catholic schools all helped to intensify these sensitivities. Moreover, the current Minister of War, General Auguste Mercier, had proved himself to be somewhat accident prone and his position was not secure.

In a wider perspective, the stability of the Third Republic seemed to be threatened by a variety of factors, including an economic recession partly accentuated by the spread of the phylloxera disease in France's vineyards, a succession of bank failures and financial scandals, the emergence of a parliamentary socialist party, industrial unrest and a wave of anarchist atrocities culminating with the assassination of President Sadi-Carnot (24 June 1894). In addition, the death of Tsar Alexander III (20 October

1894) seemed to threaten France's recently negotiated diplomatic alliance and military convention with Russia, which had enabled France to break out of the diplomatic isolation from which she had suffered since 1870. For all these reasons, the authorities were highly embarrassed by the evidence of a traitor in the army officer corps and anxious to deal with the case as rapidly and firmly as possible.

What role did anti-Semitism play? According to Guy Chapman, 'Anti-Semitism no doubt existed, but it cannot be shown to have played a dominant part in the arrest and trial of Dreyfus' (Chapman, 1955, p. 64). In contrast, Stephen Wilson has written: 'There is little doubt that Dreyfus's original arrest and condemnation stemmed from the anti-Jewish prejudice of the officer corps' (Wilson, 1982, p. 4). Certainly, some officers who initially dealt with the case, such as Colonel Sandherr (head of the Statistical Section), were anti-Semitic; and almost at once anti-Semitism became a factor in the Dreyfus Affair. On 28 October 1894 Edouard Drumont, editor of an anti-Semitic newspaper, *La Libre Parole*, received a note from Major Henry that Captain Dreyfus had been arrested on a charge of espionage. The next day *La Libre Parole*, which had been campaigning against the presence of Jews in the army officer corps, reported that an extremely important arrest had been made in connection with military espionage, and challenged the military authorities to break their silence on the matter. Other newspapers took up the cry, and on 1 November 1894 *La Libre Parole* published an article headed: 'High Treason: Arrest of the Jewish Officer, A. Dreyfus'. The article published on 3 November in *Le Petit Journal*, one of the four main Paris daily newspapers, while disclaiming anti-Semitic prejudice and condemning the stirring up of social hatreds, nevertheless assumed that Dreyfus was guilty before his trial, condoned the view that Dreyfus should never have been allowed to become an officer, and suggested that a small minority of French Jews thought and behaved in a manner that made them appear as foreigners.

Document 3.4 The Degradation of Dreyfus (5 January 1895)

The 'execution parade' began at eight forty-five in the morning in the main courtyard of the Ecole Militaire, which was full of troops. In accordance with the procedures laid down in the military penal code, all the regiments of the Paris garrison had sent a detachment.

I took part in the ceremony, wearing the uniform of an artillery lieutenant: Colonel Sandherr had given me permission to join his officers.

It was a freezing morning. Suddenly, under the pale sky, a bitter and cutting north wind threw large snowflakes in our faces: the scene was sinister.

In front of the iron railings of the courtyard, in the Place de Fontenoy, there was an enormous crowd, scarcely contained by the police, which stamped their feet, got excited, whistled , and shouted 'Death to the Jews! . . . Death to the traitor! . . . Death to Judas!'

Nine o'clock struck. General Darras, on horseback, followed by his staff, drew his sword. There was a roll of drums. 'Attention! . . . Present arms!'

In a dreadful silence, in which thousands of men seemed to be holding their breath, Dreyfus appeared from the right corner of the courtyard, surrounded by a bombardier and four artillerymen, sabres drawn and carrying revolvers. He advanced with a firm pace, head held high, as though he were in command of his escort.

Brought before General Darras, he halted, heels together in the military position; the escort stepped back four paces.

The General then rose in his stirrups and, holding high his sword, declared: 'Alfred Dreyfus, you are no longer worthy to carry arms. In the name of the French people, we degrade you!'

Immediately, an adjutant of the Republican Guard, a giant called Bouxin, approached the immobile condemned man, and, in a furious manner, stripped the stripes from the képi and the sleeves, the buttons from the tunic, the epaulettes from the shoulders, and all the insignia of rank, which he threw into the mud. When Dreyfus had been reduced to a state of rags and tatters, the giant seized his sword and scabbard, which he broke with a blow against his own knees. The frightful torture seemed to be interminable . . .

Dreyfus, in rags, as grotesque in his appearance as he was pitiable, went back to his place among the artillerymen of his escort. In this manner he marched in front of all the regiments on parade, which took a long time, since there were at least four thousand men.

During this march, a veritable martyrdom, Dreyfus did not resort to any act of defiance or revolt; his pace was as firm and as in step as that of the artillerymen who surrounded him. Twice I heard him shout: 'I am innocent!'

At the end of his march he passed in front of our group. In a dry, mechanical, expressionless voice he shouted again: 'I am innocent!'

When he finally arrived at the end of the courtyard, two gendarmes seized him, handcuffed him and heaved him into a prison van, which made off at a quick trot.

Source: G.M. Paléologue, Journal de l'Affaire Dreyfus, 1894–1899: l'Affaire Dreyfus et le Quai d'Orsay. *Paris: Plon. 1955, pp. 37–9*

After his arrest, Dreyfus was kept in solitary confinement and repeatedly interrogated and subjected to handwriting tests by Major Du Paty de Clam. However, Dreyfus made no confession; a search of Dreyfus's Paris flat and an investigation of him produced nothing incriminating; and the German, Italian and Austro-Hungarian embassies denied any connection with Dreyfus. All that remained was the alleged similarity of the handwriting of the *bordereau* with that of Dreyfus, about which expert opinion disagreed. However, from the beginning of November 1894 nationalist and anti-Semitic newspapers such as *La Libre Parole, L'Intransigeant* and *La Patrie*, and a Catholic newspaper controlled by the Assumptionist Order, *La Croix*, not only campaigned for the condemnation and even execution of Dreyfus, but against General Mercier for having allegedly mishandled the Affair. Under enormous pressure, Mercier decided that Dreyfus had to be found guilty and punished severely. On 28 November a conservative newspaper, *Le Figaro*, published the text of an interview with Mercier, in which he claimed that the evidence against Dreyfus was overwhelming; and on 19 December Dreyfus was committed to trial by a military tribunal presided over by seven army officers acting as judges. The trial ended on 22 December when the judges unanimously found Dreyfus guilty and sentenced him to deportation for life in a fortified place, forfeiture of his military rank and public degradation, the heaviest sentence possible.

The arrest and trial of Dreyfus were unsatisfactory on a number of grounds. Dreyfus had been arrested without being charged with a specific offence; he had been held in solitary confinement without at first being allowed to communicate with anybody; the family of Dreyfus were similarly kept in the dark; pre-trial publicity in several Paris newspapers was severely prejudicial to a fair trial, partly because of Henry's leak and Mercier's interview; the proceedings of the military tribunal were held in secret; only three out of five experts pronounced that the *bordereau* was in the handwriting of Dreyfus; and a file of documents of very dubious worth, which allegedly helped to incriminate Dreyfus, was communicated to the judges but not to the defence. Nevertheless, the verdict was almost unanimously welcomed by the newspaper press and public opinion; and the public degradation of Dreyfus duly took place on 5 January 1895, followed by his removal from Paris on 18 January for his eventual place of detention, Devil's Island, a former leper colony off the coast of French Guiana.

Document 3.5 The Nationalism of Bernard Lazare

What does the word nationalism mean for a Jew, or rather what should it mean? It ought to mean freedom. The Jew who today will say: 'I am a nationalist', will not say in a clear, precise and specific manner: 'I am a man who wants to reconstitute a Jewish state in Palestine and who dreams of reconquering Jerusalem.' He will say: 'I want to be a completely free man, I want to enjoy the sunshine, I want to have my right to human dignity. I want to escape the oppression, insult and contempt which people want to impose upon me.' At certain times in history, nationalism is for groups of human beings the manifestation of the spirit of freedom . . .

Am I therefore in contradiction with internationalist ideas? Not at all. How am I therefore in agreement with them? Simply by preventing myself from giving to words a significance and a meaning that they do not have. When the socialists oppose nationalism, in reality they oppose protectionism and national exclusiveness; they oppose this chauvinistic, narrow, absurd patriotism, which encourages peoples to confront each other like rivals or adversaries determined to grant neither pardon nor mercy. This is the egoism of nations, which is as odious and contemptible as the egoism of individuals. What does internationalism now involve? It obviously involves nations. What does being an internationalist mean? It means establishing between the nations ties not just of diplomatic friendship but of human fraternity.

Source: B. Lazare, Publications du Kadimah, *No. 1, 1898; J.-D. Bredin,* Bernard Lazare. *Paris: Fallois. 1992, pp. 302–3*

At first few were convinced of the innocence of Dreyfus, apart from his lawyer, Edgar Demange, and members of his family, notably his brother Mathieu. In February 1895 Mathieu Dreyfus first met Bernard Lazare, a fellow Jew from Nîmes who had completed his education at the Ecole Pratique des Hautes Etudes in Paris and become a journalist. In his newspaper articles Lazare wrote from a socialist standpoint, and even with some sympathy for anarchism. He also became a critical commentator on Jewish topics, for instance disclaiming any sense of solidarity with Jewish immigrants in France and partly blaming anti-Semitism on the allegedly exclusive attitudes of Jews. In 1894 he published a book, *Anti-Semitism, its History and its Causes*, in which he again partly blamed anti-Semitism on the alleged vanity and exclusiveness of Jews, maintained that there were not separate races, just separate peoples and nations, and argued that the future goal of Jews should be assimilation.

During the 1890s anti-Semitism became a significant phenomenon in France. Thirty-nine deputies in November 1891 supported a parliamentary proposal which would have led to the expulsion of all Jews from France. In April 1892 Edouard Drumont, the author of *La France juive* (1886), *La France juive devant l'opinion* (1886) and other anti-Semitic publications, founded *La Libre Parole*, an anti-Semitic daily newspaper, to expose the role of two corrupt Jewish financiers, the Baron de Reinach and Cornelius Herz, in scandals involving the construction of the Panama Canal. The newspaper became phenomenally successful, achieving at one point a circulation of approximately 500,000 and spawning an illustrated edition (July 1893–September 1897); and in August 1893 Drumont was elected in the Somme to the Chamber of Deputies, to which twenty-three declared anti-Semitic candidates were elected in May 1898. Drumont attacked Jews on the grounds that they constituted a nation within a nation, that they could never be loyal to France, and that they exploited France and were parasites. These views were repeated in other newspapers, such as the Assumptionist *La Croix* (which sold 170,000 copies in 1895 and had numerous regional editions, bringing the total readership of the Assumptionist press to approximately 500,000) and Henri Rochefort's *L'Intransigeant* (which had a circulation of around 200,000 in the late 1890s). In addition, the Union Nationale (founded in the early 1890s with a membership of some 12,500 by 1895) called for the exclusion of Jews from public employment, for the withdrawal of full rights of citizenship from Jews, and even for their expulsion from France; and in 1897 Jules Guérin founded the French Anti-Semitic League, of which the 5,000 or so members engaged in acts of occasional violence against Jews and Jewish-owned property.

Through his conversations with Mathieu Dreyfus, Lazare became convinced that Captain Dreyfus was the victim of a miscarriage of justice; and the extent of anti-Semitism in France forced Lazare to denounce anti-Semitism much more vigorously and unequivocally than before, and to argue that Jews lost much through becoming assimilated and that assimilation was not, and could not be, the answer. In November 1896 Lazare published in Brussels 3,500 copies of a pamphlet entitled *A Judicial Error:*

the truth about the Dreyfus Affair, which he had distributed to members of the Senate and the Chamber of Deputies, to journalists and to other public figures. A new edition, with evidence from handwriting experts that Dreyfus had not written the *bordereau*, appeared in Paris in 1897. Besides striking a major blow in support of Dreyfus, these pamphlets made Lazare a hero for French and foreign Jews, at a time when Zionist ideas were beginning to take concrete form.

At the first Zionist Conference, held in Basle at the end of August 1897, it was agreed to create a legally protected refuge for the Jewish people in Palestine. Lazare was unable to attend this conference, but he did attend the second Zionist Conference, again held in Basle a year later, and was elected to its council and action committee. Under the leadership of Theodor Herzl (who had observed the degradation ceremony of Dreyfus as the Paris correspondent of the *Neue Freie Presse* of Vienna), the conference approved the setting up of a Jewish Bank to finance Jewish settlement in Palestine. Lazare, however, believed that Jews should be concerned, not with establishing a Jewish colony and perhaps eventually a Jewish state in Palestine, which he thought would resemble all the other nation states, but rather with human rights and human values and with the persecution and oppression of communities, such as the Jews in Romania and the Armenians in Turkey.

Document 3.6 The Nationalism of Maurice Barrès

We are nationalists.

At the summits of society as in the depths of the provinces, in the moral order as in the material order, in the commercial, industrial and agricultural worlds, even in the building sites where he competes with French workers, the foreigner, like a parasite, poisons us.

An essential principle, according to which the new French policy should be based, is to protect all French nationals against this invasion, and also that it is necessary to beware of this socialism which is too cosmopolitan, or rather too German, and which undermines the defence of the fatherland.

The Jewish question is bound up with the national question. Assimilated by the Revolution to those who are French by origin, the Jews have preserved their distinctive character, and, from being persecuted as they once were, they have become domineering. We are in favour of the most complete freedom of conscience; in addition, we would consider it a serious danger to give the Jews the opportunity to invoke, and therefore to appear to defend, the principles of civil liberty proclaimed by the Revolution. But they violate these principles by isolationist behaviour which is their distinctive feature, by their tendency to monopolize and speculate, and by their cosmopolitan character. Besides, in the army, in the judiciary, in the civil service, in all our administrations, Jews infinitely exceed the normal proportion to which their number might entitle them. They have been appointed prefects, judges and financial officials because they have the money which corrupts. Without even changing the law, by insisting on more balanced recruitment from those who govern, it should be possible to correct a dangerous imbalance and secure more respect for our genuine nationals, children of Gaul and not of Judea.

Above all it is essential to make it more difficult to acquire French nationality. It is through the lax process of naturalization that the worst Jews and so many mediocrities have acquired French nationality.

Statistics indicate that 90 per cent of foreigners who acquire French nationality do so only when they are no longer liable for military service. Let it be proclaimed that military service is the condition for naturalization. In addition, those who are naturalized (apart from those from Alsace-Lorraine) should just possess personal rights and only their descendants should be assimilated to the native French and enjoy political rights.

For the last twenty years the opportunist system has favoured the Jew, the foreigner, the cosmopolitan. Those who committed this criminal error argued that these exotic immigrants contributed vigorous ingredients to France. What attractive ingredients, these Reinach, these Cornelius Herz, these Alfred Dreyfus, who almost succeeded in corrupting us! The real truth is that the vigorous ingredients which French society genuinely needs will be found within it, by encouraging the upward social mobility of the most disadvantaged and the most impoverished through improving their standard of living and their level of education and training.

It can thus be seen how nationalism necessarily gives birth to socialism. We define socialism as 'the material and moral improvement of the most numerous and the most impoverished class.'

After centuries, the French nation has achieved the provision of political security to its members. It is now necessary that it protects its members against the economic insecurity from which they suffer at all levels.

Source: L'Action Française, *15 September 1900; M. Barrès,* Scènes et doctrines du nationalisme. *Paris: Félix Juven. 1902, pp. 432–4*

Brought up in Lorraine in a middle-class family, Maurice Barrès as an eight-year-old experienced the German occupation during the Franco-Prussian War, an experience that he never forgot and that helped to make him a life-long opponent of Germany and an ardent French nationalist. Like Bernard Lazare, Barrès moved to Paris as a young man and became a journalist and literary figure, though his political development was very different from that of Lazare. He held national decadence as being at least partially responsible for France's defeats of 1870–1, he passionately sought the recovery of Alsace-Lorraine, he believed that France would be avenged by a strong charismatic leader such as Joan of Arc or Napoleon, and he admired the French army as embodying authority, tradition and French nationhood. For all these reasons, he became a fervent supporter of General Boulanger and as a Boulangist deputy represented Nancy from 1889 to 1893. Throughout the Dreyfus Affair he was violently anti-Dreyfusard, attacking Jews, defending the army and denouncing parliamentarianism. He also developed a concept of nationalism, particularly in a novel, Les Déracinés or The Uprooted (1897), in which he suggested that the genuine

Frenchman was rooted in the land where his ancestors had been buried. In other words, nationalism was the product of roots, of ties to the soil and to an ancestral legacy, of an identification with national institutions such as the army and the Catholic Church and with a national culture and consciousness. From this it followed that foreigners, Jews (non-Catholics and allegedly rootless and cosmopolitan) and even many French intellectuals (also allegedly rootless and cosmopolitan) were not, and could not be, French in any meaningful sense.

Between 1893 and 1906 (when he was re-elected in a conservative Paris constituency, which he continued to represent until his death in 1923), Barrès stood unsuccessfully in a series of parliamentary elections, attempting to win votes by appealing to the electorate's xenophobia and anti-Semitism. As early as 1893, in a campaign brochure, *For the Protection of French Workers*, Barrès proposed that immigrant workers should be liable to French military service, that French employers of immigrants should be taxed, that immigrant workers should be denied jobs in government-subsidized projects, and that immigrant workers should be deported if they applied for poor relief. Similarly, in his 1900 Nancy Programme Barrès advocated protection against foreign imports and foreign workers and against the 'feudalism' of international finance, the establishment of a pension fund (to be financed by taxes on foreign imports and foreign workers), the introduction of a fairer tax system, the promotion of agricultural savings banks and industrial co-operatives, the improvement of technical education, and the revision of the Constitution so as to permit referenda at the municipal level. This amounted to a brand of socialism, though Barrès remained unsympathetic to trade unions and strikes.

In his Nancy Programme Barrès accepted that the full rights of French citizenship should be granted to the descendants of foreign immigrant workers, suggesting that his concept of French nationalism was culturally rather than racially based. However, his antipathy to Jews by this time was racial as well as cultural, and from 1905 he opposed intermarriage in Alsace-Lorraine between French and Germans.

Notwithstanding the Dreyfus Affair, the obsession of Barrès and of many other anti-Dreyfusards with Jews is a little surprising, since the Jewish community in metropolitan France numbered only about 100,000 by 1900, though admittedly Jews were quite prominent in Paris and in some banking, business and professional circles. Similarly, provincial departments with virtually no Jewish residents sometimes elected anti-Semitic candidates to the Chamber of Deputies. Anti-Semitism in France at this time has been interpreted as an expression of revolt against all the changes caused by the development of a modern industrial society, of which to many the Jew was a symbol. The Jew as the rootless intellectual, the wandering cosmopolitan and the international capitalist could also be a symbol of a corrupt and corrupting civilization (Bredin, *Bernard Lazare*, 1992, pp. 101–2). However irrational, the ideas of Maurice Barrès exercised a profound influence on the French Right throughout the twentieth century.

Document 3.7 Emile Zola and the Press

We have seen the gutter press on heat, minting money with its unhealthy curiosity, upsetting the masses to sell its newsprint, which ceases to sell as soon as the nation is calm, sensible and strong. They are the dogs that bark in the night, the depraved newspapers which grab passers-by with their headlines in block capitals, promising debaucheries. These newspapers were only behaving as they usually do, but with a remarkable impudence.

Further up the ladder, we have seen the popular press, the newspapers costing one *sou*, those which target the greatest number and which form mass opinion, we have seen them fan terrible passions, furiously wage sectarian campaigns, killing in our dear people of France all generosity, all concern for truth and justice. I would like to believe in their good faith. But what a sad spectacle, these minds belonging to aged polemicists, demented agitators and narrow patriots, who have become opinion-formers, committing the blackest of crimes, that of confusing the public conscience and misleading an entire people! This job is even more atrocious because it is carried out, in certain newspapers, with an habitual tendency to lie, defame and denounce, which will remain the great shame of our epoch.

Finally, we have seen the heavy press, the so-called serious and honest press, join in all this with an impassive, even serene, manner which I declare to be stupefying . . .

Above all we have observed this – because in the midst of so many horrors it should suffice to choose the most revolting – we have seen the press, the squalid press, continuing to defend a French officer [Esterhazy] who has insulted the army and spat on the nation. We have witnessed some newspapers excusing him and other newspapers qualifying their condemnation of him. Why has there not been a universal cry of revulsion and execration? What has happened that this crime, which at another time would have prompted a furious demand for immediate action from the public conscience, has been excused on the grounds of extenuating circumstances by the very same newspapers which are so sensitive on matters of felony and treason?

Source: Emile Zola in Le Figaro, *5 December 1897; J.-D. Bredin,* Emile Zola: l'Affaire Dreyfus, la vérité en marche. *Paris: Imprimerie Nationale. 1992, pp. 58–9*

Newspapers played a crucial role in the Dreyfus Affair and, more generally, in the political life of the Third Republic. They broke the news of the arrest of Dreyfus, launched an anti-Semitic campaign against him, pressured the authorities to condemn and severely punish him, and thereafter continued to villify Dreyfus, to denounce his supporters (known as the Dreyfusards) and to defend his opponents (known as the anti-Dreyfusards), even including Major Esterhazy. In the absence of radio and television, newspapers provided the main source of information on current events and the main influence on shaping public opinion. They also took the initiative in a variety of spheres by promoting and organizing sporting events, subscriptions for popular causes, and referenda or opinion polls on pressing political and cultural issues. At the same time, journalism could contribute to the reputations and incomes of aspiring and established politicians and literary figures. Railways, the telegraph and later the telephone, improvements in the processes of manufacturing newsprint and newspaper printing, and the advertising and news information services offered by the Havas Agency, made possible the rapid gathering of news from most parts of the world and the cheap and efficient production and distribution of mass-circulation newspapers. The liberal press law of 29 July 1881 and soaring literacy rates due to compulsory primary education further contributed to a favourable climate for newspapers. Between 1880 and 1900 there was a threefold increase in the number of Paris newspapers, a handful of which were astonishingly successful, such as *Le Petit Journal*, with a daily circulation of a million copies in 1897 and perhaps 5 million readers.

At the time of the Dreyfus Affair, Emile Zola was one of France's most distinguished novelists. The son of an Italian immigrant (which led to accusations that he was not really French), by 1897 Zola had published some forty novels, notably a twenty-volume cycle on the lives of the fictional Rougon-Macquart family during the Second Empire, which explored such themes as working-class Paris (*L'Assommoir*, 1877), coal mining and coal miners (*Germinal*, 1885), peasants (*La Terre*, 1887), railways (*La Bête humaine*, 1890) and war (*La Débâcle*, 1892). Through these novels Zola gained the reputation of being a left-wing critic of French society and of institutions such as the French army. From the 1860s he also contributed reviews and articles to several newspapers, including *Le Figaro*, a conservative newspaper with a circulation of over 80,000 which around 1880 had abandoned monarchism for moderate republicanism and which tended to be Dreyfusard until 1898. Zola was first drawn into the public debate on the Dreyfus Affair by his opposition to anti-Semitism, which he condemned in an article published in *Le Figaro* on 26 May 1896, though he did not really join the Dreyfusard camp until a year and a half later.

During the summer and autumn of 1896 the case against Dreyfus began to unravel. On 27 August 1896 Colonel Picquart, who had succeeded Sandherr as head of the Statistical Section, acquired a letter written by Esterhazy and realized that Esterhazy's handwriting was identical to that of the *bordereau*; on 3 September the London *Daily Chronicle* published a deliberately misleading report that Dreyfus had escaped from Devil's Island, in order to focus public attention on Dreyfus once again; on 15 September a newspaper called *L'Eclair*, attempting to support the Army General Staff, revealed that at the trial of Dreyfus the judges, but not the defence, had seen a secret file of documents allegedly incriminating Dreyfus; and on 10 November, following the circulation of Bernard Lazare's *A Judicial Error* to politicians and journalists, *Le Matin* published a facsimile of the *bordereau*, thereby bringing it into the public domain and questioning its authorship. Picquart, wrongly suspected of having leaked a copy of the *bordereau* to *Le Matin*, was sent on tours in the provinces and then in Tunisia; and Major Henry in the Statistical Section began to forge documents to strengthen the crumbling case against Dreyfus. However, Picquart's convictions were communicated to Auguste Scheurer-Kestner, a Protestant from Alsace and

Vice-President of the Senate; and the summer and autumn of 1897 witnessed the formation of a small but influential group of Dreyfusards, which Scheurer-Kestner invited Zola to join on 13 November.

After some hesitation, Zola contributed a series of Dreyfusard articles to *Le Figaro*, defending Scheurer-Kestner against attacks from the anti-Dreyfusards (25 November), denouncing the anti-Dreyfusard claim that a Jewish conspiracy or 'syndicate' had been formed to defend Dreyfus (1 December) and condemning the French press for its prejudiced, irresponsible and anti-Semitic coverage of the Dreyfus Affair (5 December). Certainly, several French newspapers were openly and violently anti-Semitic, such as *La Croix*, *L'Intransigeant* and *La Libre Parole*, the majority of Paris and provincial newspapers was still anti-Dreyfusard, and some newspapers pandered to popular prejudices in order to attract readers. On the other hand, serious and balanced coverage of the Dreyfus Affair could be found in newspapers such as *Le Temps* and *Le Journal des Débats*, articles favourable to the Dreyfusards were published in newspapers such as *Le Figaro*, and some newspapers openly supported the Dreyfusards, such as *L'Aurore*, edited by Georges Clemenceau.

Zola continued his Dreyfusard campaign with public letters published as pamphlets: 'Letter to Youth' (14 December 1897), censuring nationalist demonstrations against Scheurer-Kestner; and 'Letter to France' (6 January 1898), criticizing the procedures for the forthcoming trial of Esterhazy.

Document 3.8 Emile Zola's 'J'Accuse . . . !' (13 January 1898)

I accuse Lieutenant-Colonel du Paty de Clam of having been the diabolical agent of the judicial error – unwittingly, as I would like to believe – and then of having defended his iniquitous work for three years, by means of the most preposterous and shameful machinations.

I accuse General Mercier of having made himself an accomplice to one of the greatest crimes in history, at the very least by feeble-mindedness.

I accuse General Billot of having had decisive evidence of the innocence of Dreyfus in his hands, of having suppressed it, and of having made himself guilty of this crime against humanity and against justice for political reasons, to save the compromised General Staff.

I accuse General de Boisdeffre and General Gonse of having made themselves accomplices to the same crime, the former no doubt because of his passionately held Catholicism, the latter perhaps through the *esprit de corps* which turns the offices of the Ministry of War into the Holy Ark, totally above criticism.

I accuse General de Pellieux and Major Ravary of having carried out a wicked inquiry, by that I mean an inquiry of the most monstrous partiality, which produced, in the second report, an imperishable monument of naïve effrontery.

I accuse the three handwriting experts, Messrs Belhomme, Varinard and Couard, of having made deceitful and fraudulent reports, unless a medical examination certifies them to be suffering from diseased eyesight and judgement.

I accuse the offices of the Ministry of War of having pursued a vicious campaign in the press, particularly in *L'Eclair* and *L'Echo de Paris*, in order to lead public opinion astray and to cover up their own misconduct.

I accuse, finally, the first military tribunal of having infringed the law by convicting an accused man on the basis of a secret document, and I accuse the second military tribunal of having covered up this illegality, on orders, committing in its turn the judicial crime of knowingly acquitting a guilty man.

Source: J.-D. Bredin, Emile Zola: L'Affaire Dreyfus: la vérité en marche. *Paris: Imprimerie Nationale. 1992, pp. 105–6*

Zola's intervention in the Dreyfus Affair coincided with the unmasking of Esterhazy. Having been shown examples of the handwriting of Esterhazy by a banker who happened to have some letters written by him, and having been convinced that Esterhazy was the author of the *bordereau*, on 15 November 1897 Mathieu Dreyfus wrote a letter to General Billot, Minister of War since April 1896, declaring that Esterhazy had written the *bordereau*, the sole piece of evidence against his brother, and demanding justice without delay. General Billot therefore ordered General de Pellieux to investigate Esterhazy. However, the Army General Staff (headed by General Boisdeffre) had decided to protect Esterhazy in order to prevent any reopening of the Dreyfus case: Major Henry began forging documents to try to incriminate Picquart; and General de Pellieux submitted a report to the government, claiming that there was no evidence of treason against Esterhazy, whereas Picquart was guilty of having leaked official letters, and probably secret documents. General de Pellieux then interrogated Picquart on 26 and 27 November. He proceeded to submit a second report, confirming Picquart's guilt, but on 28 November *Le Figaro* published letters by Esterhazy to his mistress in which he revealed a murderous hatred of the French. This may have prompted the government to initiate judicial proceedings against him; and, amid numerous demonstrations of nationalist anti-Dreyfusard sentiment, Esterhazy appeared before a military tribunal in Paris on 10 January 1898. Major Ravary, who was in charge of the prosecution, produced three handwriting experts (Belhomme, Couard and Varinard), who argued that Esterhazy had not written the *bordereau* since he had not disguised his handwriting, as any real spy would have done; and the trial was turned into a trial of Picquart, against whom Major Henry and General Gonse (deputy head of the Army General Staff) testified. After a trial lasting only two days, the seven military judges took just three minutes to agree to acquit Esterhazy, while Picquart was arrested the following day and sent to the Mont-Valérien prison.

On 6 January 1898, convinced that Esterhazy would be acquitted and outraged by this travesty of justice, Zola began writing what was to become '*J'accuse!*', an open letter addressed to the President of the Republic. Originally intended to be another pamphlet, it was published in *L'Aurore* on 13 January. Zola's accusations covered the whole Dreyfus Affair, not just the trial of Esterhazy. He specifically accused a long list of individuals of incompetence, perversion of the course of justice and even criminal acts: Lieutenant-Colonel du Paty de Clam, for mishandling the initial proceedings against Dreyfus; Colonel Sandherr, for misidentifying the author of the *bordereau* due to an uncritical examination of the document; the Ministers of War, General Mercier and General Billot, and the head of the Army General Staff, the Jesuit-educated and ultra-Catholic General Boisdeffre and his deputy, General Gonse, for their failures to take responsibility, their refusal to acknowledge the guilt of Esterhazy, and their cynical and disreputable persecution of Picquart; General de Pellieux and Major Ravary, for their iniquitous handling of the proceedings against Esterhazy; and the handwriting experts, for their absurd conclusions about the handwriting of the *bordereau*. Finally, he accused the Ministry of War for having incited a press campaign to mislead public opinion and to cover up their mistakes, and the first military tribunal for its condemnation of Dreyfus on the basis of a secret document, and the second military tribunal for having acted under orders in knowingly acquitting the guilty Esterhazy. It was a remarkable indictment and on the whole accurate, apart from its failure to appreciate the role of Major Henry; and it was written with great verve, with such telling phrases as 'Truth is on the march and nothing will stop it' ('*la vérité est en marche et rien ne l'arrêtera*').

The publication of '*J'Accuse . . . !*' made a sensational impact. Over 200,000 copies of the issue of *L'Aurore* were sold. The Dreyfusard cause immediately became a crusade for many intellectuals and others, while nationalists claimed that Zola had outraged the honour of the French army and a wave of anti-Semitic riots hit many towns in France and Algeria. The government could not avoid putting Zola on trial, though, to prevent a reopening of the Dreyfus case, the charge against him was limited to the libellous accusation that a military tribunal had acquitted Esterhazy on the orders of the Ministry of War. Following violent exchanges in parliament between Jules Méline, the Prime Minister, and Jean Jaurès, a leading socialist, and in an atmosphere of great excitement, Zola went on trial before a civilian court on 7 February 1898. The trial once again revealed many of the weaknesses of the case against Dreyfus, but the jury, overwhelmed by the complexities of the case and the large number of different testimonies, and reminded by General Boisdeffre that the nation needed to have confidence in its army chiefs, found Zola guilty. On 23 February Zola was sentenced to one year in prison and a fine of 3,000 francs. The Court of Appeal overturned this judgement on 2 April 1898 on a technicality, but fresh proceedings were launched against Zola and on 13 May 1898 he went on trial again. After weeks of legal wrangling and fearing a second condemnation, Zola on 18 July left Paris for London, where he remained in voluntary exile for eleven months.

Document 3.9 The Rennes Retrial (7 August–9 September 1899)

Tinkle goes the bell; judges and prisoner come in again. The Registrar reads the Act of Accusation of the first trial; it is long, and has been public property for a year and a half – and we got up at five. But when it is over comes the moment of the day. The President addresses the prisoner in a voice suave yet sharp, and Dreyfus stands up. He is round-shouldered, yet he stands bolt upright, and looks his judge hard in the face. A paper is handed to him – the *bordereau*, at once the act and evidence of treachery. Did he write that?

Again an instant's dead silence – and then again the dry, split, dead man's voice. It is the voice of a man who has forgotten how to speak, who is struggling desperately to master tones which crumble and fail him. The voice rises – half a shriek and half a sob. But the words you hear are, 'I am innocent, my colonel.' Then the colonel's soft tones again and more answers. The brake of the 120-millimetre gun, the artillery firing-manual, Dreyfus's journeys to Alsace, a suggested trip to Brussels, his relations with an Austrian mistress, his alleged confession – a string of cross-examination. It is difficult to follow the questions; but after five minutes the answers are heard in every corner of the hall. He has found his voice, and it is thick and full. No; no, my colonel; never; I never played; I do not know him; I never said so – the denials follow on the questions sharply, instantly, eagerly. Now and again a white-gloved hand is raised in emphasis, while the white left-hand fingers twitch on the képi. Now and again comes a sentence – precipitate, almost breathless, as if he feared to lose one second of his chance to be heard. Every moment his back stiffens, his voice deepens, his hand is raised more appealingly, his protestations burst out more fervently. It is a man fighting for his life against time.

Source: G.W. Steevens, The Tragedy of Dreyfus. *London and New York: Harper and Brothers. 1899, pp. 70–2*

With the conviction of Zola the Dreyfus cause experienced another defeat, both in judicial terms and so far as majority public opinion was concerned. In the general parliamentary elections of 8 and 22 May 1898 anti-Dreyfusard candidates such as Edouard Drumont and Paul Déroulède were elected, while Dreyfusard candidates such as Jean Jaurès and Joseph Reinach were defeated; and prominent Dreyfusards suffered a variety of official sanctions and popular rejections, with, for instance, the Senate not re-electing Scheurer-Kestner as its Vice-President. However, the identification of the nationalists and anti-Semites with the Right in the May 1898 parliamentary elections encouraged the French Left to break with extreme nationalism and anti-Semitism. This became more significant after the fall of the Méline government (14 June 1898) and the formation of a more left-wing government in which Godefroy Cavaignac, reputed to be both a republican and a nationalist, was the Minister of War.

Convinced that Dreyfus was guilty and had acted as an accomplice of Esterhazy, Cavaignac in a parliamentary speech of 7 July read out the texts of documents forged by Major Henry, not knowing that they were forgeries, and stated that Dreyfus had made a confession admitting his treason. Jaurès immediately responded with a letter to Cavaignac, published in *La Petite République* on 8 July, pointing out that at the Dreyfus trial secret documents had been shown to the judges but not to the defence, that the evidence for a confession by Dreyfus was unsound, and that the documents to which Cavaignac had referred were forgeries. The last point was confirmed by a letter from Picquart to the Prime Minister published in *Le Siècle* the following day. This prompted new legal proceedings against Picquart, but at the same time details began to emerge of the Army General Staff's collusion with Esterhazy. In addition, Jaurès on 10 August began publishing in *La Petite République* a series of articles (later collected in a pamphlet entitled *Les Preuves*) in which he repeated and elaborated his previous accusations; and, crucially, on 13 August an officer examining the documents in the secret Dreyfus file detected one of Henry's forgeries. Informed of this unwelcome discovery, on 30 August Cavaignac interrogated Henry (now a colonel and head of the Statistical Section) and extracted from him an admission of forgery. Henry was immediately arrested and imprisoned, while General Boisdeffre (who had been present at the interrogation) resigned. The next day Henry committed suicide in prison. His confession and suicide, and Boisdeffre's resignation, made revision inevitable, particularly as Esterhazy had precipitately fled Paris for London. On 3 September the government advised Mathieu Dreyfus to file a request for revision and Cavaignac resigned.

Anti-Dreyfusards did not give up: they converted Henry into a martyr and organized a public subscription for his widow; and the ultra-nationalist Paul Déroulède promoted a series of noisy demonstrations, and even tried to subvert the military escort at the funeral of President Félix Faure (23 February 1899). However, legal proceedings for a revision, formally initiated on 29 October 1898, continued gradually until 29 May 1899, when the Appeal Court ruled that Dreyfus should be committed for retrial by a military tribunal at Rennes (the provincial capital of conservative and Catholic Brittany).

On 9 June Dreyfus finally left Devil's Island and, still treated as a prisoner, was transported to France in a French warship. The retrial opened on the morning of 7 August in the hall of the *lycée* at Rennes in the presence of a large audience, which included many foreign journalists. All the evidence ever collected against Dreyfus was re-examined, as were nearly all the participants in the Dreyfus Affair (except Sandherr and Henry, who were dead, and, for obvious reasons, Schwarzkoppen and Esterhazy). The military witnesses (except Picquart) reasserted their conviction that Dreyfus was guilty, but the case against Dreyfus was now very weak. Nevertheless, the military judges by a majority of five to two found Dreyfus guilty, though with extenuating circumstances, and he was sentenced to ten years' imprisonment. This verdict and sentence were received with widespread incredulity in France and with universal condemnation abroad. Partly to avoid an international boycott of the Universal Exhibition, due to open in Paris in April 1900, Dreyfus was granted a presidential pardon on 19 September 1899, though he was not finally rehabilitated until 12 July 1906.

George W. Steevens, the author of a well-informed contemporary account of the Dreyfus Affair, covered the Rennes retrial as the *Daily Mail*'s correspondent. As a war correspondent, he had already covered Kitchener's campaign in the Sudan, and he was to die tragically young from a fever in Ladysmith while reporting the Boer War.

Document 3.10 Fashoda (September–November 1898)

We were the first to arrive at Fashoda, and we have captured it only from barbarism, from which you proceeded to liberate Khartoum two months later. To ask us to evacuate it prior to all discussions would amount to issuing an ultimatum. – Very well! Who, then, knowing France could be in any doubt as to my reply? You are not ignorant of my desire for an entente with England, an entente which would be as advantageous for England as for France, nor my conciliatory sentiments. I have affirmed them so freely only because you yourself know that they will not take me beyond the bounds indicated by national honour. I can make sacrifices of material interest to the entente between the two countries, but in my hands the national honour will remain intact. Nobody in my place would speak to you in any other terms and perhaps would not offer you the same friendly disposition.

Source: Théophile Delcassé to Sir Edmond Monson, 3 October 1898; Le Figaro, *24 October 1898, pp. 1–2*

Traditional Franco-British colonial rivalry reached a peak towards the end of the nineteenth century. A combination of state bankruptcy and nationalist riots in Egypt had led to British armed intervention in July 1882. France had not participated, because a majority in the Chamber of Deputies had voted against an Anglo-French occupation of the Suez Canal Zone (31 July 1882), so Britain proceeded to become the sole occupying power in Egypt, a situation much resented in France, where Napoleon's victories in Egypt were still remembered. There followed the so-called 'scramble for Africa', in which France was an eager and successful participant, acquiring Tunisia, the French Congo, Guinea, the Ivory Coast, Dahomey (between Togoland and Nigeria), the island of Madagascar, and various territories in Equatorial Africa. In this process, local initiatives by colonial administrators and army officers on the spot, and the influence of colonial pressure groups such as the Committee of French Africa (formed in 1890) and the French Colonial Union (formed in 1893), played an important role.

Théophile Delcassé, a journalist and disciple of Gambetta who had gained election to the Chamber of Deputies in September 1889, supported French colonial expansion, believing that colonies could provide France with important markets and sources of raw materials and with enhanced national prestige. As a youthful Under-Secretary for Colonies (January–November 1893) and Minister for Colonies (May 1894–January 1895), Delcassé had promoted French territorial expansion in Africa, had helped to prepare the French occupation of Madagascar, and had begun planning an expedition to Fashoda on the White Nile to challenge the British position in Egypt. The French government did not authorize the expedition to Fashoda until November 1895, by which time Delcassé was out of power, but when he returned to office as Minister of Foreign Affairs in June 1898 the expedition was well on its way. After an epic trek from the Congo, Captain Marchand and 130 men arrived at Fashoda on 10 July 1898. However, on 19 September 1898 General Kitchener, at the head of a large Anglo-Egyptian army and fresh from his victory over the Dervishes at Omdurman

(2 September), also arrived at Fashoda; and Marchand was not joined, as had been planned, by another French expedition launched from Jibuti on the Red Sea.

The British government was determined to exclude France from the Sudan; Marchand himself was in a hopeless position; in the event of war, Britain's naval superiority over France would have been formidable; and other powers, such as Russia and Germany, were not prepared to confront Britain in order to support France in the Sudan. Delcassé and the French government therefore had to climb down: after a tense stand-off, on 2 November Delcassé ordered Marchand and his men to evacuate from Fashoda; and in March 1899 Delcassé signed an agreement with Britain acknowledging French exclusion from the Nile valley. Fashoda has been described as 'the worst crisis in Anglo-French relations since Waterloo' (Andrew, 1968, p. 78) since, for Delcassé and many of his compatriots, it seemed as though French pride and honour had been humiliated by Britain. However, Delcassé's concern for French colonial expansion was more than matched by his concern to break out of the diplomatic isolation from which France had suffered since 1870 by forming alliances, first with Russia and then with Britain. Hence, to the British ambassador in Paris he professed both his desire for an entente with Britain and his concern to defend France's honour, at a time when French politicians still believed that the defence of honour might require a nation to go to war or an individual to fight a duel.

Document 3.11 The Boer War (October 1899–May 1902)

APPEAL TO THE FRENCH
For a long time the nations have indicated their desire to oblige England to make an honourable peace with the Boers or to submit to arbitration.

For a long time, the governments refuse to take the appropriate initiatives to give expression to this objective of the peoples.

For a long time we have been convinced that, in employing against the English all the means in our power, we will not only act for the good of humanity, but in the interests of a well-understood policy, thereby safeguarding the moral and economic interests of our own nation.

That is why we adopt the following resolutions, which we urge people, through press publicity and public meetings, to approve and execute with us:

We, Frenchmen, from today consider the English as our enemies.

If the government does not put the army at the disposal of the people to carry out its will by armed force, the people will show that it will not be abused.

A – ON LAND

We will fight the English by means of an economic and social boycott:

1 We will no longer buy English products;
2 We will no longer even buy anything from shops selling English products;

3   We will ask restaurant and hotel managers to put up a notice at the entrance of their establishments: Entry forbidden to the English;
4   We will ask investors to sell all their English investments and to withdraw their investments from England;
5   We will ask jewellers to stop buying diamonds from the de Beers Company.

B – ON THE SEAS

We will ask the Transvaal government to distribute letters of marque [licences to fit out armed vessels]. Many sea captains are, in fact, ready to become armed corsairs in order to destroy England's maritime trade.

Source: Le Cri du Transvaal, *28 July and 3 August 1901, p. 2*

After Fashoda Anglo-French relations reached another low point with the Boer War. Following the outbreak of hostilities in October 1899 between Britain and the two South African Boer republics, the Transvaal and the Orange Free State, a passionate wave of pro-Boer and anti-British sentiment swept France. Conscious of French divisions and weakness as a result of the Dreyfus Affair, resentful over the outcome of the Fashoda Incident, and seeing the Boer War as a David/Goliath struggle, the French public demonstrated their pro-Boer and anti-British sentiments in a variety of ways. Paris fashion houses sought inspiration in Boer dress; President Kruger was enthusiastically received when he visited France in November 1900; and some French volunteers even fought on the side of the Boers in the Transvaal. The wives of eighteen public figures, including Mmes Paul Bert, Armand Colin, Victor Duruy, Jules Ferry, Ernest Lavisse and the Comtesse de Jouvencel, organized a public appeal, the *Sou des Boers*, to which 8,000 subscribers contributed 22,815 francs in fifteen months (*Le Cri du Transvaal*, 21 July 1901, p. 2). Supporters of the pro-Boer campaign included nationalists such as Maurice Barrès, Edouard Drumont (who, predictably, blamed the war on the insatiable greed of Jewish financiers), General Parmentier and Henri Rochefort, but also figures such as Jules Lemaître (member of the French Academy) and Gabriel Monod (Professor of History and a founding member of the League of the Rights of Man), though not many French socialists. The campaign also had an international dimension: between 9 and 12 March 1901 representatives from Germany, the United States, Austria-Hungary, Belgium, Spain, France, Italy, The Netherlands, Russia and Switzerland attended a meeting in Paris of delegates of committees in favour of the independence of the Boers.

Le Cri du Transvaal, an ephemeral Paris newspaper first published on 21 July 1901, publicized the pro-Boer campaign. The newspaper emphasized the unequal and brutal nature of the conflict ('*une poignée de Boërs héroïques méthodiquement et froidement assassinés par les armées de l'une des plus puissantes nations du globe*'), criticized the British forces ('*les uniformes maudits des hordes de Kitchener*') and the forcible detention of Boer women and children in concentration camps (citing in translation the published reports of the Englishwoman Emily Hobhouse), claimed that Britain was just interested in acquiring gold and diamond mines, and warned that a British annexation of the Boer republics would threaten the French position in Madagascar.

The proposals for a French boycott of British goods and tourists were not sensible given the substantial surplus in trade and tourism France enjoyed over Britain and the danger of British retaliation – indeed, following the example of Queen Victoria, British tourists stayed away from the Riviera; and even less sensible was the proposal for piratical attacks on British merchant ships on the high seas. Yet French press criticism of Britain over the Boer War certainly had an impact: the publication on 28 September 1901 in a satirical Paris weekly, *L'Assiette au Beurre*, of a cartoon depicting the face of King Edward VII on the naked bottom of a shameless woman representing Albion led to British protests at the highest level. More seriously, Delcassé considered trying to form a continental European coalition against Britain, which seemed possible given widespread pro-Boer sympathies and the well-publicized telegram of support which the Emperor William II had sent President Kruger (3 January 1896).

However, no European state was prepared to risk war with Britain over South Africa; the outbreak of the Boxer Rising in China in June 1900 led to Britain co-operating with Germany, Russia and France in suppressing the rising; and the Boer War formally ended with a British victory in May 1902, after which the conflict ceased to be an international issue.

Document 3.12 The Separation of Church and State (9 December 1905)

LAW OF 9 DECEMBER 1905 CONCERNING THE SEPARATION
OF CHURCH AND STATE
FIRST CHAPTER
Principles

First Article. – The Republic guarantees freedom of conscience. It guarantees the free exercise of religious worship subject only to the restrictions hereinafter enacted in the interests of public order.

Article 2. – The Republic does not recognize or financially support or subsidize any religious denomination. Consequently, from the first of January which will follow the promulgation of this law, all expenses relating to religious worship will be deleted from the budgets of the state, the departments and the communes. The costs relating to chaplaincy services designed to ensure the free exercise of religious worship in public institutions such as *lycées*, colleges, schools, hospices, refuges and prisons will still be able to feature in the aforementioned budgets.

Public institutions of religious worship are suppressed, subject to the dispositions set out in article 3.

CHAPTER II
Allocation of property – pensions

Atricle 3. – The establishments, the suppression of which is specified by article 2, will continue provisionally to function, in conformity with the regulations which currently govern them, until the allocation of their property to the associations provided for in chapter IV and at the latest until the expiry of the deadline indicated below.

As soon as this law has been promulgated, the agents of the state property department will proceed to make a descriptive inventory and valuation of:

1   The movable goods and fixed assets of the afore-mentioned establishments;
2   The properties of the state, the departments and the communes of which the aforementioned establishments have the use.

This double inventory will be drawn up after due hearing of the parties with the legal representatives of the ecclesiastical establishments or those duly summoned by a notification drawn up in the administrative manner.

The agents responsible for the inventory will have the right to require all titles and documents useful to their operations to be communicated to them . . .

Article 11. – Clergymen who, at the time of the promulgation of this law, will be more than sixty years old and who will have served as state-paid ecclesiastics for at least thirty years will receive an annual pension for life equivalent to three-quarters of their salary.

Those who are over forty-five years old and who will have served at least twenty years as state-paid ecclesiastics, will receive an annual pension for life equivalent to half their salary . . .

Article 12. – The buildings which have been placed at the disposition of the nation and which, by virtue of the law of 18 Germinal Year X (8 April 1802), are used for the public exercise of religious worship or for the accommodation of the clergy (cathedrals, churches, chapels, temples, synagogues, residences of archbishops, bishops, clergy and seminary students), as well as their fixed assets and the movable objects which furnished them when they were handed over for religious worship, are and remain the property of the state, the departments and the communes.

Source: M. *Larkin,* Church and State after the Dreyfus Affair: the separation issue in France. *London: Macmillan. 1974, pp. 227–32*

Throughout the nineteenth century, Church–state relations in France were based on the Concordat agreed between Napoleon and Pope Pius VII on 15 July 1801 and amended by Napoleon on 8 April 1802 so as to ensure the subordination of the Pope and the Roman Catholic Church in France to the French state. By the Concordat, the Roman Catholic Church in France accepted the loss of ecclesiastical land sold during the Revolution and agreed that Napoleon should have the right to nominate bishops and archbishops. In return, Roman Catholicism was recognized as the religion of the great majority of French citizens (but not as the exclusive or state religion in France), Catholic cathedrals and churches were reopened for Catholic worship, and the payment of salaries to archbishops, bishops and parish clergy became a state responsibility. By the so-called Organic Articles of 8 April 1802, French government approval was required in France for the publication of papal bulls or documents, for the intervention of any papal representative, and for the holding of any ecclesiatical synod or council. In addition, all the clergy had to swear an oath of allegiance to the state, and they became subject to numerous state regulations that even covered clerical dress.

The Concordat worked quite well (except under Napoleon), but at the end of the nineteenth century it came under attack. By 1898 nearly 20 per cent of the entire male secondary-school population was taught in schools run directly or indirectly by religious orders, while a further 22 per cent attended other Catholic schools (Larkin, 1995, p. 29), an intolerably high percentage for the anti-clerical Left who wanted French schoolchildren to receive a republican education. Moreover, during the Dreyfus Affair French army officers educated at Catholic schools had revealed an apparent contempt for republican values and loyalties; and elements of the Catholic Church, particularly the Assumptionist Order and its newspaper, *La Croix*, had discredited the entire Catholic Church in the opinion of much of the French Left by their extreme anti-Dreyfusard position and by their hysterical campaigns against Jews, Protestants, Freemasons and socialists. The coming to power in June 1899 of a left-wing government headed by Waldeck-Rousseau led to the dissolution of the Assumptionists as an unauthorized order in January 1900 and to a law of 1 July 1901 requiring all religious orders to submit themselves for government authorization. Anti-clerical policies intensified after June 1902, when Emile Combes became Prime Minister and Minister of the Interior and Public Worship. Combes interpreted the law of 1 July 1901 very severely and he was responsible for a law of 7 July 1904 prohibiting authorized regular clergy from teaching and ordering the closure of their schools within ten years. As a result, approximately a third of all private Catholic schools in France had to close, while the remainder had to be run (at least nominally) by laymen, and over 200 million francs' worth of church property was confiscated. Combes also quarrelled with the Vatican over episcopal appointments and a state visit by President Loubet to Rome, and he promised to bring the whole question of the separation of Church and state before parliament. Although Combes had to resign in January 1905 because of a scandal over army promotions, a separation bill was introduced in parliament on 21 March and eventually passed the Chamber of Deputies and the Senate, becoming law on 9 December 1905.

The Separation Law abolished the Concordat: the payment out of public funds of subsidies to the Catholic Church and salaries to its clergy was ended, though some clergy qualified for state pensions; the property of the Catholic Church, after it had been inventoried and valued, was transferred to the state, apart from property acquired from private funds since April 1802, which was transferred to cultural associations; and these cultural associations were given the rent-free use of cathedral and church buildings, which nevertheless remained state property, subject to state control. This amounted to the most severe blow suffered by the Catholic Church in France since the Revolution, and the reaction of the Vatican made its impact even worse. The papal encyclical *Vehementer nos* (11 February 1906) condemned the unilateral abolition of the Concordat and the concept of cultural associations, because it took no account of the Constitution and hierarchical structure of the Catholic Church; and a further papal encyclical of 10 August 1906 forbad Catholics from forming cultural associations, which meant that the Church suffered massive and unnecessary property losses. Ironically, the Concordat survived untouched in German-ruled Alsace-Lorraine, but in the rest of France the Third Republic inflicted a deep wound on the Catholic Church.

CHRONOLOGY

1890
12 November   Toast of Algiers

1891
23 July   Official visit of French naval squadron to Kronstadt (Russia)

1892
16 February   Papal encyclical *Au milieu des sollicitudes*
July   Franco-Russian military agreement

1894
24 June   Assassination of President Carnot by an anarchist
15 October   Arrest of Captain Dreyfus
1 November   Arrest of Dreyfus reported in *La Libre Parole*
19–22 December   First trial of Dreyfus

1895
5 January   Degradation of Dreyfus at the Ecole Militaire
17 January   Félix Faure elected President of the Republic
13 April   Arrival of Dreyfus at Devil's Island
1 October   Madagascar proclaimed a French protectorate

1896
3 September   Report of escape of Dreyfus published in London *Daily Chronicle*
10 November   Facsimile of the *bordereau* published in *Le Matin*

1897
14 July   Announcement in Senate by Scheurer-Kestner that he is convinced that Dreyfus is innocent
15 November   Esterhazy denounced by Mathieu Dreyfus

1898
2 January   Esterhazy committed for trial
11 January   Acquittal of Esterhazy
13 January   Publication of Zola's *'J'Accuse . . . !'* in Clemenceau's *L'Aurore*
14–24 January   Anti-Semitic riots in several French cities and in Algiers
7 February   Trial of Zola begins

23 February	Condemnation of Zola
26 February	Dimissal of Picquart from the army with loss of pension rights
8 and 22 May	General parliamentary elections
4 June	Founding of the League of the Rights of Man
7 July	Parliamentary speech by Cavaignac citing Henry forgery
10 July	Arrival of Captain Marchand at Fashoda
18 July	Departure of Zola from Paris for exile in London
30 August	Interrogation and confession of Colonel Henry
31 August	Suicide of Henry
1 September	Flight of Esterhazy to Belgium and London
3 September	Application for a review of the Dreyfus case
19 September	Arrival of Kitchener at Fashoda
20 September	Initiation of proceedings against Colonel Picquart
2 November	French evacuation from Fashoda ordered by Delcassé
14 December	Public subscription for Henry's widow opened by *La Libre Parole*

1899

16 February	Death of President Félix Faure
18 February	Election of Emile Loubet as President
23 February	State funeral of Félix Faure and failed *coup* by Déroulède
21 March	Franco-British agreement on Africa
3 June	Dreyfus committed for retrial by a military tribunal at Rennes
22 June	Formation of Waldeck-Rousseau government
7 August	Opening of Rennes retrial
9 September	Dreyfus found guilty by five-to-two verdict, with extenuating circumstances
19 September	Dreyfus pardoned by President Loubet

1900

14 April	Opening of the Universal Exhibition in Paris

1901

1 July	Law enforcing government authorization for religious orders

1902

27 April–11 May	General parliamentary elections
6–10 June	Formation of Combes government

1904

7 July	Law forbidding members of religious orders from teaching
30 July	Rupture of diplomatic relations between France and the Vatican

1905

24 January	Resignation of Combes and formation of Rouvier government
6 June	Resignation of Delcassé
9 December	Law on the separation of Church and state

1906

11 February   Papal encyclical *Vehementer nos*
12 July   Dreyfus officially rehabilitated
21 July   Dreyfus awarded the Legion of Honour

BIBLIOGRAPHY

Andrew, C., *Théophile Delcassé and the Making of the Entente Cordiale: a reappraisal of French foreign policy, 1898–1905*. London: Macmillan. 1968.

Arendt, H., *The Origins of Totalitarianism*. London: George Allen & Unwin. 1967.

Birnbaum, P. (ed.), *La France de l'Affaire Dreyfus*. Paris: Gallimard. 1994.

Bredin, J.-D., *The Affair: the case of Alfred Dreyfus*. London: Sidgwick & Jackson. 1987.

—— *Emile Zola: l'Affaire Dreyfus, la vérité en marche*. Paris: Imprimerie Nationale. 1992.

—— *Bernard Lazare*. Paris: Fallois. 1992.

Brogan, Sir D., *The Development of Modern France, 1870–1939*. London: Hamish Hamilton. 1967.

Burns, M., *Rural Society and French Politics: Boulangism and the Dreyfus Affair, 1886–1900*. Princeton, NJ: Princeton University Press. 1984.

—— *Dreyfus: a family affair, 1789–1945*. London: Chatto & Windus. 1992.

—— (ed.), *France and the Dreyfus Affair: a documentary history*. Boston and New York: Bedford and St Martin's Press. 1999.

Cahm, E., *The Dreyfus Affair in French Society and Politics*. London and New York: Longman. 1996.

Chapman, G., *The Dreyfus Case: a reassessment*. London: Rupert Hart-Davis. 1955.

—— *The Dreyfus Trials*. London: B.T. Batsford. 1972.

Derfler, L. (ed.), *The Dreyfus Affair: tragedy of errors?* Boston: D.C. Heath. 1963.

Dreyfus, A. (ed. P. Oriol), *Carnets, 1899–1907*. Paris: Calmann-Lévy. 1998.

Fitch, N., 'Mass Culture, Mass Parliamentary Politics, and Modern Anti-Semitism: the Dreyfus Affair in rural France', *American Historical Review*, 97 (1992), 55–95.

Griffiths, R., *The Use of Abuse: the polemics of the Dreyfus Affair and its aftermath*. Oxford: Berg. 1991.

Hoffman, R.L., *More than a Trial: the struggle over Captain Dreyfus*. New York and London: The Free Press and Collier Macmillan. 1980.

Hyman, P., 'The Dreyfus Affair: the visual and the historical', *Journal of Modern History*, 61 (1989), 88–109.

Jaurès, J., *Les Preuves. Affaire Dreyfus*. Paris: La Découverte. 1998.

Johnson, D., *France and the Dreyfus Affair*. London: Blandford. 1966.

Johnson, M.P., *The Dreyfus Affair*. London: Macmillan. 1999.

Joly, B., 'Le Parti royaliste et l'Affaire Dreyfus (1898–1900)', *Revue Historique*, 269 (1983), 311–64.

—— 'Les Antidreyfusards croyaient-ils Dreyfus coupable?', *Revue Historique*, 291 (1994), 401–37.

Kaplan, R.E., *Forgotten Crisis: the fin-de siècle crisis of democracy in France*. Oxford: Berg. 1995.

—— 'Making Sense of the Rennes Verdict: the military dimension of the Dreyfus Affair', *Journal of Contemporary History*, 34 (1999), 499–515.

Kedward, R., *The Dreyfus Affair: catalyst for tensions in French society*. London: Longman. 1969.

Larkin, M., *Church and State after the Dreyfus Affair: the separation issue in France*. London: Macmillan. 1974.

—— 'La République en danger?: the pretenders, the army and Déroulède, 1898–1899', *English Historical Review*, 100 (1985), 85–105.

—— *Religion, Politics and Preferment in France since 1890: La Belle Epoque and its legacy*. Cambridge: Cambridge University Press. 1995.

Mandell, R.D., 'The Affair and the Fair', *Journal of Modern History*, 39 (1967), 253–65.

Marrus, M.R., *The Politics of Assimilation: a study of the French Jewish community at the time of the Dreyfus Affair*. Oxford: Clarendon Press. 1971.

Mayeur, J.-M., 'Les Catholiques dreyfusards', *Revue Historique*, 261 (1979), 337–60.

Mayeur, J.-M. and Rebérioux, M., *The Third Republic from its Origins to the Great War, 1871–1914*. Cambridge: Cambridge University Press. 1984.

Millman, R., 'Jewish Anticlericalism and the Rise of Modern French Antisemitism', *History*, 77 (1992), 220–36.

Mitchell, A., 'The Xenophobic Style: French counterespionage and the emergence of the Dreyfus Affair', *Journal of Modern History*, 52 (1980), 414–25.

Oriol, P., *'J'Accuse . . . !'; Emile Zola et l'Affaire Dreyfus*. Paris: Librio. 1998.

Rutkoff, P.M., 'The Ligue des Patriotes: the nature of the radical right and the Dreyfus Affair', *French Historical Studies*, 8 (1974), 585–603.

Snyder, L.L., *The Dreyfus Case: a documentary history*. New Brunswick, NJ: Rutgers University Press. 1973.

Soucy, R., *Fascism in France: the case of Maurice Barrès*. Berkeley: University of California Press. 1972.

Sternhell, Z., 'Paul Déroulède and the Origins of Modern French Nationalism', *Journal of Contemporary History*, 6 (1971), 46–70.

—— *Maurice Barrès et le nationalisme français*. Paris: Colin. 1972.

—— 'National Socialism and Antisemitism: the case of Maurice Barrès', *Journal of Contemporary History*, 8 (1973), 46–66.

—— *The Birth of Fascist Ideology*. Princeton, NJ: Princeton University Press. 1994.

Sutton, M., *Nationalism, Positivism, and Catholicism: the politics of Charles Maurras and French Catholics, 1890–1914*. Cambridge: Cambridge University Press. 1983.

Wilson, N., *Bernard Lazare: antisemitism and the problem of Jewish identity in late nineteenth-century France*. Cambridge: Cambridge University Press. 1978.

Wilson, S., 'The Antisemitic Riots of 1898 in France', *Historical Journal*, 16 (1973), 789–806.

—— 'Catholic Populism in France at the Time of the Dreyfus Affair: the *Union Nationale*', *Journal of Contemporary History*, 10 (1975), 667–705.

—— 'Antisemitism and Jewish Response in France during the Dreyfus Affair', *European Studies Review*, 6 (1976), 225–48.

—— 'Le Monument Henry: la structure de l'antisémitisme en France, 1898–1899', *Annales, E.S.C.*, 32 (1977), 265–91.

—— *Ideology and Experience: antisemitism in France at the time of the Dreyfus Affair*. London and Toronto: Associated University Presses, 1982.

4 | Women and the family

Approximately half of the French population was female, yet women played a subordinate public role since they suffered from social, legal, political and economic discrimination. The traditional social view of women, reinforced by the teachings of the Roman Catholic Church, was that they should be pious, modest, virtuous and chaste, devoted to the care of their husband, home and children, and emerging from this private sphere only to serve the Church and engage in charitable activities. Such attitudes had influenced the Civil Code, which gave women few legal rights and placed married women under the authority of their husbands. Similarly, women were not allowed to vote in local or parliamentary elections, or to hold any elected public office; and women's employment opportunities were largely restricted to menial jobs, in which they earned substantially less than their male counterparts.

However, after 1870 a number of factors helped to change the position of women in French society. The authority and attitudes of the Roman Catholic Church came under sustained attack from republicans and anti-clericals, while feminists developed new ideas about the role of women and demanded an end to discrimination. Expanding provision for female education encouraged women to gain access to jobs and professions that had hitherto been male preserves. Industrialization created many new employment opportunities for women, as did the huge expansion in service industries, so that women could become more mobile and more independent. Nevertheless, improvements in the legal rights and status of women between 1870 and 1914 proceeded at a relatively modest and gradual pace, and could generate considerable conflict.

Like the role and rights of women, the institution of the family featured as a subject of debate. Traditionalists saw the family as one of the principal foundations of society and even of civilization, as an institution sanctified by the Church, and as a crucial factor in determining an individual's wealth and social status. Critics viewed the family as a bourgeois institution that encouraged the sacrifice of love, morality and happiness for social and financial advancement. This view led to distrust of the Church's influence over family life, to support for the reintroduction of divorce, and to concerns regarding illegitimate children and prostitution.

Document 4.1 Women and the Paris Commune of 1871

Is it credible that it is possible to make the Revolution without women?

For twenty years this has been attempted and the Revolution has not been accomplished.

The first Revolution [of 1789] accorded women the title of female citizens [*citoyennes*], but did not give them the rights of citizens. Women were left excluded from liberty and equality.

Rejected by the Revolution, women returned to Catholicism, and, under the influence of the Church, formed that immense reactionary force imbued with the spirit of the past which stifles the Revolution every time it wants to revive.

When will people realize that this has lasted long enough? When will the intelligence of male republicans be raised so as to understand their principles and serve their interests? They demand that women should no longer be under the yoke of priests, yet they do not like to see women become free-thinkers. They certainly do not want women to work against them, yet they reject the assistance of women when it is offered. Why is this?

The reason is that many male republicans – I except the genuine ones – have dethroned the Emperor and the good Lord . . . only to put themselves in their places. Naturally, in this role they need subjects, or at least female subjects. Women should no longer obey priests; but women should not assert themselves any more than previously. Women should remain neutral and passive, under the direction of men, so that they just change their confessor . . .

The Revolution, if it is to be true to itself, stands for the rights and responsibilities of every human creature, without any restriction except the rights of the community, and without any privilege of race or gender.

Women will only abandon the old faith in order to embrace the new faith with enthusiasm. They do not want to be, and they cannot be, neutral. A choice has to be made between their hostility and their devotion . . .

However, who suffers most from the present crisis, from the food shortages, from the high unemployment? Women, and above all single women, in whom the present regime is not interested, just like previous regimes.

Who has nothing to gain, at least in the short term, from the success of the Revolution? Women again. The current issue is the liberation of men, not the liberation of women.

Source: André Léo (Léodile Champseix) in La Sociale, *8 May 1871; M. Albistur and D. Armogathe (eds),* Le Grief des femmes: anthologie de textes féministes du second empire à nos jours. *Poitiers: Editions Hier et Demain. 1978, pp. 44–8*

During the Revolution of 1789, women participated in riots and demonstrations over the price and availability of food and in the march to Versailles of October 1789, when the royal family were forced to move to Paris; demands for women's rights were made by the Marquis de Condorcet and by feminists such as Olympe de Gouges, Etta

Palm d'Aelders, Théroigne de Méricourt, Pauline Léon and Claire Lacombe; and an embryonic women's movement developed in Paris, with feminist clubs, societies and newspapers. Yet the Revolution did very little for women, apart from ending primogeniture; and in the autumn of 1793 the Jacobins, whom some women had supported, vigorously cracked down on the feminist movement and ignored women's economic and political demands. As a result, many women returned to the Roman Catholic Church, with some engaging in counter-revolutionary activities. Consequently, throughout the nineteenth century women tended to be identified with political conservatism and with the Roman Catholic Church.

Feminism and a radical women's movement in Paris briefly re-emerged during the revolution of 1848 and during the Paris Commune of 1871. During the Commune, women helped to frustrate the removal of cannon from Montmartre on the morning of 18 March, organized themselves through the Union of Women for the Defence of Paris and the Care of the Wounded and the Women's Vigilance Committee of Montmartre (whose members included Louise Michel and André Léo), and even formed a women's battalion (the Légion des Fédérées) and other organized and armed units of women who fought and died on the barricades. The male-dominated Commune tended to disapprove of female armed combatants and did not grant women political rights, though the Commune did grant pensions to common-law spouses and their offspring and food rations to women legally separated from their husbands. The Commune also intended to improve the education of girls and set up a committee, which included André Léo, with this remit.

André Léo was a female novelist and disciple of the socialist Pierre Leroux, and had become a radical journalist during the siege of Paris. Her case, that women were suffering more than men, that male republicans were not interested in the liberation of women, and that the goals of the Revolution could not be achieved without the support and the liberation of women, was a strong one.

Document 4.2 Moderate Feminism

The establishment of the true conditions for morality is a matter of urgency, that is to say the repeal of certain laws and the introduction of new laws, so that finally there will be only one code of morality equally applicable to all, irrespective of the sex of the individual.

We have been assured that the Germans defeated us because they are more moral than the French; that among Germans marriage is more respected and that the family occupies a more important place in their lives than in ours . . .

Any society that regards prostitution as a necessity is a society whose foundations are undermined; it carries in its side a virus, its downfall is pronounced in advance.

However, this downfall can to a greater or lesser extent be delayed. Prostitution in its multiple forms is simply disguised polygamy.

When men abandon themselves to systematic immorality, dissolution will soon spread to all ranks of society.

Debauchery is far from being confined within the limits designated by the police. It insinuates itself wherever there is a young girl without experience, without supervision, and without protection. Female apprentices, industrial workers, shop assistants, domestic servants, entertainers are all so many potential recruits to prostitution. Later, after they have become courtezans, these young girls in their turn sow the seeds of scandal and licentiousness. The circle of virtue daily becomes smaller, and the time is near when a flourishing society will rot on its feet and become irredeemably lost, if it is not thoroughly purified by some heroic remedies . . .

These are the remedies:

1 Paternity suits to be legally allowed;
2 Wives to be able to sue their husbands for separation or divorce if their husbands are guilty of adultery, even if the mistress does not live in the marital home;
3 Recognition of the civil rights of women;
4 Equal pay for equal work; admission of women into all the liberal professions as soon as they are qualified.

The promulgation of these laws would lead to a 100 per cent improvement in morality and would then achieve the regeneration of France.

Source: M. Deraismes, 'La Régéneration de la France', L'Avenir des Femmes, 5 November 1871; M. Deraismes, Ce Que Veulent Les Femmes: articles et conférences de 1869 à 1891. Paris: Syros. 1980, pp. 55–7

This moderate feminist programme is a protest against the double standards inherent in the Civil Code, in educational and career opportunities, and in employment practices, and against the alleged immorality of official policy towards prostitution. If a wife committed adultery, she could be sentenced to serve between three and twenty-four months in prison, whereas an adulterous husband could be punished only if he brought his mistress into the marital home, and even then he risked just a fine of between 100 and 2,000 francs. If a husband discovered his wife in the act of committing adultery, he could kill her in the knowledge that the courts would excuse his 'crime of passion', whereas a wife who killed her husband in the same circumstances was guilty of murder. Similarly, women who had one or more children outside of marriage were not allowed to bring paternity suits against the father or fathers, and an illegitimate child had no inheritance rights over his or her father's estate unless the father had legally recognized the child. The law also treated a married woman as a minor: in all legal, business and financial matters her husband's signature was required, and she had no legal rights over her children, unless she became a widow and did not remarry.

Very small numbers of women were just beginning to gain admission to universities, but the liberal professions still remained virtually closed to them. On the other hand, large numbers of women worked in low-paid and low-status jobs, with little or no job security, so that many of them drifted into prostitution. In Paris between 1871 and 1903 some 155,000 women registered as prostitutes, and the police arrested a further 725,000 suspected of prostitution (Zeldin, 1973, p. 308). A vice squad (*police des moeurs*) regulated the prostitution industry, and in 1870 there were 145 official brothels in Paris, though the number subsequently declined as clandestine brothels multiplied. Feminists objected that official regulation of brothels and prostitutes implied official approval of prostitution, but it also meant prostitutes received medical examinations and treatment and avoided the worst forms of maltreatment and exploitation.

This emphasis on double standards and morality, and omission of any reference to political rights, reflected both the widespread opinion that moral decadence had been at least partly responsible for France's defeat in the Franco-Prussian War and the discrediting of more militant brands of feminism by the whole experience of the Paris Commune. The programme's author, Maria Deraismes, was a writer and journalist who in 1866 had helped to found the Society for the Demand of Women's Rights, which has been described as 'the first feminist group in France' (Sowerwine, 1982, p. 7). With a male journalist, Léon Richer, in 1869 she founded a feminist newspaper, *Le Droit des femmes* (retitled *L'Avenir des femmes* in 1871), and in April 1870 the Association for the Future of Women. Thereafter Maria Deraismes and Léon Richer organized feminist banquets, the first French international conference on the rights of women (July 1878), and another feminist conference to coincide with the Universal Exhibition and the centennial of the Revolution of 1789 (June 1889). Deraismes and Richer subscribed to what was known as the strategy of the breach (*la politique de la brèche*), the conduct of piecemeal attacks against the 'wall' of male prejudice so as gradually to achieve legal and educational reforms. This policy had its successes, particularly in the spheres of educational reform and divorce legislation. However, other reforms came much more slowly: only in 1912, for instance, was a law introduced permitting in certain circumstances single mothers or illegitimate children to track down wayward fathers and sue for financial support. Indeed, because of their failure to press for women's political rights, and because of the priority they gave to republicanism, anti-clericalism and (in the case of Deraismes) even Freemasonry, Deraismes and Richer can be represented as 'traitors to the feminist cause' (McMillan, 1981, p. 373).

Document 4.3 Radical Feminism

Programme of the Society for Women's Rights (1876–1880)

The Society, believing that women's political emancipation is the sole means of obtaining women's legal and economic emancipation, inscribes into its programme the right of women to vote and to be eligible for elected office on a local and a national level.

The Society inscribes into its programme the creation of an integrated educational system for girls. There is no need to burden the budget to achieve this goal, since it is sufficient to make *lycées* and other existing schools co-educational, open to both girls and boys.

The Society demands access for women to all careers and professions, and equal pay for equal work.

The Society demands that women have the right to file paternity suits.

The Society believes that marriage should be an association both freely contracted and based on equality between spouses. At the present time, the Society advocates the separate ownership of property by husband and wife.

Like every association, marriage should be dissolvable, since a human being can much less give up his person and his freedom than his interests.

The right of spouses to separate does not lessen the duty imposed on them to bring up their children.

The Society, seeking impartial justice, wants women to be appointed consular judges, civil judges and jurors.

Finally, the Society wants the recognition and exercise of all rights for women, who are required to carry out all duties, and the equality of the two sexes before the law.

Source: H. Auclert, Historique de la Société le Droit des Femmes, *1876–1880. Paris: Robert et Buhl. 1881, pp. 6–7*

Radical feminism in France suffered a major setback with the suppression of the Paris Commune and the leadership vacuum created by the exile of Paule Mink and the transportation of Louise Michel to New Caledonia in the South Pacific. However, Maria Deraismes and Léon Richer soon had a radical rival in Hubertine Auclert. Financially independent, but from a prosperous peasant rather than a bourgeois background (like the wealthier and better-educated Deraismes and Richer), Auclert had arrived in Paris in 1873 and had joined Deraismes and Richer, only to conclude that they were too moderate because of their refusal to press for women's political rights or to resort to any illegal tactic. Auclert therefore broke away and between November 1876 and February 1877 formed her own feminist group, the Society for Women's Rights (Le Droit des Femmes), for which she virtually dictated the statutes and programme.

A few women had participated in the elections to the Estates General of 1789 (as female nobles, land-owners and heads of religious houses), but since 1789 women in France had been deprived of all political rights except the right to petition politicians, parliament and (after 1875) the President. According to a rarely enforced law, they were even legally prohibited from attending political meetings, and women journalists were debarred from the press gallery of the Chamber of Deputies. Auclert became convinced that to pursue the strategy of the breach, pressing for piecemeal reforms from an exclusively male political establishment, would achieve little in the short or even medium term. Instead, she advocated an assault strategy (*la politique de l'assaut*), according to which women should demand the vote and, having gained political power, should then use that power to establish full equality between men and women. Opponents of women's suffrage argued that women should not have the vote because they were insufficiently educated, they were subject to the reactionary influence of the Catholic Church, they did not perform military service, they lacked any interest in, or aptitude for, politics, they ought to concentrate on their domestic duties, and because married women were politically represented by their husbands. Auclert countered by maintaining that women's reproductive and home-caring roles were as important as those of any male worker; that moral and intellectual qualities were not determined by an individual's gender; that maternity was no more an obstacle to political activity than to the exercise of an artistic or business skill; that the enfranchisement of women would bring to an end the oppression and exploitation of women and would generally promote morality in politics; that a mother with forty years' experience of life was much better prepared to exercise her political rights than her twenty-one-year-old son; that not all men performed military service, while in desperate situations some women became soldiers; that the reactionary influence of the Catholic Church did not electorally disqualify devout religious men, or male priests and pastors; and that women qualified for the vote because they had to obey the law and pay taxes, just like men.

As regards tactics, Auclert organized demonstrations, disruptive public protests and tax boycotts, and on one occasion (3 May 1908) she even overturned a ballot box in a Paris polling station, though, unlike some of the British suffragettes, she never resorted to acts of violence against people or property. However, neither her programme nor her tactics enjoyed significant public support. The membership of the Society for Women's Rights never exceeded about 150, while the circulation of her newspaper, *La Citoyenne* (1881–91), never exceeded about a thousand.

Document 4.4 Feminism and Socialism

The Workers' Socialist Congress of Marseilles (October 1879)

In view of all the advantages which accrue to the proletariat by treating sympathetically the assistance of women in its struggle against the privileged, Congress expresses the wish that special attention is devoted to the subject of the civic education of women. Men will admit women into their meetings, study circles and socialist electoral meetings, where they will have the right to vote.

Congress, considering that men and women are equivalent before nature, considering that they are equally indispensable for the perpetuation of society, declares that they should rule this society together and share the exercise of the same rights, publicly and privately.

Congress, following the principle of the absolute equality of the two sexes, accords to women the same social and political rights as to men.

Rights entail responsibilities: women should work, being a consumer and no less suited to production than men. Congress expresses the wish that the same work opportunities exist for the two sexes and that this economic formula is rigorously applied: equal pay for equal work.

With regard to women's work in factories, mills and workshops, Congress, not wishing to restrict the freedom to work, can only express the wish that the systems established in the factories, mills and workshops for male and female workers are replaced by other systems based on hygienic principles. In addition, Congress expresses the wish, and this is in the interests of all, that an equitable division of labour is made, so that those who are not strong, whether men or women, are assigned work which requires skill, while those who are strong are assigned work which requires strength.

With regard to prison and convent work, it would be puerile for Congress to express a wish that it should be suppressed. It is not the symptom, but the cause, which should be destroyed.

Congress, considering that convents are only a refuge offered to idleness and demoralization, decides that they should be suppressed.

Source: M. Albistur and D. Armogathe (eds), Le Grief des femmes: anthologie de textes féministes du second empire à nos jours. *Poitiers: Editions Hier et Demain. 1978, pp. 68–9*

During July and August 1878 Léon Richer organized an international congress on the rights of women in Paris to coincide with an international exhibition in Paris. It was the first major international demonstration of French feminism during the Third Republic, with 220 official delegates attending from eleven countries, and with audiences at some sessions exceeding 600. Among the participants was Hubertine Auclert, but, with the support of the congress, Richer refused to allow her to deliver her prepared speech on votes for women or even to allow the subject of women's suffrage to be discussed. 'The congress of 1878 became the funeral of Auclert's political innocence' (Hause, 1987, p. 43). She resigned her membership of congress committees and decided to focus her campaign for women's political rights on the French socialist movement, establishing links with *Le Prolétaire*, a socialist newspaper that first appeared in November 1878.

As an official delegate, Auclert attended the French Socialist Workers' Congress held in Marseilles between 20 and 31 October 1879. She had been appointed a member of a special committee to consider the equality of women and was permitted to address the congress on this subject for an hour. She argued that women could be exploited by all males, both rich and poor, and that the principle of women's equality with men must be recognized. Her speech was rapturously received; she was invited to chair a committee with a brief to draft a statement on women's rights; and the statement she produced, affirming that women should have the same social, legal, political and employment rights as men, was approved by the congress. However, the alliance between French radical feminism and French socialism proved to be short lived: the 1878 Socialist Congress, held when French socialists were still politically marginal, with seemingly no prospect of exercising any real power, was untypically radical; many socialists regarded women as conservative and priest-ridden, and socialists generally tended to be alienated by the middle-class character of French feminism; male French workers were often indifferent, or even hostile, to women's rights; and male French socialists soon became convinced that winning the class struggle was the priority and that campaigns for women's rights were a distraction.

Document 4.5 The Roman Catholic View of Women

Without any doubt, the great merit, the incomparable honour, of a woman is to bring up her children and to produce men, just as her sweetest joy and her first duty are to make her husband happy. However, to make her husband and children good and happy, to produce men, 'brave young lads, who believe in God and do not fear cannon' (as Joseph de Maistre aptly put it), it is necessary to have women who are strong in intelligence, judgement and character, and who are assiduous, industrious and attentive; it is necessary, as the Holy Scriptures teach us, that this caring, this beauty and this kindness, which adorn and embellish everything in a home, are illuminated from on high. *As the sun shines on the world, so a good woman ornaments her home.* It is necessary that this hand, which holds the spindle and which devotes itself to domestic matters, is controlled by a head which thinks and governs. The image depicted by Solomon is not that of a woman uniquely devoted to domestic life, but of a capable woman; and if her children rise up to proclaim her happy and glorious, it is because she has an elevated sense of life's details, of far-sightedness with respect to the future, and of the care of souls; because she is in all things at the level of the noblest duties and the most serious thoughts, in a word, the worthy and intelligent companion of a husband.

Source: F.A.P. Dupanloup, Lettres sur l'éducation des filles et sur les études qui conviennent aux femmes dans le monde. *Paris: Julen Gervais. 1879, p. 42*

Frequently long lived, and normally secure in the posts they occupied, Roman Catholic clergy could remain public figures for extended periods in nineteenth-century France. Born in 1802, Félix Dupanloup had become a prominent priest in Paris as far back as the 1820s. Serving the fashionable parishes of La Madeleine and St Roch, and subsequently the Cathedral of Notre Dame as a canon, he had made a name for himself as a writer, preacher and educator and as Talleyrand's death-bed confessor. In 1849 he was appointed Bishop of Orleans, where he energetically supervised his diocese until his death nearly thirty years later. He also became involved in politics: in the National Assembly elections of February 1871 he was elected a deputy for the Loiret, and he was one of the new life senators elected in 1876.

Dupanloup is difficult to categorize politically: he regretted the overthrow of the Bourbon monarchy in 1830 and worked for a Bourbon restoration in the 1870s, yet he was the only French bishop not to condone Louis-Napoleon's *coup d'état* of December 1851 and he did not welcome the doctrine of papal infallibility. One of his great interests was education, and in this field he was a Catholic traditionalist. From the 1840s he consistently campaigned for Catholic education and he helped to frame the Falloux law of March 1850, which gave the Catholic Church a considerable role in French education. He also vigorously and publicly opposed a national scheme launched in 1867 by Victor Duruy, Minister of Education, whereby young ladies, accompanied by their mothers or maids, could attend academic courses, usually taught by male *lycée* teachers in town halls. Dupanloup insisted that advanced academic courses were morally dangerous for girls and that it was also morally dangerous to allow girls to be taught by male teachers.

The Roman Catholic Church traditionally had two ideals of woman – the chaste virgin devoted to God and the tender mother devoted to her child or children – the two ideals being conveniently combined in the Virgin Mary. From this it followed that, since women should not have jobs or careers outside the home, the education of girls should focus, not on academic study, but on the acquisition of domestic skills and on the inculcation of religious piety and moral values. Dupanloup wanted girls to receive an education that 'toughened the body and fortified the soul'. They should be inspired with 'the love of duty and the need to make sacrifices for duty'; they should be encouraged to be modest, respectful, charitable, pure and truthful; and they should be taught to despise vanity, egoism, pride and ingratitude (Dupanloup, 1879, pp. 343, 354, 356, 371 and 374). Such a view was evidently conservative (significantly, Dupanloup cites the ultra-royalist Joseph de Maistre as an authority), but it did assign to women crucial roles at home and in the family and as moral guardians. The influence of this Catholic view of the role of women and of the character of girls' education, which extended well into the twentieth century, helps to explain why a disproportionate number of those active in French feminism were non-Catholics – Protestants, Jews, free-thinkers and atheists.

Document 4.6 Secondary School Education for Girls

THE LAW OF 21 DECEMBER 1880

Article 1 Establishments for the secondary-school education of young girls will be founded by the state, with the co-operation of departments and communes.

Article 2 These establishments will be day schools. Boarding annexes may be added, if requested by municipal councils and with the agreement of the state. They will be subject to the same regulations as the colleges in the communes.

Article 3 Scholarships will be founded by the state, the departments and the communes, for pupils, both day-girls and boarders, and for student teachers. The number of these scholarships will be determined in the statutes drawn up between the ministry and the department or commune in which the school is located.

Article 4 The curriculum will include:
1 Moral instruction;
2 The French language, reading aloud, and at least one living language;

3 Classical and modern literature;
4 Geography and cosmography [the study of the universe];
5 French history and some general history;
6 Arithmetic and the principles of geometry, chemistry, physics and natural history;
7 Hygiene;
8 Domestic science;
9 Needlework;
10 Elementary common law;
11 Drawing;
12 Music;
13 Gymnastics.

Article 5 Religious education will be given, if requested by parents, by the ministers of the different denominations, in the school buildings but outside class hours. The ministers of the different denominations will be certified by the Ministry of Education. They will not live in the school.

Article 6 A course in education can be added to the curriculum.

Article 7 No pupil can be admitted to a state secondary school without having passed an examination demonstrating her ability to follow the academic programme.

Article 8 Young girls who have successfully completed an academic programme at a state secondary school and who have passed an examination will be awarded a diploma.

Article 9 Each state secondary school for girls will be placed under the authority of a female director.

Teaching will be provided by qualified male or female teachers.

Source: C. Sée, Lycées et collèges de jeunes filles: documents, rapports et discours à la Chambre des Députés et au Sénat. *Paris: Léopold Cerf. 1884, pp. 434–5*

The Catholic view of women and of girls' education, which influenced government educational policy in France until the 1880s, resulted in inadequate educational provision for girls and women. State primary-school education for girls had not been introduced until 1836 and remained far from universal. There were no state secondary schools for girls, for which a limited number of private and convent schools, distributed throughout France in a somewhat random manner and often staffed by academically unqualified teachers, were a poor substitute. In 1870 France had only nineteen teacher-training schools for aspiring female primary-school teachers, so that even state primary schools had to rely partly on nuns. Universities were only just beginning to open their doors to the occasional female student: by 1879 three Frenchwomen were arts graduates and five Frenchwomen were medical graduates. The general level of female education therefore remained relatively low. In 1872 only 65 per cent of French brides could write their names, compared with 80 per cent of French bridegrooms and military recruits, and at least 40 per cent of Frenchwomen must have been functionally illiterate.

Republicans and anti-clericals believed, like Jules Michelet, that the influence of the Roman Catholic Church on women and on girls' education was politically and socially harmful, and that the introduction of a state secular educational system for boys and girls was an essential precondition for the security and permanence of the Third Republic. Also, Protestants tended to value girls' education and educated women. In 1866 Jean Macé had founded the Education League (Ligue de l'Enseignement), which became a powerful pressure group for republican and secular education, particularly after the republican electoral victories of 1877–9. The realization of the objectives of the Education League was largely the work of Jules Ferry, who was appointed Education Minister in February 1879, though a left-wing republican deputy for the Seine and friend of Jules Ferry, Camille Sée, was mainly responsible for the law of 21 December 1880.

The law itself established state secular secondary schools for girls, with admission requirements and qualified teaching staff to maintain academic standards. However, the exclusion of Latin, the inclusion of hygiene, domestic science, needlework, drawing and music, and the introduction of a diploma instead of the *baccalauréat* awarded to male *lycée* students meant that girls were offered a state secondary education that was separate, different and academically inferior to that of boys. Indeed, Hubertine Auclert complained that all state secondary schools should have been made co-educational and that girls should have been allowed to follow the same academic syllabus, and sit the same examinations, as boys. Also, state secondary schools for girls became fee-paying (like boys' *lycées*), except for those who qualified for scholarships.

Nevertheless, this law, together with the introduction of free and compulsory primary education for boys and girls (law of 16 June 1881), marked a great advance for female education in France; and the requirement (law of 9 August 1879) that each department should have at least one teacher-training school for aspiring female primary-school teachers, the opening of institutions exclusively for women at Fontenay-aux-Roses (for future teachers at teacher-training schools) and at Sèvres and Saint-Cloud (for future teachers at girls' secondary schools), and the creation of jobs for teachers in girls' secondary schools established new professional career opportunities for women.

Document 4.7 Divorce

Since 1789 marriage can be considered only as a contract based on the freely expressed wishes of the contracting parties. However, it is in the nature of all contracts that they can become void, either by agreement with the consent of the contracting parties, or by the wish of one of the contracting parties, if the other contracting party has not fulfilled the conditions of the contract. . . .

Marriage is not a coercive law. It is true that the Civil Code clearly proclaims that the husband owes protection to his wife, that the wife owes obedience to her husband, and that the wife is obliged to follow her husband wherever he pleases to take her.

But where is the sanction that compels spouses to carry out these reciprocal duties? If the husband does not want to protect his wife, if the wife does not want to obey her husband, if even one of the spouses abandons the marital home, what forces them to return to the path of duty? A husband, it is true, can force his wife to return to the marital home by employing the police against her; but what happens if she leaves the marital home again as soon as the police have left? A wife can similarly force her husband to receive her in the marital home; but what happens if the husband chases her out of the marital home as soon as the police have left? Will a resort to authority be made a second, third or fourth time? This is clearly impossible. In cases of this nature there will be judicial proceedings and the matter will be settled by a legal separation.

When a spouse wants to abandon his or her partner, whether the partner consents or otherwise, there is therefore no social authority which can prevent the spouse. We are therefore entitled to claim that, if the immense majority of spouses remain together, it is for reasons quite other than the stipulations of the law.

Spouses remain together because habit and, if there is no passion, the friendship which they feel for each other make it a necessity for them; they remain together because they have a lively affection for their children, and because this affection is for them a much stronger tie than any article in the Civil Code; they remain together because they have financial obligations towards each other that make separations very expensive. But legal obstacles never keep them together.

Source: A. Naquet, Le Divorce. Paris: E. Dentu. 1881, pp. 19 and 48–9

For historical reasons, divorce in France had become linked to republicanism and anti-clericalism. Before 1789, Roman Catholic dogma determined the legal framework of marital relations and divorce did not exist. In the event of the breakdown of a marriage, the rich and influential could obtain a legal separation through the courts, while the poor could in effect end their marriages by abandoning their partners. The Declaration of the Rights of Man and Citizen (1789), the Revolution's attack on the Roman Catholic Church, the definition of marriage in the 1791 Constitution as a civil contract rather than as a religious sacrament, and the dramatic radicalization of the Revolution during the summer of 1792 all led to the divorce law of 20 September 1792. This introduced legal divorce by mutual consent. In addition, one partner could petition for divorce on a wide variety of grounds; and a divorced person could remarry a year after his or her divorce. Subsequent revolutionary legislation and the Napoleonic Civil Code made divorce legislation less liberal, but divorce remained a legal possibility until it was abolished by a law of 8 May 1816 as part of the royalist and clerical reaction following the second restoration of the Bourbon monarchy in 1815. Attempts to reintroduce divorce were blocked by the Chamber of Peers after the revolution of 1830 and by the National Assembly after the revolution of 1848, so that the issue resurfaced after the establishment of the Third Republic.

During the Paris Commune of 1871 several feminists and revolutionary clubs demanded the re-establishment of divorce, and thereafter Léon Richer and Alfred Naquet campaigned for a divorce law. In *Le Divorce* (serialized in *L'Avenir des femmes* from April 1872 and subsequently published as a book) Richer argued that current legislation led to high illegitimacy rates and encouraged double standards, and he advocated divorce if one or both of the spouses wanted it. Naquet, a Jewish deputy for the Vaucluse influenced by the ideas of the radical socialist Charles Fourier, submitted to the Chamber of Deputies in June 1876 a proposal to restore the divorce law of September 1792. When this failed, in May 1878 he proposed resurrecting a modified version of the divorce legislation in the Napoleonic Code. With considerable energy and great persistence, he piloted his divorce bill through the Chamber of Deputies and the Senate (to which he gained election in July 1883), while at the same time conducting a pro-divorce law propaganda campaign through speeches and banquets in Paris and the provinces, and through articles in newspapers and publications such as *Le Divorce* (1877; second edition 1881).

Naquet took an anti-clerical line, asserting that current legislation reflected Roman Catholic dogma and was offensive to non-Catholics, that marriage was a legal contract, not a religious sacrament, and should be subject to the same rules as any other contract, and that the Catholic concept of marriage as an indissoluble union based on vows made in the presence of God was in practice unenforcible. Catholics and opponents of divorce argued that the reintroduction of divorce would help to undermine the principles of property, religion and the family, would permit men to become serial husbands and women serial victims, and would be socially divisive, since only the rich would be able to afford divorce. The Bishop of Angers even claimed that Naquet's divorce bill represented a Jewish plot to divorce the Third Republic from the Catholic Church. However, a majority of legislators saw a divorce law as extending personal rights, as undermining the authority of the Catholic Church, and as strengthening the institutions of marriage and the family. A divorce bill therefore eventually passed both the Chamber of Deputies and the Senate, becoming law on 19 July 1884. This law was quite conservative, permitting divorce solely on the grounds of matrimonial fault (adultery, physical violence, moral cruelty or conviction and imprisonment for a serious crime), not of consent, and forbidding an adulterer to marry his or her lover. A law of 15 December 1904 removed the latter prohibition, and in other respects divorce legislation gradually became more liberal. Nevertheless, divorce remained a minority and widely disapproved-of process until well into the twentieth century – there were just 4,000 divorces in France in 1885 and 16,000 in 1900 (Copley, 1989, p. 126). The concept of the no-fault divorce did not enter French legislation until 1975.

Document 4.8 Depopulation and the Birth Rate

For some years a cry of alarm has been raised and has shaken the whole of France. The word depopulation has been pronounced and has sounded in all our hearts. It is said that the birth rate is in decline, that the French population is becoming smaller, that this is a sign of decadence . . .

As the French nation becomes more and more infertile, so foreigners invade us and on our soil come to take the place of our nationals.

Workers from Spain and Italy flood into the South of France, from Belgium into Northern France, from Germany into Paris and the eastern departments. The number of non-naturalized foreigners has risen for twenty years and has now reached a figure of one million one hundred thousand. We are therefore right to develop a sense of patriotic concern and to seek out the causes of France's low birth rate.

When the genetic instinct weakens, when the irresistible attraction of transmitting life loses its intensity, when the desire to pass on to a human being produced by oneself, not only the fruit of one's labours, but of one's ideas, feelings, loves and hatreds, when, I repeat, this desire is dulled, there must be some very important reasons.

The explanation certainly cannot lie in physiological degeneration or in a waning of dynamism.

Other explanations put forward have included the pursuit of individual well-being, the unbridled love of luxury, the family pride which does not want to divide the family inheritance, the exaggeration of paternal love anxious to assure the happiness of a single child, the preoccupation of women with their appearance, etc. . . . , etc. . . . All these factors, however, have always existed, so they do not suffice to explain the current siuation.

Source: M. Deraismes, 'La Dépopulation et la natalité', Le Républicain, 22 and 26 March 1883; M. Deraismes, Ce Que Veulent Les Femmes: articles et conférences de 1869 à 1891. Paris: Syros. 1980, pp. 65–7

The French birth rate began to decline at the end of the eighteenth century and remained at a relatively low level until the Second World War, while in the same period French citizens did not emigrate from France in significant numbers. Between 1871 and 1911, the French population increased by about 3 million, from approximately 36.1 million to nearly 39.2 million, taking into account the 1.6 million inhabitants lost by the German annexation of Alsace-Lorraine. This represented an average annual growth rate of just 0.2 per cent, which was lower than that of any other European state, despite, in many cases, much higher emigration rates. For instance, between 1881 and 1911 the population of the German Empire rose from 45.2 million to 64.9 million and the population of the Russian Empire from 97.7 million to 160.7 million.

France's demographic performance alarmed many French people, who saw it as a symptom of national decadence and, in an age of mass military conscription, as a crippling handicap in any future conflict with Germany. A parallel cause for alarm was the influx of foreign immigrants into France. Certainly, as the feminist Maria Deraismes points out, significant numbers of Belgians settled in northern France, particularly in the industrial towns of Lille, Roubaix and Tourcoing, Italians and Spaniards moved into southern France, and Paris attracted immigrants from many countries. However, migration within France was more important, from rural areas to towns and cities; and without foreign immigration, France would have experienced labour shortages and an even slower population growth.

Contemporaries often blamed France's slow population growth on their particular social concerns – 'conscription, capitalism, clerical celibacy, urbanization, secularization, taxation, equal inheritance, Free Masonry, overeating, bicycling, alcoholism, absinthe, tobacco, and both the emancipation and subjugation of women' (McLaren, 1976, p. 491), to which might be added syphilis, the weakening of moral and religious principles, and the pursuit of pleasure and material well-being. Feminists tended to support the availability to women of contraception and abortion (a criminal offence since 1810, according to article 317 of the Criminal Code), while arguing that women should be given incentives to bear children by granting them the right to pursue the fathers of their children for child support, the right to claim welfare benefits as mothers, and the right to the same legal and political status as men. Around the turn of the century a French pro-natalist movement began to emerge, with, for instance, the founding of the National Alliance for the Increase in the French Population in 1896 and of the League against Child Mortality in 1902, organizations that campaigned for such measures as family allowances, taxes on unmarried adults, and improvements in public health and hygiene. Legislation gradually began to reflect these concerns, with laws introducing free hospital admission to women in childbirth (1893), payments for destitute children (1904), low-income housing (1906), maternity leave rights (1909 and 1913), and assistance for families with large numbers of children (1913 and 1914). However, the French birth rate remained stubbornly low for reasons which may never be fully understood, but which may have included equal inheritance laws and the relatively cramped housing conditions experienced by most urban French households.

Document 4.9 Women and Capitalism

This futile and frivolous being who lives only for a piece of lace or jewellery, the fashionable woman, is for her husband or lover merely a luxury object or an advertisement.

The wealthy capitalist has a beautiful woman just as he has a beautiful horse. But, it will be pointed out, men prefer these pretty little dolls who, outside the chatter of the salons, have not two ideas in their heads, to serious and educated women, to working women. This observation in general is unfortunately true. Lots of men disapprove of women who work and who think, under the pretext that this is not their role, but in fact through fear of intellectual equality. Equality which could only compromise what is understood by the term masculine superiority . . .

Ah!, in this Paris where so much grandeur mixes with so much baseness, there are women, martyrs of a heartless society, whose lives are just a long tissue of suffering, sorrows and tears! These women are worthy of the most profound compassion, but their martyrdom will not end until the social revolution which, in including all humanity, will liberate the eternally oppressed woman. To be a feminist and not to be a revolutionary is therefore ridiculous. Feminism alone is an absurdity, because only when all human beings have been liberated by the Revolution will oppressed women regain their freedom and dignity . . .

Everything at the moment is against women. Family, education, religion, the law, all the moral and social authorities contribute to her oppression. Barely escaped from the tyranny of the family, the young girl falls under the yoke of marriage. Obedience, an odious and degrading word, flaunted in the Civil Code, makes marriage the most cruel of chains . . .

At present there exists, nobody can deny it, gender rivalry just as there is class rivalry or even rivalry within the working class. Men and women are rivals, that is to say adversaries, because their interests are different and because this monstrous society is entirely based on the competition between individuals.

Source: Suzanne Carruette, 'La Femme de demain', Le Libertaire, 22 April 1900; M. Albistur and D. Armogathe (eds), Le Grief de femmes: anthologie de textes féministes du second empire à nos jours. Poitiers: Editions Hier et Demain. 1978, pp. 78–81

Marxist concepts of the class struggle between a parasitic and exploitative bourgeois class and a working and starving proletariat were transferred by revolutionary feminists such as Suzanne Carruette to the debate about the position of women and to the concept of a gender struggle between men and women. Carruette argued that capitalism oppressed and exploited women just as it oppressed and exploited workers. Rich men turned young and beautiful women into 'trophy wives' or mistresses. They might be pampered, indulged and well dressed, but they were uneducated, led pointless lives, and were little more than rich men's playthings and status symbols. Meanwhile, women workers had to suffer the more obvious forms of capitalist oppression – low pay, long hours of work, and a miserable standard of living. The solution was not feminism but revolution, which alone could overthrow capitalism, liberate both men and women, and construct a new society in which there was no oppression and no exploitation. Carruette looked forward to the woman of tomorrow, 'freed from all hindrance, control and prejudice, emancipated in her body, heart and mind, sovereign mistress of herself, liberated, loved and respected' (Albistur and Armogathe, 1978, p. 81).

This approach raised a number of questions: whether change should come through revolutionary struggle and upheaval or through government action and parliamentary legislation; whether working women should seek allies among male workers, socialists or feminists, relying on working-class solidarity, ideological solidarity or sisterhood solidarity; and whether for women economic and social disabilities were more important than legal and political disabilities, class differences than gender differences.

Such questions were hotly debated among French feminists, but most would have agreed with Suzanne Carruette's emphasis on the general male prejudice towards intellectual and career women, on the resemblance of a female prostitute to a woman who in effect sold herself in marriage to a rich husband, on the courage and perseverance of women who did work in manual or professional jobs, and on the inability of many women to gain a good education and to become intellectually and financially independent.

Document 4.10 Women and Work

The male bourgeois thought and still thinks that the wife should stay at home and devote herself to looking after and managing the home, caring for the husband, and feeding and clothing the children. Long ago Xenophon, when the bourgeoisie was emerging and taking shape in classical antiquity, traced the main outlines of his ideal woman. If over the centuries this ideal could appear to be reasonable, it was only because it corresponded to prevailing economic conditions, and it is no more than an ideological survivor from the period when those conditions ceased to exist.

The domestication of woman presupposes that she fulfils in the household multiple functions, which absorb all her energy. However, the most important and the most demanding of these domestic tasks – the spinning of wool and linen, knitting, the tailoring and making of clothes, laundry-work, bread-making, etc. – are today carried out by capitalist industry. It equally presupposes that men by their marriage settlements and their earnings can provide for the material needs of their families. However, among the wealthy bourgeoisie marriage is as much an association of capital as a union of individuals, and often the value of the marriage settlement of the bride is superior to that of the groom; and among the lower middle class the earnings of the male head of the family have often fallen so low that the children – boys and girls – are forced to earn their means of existence in business, in administrative posts with railway companies, in banks, in teaching, in the post office, etc.; and it often happens that young married women continue to work outside the home so as to contribute to the household income, because the earnings of the husband are not sufficient to cover household expenses . . .

Capitalism has not snatched women from the domestic hearth and thrown them into social production to emancipate them, but to exploit them even more ferociously than they were exploited by men. Also, great care has been taken not to overthrow the economic, legal, political and moral barriers put in place to shut away women in the marital home. Women, exploited by capitalism, suffer the misery of the free market and in addition are burdened with the chains of their past. Their economic misery is intensified. Instead of being looked after by a father or husband, to whose authority they continue to be subject, they must earn their own livings; and when their daily work in the workshop, office or school is finished, their domestic work begins.

Maternity, the sacred labour, the most elevated of social functions, becomes in capitalist society a cause of horrible economic and physiological miseries. The intolerable condition of women is a danger for the reproduction of the species.

Source: P. Lafargue, La Question de la femme. *Paris: L'Oeuvre nouvelle. 1904, pp. 3–5 and 21–2*

For the socialist Paul Lafargue, the impact of capitalism and of work outside the home on women was mixed. On the one hand, capitalism had liberated women from many domestic tasks and had created many new employment opportunities for women, who were now able to be economically independent or important contributors to the household income. On the other hand, capitalism meant that marriage for the wealthy was based on money, not love, while poor women were forced to suffer exploitation in the labour market, and experienced maternity and motherhood in intolerable circumstances. Certainly, technology was liberating women from many household chores, a process which has continued to the present; and new employment opportunites for women were being created in department stores, post offices, banks, teaching and public transport, while female employment in a number of industries, including food, chemicals, paper, publishing and metalwork, was expanding. Altogether, excluding women employed in agriculture, by 1906 some 4,356,000 women were employed in the French labour force, forming 36.6 per cent of all non-agricultural workers (McMillan, *Housewife*, 1981, p. 37).

However, conditions of work for women remained poor, particularly in traditional areas of female employment such as textiles, clothes production and domestic service; and women generally were paid roughly half of what men were paid. Between 1891 and 1893 the average daily wage was six francs and fifteen centimes for men and three francs for women in the department of the Seine, and three francs and ninety centimes for men and two francs and ten centimes for women in the provincial departments. Only cutters and polishers of precious stones in the department of the Seine earned the same wage, whether they were men or women (Guilbert, 1966, pp. 17–18).

Legislators could be more concerned with female morality than with female welfare, as indicated, for instance, by the laws prohibiting night-work for girls and women up to the age of twenty-one (19 May 1874) and for all female workers (2 November 1892). Trade unions remained male dominated and not over-concerned with specifically women's issues (though unions often welcomed the support of women during strikes), and a large proportion of working women did not belong to a trade union, so that only 5.3 per cent of trade union membership was female in 1900 (Guilbert, 1966, p. 432).

Even Paul Lafargue's concern for the plight of women workers seems to have stemmed partly from his fears regarding the French birth rate. The traditional line that a wife should look after her husband and children rather than go out to work was followed by some members of the French Left (and by many working-class women – female factory-workers tended to be young and unmarried), while others on the French Left argued that it was better for women to stay at home instead of working for a derisory wage. Female workers could also be resented by their male counterparts, fearful of having their jobs 'poached' by cheap labour. However, the gradual process of accepting women workers and integrating them fairly into the labour force had begun by the eve of the First World War.

Document 4.11 Joan of Arc

To attribute Joan of Arc's extraordinary vocation exclusively to her love for her country is to falsify history and to substitute a conventional figure for the real Joan of Arc.

This generous sentiment of patriotism undoubtedly occupied a large place in her heart. For a long time she suffered, with inexpressible anguish, the sorrow of knowing that her country had been invaded, her king dethroned, and the national cause almost despaired of; and when finally given the opportunity to act and to sacrifice herself, she certainly demonstrated the passion of her wholly French spirit.

I repeat, nevertheless, that her personality is seriously distorted if, through lack of faith and fear of the divine, people insist in seeing in her simply a sort of virginal and intrepid amazon, . . .

If Joan of Arc was the incomparable female warrior who attracted the respect and admiration of the bravest military commanders of her time, she was above all a person sent by God, not in a poetic or metaphoric sense which can be interpreted in any way, but in the strictest and most precise meaning of the term. In this alone lies the fundamental explanation for the outstanding services for which France is indebted to her.

Source: Mgr Perraud, Panegyric on Joan of Arc, 8 May 1887; Abbé P. Fesch, Jeanne d'Arc, vierge et martyre. *Paris: Tolra. 1894, p. 380*

Since the beginning of the nineteenth century, the symbolism of Joan of Arc had been exploited for political reasons. Following his Concordat with the papacy and anxious to consolidate good relations between his regime and the Catholic Church, on 30 January 1803 Napoleon authorized the celebration of a Joan of Arc feast at Orleans on 8 May (the anniversary of the relief of Orleans) and the construction of a new monument to her. Interest in Joan of Arc increased with the publication from 1841 of scholarly editions of documents associated with her by the Society of the History of France, and with the attention she received from writers such as Alphonse de Lamartine, who portrayed her as a Romantic heroine (1852), and Jules Michelet, who identified her with French nationalism (1853). Military defeat and loss of territory in 1870–1, and the subsequent Catholic revival, gave further impetus to the nationalist and Catholic cults of Joan of Arc, the peasant-girl from Lorraine (now largely annexed to the German Empire) who had inspired the liberation of France from the English allegedly on the promptings of heavenly voices. By the 1890s publications on Joan of Arc had become a flood, and her birthplace in Domremy had become a site of national pilgrimage. In 1904 a National Joan of Arc League was founded, and publications on Joan of Arc continued, notably a two-volume life by Anatole France (1908), reprinted many times, and a study by Charles Péguy (1910).

The Joan of Arc cult had, however, different claimants. For nationalists, she was the liberator of enemy-occupied French territory; for Catholics, a saint and martyr; and for feminists, a woman who had worn men's clothes and armour and who had succeeded in a man's world. Cardinal Perraud is here emphasizing that Joan of Arc was motivated more by her religion than her patriotism as part of a campaign to canonize her, a campaign which eventually succeeded. Declared Venerable in 1894 and Blessed in 1909, she was finally canonized in 1920 amid the political conservatism and Catholic revivalism of the immediate post-First World War years in France. However, her symbolism continued to be disputed. Charles Maurras and Action Française emphasized her royalism, patriotism and Catholicism, while the Left delighted in pointing out that this peasant-girl had been betrayed by her king and condemned to be burnt at the stake as a heretic by Catholic judges. Similarly, during the Second World War in different ways French fascists, German occupiers and Charles de Gaulle all tried to exploit Joan of Arc for propaganda purposes.

Document 4.12 Sex and Marriage

Marriage, as it is instituted in our customs, is essentially about uniting a woman who is a virgin to a man who is sexually experienced, and entrusting the sexual education of the bride to the experience of the groom. The system is based on the principle or, in my opinion, on the prejudice about female virginity. However, in agreeing that women should come to marriage in this pure and ignorant state, it is particularly important that these novices should find good teachers, and that their preparation for marriage should be entrusted to competent hands. The current system prevents women from acquiring before marriage even a theoretical experience of physical love. On the other hand, in a roundabout way, the system prevents the majority of men from gaining in suitable conditions this experience, which at least one of the two spouses should possess. If young men, in the period of freedom which precedes marriage, are constrained to seek their lessons from prostitutes, is that due on their part to a free choice, a preference? On the contrary, would they not prefer to find within their reach, among their close friends, the sexual partner which they are obliged to seek by chance? Instead of turning their youthful ardour into financial transactions in brief and chance encounters, would they not prefer to bring their youthful ardour to a girl friend who would be their equal, so that a mutual tenderness could prepare them for the development and exchange of desire? However, this is precisely what social convention prohibits as if it were the most dreadful and reprehensible act, and, if this convention is evidently justified by our moral codes, is not the inevitable consequence to throw young men to venal pleasure, to dubious associations, to vicious habits, and to the ignoble passivity which this form of pleasure entails? Under the most severe penalties, you forbid young women to come to marriage already instructed in the arts of love-making, but at the same time you ruin their future teachers. This is to commit too many mistakes simultaneously.

Source: L. Blum, Du Mariage. *Paris: Librairie Paul Ollendorff. 1907, pp. 87–8*

Léon Blum, the future leader of the majority Socialist Party and the Socialist Prime Minister in the Popular Front governments of 1936–8, came from an Alsatian Jewish family. His father had moved to Paris shortly before 1848 and had eventually set up as a cloth merchant in the rue Saint Denis. After a successful school career and some false starts in higher education, Blum established for himself a reputation as a writer through articles published in *La Revue Blanche* while at the same time qualifying as a lawyer. In 1896 he was appointed to a post at the Conseil d'Etat, and thereafter pursued his legal career, became a distinguished theatre critic, and, influenced by Lucien Herr (librarian at the Ecole Normale Supérieure), Georges Clemenceau and Jean Jaurès, became attracted to left-wing politics. In 1897 Blum joined the Dreyfusard camp as an active member.

Not surprisingly, given his intellectual and political development, the main influences on Blum in writing *Du Mariage* were the socialist Charles Fourrier and writers such as Balzac, Stendhal and Tolstoy, rather than feminism or the ideas of Freud. Blum considered that, while happily married himself, marriage in general was a badly functioning institution. Although attracted to the concept of 'free love', he decided that, in effect, 'free love' should be enjoyed only by young men and young women before marriage, to enable them to gain sexual experience within loving relationships. This would result, he maintained, in a better preparation for happiness in marriage than the current practice, whereby brides were virgins and grooms had received their sexual initiation from prostitutes. An alternative solution, advocated by Tolstoy, was that both bride and groom should be virgins; and Blum does not seem to consider practical problems such as the restricted availability of contraceptive devices, the illegality of abortion, and the consequent possibility of unwanted pregnancies and unwanted children. Nevertheless, Blum was ahead of his time in publicly recognizing that women could have strong sexual desires, which, if not satisfied, might lead to unhappiness, but that love and physical passion were not necessarily related; and with considerable justification he suggested that there would be less working-class prostitution if bourgeois women enjoyed sexual freedom before marriage. Blum's bold and radical ideas inevitably attracted criticism, some of it anti-Dreyfusard and anti-Semitic, though a surprising number of critics described the book as courageous. Women tended to be unenthusiastic, and Jaurès was shocked.

CHRONOLOGY

1871

11 April   Founding of the Union of Women for the Defence of Paris and the Care of the Wounded

10–15 May	Organization of the Légion des Fédérées

1874

19 May	Law prohibiting factory-work for children under 12, night-work for girls under 21 and underground work in mines, pits and quarries for all female workers and for boys under 12

1878

July–August	First French International Congress for Women's Rights held in Paris

1879

9 August	Law requiring each department to establish a school for the training of female primary-school teachers
20–31 October	French Socialist Workers' Congress held in Marseilles

1880

21 December	Law on secondary-school education for girls

1881

16 June	Law establishing free primary education for boys and girls up to age 13
14 July	Feminist demonstration led by Auclert to the Place de la Bastille

1882

18 March	Law making primary education for boys and girls compulsory

1884

27 July	Divorce law

1889

26–9 June	Second French International Congress for Women's Rights
July	Radical Feminist Congress

1892

2 November	Law prohibiting night-work for women and restricting working day to 11 hours

1900

5–8 September	International Congress on the Condition and Rights of Women
1 December	Women permitted to become barristers in France

1906

3 June	Deputies showered with suffragist handbills by Madeleine Caroline Kauffmann
1–4 November	National Congress on the Civil and Political Rights of Women

1907

13 July	Law allowing married women to dispose freely of their own incomes

August   First International Conference of Socialist Women held at Stuttgart

1908
3 May   Upsetting of a ballot box by Auclert in a Paris polling station
26–8 June National Congress on the Civil and Political Rights of Women

1909
February   Formation of the French Union for Women's Suffrage (UFSF) Law giving
           women the right to return to their jobs after maternity leave

1912
4 July   Introduction of maximum 10-hour working day for all workers
           Law introducing maternity leave: optional 4 weeks before birth,
           compulsory 4 weeks after birth

1913
14 July   Law introducing assistance to families with numerous children (*familles
           nombreuses*)

1914
5 July   Feminist demonstration in Paris to commemorate Condorcet

BIBLIOGRAPHY

Accampo, E.A., Fuchs, R.G. and Stewart, M.L., *Gender and the Politics of Social Reform in France, 1870–1914*. Baltimore and London: Johns Hopkins University Press. 1995.

Albistur, M. and Armogathe, D., *Le Grief des femmes: anthologie de textes féministes du second empire à nos jours*. Poitiers: Editions Hier et Demain. 1978.

Auspitz, K., *The Radical Bourgeoisie: the Ligue de l'Enseignement and the origins of the Third Republic, 1866–1885*. Cambridge: Cambridge University Press. 1982.

Bidelman, P.K., *Pariahs Stand Up!: the founding of the liberal feminist movement in France, 1858–1889*. Westport, Conn.: Greenwood Press. 1982.

Copley, A., *Sexual Moralities in France, 1780–1980: new ideas on the family, divorce, and homosexuality*. London and New York: Routledge. 1989.

Derfler, L., *Paul Lafargue and the Flowering of French Socialism, 1882–1911*. Cambridge, Mass., and London: Harvard University Press. 1998.

Dupanloup, F.A.P., *Lettres sur l'éducation des filles: documents, rapports et discours à la chambre des Députes et au Sénat*. Paris: Jules Gervais. 1879.

Ellis, J.D., *The Physician-Legislators of France: medicine and politics in the early Third Republic, 1870–1914*. Cambridge: Cambridge University Press. 1990.

Evans, R.J., 'Feminism and Anticlericalism in France, 1870–1922', *Historical Journal*, 25 (1982), 947–9.

Fuchs, R.G. (ed.), 'Population and the State in the Third Republic', special edition of *French Historical Studies*, 19 (1996).

Fuchs, R.G. and Moch, L.G., 'Pregnant, Single, and Far from Home: migrant women in nineteenth-century Paris', *American Historical Review*, 95 (1990), 1007–31.

Guilbert, M., *Les Femmes et l'organisation syndicale avant 1914*. Paris: CNRS. 1966.

Hanna, M., 'Iconology and Ideology: images of Joan of Arc in the idiom of the Action Française, 1908–1931', *French Historical Studies*, 14 (1985), 215–39.

Hause, S.C., *Hubertine Auclert, the French Suffragette*. New Haven, Conn., and London: Yale University Press. 1987.

Hause, S.C., and Kenney, A.R., 'The Limits of Suffragist Behavior: legalism and militancy in France, 1876–1922', *American Historical Review*, 86 (1981), 781–806.

—— *Women's Suffrage and Social Politics in the French Third Republic*. Princeton, NJ: Princeton University Press. 1984.

Hilden, P., *Working Women and Socialist Politics in France, 1880–1914: a regional study*. Oxford: Clarendon Press, 1986.

—— 'Rewriting the History of Socialism: working women and the Parti Ouvrier Français', *European History Quaterly*, 17 (1987), 285–306.

Johnson, M.P., 'Citizenship and Gender: the Légion des Fédérées in the Paris Commune of 1871', *French History*, 8 (1994), 276–95.

Krumeich, G., *Jeanne d'Arc à travers l'histoire*. Paris: Albin Michel. 1993.

Lacouture, J., *Léon Blum*. New York and London: Holmes & Meier. 1982.

McBride, T.M., 'A Woman's World: department stores and the evolution of women's employment, 1870–1920', *French Historical Studies*, 10 (1978), 664–83.

McLaren, A., 'Sex and Socialism: the opposition of the French left to birth control in the nineteenth century', *Journal of the History of Ideas*, 37 (1976), 475–92.

—— 'Abortion in France: women and the regulation of family size, 1800–1914', *French Historical Studies*, 10 (1978), 461–85.

McMillan, J.F., *Housewife or Harlot: the place of women in French society, 1870–1940*. Brighton: Harvester Press. 1981.

—— 'Clericals, Anticlericals and the Women's Movement in France under the Third Republic', *Historical Journal*, 24 (1981), 361–76.

—— *Françaises: the social condition of women and the politics of gender in France, 1789–1914*. London: UCL Press. 1997.

Margadant, J.B., *Madame le Professeur: women educators in the Third Republic*. Princeton, NJ: Princeton University Press. 1990.

Miller, M.B., *The Bon Marché: bourgeois culture and the department store, 1869–1920*. London, Boston and Sydney: George Allen & Unwin. 1981.

Nord, P., 'The Welfare State in France, 1870–1914', *French Historical Studies*, 18 (1994), 821–38.

Offen, K., 'The Second Sex and the Baccalauréat in Republican France, 1880–1924', *French Historical Studies*, 13 (1983), 252–88.

—— 'Depopulation, Nationalism, and Feminism in Fin-de-Siècle France', *American Historical Review*, 89 (1984), 648–76.

Ronsin, F., *Les Divorciaires: affrontements politiques et conceptions du mariage dans la France du XIXe siècle*. Paris: Aubier. 1992.

Schulkind, E., 'Socialist Women during the 1871 Commune', *Past and Present*, 106 (1985), 124–63.

Shafer, D.A., '*Plus que des ambulancières*: women in articulation and defence of their ideals during the Paris Commune (1871)', *French History*, 7 (1993), 85–101.

Shapiro, A.-L., *Breaking the Codes: female criminality in fin-de-siècle Paris*. Stanford, Calif.: Stanford University Press, 1996.

Smith, B.G., *Ladies of the Leisure Class: the bourgeoises of northern France in the nineteenth century*. Princeton, NJ: Princeton University Press. 1981.

Sowerwine, C., *Sisters or Citizens?: women and socialism in France since 1876*. Cambridge: Cambridge University Press. 1982.

Stuart, R., 'Whores and Angels: women and the family in the discourse of French Marxism, 1882–1905', *European History Quarterly*, 27 (1997), 339–69.

Tomlinson, R., 'The "Disappearance" of France, 1896–1940: French politics and the birth rate', *Historical Journal*, 28 (1985), 405–15.

Warner, M., *Joan of Arc: the image of female heroism*. London: Weidenfeld & Nicolson. 1981.

Zeldin, T., *France, 1848–1945: ambition, love and politics*. Oxford: Clarendon Press. 1973.

5 | The First World War

The First World War was the most traumatic experience suffered by the Third Republic between the end of the Franco-Prussian War and the outbreak of the Second World War. It marked the end of an era, perhaps even of a world, characterized, at least in contrast to the inter-war period, by political and social stability, low inflation, low taxes and low unemployment. The war itself subjected France to an unprecedented ordeal lasting over four years: some 1,397,800 Frenchmen were killed and another 4,266,000 wounded; an enormous financial and economic cost was incurred, perhaps amounting to half of France's national wealth; and large parts of north-eastern France, one of the country's most economically productive regions, were devastated by years of fighting. It was a war that led to a massive mobilization of France's human, industrial and financial resources. Approximately 8,410,000 men from France and the French colonial empire were mobilized to serve in France's armed forces, while millions of French men and women and a significant number of foreign and colonial workers were recruited to contribute to victory on the home front.

The whole character of the French economy was transformed: an economy run largely on *laissez-faire* capitalist lines was gradually replaced by a state-directed economy, in which the government, not private companies or market forces, determined decisions regarding imports, exports, investment, production, wages, labour and use of resouces. To meet the war's astronomical cost, tax revenues were doubled and the government borrowed on an unprecedented scale, both on the French market and from her allies, Britain and the United States.

In November 1918 victory over the German Empire crowned this colossal effort and sacrifice, though defeat had at times seemed a possibility and victory came at a heavy price. In September 1914 and again during the early summer of 1918 German advances threatened Paris, while in May and June 1917 industrial strikes and army mutinies brought France close to collapse. Moreover, besides the human, economic and financial cost of the war, the national patriotic unity, proclaimed and almost universally accepted in August 1914, gradually became eroded by an anti-war movement within the French Left; and the Russian alliance, so crucial in terms of French diplomacy, military planning and foreign investment, evaporated with the overthrow of the Tsarist regime, the seizure of power by the Bolsheviks, and the partial break-up of the Russian Empire.

Of course, the extent to which the First World War marked a rupture with the past is debatable: many trends, such as the development of chemical, pharmaceutical and metallurgical industries, the formation of large industrial firms, the introduction of new technologies and new technological products such as cars and aircraft, the rise in the membership of socialist parties and of trade unions, and the changing roles of women in society and in the economy, were accelerated rather than initiated by the First World War. Nevertheless, the First World War was responsible for a profound change to that intangible concept, the French national psyche. Altogether, the war provided the Third Republic with the severest of challenges. The ultimate triumph of the Third Republic, albeit by a narrow margin, at enormous cost and with the indispensable assistance of allies, is a tribute to the loyalty it had won in the hearts of most of its citizens, to its broadly liberal and democratic character, and to its ability to adapt in order to survive.

Document 5.1 Sport and the Olympic Games

It is above all essential to preserve for athletics the noble and chivalrous character that has distinguished it in the past, so that it can continue to play effectively in the education of modern peoples the admirable role which the Greek masters gave it. Human imperfection always tends to transform the Olympic athlete into a circus gladiator. It is necessary to choose between the two athletic models which are not compatible. To defend themselves against the spirit of money and professionalism that threatens them, the amateurs, in the majority of countries, have established a complicated legal framework, full of compromises and contradictions. In addition, too often the letter rather than the spirit of the law is respected. A reform is essential and, before it is undertaken, it must be discussed. The questions which have been placed on the agenda for the Congress relate to these compromises and contradictions affecting regulations governing amateurs. The proposal mentioned in the last paragraph would be the happy expression of the international understanding that we are attempting, if not to achieve, at least to prepare for. The re-establishment of the Olympic Games, on foundations and according to conditions that are in conformity with modern life, would bring together every four years the representatives of the world; and it is reasonable to believe that such polite and peaceful competitions constitute the best form of internationalism.

Source: Circular of the Baron de Coubertin to French and foreign sporting and athletic societies, 15 January 1894; P., Baron de Coubertin, Une Campagne de vingt-et-un ans, 1887–1908. *Paris: Librairie de l'Education physique. 1909, p. 91*

The years leading up to the First World War witnessed two apparently contradictory tendencies: on the one hand, increasing international contact and interdependence; on the other hand, increasing international competition and rivalry. Both of these tendencies can be found in the development of sport and of the modern Olympic movement.

The development of sport in France after 1870 was influenced by the French defeat in the Franco-Prussian War, the introduction of team sports from England, the gradual rise in the standard of living and in the availability of leisure, and by the technological innovation and production skills responsible for bicycles, cars, yachts and aircraft. The French defeat led to a new emphasis on sports with an obvious military relevance, such as horse-riding, rifle-shooting and gymnastics. Even the French Alpine Club, founded in 1874, was intended to provide 'a school of physical energy and moral vigour', training French youth to be 'more virile, more apt to bear military life, more prepared to face a long conflict without discouragement' (Weber, 1971, p. 72). This approach to sport attracted nationalists such as Paul Déroulède (who organized the national shooting competitions out of which in 1886 arose the Union des Sociétés de Tir de France) and republican politicians such as Jules Simon (who helped to ensure that gymnastics and physical exercises became compulsory in state schools from 1880).

England pioneered a series of team sports such as cricket, football, rugby and rowing, and developed other sports such as boxing, fencing and tennis. All these sports (with the notable exception of cricket) soon spread to France, one of the first French football clubs being Le Havre Athletic Club (founded in 1872). International competitions eventually followed. In 1893 French rowers competed at Henley and a French football team played against an English team in London.

On a technological level, the development of a modern-style bicycle during the 1890s, with pneumatic detachable tyres thanks to the work of John Boyd Dunlop and the Michelin brothers, was crucial. The Tour de France was first competed for in 1903 and rapidly became a national institution. Whereas before 1870 newspapers barely mentioned sport, by 1914 they were devoting pages to the subject, and numerous publications were now exclusively focused on sport. Commercial sponsorship of sport had also arrived by 1914.

Like many of his contemporaries, the Baron de Coubertin's attitude to sport was influenced by British (and later American) example, but he was exceptional in his devotion to the revival of the Olympic Games and to his moral vision of sport and of international sporting contests. The development of organized sporting activities in many countries and archaeological discoveries in Greece helped to create a favourable climate for a revival of the Olympic Games of ancient Greece, which Coubertin began to campaign for in 1887. In November 1892 he organized a French conference to support a projected Olympic Games, and this was followed by an international conference held in Paris in June 1894. Seventy-nine delegates representing forty-nine organizations from nine countries unanimously endorsed Coubertin's project and his ideal – that competitors should be amateurs, not professionals, that they should compete according to the highest standards of sportsmanship, and that the aim should at least in part be the promotion of international peace and fellowship. Coubertin's insistence on the amateur status of competitors, and his opposition to the inclusion of women in Olympic competitions, helped to influence the development of international sporting competitions, though from the start the Olympic Games arguably promoted national rivalry as much as international peace and fellowship.

The first modern Olympic Games were held in Athens in April 1896, and thereafter in Paris (1900), St Louis, Missouri (1904), London (1908) and Stockholm (1912). The Olympic Games due to be held in 1916 were one of the many casualties of the First World War, but the Games were revived in 1920. As the most prominent early advocate and organizer of the Olympic movement, and as chairman of the International Olympic Committee from 1897 to 1924, Coubertin was very much the father of the modern Olympic movement.

Document 5.2 The Franco-British Entente Cordiale

Our arrangements with England have been quite well handled. I am astonished by the ease with which public opinion accepts this reasonable idea that, not being able to expel the English from Egypt, it was time to accept an accomplished fact against which we were powerless and to secure something in exchange for our support. Delcassé has had the audacity to say out loud what everybody privately thought and the good luck to enjoy a unique combination of circumstances for dealing with the English.

We must not ignore the fact that, without the Transvaal War, which has bloodied and sobered Great Britain, without the conflict in the Far East, which has caused those on both sides of the Channel to reflect and has inspired in everybody a strong desire to limit the conflict, our agreements would not have been possible or would not have been favourably accepted by public opinion. There was, then, a happy combination of circumstances, but it is not enough to have opportunities in life or even to want to exploit them, it is necessary to be ready to exploit them. We were, however, ready, thanks to conversations pursued without interruption for many years.

Source: Paul Cambon to his son, 16 April 1904; P. Cambon, Correspondance, 1870–1924. Paris: Bernard Grasset. 1940, II, p. 134

Due to the mistakes and failures of Napoleon III's foreign policies, France was diplomatically isolated at the time of the Franco-Prussian War; and, due largely to the skill of Bismarck's diplomacy, France remained diplomatically isolated after 1870. However, at the beginning of the 1890s France began to break out of this isolation. At a time when relations between Germany and Russia were deteriorating, the French government signalled its wish to have closer relations with Russia by arresting Russian and Polish revolutionaries resident in France (May 1890) and by sending a naval squadron on a courtesy visit to the Russian naval base at Kronstadt (July 1891). This visit coincided with the granting of a French financial loan to Russia; and in an exchange of letters on 27 August 1891 the French and Russian governments agreed to consult if peace were threatened. On these slender foundations a Franco-Russian alliance was gradually constructed: a Russian naval squadron visited Toulon in October 1893; a Franco-Russian military convention was agreed in January 1894; more French loans were granted to Russia, particularly for railway construction; and Tsar Nicholas II and his wife made a successful state visit to France in October 1896.

As the Franco-Russian alliance became ever more substantial, so Franco-British relations became more problematic, since both France and Russia were major imperial rivals of Britain, and a Franco-Russian alliance could be presented as being directed as much against Britain as Germany.

After the Crimean War Britain had retreated into 'splendid isolation', but by the beginning of the twentieth century such a policy was no longer practical. British interests in China were threatened by the expansionist policies of both Russia and Japan and by the anti-European Boxer Rising (June–August 1900), while the Boer War exposed British military weakness and diplomatic isolation. Various attempts to secure an Anglo-German alliance failed, and the German decision in 1898 to build a high seas fleet potentially challenged British naval supremacy. In January 1902 Britain negotiated an alliance with Japan, but this meant that when the Russo-Japanese War broke out in February 1904 Britain and France were, at one remove, on opposing sides. Resentment over the British occupation of Egypt and the Sudan, colonial conflicts such as the Fashoda Incident, and pro-Boer sympathies did not predispose French public opinion to welcome an *entente* with Britain. The value to France of such an agreement was nevertheless recognized by Théophile Delcassé (Minister of Foreign Affairs, 1899–1905), particularly as France did not want to be drawn into any conflict with Britain through her alliance with Russia, and because France needed British support for her expansionist designs on Morocco.

State visits by King Edward VII to Paris (May 1903) and by President Loubet to London (July 1903) helped to win over French public opinion. Between July 1903 and April 1904 Franco-British negotiations settled colonial disputes over Morocco, Egypt, Siam, the Suez Canal, Newfoundland fisheries, frontiers in West Africa, and the administration of the New Hebrides in the South Pacific. The agreement signed on 8 April 1904 was much more, though, than a settlement of colonial disputes: it was the foundation for a diplomatic and military alliance that contributed to the outbreak of the First World War by helping to divide up the Great Powers of Europe into two opposing camps (the Triple Alliance of Germany, Austria-Hungary and Italy, and the Triple Entente of France, Russia and Britain), by permitting the French to pursue their Moroccan ambitions despite German opposition, and by encouraging the Germans to develop new war plans that involved an offensive strike against France.

With considerable justification, Paul Cambon could claim responsibility for the achievement and maintenance of the Franco-British Entente Cordiale during his remarkably long period as the French ambassador in London (1898–1920). He shared Delcassé's related objectives of securing better relations with Britain and promoting French expansion in North Africa (Paul Cambon had been one of the architects of the French protectorate over Tunisia and his brother, Jules Cambon, had served as Governor General of Algeria, 1891–6). In 1901, acting on his own initiative, Paul Cambon had opened negotiations in London over a possible French recognition of the British position in Egypt in return for British acceptance of French expansion in Morocco; and he set out to arouse the interest of the British government and of British public opinion in such an arrangement by having *The Times* publish a report on the subject in February 1903. Paul Cambon, though, declined to speak English in diplomatic conversations, had a limited circle of British contacts, and always tended to overestimate Britain's commitment to France.

Document 5.3 Anti-militarism and Anti-colonialism of the Left

Workers,

Tomorrow, perhaps, we will be faced with a *fait accompli*: war DECLARED!

For five years a French colonial party, for whom Delcassé was the henchman, has prepared the conquest of Morocco. Capitalists and army officers press for the invasion of this country, some to speculate and enrich themselves, others to pick up promotions and decorations in the fighting.

Capitalist and imperialist Germany, wishing to have her share of the loot, has intervened.

The German and French governments, faithful servants of capitalist interests which alone are involved, have elevated these quarrels among speculators to the level of a bitter conflict.

To satisfy the inexhaustible appetites of this coalition of interests, the rulers of the two countries are ready to throw the working masses of Germany and France against each other.

Who does not shudder at the horror of the carnage? Thousands of men colliding with each other . . . rapid-fire rifles, artillery and machine-guns accomplishing their work of death . . .

Who could calculate the billions squandered, billions snatched from the labour of peasants and workers?

This picture is not exaggerated. At this very moment the naval bases are preparing for war and the army is ready to leave.

In June 1905 the declaration of war was avoided only by the resignation of Delcassé. Since then war has been at the mercy of the smallest incident. It is absolutely true that on 19 December 1905, after the French government had learnt that the German ambassador in Paris had been recalled, all telephone communications were suspended for four hours so that the government could, if necessary, send out mobilization orders with maximum speed.

The press knows these facts . . . and remains silent.

Why? The reason is to put the people under an obligation to march to war, under the pretexts of NATIONAL HONOUR and of a war that is inevitable because it is defensive.

And the Algeciras Conference, which is presented to us as leading to a peaceful solution to the conflict, could result in war.

However, *the people do not want war!* If the people were consulted, they would unanimously affirm their desire for Peace.

The working class has no interest in war. It alone bears all the costs, – paying with its labour and with its blood. It is therefore to the working class that it is incumbent to say out loud THAT IT WANTS PEACE AT ANY PRICE!

Source: La Voix du Peuple, *14–21 January 1906; J.-J. Becker,* Le Carnet B: les pouvoirs publics et l'antimilitarisme avant la guerre de 1914. *Paris: Klincksieck. 1973, p. 187*

The so-called French 'colonial party' comprised societies such as the Committee of French Africa (formed in 1890), the French Colonial Union (formed in 1893), the Committee of French Asia (formed in 1901), the Committee of Morocco (formed in 1904), the French Colonial League (formed in 1907) and the Franco-American Committee (formed in 1910), together with members of the Chamber of Deputies who belonged to a 'colonial group' (mostly representatives of Algerian and colonial departments and of French towns with colonial interests) and a band of officials, army officers, journalists and other colonial enthusiasts. Generally, though, French public opinion tended to show little interest in France's colonial empire, unless a colonial conflict coincided with a European rivalry such as Fashoda with Britain or Morocco with Germany; and the economic importance to France of her colonial empire remained limited – in 1914, French colonies accounted for a mere 11 per cent of French exports, 9 per cent of French imports and 9 per cent of her foreign investment (Keiger, *France*, 1983, p. 9). This was reflected in the relatively small memberships of the French colonial societies. Individual members of the 'colonial party' could still exercise a considerable amount of influence, such as Eugène Etienne (deputy for Oran in Algeria, 1881–1919, founding member of several colonial societies, Under-Secretary of State for the Colonies, 1887 and 1889–92, Minister of the Interior, 1905, and Minister of War, 1905–6 and 1913) and General (later Marshal) Lyautey (who, after military service in Indo-China, Madagascar and Algeria, was appointed Resident General in Morocco in 1912, and who gained, through his colonial career and his writings, an important reputation in France). The 'colonial party' was particularly influential in promoting the Fashoda expedition, in backing Delcassé in his bid for a colonial agreement with Britain, and in pressing for French expansion in Morocco.

Having secured British, as well as Spanish and Italian, consent to French expansion in Morocco, Delcassé believed that he could proceed without reference to Germany. At the end of 1904 the Sultan of Morocco was persuaded by France to accept a series of reforms and a French mission to oversee the implication of these reforms. This was in contravention of the Madrid Convention of 1880, whereby France, Germany and other states had guaranteed the independence of Morocco. Therefore, on 31 March 1905 the Kaiser interrupted his annual Mediterranean cruise to land at Tangier and give a speech, in which he asserted Germany's demand for free trade and equal rights in Morocco and confirmed the status of the Sultan of Morocco as the ruler of an independent country. There followed a major diplomatic crisis, with Germany issuing an ultimatum for the dismissal of Delcassé at the end of May. Faced with the prospect of war with Germany, the French government decided to accept Delcassé's resignation on 6 June 1905, whereupon the German Chancellor, von Bülow, was promptly made a prince. The German government then insisted that an international conference should be held to settle the Moroccan question. However, at the Algeciras Conference (16 January–7 April 1906), attended by representatives of thirteen nations, only Austria-Hungary and Morocco supported Germany, so France more or less achieved her objectives: France and Spain were assigned the responsibility of policing Morocco, and France gained the major stake in the Moroccan state bank. Moreover, in contravention of the 1906 agreement, German firms subsequently found it difficult to secure contracts in Morocco, and in 1911 the French used rioting in Fez as a pretext for a French military occupation of the Moroccan capital.

French expansion into Morocco encountered virtually no opposition in France, except from the Confédération Général du Travail or CGT (equivalent to the British TUC) and from some socialists. The text of this anti-war poster, published by the CGT on 11 January 1906, is an example of the pacifist, anti-militarist and anti-imperialist position of much of the pre-First World War French Left, which generally claimed that the workers had no country, that class divisions were more important than national divisions, and that wars were invariably fought in capitalist and imperialist interests and against the interests of the working class. Similarly, at the annual conference of the CGT held at Amiens between 8 and 16 October 1906, a resolution was passed approving the distribution of anti-militarist and anti-patriotic propaganda, on the grounds that the army in strike situations was always on the employers' side and that, in all national and colonial wars, the working class was duped and sacrificed by the parasitic bourgeois-employer class. The next annual conference of the CGT, held at Marseilles between 5 and 12 October 1908, went even further by agreeing that, in the event of a war breaking out between states, the workers in the belligerent states should respond to the declaration of war with a declaration of a revolutionary general strike, so as to halt hostilities and promote a revolutionary situation. However, the rhetoric of the French Left was often more radical than its policies and decisions in practice. Nor was the French working class, though generally hostile to militarism and war, necessarily unpatriotic.

Document 5.4 The Caillaux Trial

THE TORMENT OF A WOMAN

No drama can offer more intense emotion, and this was an extraordinarily moving audience, the atmosphere of which cannot be conveyed. The official record will report accurately what was said, but will not be able to convey the drama that was enacted. It was one of those plays that should not be read but which must be seen. It was all magnificent. The scene was the Assize Court. A woman who had divorced her husband because she had fallen in love with another man; her second husband, opposite, who had betrayed and abandoned her; and this second husband is a former government minister, a former prime minister, who has held the destinies of France in his hands; the rival woman, now married, in the dock accused of murder. That is the cast.

Source: Le Figaro, *24 July 1914, p. 1*

On 28 June 1914 the Archduke Francis Ferdinand, heir apparent to the throne of the Austro-Hungarian Empire, was assassinated together with his wife in the Bosnian capital, Sarajevo, by a Bosnian Serb. It was not immediately apparent that this atrocity would have any serious consequences for France, at least until 23 July 1914, when Austria-Hungary sent an uncompromising ultimatum to Serbia. Even then French newspapers devoted less space to the rapidly unfolding crisis in the Balkans than to the trial of Henriette Caillaux, which had begun on 20 July and continued for eight days.

Henriette Caillaux was the second wife of Joseph Caillaux, Radical deputy for the Sarthe, 1899–1919, who had served four times as Minister of Finance (June 1899–June 1902, October 1906–July 1909, March–June 1911, December 1913–March 1914) and once as Prime Minister and Minister of the Interior (June 1911–January 1912). For many conservatives, Joseph Caillaux was a controversial figure: as Minister of Finance, he had attempted to introduce an income tax (a measure successfully blocked by the Senate); and as Prime Minister, he had defused the Second Moroccan Crisis when, following the French military occupation of Fez and the arrival of a German gunboat, *The Panther*, at Agadir (1 July 1911), he had negotiated an agreement with Germany (4 November 1911), whereby Germany accepted the French protectorate in Morocco in return for two strips of territory in the French Congo. Moreover, Joseph Caillaux had publicly flouted convention in his private life. In 1908 Henriette Caillaux had divorced her first husband to marry Joseph Caillaux, with whom she had been having an affair for about a year. Joseph Caillaux, though, was also married, and his first wife delayed the marriage of Henriette and Joseph Caillaux until October 1911. Consequently, conservatives accused Caillaux of having threatened private wealth with a revolutionary income tax, of having sold out to the Germans by ceding to them French colonial territory, and of having undermined family values by living publicly with his mistress. When Joseph Caillaux was reappointed Minister of Finance in December 1913, the conservative newspaper, *Le Figaro*, launched a virulent press campaign against him, claiming that he was morally unfit to hold ministerial office.

On 13 March 1914 *Le Figaro* published on its front page the text of an intimate letter written by Joseph Caillaux in 1901 to the lady who became his first wife, but who was then his mistress and the wife of a cabinet colleague. Fearing that *Le Figaro* had more letters of a similarly compromising nature, which would in due course be published, and perhaps jealous and resentful of her husband's political career, Henriette Caillaux on 16 March 1914 gained admission to the office of Gaston Calmette, editor of *Le Figaro*, and shot him dead with a pistol. This crime and the subsequent trial captured the interest of the French newspaper-reading public. The affair involved the perennially fascinating combination of sex, violence, wealth and high politics. Also, there was much French interest at this time in crimes of passion, in the defence of honour and in the psychology and behaviour of women. The French traditionally adopted a tolerant attitude towards a crime of passion, which was what Henriette Caillaux claimed she had committed. According to aristocratic and masculine values, the defence of personal and national honour was always a duty, and

Henriette argued that she had been defending her honour. In doing so, Henriette had acted emotionally, but this was not surprising since women were supposed to be subject to ungovernable emotions; and current trends in psychology, an increasingly fashionable discipline, suggested that individuals were not always responsible for their actions, since unconscious motivation could lead to the uncontrollable act. The prosecution, on the other hand, maintained that Henriette had committed a premeditated and brutal murder: she had purchased and tested a Browning automatic pistol, she had written a note to her husband announcing her intentions, and she had fired five times at Gaston Calmette. Moreover, during her trial Henriette displayed, not hysterical emotion, but a 'lucid calm', a 'mysterious sang-froid' and a 'prodigious assurance' (*Le Figaro*, 21 July 1914, p. 1). Nevertheless, on 28 July 1914 the jury found Henriette Caillaux not guilty.

Document 5.5 The Sacred Union

For more than forty years, the French, in a sincere love of peace, have repressed from the bottom of their hearts the desire for legitimate reparations.

They have given to the world the example of a great nation, which, having clearly recovered from defeat through determination, patience and industry, has used its recovered and rejuvenated power only in the interests of progress and for the well-being of humanity.

Since the Austrian ultimatum opened a threatening crisis for the whole of Europe, France was determined to follow and to recommend to all a policy of prudence, wisdom and moderation. No action, gesture or statement can be imputed to France which was not pacific or conciliatory. As fighting begins, France has the right solemnly to declare this truth that, up to the last moment, she made the utmost efforts to avert the war that has just broken out and for which the German Empire will bear, before history, the overwhelming responsibility.

The very day after we and our allies publicly expressed the hope of witnessing the peaceful pursuit of the negotiations initiated under the auspices of the British government, Germany suddenly declared war on Russia, invaded the territory of Luxembourg, outrageously insulted the noble Belgian nation, our neighbour and friend, and traitorously tried to surprise us while in the midst of diplomatic conversations . . .

The President of the Republic, interpreter of the unanimity of the country, conveys to our servicemen on land and at sea the admiration and confidence of all French people.

Firmly united in the same sentiments, the nation will persevere in the calm determination which it has displayed every day since the crisis began . . .

In the war that is starting, France will have right on her side, giving her an eternal moral strength which peoples, no more than individuals, cannot underestimate with impunity. France will be heroically defended by all her sons, whose sacred union before the enemy nothing will break, and who are today fraternally assembled in a shared indignation against the aggressor and in a shared patriotic faith.

Let us lift up our hearts and long live France!

Source: Presidential message to the Chamber of Deputies, 4 August 1914;
R. Poincaré, Au Service de la France: neuf années de souvenirs, *vol. 4,*
L'Union Sacrée. *Paris: Plon. 1927, pp. 544–6*

The diplomatic crisis escalated rapidly after the dispatch on 23 July 1914 of the Austro-Hungarian ultimatum to Serbia, Austria-Hungary's delayed response to the assassination of the Archduke Francis Ferdinand on 28 June. Serbia failed to satisfy all of Austria-Hungary's stiff requirements, whereupon Austria-Hungary, ignoring a British proposal for Great Power mediation of the Balkan Crisis, declared war on Serbia on 28 July. Germany opposed British attempts at mediation, supported Austria-Hungary's moves against Serbia, and responded to Russian mobilization by declaring war against Russia on 1 August. German war plans assumed that Germany would have to fight France and Russia simultaneously, so Germany had adopted the Schlieffen Plan whereby France would be knocked out by a lightning strike to Paris through Belgium and Luxembourg, after which the main resources of the German army could be deployed against the numerically superior Russians. On 1 August Germany insisted not just on French neutrality, but on the surrender of her principal fortresses along her eastern frontier as a guarantee of her 'sincerity'. The French government could not comply with this demand, so the Schlieffen Plan went into operation. On 2 August Germany invaded Luxembourg and demanded free passage for her troops through Belgium, falsely claiming that a French attack on Germany through Belgium was imminent; and on 3 August Germany declared war on France, this time falsely claiming that French aircraft had violated German airspace over Nuremberg.

For the French government, an important factor in this crisis was the attitude of the French Left. Generally, the French Left had tended to oppose armaments, support the replacement of standing armies with popular militias, and urge the settling of disputes between states by international arbitration. In 1913 both socialists and trade unionists opposed the extension of the term of compulsory military service from two to three years. Although a majority in the Chamber of Deputies passed the relevant bill on 19 July 1913, this opposition continued until July 1914. Similarly, at a conference held in Paris between 14 and 16 July 1914, French socialists agreed to use every means at their disposal, including the general strike, to prevent a European war. This resolution provoked conservative and nationalist newspapers to launch a bitter anti-socialist campaign, in which *L'Action Française* even hinted that the socialist leader, Jaurès, should be assassinated. In the emotionally charged atmosphere created by the crisis, it is perhaps not surprising that a nationalist fanatic did in fact assassinate Jaurès, while he was dining at a Paris café on the evening of 31 July 1914. Ironically, on the same day the leaders of the CGT decided not to call a general strike; and Jaurès by this time had become convinced that the French government was committed to peace and did not believe that a general strike should be unleashed on a pacific government.

Raymond Poincaré had served as Prime Minister and Foreign Minister between January 1912 and January 1913, when he had been elected President of the Republic, a post he held until February 1920. As a Lorrainer, Poincaré wanted the return of the lost provinces, and he supported the three-year military service bill. However, he was prepared to compromise with Germany over issues such as the Liman von Sanders Affair and the Baghdad railway, and he was the first French President to dine at the German Embassy in Paris (19 January 1914). During July and early August 1914 Poincaré's objectives were, above all, to keep France united and to maintain the Russian and British alliances. On 16 July Poincaré, together with René Viviani (both Prime Minister and Foreign Minister) embarked at Dunkirk on the battleship *France* for a pre-arranged state visit to Russia, Sweden, Denmark and Norway. Because of the crisis, the visits to Denmark and Norway were cancelled, but the French leaders still did not return to France until 29 July, so for a crucial period they were out of France, dependent upon unsatisfactory radio communications, 'literally and metaphorically at sea' (Keiger, *France*, 1983, p. 147).

Poincaré has been accused of having failed to restrain Russia. However, the Austrian ultimatum to Serbia was carefully timed so as to follow the departure of Poincaré and Viviani from Russia on 23 July; and the French ambassador at St Petersburg, Maurice Paléologue, failed to keep Paris adequately informed of the Russian military mobilization on 29 and 30 July. German military activity virtually forced French mobilization on 1 August, and the German invasions of Luxembourg, Belgium and France made war inevitable between France and Germany. Distracted by the Caillaux Affair, overtaken by the rapidity of events, the French public reacted with shock and resignation to the mobilization and the declaration of war, but not with panic or resistance. It was widely believed that the French government had tried to avoid war and that France was the victim of German aggression and had to be defended. Military mobilization itself disorganized trade unions and political parties, and discouraged any immediate effective resistance to the war. The funeral of Jaurès (4 August 1914) in effect became an expression of national unity: Poincaré, Viviani and the Presidents of the Senate and the Chamber of Deputies all gave addresses; the Secretary General of the CGT gave a patriotic speech; and even Maurice Barrès and members of the right-wing Patriotic League attended the funeral service. In addition, Poincaré helped to promote national unity by not arresting suspected pacifists and anti-militarists (those on a list compiled by the authorities and known as the 'Carnet B'), by suspending a decree ordering the closure of various religious establishments, and by granting an amnesty to revolutionaries condemned for violation of the press laws. Thus Poincaré could claim with considerable justice on 4 August that Frenchmen were united in a 'sacred union', which he himself had helped to achieve.

Document 5.6 Opposition to the Sacred Union

The national conference of French trade unions . . . affirms that it is a duty, after a year of the most appalling and atrocious carnage that mankind has known, to determine clearly the current and future action of the French trade unions towards the war and its consequences.

The Conference declares:

THIS WAR IS NOT OUR WAR! . . .

Far from being exclusively, as is endlessly claimed, the war of German imperialism against Europe, it is simply the product of the clash of all the national imperialisms that have intoxicated all states, large and small, and that have taken root in the boundless and essentially egotistical ambitions of the ruling classes.

Confronted by the horrifying abyss opened by the war, all governments blamed the immediate responsibility on others. However, if it currently seems that Austria and Germany are the immediate and much sought-for aggressors, the Conference cannot forget that the war is the product of the political and economic conflicts that have long developed in the heart of capitalist society and for which each belligerent state has its overwhelming role of direct responsibility: France, by launching herself into the Moroccan adventure; Italy, by carrying out the conquest of Libya; Austria-Hungary, by throwing herself on the Balkan markets; Russia, by pursuing her secular dream of the conquest of Constantinople; Germany and England, by their permanent industrial and commercial rivalry . . .

It is therefore, undeniably, through the fault of all governments that for over a year the blood of the workers has flowed in torrents. On numerous fronts, where the scourge of war has laid waste, there are 4 million corpses and even more wounded, crippled and mutilated. Everywhere ruins pile on ruins. Everywhere households are devastated and an incalculable number of widows and orphans increases horrifyingly each day. Everything bears witness to the horror of this conflagration, into which each of the belligerent camps tries to make other nations enter.

No conquest, no booty, no victory, no war gain can ever compensate for all this material and moral suffering or make up for the destruction and the incomparable losses. And, after the war, it will be the proletariat again that will carry the immense burden of the liquidation of this criminal war . . .

For these reasons, Conference decides that the CGT should participate in all proletarian action for peace, having as basic principles:

1   The liberation of invaded territories, including Belgium;
2   No annexations without consulting the populations concerned;
3   The political and economic independence of every nation;
4   Disarmament;
5   Compulsory arbitration . . .

Conference demands the immediate discussion of the peace terms.

Conference denounces the sacred union which, in all countries, has been the most effective way of stifling the most sound and politically conscious section of the proletariat, and it demands the re-establishment of trade union rights, of the freedom of the press and assembly, etc.

Conference declares that at no moment should the CGT renounce its principal objective and its *raison d'être*: the class struggle.

Source: Resolution submitted by Alphonse Merrheim and Albert Bourderon to a trade union conference held in Paris on 15 August 1915; A. Rosmer, Le Mouvement ouvrier pendant la guerre: de l'union sacrée à Zimmerwald. *Paris: Librairie du Travail. 1936, pp. 351–4*

In the spirit of the Sacred Union, parliament passed all the government's war measures and witnessed the public reconciliation of the ex-Communard Edouard Vaillant with the royalist Albert de Mun, mobilization proceeded without any significant resistance, industrial strikes became almost unknown, and a new government was formed (26 August 1914), with Viviani still the Prime Minister but including two socialists – Marcel Sembat (Public Works) and Jules Guesde (Minister without Portfolio). Early assumptions that the war would be brief and victorious were replaced by a realization that France had embarked on a long-drawn-out war of attrition, the costs of which would be unprecedented. This encouraged some elements of the French Left to question, challenge and even condemn the Sacred Union.

The Sacred Union has been interpreted as the climax of a national patriotic revival that had allegedly swept over France in the years leading up to 1914, but also as a betrayal of the proletariat by the Second International, the CGT and the French Socialist Party. While there was a general consensus that French territory and French republican values had to be defended against German aggression, militant nationalism seems to have been confined to a small minority; and between 26 July and 3 August acts of opposition to the war – meetings, demonstrations, distribution of anti-war leaflets and posters, occasional violent protests – occurred in Paris and in thirty-six provincial departments (Becker, 1977, pp. 149–88). On the Left, the main socialist party, known as the SFIO (Section Française de l'Internationale Ouvrière), had been formed in 1905 through an amalgamation of the moderate socialists led by Jean Jaurès, who believed in reformism, and the more radical socialists led by Jules Guesde, who believed in the class struggle. Socialists, though, remained divided, notably over how to respond to the prospect of a European war. Thus the SFIO Conference of July 1914 endorsed the general strike stategy by a fairly narrow margin (1,690 votes for, 1,174 votes against, 83 abstentions, 24 absentees) (Becker, 1977, p. 114). The CGT tended to be more radical than the SFIO and was theoretically bound by the anti-war resolutions passed at the CGT congresses held at Amiens (1906) and Marseilles (1908), but the CGT decision of 31 July 1914 not to call a general strike reflected a lack of support for the measure among French workers, many of whom were not trade union members.

Towards the end of October 1914, a small number of left-wing socialists and trade unionists began to meet regularly in Paris. Besides encouraging the publication of pacifist articles in trade union newspapers, their activities were mainly directed towards building up an anti-war group within the French trade union movement. Among those involved were Alphonse Merrheim, the Secretary of the French Metalworkers' Union, and Albert Bourderon, the Secretary of the Barrel Makers' Union. In February 1915 Merrheim attended an inter-Allied socialist conference in London in order to argue in favour of an early, negotiated end to the war and to oppose the majority of the CGT delegation, who supported the Sacred Union. On 1 May 1915 Merrheim, together with Bourderon, produced the first wartime issue of the Metalworkers' Union newsletter without submitting it to state censorship. The newsletter publicized the slogan 'This war is not our war', outlined a programme which included no imposed annexations, national self-determination, disarmament and compulsory arbitration of international disputes, and condemned the 'collaboration' of the CGT with the French state.

The resolution submitted by Merrheim and Bourderon to the trade union conference held in Paris on 15 August 1915 repeated this programme. By claiming that all belligerent countries, including France, were responsible for the outbreak of the First World War, the resolution undermined the moral case for the Sacred Union. By stressing the appalling human and material cost of the war, the resolution emphasized the pointlessness of the struggle. By presenting a programme for securing an immediate and lasting peace, the resolution made a bid for the moral high ground. Finally, by denouncing the Sacred Union, demanding the restoration of civil liberties and urging a return to the class struggle, the resolution appealed to radical sympathies. The conference rejected the resolution by 81 to 27, with 10 abstentions. Nevertheless, opposition to the Sacred Union had won significant support; and the French Left was now divided into *majoritaires* (the majority who supported the Sacred Union) and *minoritaires* (the minority who opposed it).

Document 5.7 Industrial Mobilization

On the day of mobilization the workshops were almost completely deserted. All the strongest men, all those who were the muscle and brain of the workshops, were mobilized, and the greater number of the workshops were closed. The men had been mobilized, called to that military service which so many of them had been accustomed to criticize at our meetings and conferences. They had been mobilized, they the keenest of anti-militarists, the most active members of the International Labour Confederation. They had been mobilized, and were setting out to war with enthusiasm, in the knowledge that their country had been attacked. Those who would never have tolerated aggression against another country, who would never have consented to provoke a war, were ready to sacrifice their lives for the defence of their homes and country. They want to fight in that spirit, knowing as we all do that they must all give their blood, their life, for the defence of the nation.

But at the end of only a few weeks the enormous consumption of ammunition at the Battle of the Marne revealed the necessity of organizing, in the midst of war, an industrial programme which surpassed everything which, until then, could have been imagined necessary for the needs of the country. That is how it came about that workers who had set out to fight on the battlefield were suddenly called back to the workshops and are now doing their share as soldiers in the industrial army . . .

But since the War I affirm, with full knowledge, that there has not been a single strike in France, not even one of these little twenty-four-hour strikes by means of which workpeople show their discontent. If here and there a disagreement arose it was sufficient to send to the place a Government representative or a friendly member of Parliament, or even one of the trade unionists who every day are sharing in the work for national defence; and a peaceful settlement was brought about at once . . .

Some days ago, at St Etienne, in a friendly meeting which I had with the members of the Union of State Workers, I spoke of the necessity of introducing female labour into the national factories. They reminded me of how for fifteen to twenty years they had resisted the introduction of women into the factories, and had even fought to prevent it. But now, with the guarantee which I gave them that for equal work there should be equal pay, to use the old Union claim, they consented to the entry of women into the St Etienne workshops, and to-day several hundred women are already to be found employed there.

Source: Speech by Albert Thomas delivered at the British Ministry of Munitions, 6 October 1915; A. Thomas, French Munition Workers' Sacrifices and Aims. London: Munitions Parliamentary Commission. 1915, pp. 4–6

The German invasion and occupation of French territory, and the formation of the Western Front war zone, had a devastating impact on the French economy. Prior to August 1914, the area directly affected had accounted for approximately two-thirds of French iron and steel production, three-quarters of coal and coke production, four-fifths of pig-iron and woollen production, and over 90 per cent of the output of linen goods and copper (Lawrence, Dean and Robert, 1992, p. 582). The war also cut off France from Alsace-Lorraine, Belgium, Germany and Central Europe, while her maritime trade became subject to attack, disruption and a shortage of ships, which intensified after the German adoption of a policy of unrestricted submarine warfare (31 January 1917). The mobilization of troops for the army (2,887,000 men joined the French army in the first two weeks of the war), the accompanying disruption of the railways, the return of foreign workers to their home countries, and a drying up of credit rapidly led to a sharp decline in industrial output and to massive unemployment. By the end of August 1914 approximately half of France's factories had closed down, including the military workshops of Bourges and St Etienne (Godfrey, 1987, p. 47); and by October 1914, unemployment had risen to a monthly average of 35 per cent, and it was still at 20 per cent in January 1915 (Horne, 1991, p. 87). Yet the French military, who had planned for a three-month campaign, at once demonstrated a seemingly insatiable demand for ammunition and *matériel*.

On 20 September 1914 Alexandre Millerand, the new Minister for War, summoned leading bankers, industrialists and representatives of the railway companies to Bordeaux for a conference to draw up plans for the immediate economic mobilization of France. Following this conference, French governments, responding to the crisis situation and to pressure from their principal ally, Britain, increasingly attempted to impose civilian political leadership over the nation's economic war effort. This came to involve state requisitioning of vital necessities, state direction of the labour force, investment and raw materials, state regulation of wages and prices, and state control of imports, exports and transport. A key figure in this policy was Albert Thomas, a socialist deputy for the Seine since May 1910, who, after recruiting skilled workers for war industries (October 1914–May 1915), from May 1915 until September 1917 organized arms production as head of the Under-Secretariat of State for Artillery and Munitions (from December 1916, the Ministry of Armament and War Production).

On 11 October 1914 French army commanders received government orders to release skilled workers for factory work, and by the end of 1915 approximately 500,000 conscripted soldiers had been returned to industry (Fridenson, 1992, pp. 61 and 73). The war industries' labour force was reconstituted and enormously expanded, from 50,000 in August 1915 to 1.7 million in November 1918. The latter figure included 430,000 women, 133,000 workers under eighteen years of age, 108,000 foreigners, 61,000 colonial workers and 40,000 prisoners of war (Fridenson, 1992, p. 62; Godfrey, 1987, p. 186). This labour force achieved remarkable results: output of aeroplane engines at the Gnôme et Rhône factories rose from 15 in September 1914 to 243 per month by 1915 (Fridenson, 1992, p. 143); and shell production for the 75-mm gun increased from 13,500 to 212,000 per day and for the 155-mm gun from 405 to 45,000 per day (Godfrey, 1987, pp. 186–7). Altogether, until the end of the war, France remained the largest Allied producer of arms. Inevitably, there were costs. Thomas was accused of attaching more importance to production figures than to workers' wages, rights and conditions of work or to the allegedly excessive profits of capitalist companies; and France lost its generally strike-free status in 1916, and suffered massive strike waves in 1917 and, to a lesser extent, in 1918. Nevertheless, the French ability to supply and equip its armed forces and to feed its population contributed substantially to the Allied victory.

Document 5.8 The Western Front

'They are attacking!'

Gilbert and I have leapt up together, deafened. Our hands blindly search for our rifles and tear back the canvas which blocks the entrance.

'They are in the trench!' The cemetry reverberates with the explosion of grenades and the rattle of machine-gun fire. It is like some mad display of flames and noise that suddenly shatters the night. Everybody opens fire. Nobody knows what is happening, there are no orders: they are attacking, they are in the trench, that is all . . .

A man runs past in front of our dug-out and falls down, as if he had stumbled. Other shadowy figures pass, run, advance, retreat. From a ruined chapel, red flares shoot up, signalling for an artillery barrage. Then the day suddenly seems to dawn; large pale stars explode above us, and, as though in the beam of a lighthouse, phantom-like figures appear, rushing between the cemetery crosses. Grenades explode, thrown from all directions. A machine-gun slides under a tombstone, like a snake, and begins to fire rapidly, mowing the ruins with its bullets.

'They are in the trench!' voices repeat.

And, flattened against the embankment, men continue to throw grenades, without stopping, from the other side of the wall. Above the parapet men fire without aiming. All the tombs have opened, all the dead have risen up, and, still blind, they kill in the dark, without seeing anything, they kill the dark or they kill men.

Source: R. Dorgelès, Les Croix de bois. *Paris: Albin Michel. 1919, pp. 253–4*

In accordance with the Schlieffen Plan, on 2 and 3 August 1914 the German army launched a massive offensive through Luxembourg and Belgium. Resistance was swept aside, though the fortresses of Liège, Naumur, Antwerp and Maubeuge held out for a time, and by 4 September German cavalry were within sight of the Eiffel Tower. Since the Germans had successfully repulsed French attacks in Lorraine, it looked as though Paris, and even France, might fall. Perhaps as many as half a million people fled the capital, while the government itself decided to evacuate to Bordeaux on 2 September. However, the French armies had managed to retreat in more or less good order; the Germans had swung left in front of Paris, instead of trying to encircle the city (as the Schlieffen Plan had envisaged); two German army corps were transferred from the Western Front after a Russian invasion of East Prussia; the French railway system coped remarkably well with the demands of war; and on 5 September General Joffre, commander-in-chief of French forces on the Western Front, began a counter-attack on the overextended German lines. In the so-called 'miracle of the Marne', German troops were pushed back to a line north of Soissons, Rheims and Verdun. There followed between 12 September and 13 November the 'race to the sea', ending with the creation of an unbroken line of fortified trenches from a corner of Belgium to the Swiss frontier.

In the four years of trench warfare that followed on the Western Front, the French tended to be at a disadvantage, at least until the beginning of the final German retreat in July 1918. Well-entrenched troops, protected by barbed wire and defended by machine-guns and artillery, could usually be dislodged only at very heavy cost, and even then territorial gains were likely to be small. Moreover, the French were generally less well equipped than their German opponents and were deficient in heavy artillery. However, before 1914 the French High Command had adopted an offensive strategy, and it continued to be mesmerized by the prospect of achieving a 'breakthrough'. Psychologically, too, the French were under pressure to liberate German-occupied France. Hence, whereas the Germans mounted only two major offensives on the Western Front, the attack on the fortifications around Verdun (February–December 1916) and the Ludendorff Offensive (March–July 1918), the French and their British allies launched a series of offensives. While these were extremely costly for the

Germans, they were equally so for the Allies, and territorial gains were generally minor. Only after the end of the First World War was the full horror of the fighting on the Western Front brought home to the French public, such as in this description of a French infantry company attacked by night in the macabre location of a cemetery. The description emphasizes the confusion and the absence of orders that characterized much of the fighting. How so many soldiers put up for so long with such appalling conditions, such astronomically high casualty rates and such apparently ill-conceived and futile military operations is hard to explain.

The image of French infantrymen going over the top like lambs to the slaughter-house, automatically obeying the orders of a High Command totally indifferent to human casualty rates, has recently been challenged (Smith, 1994). Soldiers did not always obey orders, and increasingly 'interpreted' orders according to whether the prescribed objective was likely to be achieved without disproportionate cost; and the French High Command became less reckless in its use of its soldiers – the year 1915 accounted for approximately 430,000 of France's 1,397,800 total war dead. Nevertheless, most French soldiers seem to have shared a degree of national patriotism and cohesiveness that today is difficult to comprehend.

Document 5.9 The Eastern Front

As General Joffre asked, in his letter of 3 August [1915], it seems indispensable to know 'where we are going in the Near East'. It is therefore necessary to examine briefly the different possible options so as to be able to determine which directions to follow.

A If the two [French] divisions currently in the Gallipoli peninsula remain there, we can be under no illusions. They are condemned to frontal combat and to trench warfare; they can advance only very slowly, before a series of defensive Turkish lines; the *status quo* will very likely continue for a long time, perhaps until the end of the campaign, with losses suffered every day to no purpose, with all the problems already briefly outlined for resupplying the troops, with the perpetual muddle of the British forces and the perspective of a conflict in a latent state for a long time. This option should therefore be rejected.

B To make the situation in the Gallipoli peninsula less precarious, to enable us to progress along the Dardanelles, we could be given the objective of capturing the artillery batteries along the Asiatic coast . . .

[Attacks on Chanak, Smyrna and Alexandretta, in Turkish Asia Minor, considered.]

G To achieve something in the Near East, there could be, instead of an operation in Asia Minor, an intervention in Serbia following a disembarkation in Salonika.

It is not up to me to discuss whether the diplomatic situation would permit a disembarkation at this spot, with the agreement of the Greek government. Some people, however, think that, confronted by the fact of an accomplished disembarkation, Greece could only make a formal protest. Be that as it may, Salonika as a base of operations would permit an effective and profitable military intervention. Would it not, in effect, be possible to achieve thereby either a pro-Allied move by hesitant Balkan states, or at least a reinforcement of the Serbian army, which could thus receive aid and support for defensive and offensive actions?

From the military point of view, the disembarkation would operate within the same time limits as in Turkish Asia Minor, but much more easily, Salonika being a port. In addition, there is a railway line.

Source: Memorandum on the military situation in the Near East by General Sarrail, August 1915; General M. Sarrail, Mon Commandement en Orient, 1916–1918. *Paris: Ernest Flammarion. 1920, pp. 297–301*

During the First World War, two schools of thought emerged in France and Britain as to how victory could best be achieved. 'Westerners' believed that Germany should be ground down in a war of attrition on the Western Front, and that military operations elsewhere were sideshows that wasted scarce resources. 'Easterners' believed that the Western Front had become a very expensive stalemate, and that military operations in the Balkans or against the Ottoman Empire could cause the defeat of Germany's allies, which in turn would lead to the defeat of an isolated Germany. Pleas from Russia to relieve pressure on the Caucasus front encouraged 'Easterners' to plan an operation in the Dardanelles that would, it was hoped, eventually lead to the Allied capture of Constantinople. Unsuccessful naval operations in February 1915 forewarned the Turks, so that when British, French, Australian and New Zealand troops were landed on the Gallipoli peninsula from April 1915, they were pinned down by the Turks and unable to break out of their bridgeheads.

In France General Joffre and most of the French military establishment were 'Westerners', while at least some of their left-wing critics were 'Easterners'. In July 1915 Joffre dismissed General Maurice Sarrail from his command of the French Third Army, which had distinguished itself in the Battle of the Marne. Since Sarrail was reputed to be a republican and had many political and parliamentary contacts, left-wing politicians protested against his dismissal and pressured the government to offer Sarrail the command of French troops in the Dardanelles. However, Sarrail correctly appreciated that the Allied situation in Gallipoli was unpromising (the Allies eventually recognized this, evacuating Gallipoli in January 1916), and he wanted to be in charge of an operation rather than under British overall command. Therefore, in his memorandum of August 1915 he suggested landing a force in Salonika on the Mediterranean coast of north-eastern Greece.

Sarrail's suggestion was adopted, and in October 1915 he was sent to Salonika to take command of what became a mixed French, British, Serbian, Italian and Russian force. The aims of the Salonika expedition were to help Serbia, encourage Greece and Romania to join the Allies, and inflict military defeat on Bulgaria, which would have severed communications between the Central Powers and the Ottoman Empire. Sarrail had the support of the new Prime Minister, Aristide Briand, and of the new

War Minister, General Joseph Galliéni, but Joffre remained opposed, the British and the Italians were unenthusiastic and suspicious of French ambitions in the region, and Sarrail constantly complained of insufficient men and artillery. During the summer of 1917 a pro-Allies king and government were installed in Greece, and in August 1917 Romania declared war on Austria-Hungary. However, Romania was rapidly defeated and the Allies did not achieve a decisive breakthrough against Bulgaria until September 1918. Sarrail, meanwhile, had been relieved of his command on 10 December 1917 by Georges Clemenceau, who had formed a new government the previous 16 November and who was a long-time critic of the Salonika expedition and a vigorous and determined 'Westerner'.

Document 5.10 German-occupied France

On a signal from his superiors, a sentry approached with a loaded rifle. Threatened in this way, the miners had to retire. And 300 pit ponies perished from starvation in the darkness. Imagine the sufferings of these unfortunate animals, first neighing, stamping the ground with impatience; then, tortured by hunger, galloping madly along the galleries, colliding with other companions in misfortune, fighting desperately between themselves in the night, finally dying in agony at the bottom of this infernal tomb!

The Germans had polluted the mine with the stench of the decaying flesh from the 300 dead pit ponies. However, even though the mine was defiled and asphyxiated, it could still revive, live and produce again. It was a question of killing it, of suffocating it by blocking the ventilation shafts by which it breathed the air of men. The satanic plan was executed by professional killers. There was no shortage of weapons: in the sheds there were skips and wagons for the transport of coal; the soldiers seized them and threw them into the vast openings, gaping wide like hungry mouths. The mine cried out, and groaned with loud metallic moans, but it still lived; the power of fire continued to circulate in its black veins.

Then the assassins returned to their task, falling fiercely and relentlessly on their victim. The mine lay prone under their heavy boots, strangled, blinded; this time, they drowned it. With explosions of grenades thrown into the tunnel linings, they flooded the galleries and the shafts of the same pit, and slowly the water rose and rose. All resistance having become impossible, the invaded and submerged mine finally gave up and died.

In a few hours, the labour of several generations had been destroyed.

Source: E. Basly, Le Martyre de Lens: trois années de captivité. *Paris: Plon-Nourrit. 1918, pp. 38–9*

During the First World War, north-eastern France and its civilian population suffered severely. From the autumn of 1914 to the autumn of 1918, a considerable portion of the region was under German military occupation, and a broad swathe of territory endured devastating destruction and the suspension of normal civilian life in the war zones. The French were very conscious of this suffering and destruction, and developed the concept of martyred cities, among which featured Arras, Péronne, Rheims and Saint-Quentin, as well as Lens.

Lens was a small mining town north of Arras and about twenty miles from the Belgian frontier. During the First World War, it was not just under German military occupation but found itself close to some of the fiercest fighting on the Western Front, at Loos and Vimy Ridge. As a result, the town was virtually demolished and in April 1917 the Germans forcibly evacuated the civilian population of some 18,000.

Emile Basly, the mayor of Lens, wrote an account of the German occupation of Lens that was first published in *Le Petit Parisien* and then in book form. He described the requisitioning of food and accommodation, the confiscation of property (including church bells), the financial exactions (including taxes on dogs, which were eventually all killed), the imposition of curfews and restrictions on movement, the compulsory medical examinations of women, the forced labour required of civilians, and the brutal punishments, even executions, for 'crimes' such as singing and visiting a family tomb. Throughout, the German soldiers are portrayed as having behaved in an arrogant and insulting manner towards the local inhabitants, who allegedly remained brave, resilient and defiant. In the passage quoted Basly is describing the destruction by the Germans of a coal mine near Lens. By anthropomorphizing the mine and by representing its destruction as an act of murder, Basly is obviously trying to achieve the maximum dramatic and emotional effect.

Document 5.11 Revolution in Russia

It is difficult to imagine today the extraordinary enthusiasm with which all socialists greeted the news of the Russian Revolution. The *majoritaires* were among the most enthusiastic in welcoming it. They had always been slightly embarrassed in having as allies in a war of liberation for freedom and justice the most odiously despotic regime in Europe. However, now the Tsarist regime was collapsing under the weight of its mistakes and its crimes. Democrats and socialists were seizing power, scarcely encountering any opposition. Like a ripe fruit that falls from the tree at the first puff of the wind, they were picking up power without having to grab it by brute force. A huge country, larger than half of Europe, and inhabited by 140 million people, was going to attain full democracy. Everybody at that time assumed that the young revolutionary country would remain at France's side in the war. But everybody, at least among the socialists, hoped that revolutionary Russia would insist that the Allies repudiate all imperialism. Revolutionary Russia, in fact, was to launch across the world the famous slogan, which became popular so quickly, of 'Peace without annexations or conquests'. Finally, socialists were among the leaders of revolutionary Russia. It was thanks to the socialists that the revolution had triumphed. The new regime was based on the working-class masses, whom the socialists had worked on for so long. The sudden and rapid victory of revolution in Russia seemed to open unlimited hopes for the socialists.

Source: L.O. Frossard, De Jaurès à Lénine: notes et souvenirs d'un militant. *Paris: Bibliothèque de documentation sociale. 1930, pp. 31–2*

The outbreak of a revolutionary movement in Russia at the end of February 1917, the abdication of Tsar Nicholas II on 2 March, and the formation of a Provisional Government which included the socialist Alexander Kerensky, as Minister of Justice, had a profound impact on France. The French Left could rejoice in the first successful revolution in a major European state since the French Revolution of 1789, and in the replacement of the Tsarist autocracy by an apparently democratic regime, with, again apparently, socialist representation and working-class support. However, the February Revolution was generally misunderstood and misinterpreted in France, and subsequent developments in Russia were unforeseen.

Many French people thought that a liberal and democratic Russia would fight the First World War more effectively and enthusiastically than its Tsarist predecessor had done. In fact, Russia was in a desperate economic and social condition by February 1917, and war-weariness had become all pervasive. Also, the rapid emergence of soviets created a dual-power situation that challenged the authority of the Provisional Government, which itself, through its policies and mistakes, lost popular support; and separatist movements gained momentum in Finland and elsewhere. The coming to power of Lenin and the Bolsheviks in the October 1917 Revolution, and the Treaty of Brest-Litovsk of 3 March 1918 between Russia and the Central Powers, by which Russia withdrew from the First World War, meant the French had to respond to a Bolshevik revolution in Russia and to Lenin's foreign and domestic policies at a time when France herself was experiencing army mutinies and industrial unrest, increasing disillusionment with the Sacred Union, and an intensifying split within the French left between the *majoritaires* and the *minoritaires*. Developments in Russia thus became an important factor in French politics, helping to weaken the Sacred Union, to encourage anti-war, radical and even revolutionary sentiments, to undermine support for Allied war aims, and to reinforce the *minoritaires* in their conflict with the *majoritaires*. Ludovic Oscar Frossard, the author of this extract, belonged to the *minoritaires*, though, like nearly all French socialists in 1917 and 1918, he had reservations about Lenin and his methods and opposed Russia's conclusion of a separate peace.

Document 5.12 Clemenceau and Victory

I am, for the time being, the head of the republican government, and in this capacity I have doctrines to defend at this parliamentary tribune. If the Chamber of Deputies were to censure me, it would be my duty to submit my resignation to the President of the Republic.

The first of these doctrines is the principle of liberty which I have already posed.

The second, in the present circumstances, is that we are at war: we must wage war, we must think only of war, we must turn all our thoughts to war, we must sacrifice everything to the regulations which will in future promote agreement, if we are to succeed in assuring the triumph of France . . .

Today our duty is to conduct the war while at the same time safeguarding the rights of the citizen, by protecting not just liberty, but all liberties. Well, make war. Let us examine the treason trials. Say that we have acted incorrectly, say that the administrations that have preceded me have maladministered justice. That is your business. You will always find somebody to respond to you.

I am today confronted by developments that have been set in motion and which you all know about, developments on which I must concentrate and on which I must exclusively focus my thoughts twenty-four hours a day. Help me, even you, my adversaries!

Source: Georges Clemenceau in the Chamber of Deputies, 8 March 1918;
G. Clemenceau, Discours de guerre. *Paris: Presses universitaires de France.*
1968, pp. 166–7

A very critical situation developed in France during 1917. The winter of 1916–17 was abnormally cold; shortages of food and other essential commodities were becoming significant; and prices were rising much faster than wages. Between 2 August 1914 and 31 December 1916, the cost of living increased by 45 per cent, while wages rose 25 per cent in heavy industry, 22 per cent in light industry, and 16 per cent for women in light industry (Wohl, 1966, p. 87). At the same time, capitalists were widely believed to have been making inflated profits out of the war. All this encouraged a dramatic rise in industrial militancy. In 1915 there were 98 strikes involving 9,361 strikers, in 1916 314 strikes involving 41,409 strikers, and in 1917 696 strikes involving 293,810 strikers (Ligou, 1962, p. 277). Increasingly, too, strikers did not just make economic demands, but political demands such as the publication of France's war aims and the negotiation of an immediate peace on the basis of no annexations and no indemnities. Such demands were made by a growing number of socialists, disillusioned with the Sacred Union and with the supposed imperialism of Allied war aims, influenced by the anti-war stance of Merrheim and Bourderon, encouraged by developments in Russia, and alienated by the government's refusal to allow French delegates to attend a projected international socialist congress at Stockholm. On 12 September 1917 the SFIO decided that no deputy of the party should in future serve in a war cabinet.

Meanwhile, morale and discipline among French soldiers on the Western Front had come close to collapse. After over twenty months of fighting, in which the French army had sustained huge casualties usually for minimal territorial gains, General Nivelle launched a new offensive on the Western Front on 16 April 1917. Within five days, over 30,000 French soldiers had been killed and another 90,000 wounded, of whom 5,000 died through lack of medical attention. On 3 May an entire division refused to go into battle, and throughout May and into June the French army suffered indiscipline, high desertion rates and cases of outright mutiny and even revolt. Altogether, serious cases of collective indiscipline occurred in 54 divisions, out of a total of some 109

French infantry divisions on the Western Front. However, a judicious combination of firmness and reform by General Pétain eventually restored order, while France found a political saviour in Georges Clemenceau.

Clemenceau, who had appeared to be left wing over the Dreyfus Affair and over the separation of Church and state, had gained a right-wing reputation as Minister of the Interior (March–October 1906) and as Prime Minister (October 1906–July 1909). However, on issues such as railway nationalization and the introduction of an income tax and of old-age pensions, he remained quite left wing, but his use of troops to deal with strikes and his arrest of CGT militants alienated socialists and trade unionists. After resigning the premiership, Clemenceau continued to be a senator, and from 1913 he regularly contributed articles to a newspaper, *L'Homme Libre* (later renamed *L'Homme Enchaîné*). In his speeches and articles he supported the introduction of a three-year term of military service and the maintenance of a strong line against Germany. Once the First World War had begun, Clemenceau, in the press and in the Senate and its committees, became one of the most vigorous critics of a succession of French governments, condemning the tactics of the French High Command on the Western Front, opposing the diversion of resources to Salonika or the Ottoman Empire, complaining of inadequate medical services and of munitions shortages, and attacking government failures to clamp down on all forms of defeatism. This onslaught climaxed during the summer and autumn of 1917, when Clemenceau almost single-handedly brought about the resignation of Malvy as Minister of the Interior (31 August 1917); and he continued to press his attacks until President Poincaré invited him to form a government on 16 November 1917.

Prime Minister from November 1917 to January 1920, Clemenceau presided over the last and ultimately victorious year of the First World War, gaining the title of the Father of Victory ('Père-La-Victoire'). With remarkable energy and focused determination (he was sixty-seven in 1917), he rallied the national morale with his speeches and regular visits to the front; and he helped to maintain Allied unity, dangerously strained during the German offensives of March–July 1918, so that, with American assistance, the German armies could eventually be rolled back until the armistice of November 1918. However, Clemenceau's concentration on waging war on the Western Front and on securing victory over Germany had its price. Socialists did not join Clemenceau's government and the Sacred Union came to an end; Clemenceau subordinated individual rights and freedoms to the requirements of the war effort, so that socialists and some republican–socialists and left-wing Radicals constantly opposed him, even accusing him (as on 8 March 1918) of provocation of the working class (though in 1918 France experienced 499 strikes involving 176,187 strikers, fewer than in 1917) (Watson, 1974, p. 284); treason trials did not always strictly follow correct judicial procedures, through a desire to make an example and present the government as firmly anti-defeatist; government war expenditure was increased far beyond tax receipts, leading to borrowing and indebtedness on a colossal scale, with damaging long-term consequences for the country; and Clemenceau may have undermined Austro-Hungarian peace initiatives, while he certainly failed to formulate a sensible policy towards the Bolshevik regime in Russia. Nevertheless, it was highly appropriate that Clemenceau, the last surviving signatory of a protest against the surrender of Alsace-Lorraine to Germany in 1871, should have welcomed the return of the lost provinces to France in November 1918.

CHRONOLOGY

1891

23 July	Arrival of French naval squadron at Kronstadt (Russia)
27 August	Franco-Russian agreement

1894

4 January	Franco-Russian military convention

1896

April	First modern Olympic Games held at Athens
October	Visit of Tsar Nicholas II and his wife to France

1900

December	Agreement between France and Italy over Morocco and Tripolitania (Libya)

1903

1–4 May	Visit of King Edward VII to Paris
6–9 July	Visit of President Emile Loubet to London

1904

24–9 March	Visit of President Loubet to Rome
8 April	Franco-British agreement

1905

3 March	Landing of Emperor William II at Tangiers
23–5 April	Creation of SFIO at Paris congress

1906

16 January–7 April	Algeciras Conference on Morocco

1911

1 July	Arrival of German warship *The Panther* at Agadir
28 July	General Joffre appointed chief of the French Army General Staff
4 November	Franco-German treaty on Morocco, the Congo and the Cameroons

1912

30 March	Treaty of Fez establishing a French protectorate in Morocco

1913

6 March	Period of compulsory military service in France raised from two to three years

1914

17 March	Murder of Calmette, editor of *Le Figaro*, by Mme Caillaux
28 June	Assassination of the Archduke Francis Ferdinand and his wife at Sarajevo
23 July	Austro-Hungarian ultimatum to Serbia
28 July	Austro-Hungarian declaration of war against Serbia
1 August	German declaration of war against Russia and French mobilization
2 August	German invasion of Luxembourg and German ultimatum to Belgium
3 August	German declaration of war against France and invasion of Belgium
4 August	British declaration of war against Germany
5 August	French censorship law
26 August	Formation of new government under Viviani, including two socialists
2–3 September	French government and parliament leave Paris for Bordeaux
6–12 September	German advance halted at the Battle of the Marne
20 September	Conference of industrialists at Bordeaux
November	Return of government ministries to Paris
3 November	French and British declaration of war against Turkey
23 December	French parliament reassembled in Paris

1915

16 February–10 March	French offensive in Champagne
25 April	Franco-British landings at Gallipoli
9 May–16 June	Battle of Arras
18 May	Albert Thomas appointed Under-Secretary of State for Artillery and Munitions
23 May	Italian declaration of war against Austria-Hungary
5–8 September	Zimmerwald Conference
6 October	Landings of French troops at Salonika
17 October	French declaration of war against Bulgaria
29–30 October	Resignation of René Viviani and formation of new French government by Aristide Briand
25–30 December	SFIO National Congress

1916

16 January	General Sarrail appointed Commander-in-Chief of Allied troops in Salonika
21 February–16 December	Battle of Verdun
24–30 April	Kienthal Conference
1 July–8 November	Battle of the Somme

| 17 December | General Nivelle appointed Commander-in-Chief of the French armies on the Western Front |

1917

1 February	Beginning of German campaign of unrestricted submarine warfare
2 March	Abdication of Tsar Nicholas II
3 April	Entry of the United States into the First World War
16–29 April	Failure of Nivelle's Chemin des Dames Offensive
28 April	General Pétain appointed chief of the French Army General Staff
20 May	Beginning of mutinies among French troops on Western Front
2 June	French socialists refused passports to attend conference in Stockholm
6 November	Seizure of power by Bolsheviks in Petrograd
16 November	Formation of Clemenceau government

1918

8 January	Publication of President Wilson's Fourteen Points
21 March–7 July	German offensives on the Western Front
14 April	General Foch appointed Commander-in-Chief of Allied armies on the Western Front
18 July–4 August	Allied offensive in second Battle of the Marne
6 October	Request to President Wilson by Germany for an armistice
11 November	Armistice between Allies and Germany

BIBLIOGRAPHY

Abrams, L. and Miller, D.J., 'Who Were the French Colonialists? A reassessment of the *Parti Colonial*, 1890–1914', *Historical Journal*, 19 (1976), 685–725.

Andrew, C., *Théophile Delcassé and the Making of the Entente Cordiale: a reappraisal of French foreign policy, 1898–1905*. London: Macmillan. 1968.

Andrew, C.M. and Kanya-Forstner, A.S., 'The French 'Colonial Party': its composition, aims and influence, 1885–1914', *Historical Journal*, 14 (1971), 99–128.

—— 'The *Groupe Colonial* in the Chamber of Deputies, 1892–1932', *Historical Journal*, 17 (1974), 837–66.

Becker, J.-J., *1914: comment les français sont entrés dans la guerre*. Paris: Presses de la Fondation Nationale des Sciences Politiques. 1977.

—— 'Union Sacrée et idéologie bourgeoise', *Revue Historique*, 264 (1980), 65–74.

—— *The Great War and the French People*. Leamington Spa, Heidelberg and Dover, NH: Berg. 1985.

Berenson, B. *The Trial of Madame Caillaux*. Berkeley, Los Angeles and Oxford: University of California Press. 1992.

Collins, D.N., 'The Franco-Russian Alliance and Russian Railways, 1891–1914', *Historical Journal*, 16 (1973), 777–88.

Dallas, G., *At the Heart of a Tiger: Clemenceau and his world, 1841–1929.* London: Macmillan. 1993.

Darrow, M.H., 'French Volunteer Nursing and the Myth of War Experience in World War I', *American Historical Review*, 101 (1996), 80–106.

Duroselle, J.-B., *La Grande Guerre des Français, 1914–1918.* Paris: Perrin. 1995.

Dutton, D.J., 'The *Union Sacrée* and the French Cabinet Crisis of October 1914', *European Studies Review*, 8 (1978), 411–24.

—— 'The Balkan Campaign and French War Aims in the Great War', *English Historical Review*, 94 (1979), 97–113.

Flood, P.J., *France, 1914–18: public opinion and the war effort.* London: Macmillan. 1990.

Fridenson, P. (ed.), *The French Home Front, 1914–1918.* Providence, RI, and Oxford: Berg. 1992.

Godfrey, J.P., *Capitalism at War: industrial policy and bureaucracy in France, 1914–1918.* Leamington Spa, Hamburg and New York: Berg. 1987.

Goldberg, H., *The Life of Jean Jaurès.* Madison: Wisconsin University Press. 1962.

Grayzel, S.R., 'Mothers, Marraines, and Prostitutes: morale and morality in First World War France', *International History Review*, 19 (1997), 66–82.

Guillen, P., 'Les Questions coloniales dans les relations franco-allemandes à la veille de la première guerre mondiale', *Revue Historique*, 248 (1972), 87–106.

Harris, R., 'The "Child of the Barbarian": rape, race and nationalism in France during the First World War', *Past and Present*, 141 (1993), 170–207.

Hayne, M.B., *The French Foreign Office and the Origins of the First World War.* New York: Oxford University Press. 1993.

Horne, J.N., 'Immigrant Workers in France during World War I', *French Historical Studies*, 14 (1985), 57–88.

—— '*L'Impôt du sang*: republican rhetoric and industrial warfare in France, 1914–18', *Social History*, 14 (1989), 201–23.

—— *Labour at War: France and Britain, 1914–1918.* Oxford: Clarendon Press. 1991.

Howorth, J., 'French Workers and German Workers: the impossibility of internationalism, 1900–1914', *European History Quarterly*, 15 (1985), 71–97.

Keiger, J.F.V., 'Jules Cambon and Franco-German détente, 1907–1914', *Historical Journal*, 26 (1983), 641–59.

—— *France and the Origins of the First World War.* London: Macmillan. 1983.

—— *Raymond Poincaré.* Cambridge: Cambridge University Press. 1997.

Krumeich, G., *Armaments and Politics in France on the Eve of the First World War: the introduction of three-year conscription, 1913–1914.* Worcester: Berg. 1984.

Lawrence, J., Dean, M. and Robert, J.-L., 'The Outbreak of War and the Urban Economy: Paris, Berlin, and London in 1914', *Economic History Review*, 45 (1992), 564–93.

Ligou, D., *Histoire du socialisme en France, 1871–1961.* Paris: Presses Universitaires de France. 1962.

Lunn, J., '"Les Races Guerrières": racial preconceptions in the French military about West African soldiers during the First World War', *Journal of Contemporary History*, 34 (1999), 517–36.

Macaloon, J., *This Great Symbol: Pierre de Coubertin and the origins of the modern Olympic Games.* Chicago: Chicago University Press. 1981.

Noland, A., 'Individualism in Jean Jaurès' Socialist Thought', *Journal of the History of Ideas*, 22 (1961), 63–80.

Pedroncini, G., *Les Mutineries de 1917.* Paris: Presses Universitaires de France. 1967.

Philpott, W.J., *Anglo-French Relations and Strategy on the Western Front, 1914–1918*. London: Macmillan. 1996.

Rolo, P.J.V., *Entente Cordiale: the origins and negotiation of the Anglo-French Agreements of 8 April 1904*. London: Macmillan. 1969.

Seager, F., 'Joseph Caillaux as Premier, 1911–1912: the dilemma of a liberal refromer', *French Historical Studies*, 11 (1979), 239–57.

Smith, L.V., *Between Mutiny and Obedience: the case of the French fifth infantry division during World War I*. Princeton, NJ: Princeton University Press. 1994.

Stevenson, D., *French War Aims against Germany, 1914–1919*. Oxford: Clarendon Press. 1982.

—— 'War by Timetable?: the railway race before 1914', *Past and Present*, 162 (1999), 163–94.

Stovall, T., 'The Color Line behind the Lines: racial violence in France during the Great War', *American Historical Review*, 103 (1998), 737–69.

Tanenbaum, J.K., *General Maurice Sarrail, 1856–1929: the French army and left-wing politics*. Chapel Hill: North Carolina University Press. 1974.

Trachtenberg, M., 'A New Economic Order: Etienne Clémentel and French economic diplomacy during the First World War', *French Historical Studies*, 10 (1977), 315–41.

Watson, D.R., *Georges Clemenceau: a political biography*. London: Eyre Methuen. 1974.

Weber, E., 'Pierre de Coubertin and the Introduction of Organized Sport in France', *Journal of Contemporary History*, 5 (1970), 3–26.

—— 'Gymnastics and Sports in Fin-de-Siècle France: opium of the classes?', *American Historical Review*, 76 (1971), 70–98.

Williamson, S.R., *The Politics of Grand Strategy: Britain and France prepare for war, 1904–1914*. Cambridge, Mass.: Harvard University Press. 1969.

Wohl, R., *French Communism in the Making, 1914–1924*. Stanford, Calif.: Stanford University Press. 1966.

6 | France after the First World War

The First World War cast a long shadow over the Third Republic, right up to its demise during the summer of 1940. In domestic political terms the war seemed to be a triumph of the Right: during it the Radical Party had become more conservative; and the Radical Clemenceau had headed the centre-right coalition government that had led France to victory and from which the socialists had excluded themselves. The victory celebrations, and the commemoration of the war dead, tended to take a right-wing form, being dominated by conservative government and official figures and by the traditional right-wing institutions: the army and the Roman Catholic Church. The French army could rightly claim its enormous contribution to the Allied victory over Germany and could present figures such as the newly promoted marshals Joffre, Foch and Pétain as national heroes. At the same time, the Roman Catholic Church, so often a source of division and conflict in French history, could present itself as a national institution, having supported France's war effort, participated prominently in all the commemoration ceremonies for the First World War, and played a major role in the construction of ossuaries to house the remains of the unidentified dead at Douaumont and elsewhere. In contrast, by the end of the First World War the French Left was often identified with pacifism, anti-militarism and industrial disputes; and in 1920 it split, with the founding of the French Communist Party, a development that helped to keep the Left out of power for most of the inter-war period. The Treaty of Versailles, similarly, could be portrayed as a triumph of right-wing war aims: France regained German-occupied Alsace-Lorraine; Germany was disarmed and burdened with reparations; and, through the acquisition of colonial territory from Germany as League of Nations mandates, the French colonial empire achieved its greatest territorial extent.

However, victory for France in the First World War had been achieved at too high a price in human, financial, economic and psychological terms. In addition to the 1,397,800 dead or missing, there were 1,040,000 disabled, 719,000 orphans and 630,000 widows. The war dead totalled just over 10 per cent of France's active male population, a proportion higher than that of any other belligerent state, except Serbia and Romania. The vast majority of the dead were young men aged between eighteen and thirty; and the death rate was particularly high for young officers in the infantry and air corps. The lives of many of the best and brightest of France's young men had been sacrificed. Of the 346 former students of the élite academic institution the Ecole Normale Supérieure who had graduated between 1908 and 1917, 143 were killed and 85 were wounded (Hughes, 1971, p. 17). If France had not quite lost a generation, she had certainly suffered a severe demographic blow. Besides the combat casualties, the number of marriages had sharply declined, and war conditions and diseases, including an influenza epidemic, had shortened many lives. As a result, the total French population declined from 39,605,000 in 1911 to 39,210,000 in 1921, notwithstanding the addition of Alsace and Lorraine; and the shortage of young men in the labour force led to almost 2 million foreign workers going to work in France between 1920 and 1930. The erection of public war memorials, with their long lists individually naming the dead, by nearly every community in France, the annual commemoration of Armistice Day, the tomb of the unknown soldier under the Arc de Triomphe and its role in public ceremonies, the proliferation of ex-servicemen's leagues, which almost 3,500,000 veterans joined, and war burial associations, together with their attendant publications, all helped to keep alive the memory of a terrible human sacrifice.

France's material losses were equally crippling. The fighting on the Western Front had devastated a great swathe of territory across north-eastern France, while German-occupied France had suffered systematic destruction and the displacement of much of its civilian population. A significant proportion of the French merchant fleet had been sunk, and during the war years little had been spent on France's infrastructure, so that roads, railways and housing had been starved of investment. War expenditure had not been paid for by increased taxation, but by leaving the gold standard, borrowing on a massive scale, printing money and selling foreign investments. Consequently, by the end of the war France was experiencing soaring inflation, with prices more than 400 per cent higher than in 1914; the national debt stood at 175 billion francs, a fivefold increase on the 1913 figure; and France had lost approximately half of her pre-war foreign investments, due not only to compulsory sales but also to the confiscation of assets by enemy governments and by the Bolshevik regime in Russia. The shift to a war economy had created a huge armaments industry, employing by November 1918 some 1,700,000 workers, who were now largely redundant. At the same time, the production of consumer goods had been given a low priority and export markets had been lost. With the end of the war, Allied financial and economic assistance also ended, and in March 1919 the British and Americans ceased to support the French franc. Yet French war expenditure did not end with the cessation of hostilities, since reconstruction, land reclamation, war cemeteries and support for the widowed, orphaned and crippled still had to be paid for. The reintegration of Alsace and Lorraine into the French economy was obviously an asset, but France had to confront the post-war years in a severely weakened financial and economic condition.

Despite this prodigious expenditure of effort and resources, French national security was not guaranteed by the defeat of Germany or by the post-war treaty settlement. Germany had not been totally defeated by November 1918 – her armies were still intact and her territory had barely been invaded by the Allies, even though a revolutionary tide of strikes, mutinies and demonstrations swept away Emperor William II and the imperial regime. The post-war treaty settlement did require Germany to surrender territory, to disarm and to pay reparations. Yet, even after the territorial losses, the population of Germany in 1920 was nearly 62 million, compared with the French population of approximately 39 million; and, although exhausted and unstable, Germany's economic potential exceeded that of France. The provisions for disarmament and reparations, so poisonous for Franco-German relations, were probably unenforcible from the start, and were certainly unenforcible by France alone. Formerly assured by specific diplomatic and military alliances with Russia and Britain, France now depended on an isolationist United States, a toothless League of Nations and a Britain drained, like France, by the First World War and often distracted by imperial commitments. Attempts to contain Germany by forming alliances with a 'little entente' of states such as Poland, Czechoslovakia, Yugoslavia and Romania were unlikely to be a satisfactory substitute, given their weakness, their quarrels among themselves, and the fact that France could do so little for them. Nor could France afford to place much reliance on her colonial empire, with the outbreak during the 1920s of revolts in Syria and Morocco, the expansionist ambitions of Italy and Japan, and the demands made by the colonies on France's limited financial, economic and military resources. Altogether, during the inter-war period, France was still a Great Power, but one that had been fatally weakened.

Document 6.1 President Wilson's Fourteen Points

    I   Open covenants of peace, openly arrived at, after which there shall be no private international understandings of any kind but diplomacy shall proceed always frankly and in the public view.

   II   Absolute freedom of navigation upon the seas, outside territorial waters, alike in peace and in war, except as the seas may be closed in whole or in part by international action for the enforcement of international covenants.

 III   The removal, so far as possible, of all economic barriers and the establishment of an equality of trade conditions among all the nations consenting to the peace and associating themselves for its maintenance.

 IV   Adequate guarantees given and taken that national armaments will be reduced to the lowest point consistent with domestic safety.

   V   A free, open-minded, and absolutely impartial adjustment of all colonial claims, based upon a strict observance of the principle that in determining all such questions of sovereignty the interests of the populations concerned must have equal weight with the equitable claims of the government whose title is to be determined.

 VI   The evacuation of all Russian territory . . .

 VII   Belgium, the whole world will agree, must be evacuated and restored, without any attempt to limit the sovereignty which she enjoys in common with all other nations . . .

VIII   All French territory should be freed and the invaded portions restored, and the wrong done to France by Prussia in 1871 in the matter of Alsace-Lorraine, which has unsettled the peace of the world for nearly fifty years, should be righted, in order that peace may once more be made secure in the interests of all.

IX A readjustment of the frontiers of Italy should be effected along clearly recognizable lines of nationality.

X The peoples of Austria-Hungary, whose place among the nations we wish to see safeguarded and assured, should be accorded the freest opportunity of autonomous development.

XI Romania, Serbia, and Montenegro should be evacuated; occupied territories restored; Serbia accorded free and secure access to the sea; and the relations of the several Balkan states to one another determined by friendly counsel along historically established lines of allegiance and nationality; and international guarantees of the political and economic independence and territorial integrity of the several Balkan states should be entered into.

XII The Turkish portions of the present Ottoman Empire should be assured a secure sovereignty, but the other nationalities which are now under Turkish rule should be assured an undoubted security of life and an absolutely unmolested opportunity of autonomous development, and the Dardanelles should be permanently opened as a free passage to the ships and commerce of all nations under international guarantees.

XIII An independent Polish state should be erected which should include the territories inhabited by indisputably Polish populations, which should be assured a free and secure access to the sea, and whose political and economic independence and territorial integrity should be guaranteed by international covenant.

XIV A general association of nations must be formed under specific covenants for the purpose of affording mutual guarantees of political independence and territorial integrity to great and small states alike.

Source: Address by President Woodrow Wilson to a joint session of Congress, 8 January 1918; The Papers of Woodrow Wilson. *Princeton: Princeton University Press. 1984, XXXXV, pp. 536–8*

At the beginning of the First World War, French war aims were limited to the recovery of Alsace-Lorraine and of German-occupied France and to the restoration of Belgian independence. The conquest of German colonial territory, the enormous cost and prolonged duration of the war and the formulation of war aims by France's allies encouraged France to develop more ambitious war aims herself. France and Britain made preliminary agreements to partition German Togoland in August 1914 and the German Cameroons in March 1916, while the Sykes–Picot agreement of January 1916 envisaged a similar Franco-British partition of the Ottoman Empire. Meanwhile, Belgium laid claim to the Grand Duchy of Luxembourg; and Russia demanded Constantinople and the Dardanelles Straits, Prussian Poland and the break-up of the Austro-Hungarian Empire, from which along with Italy, Serbia and Romania, she hoped to gain territory. To prevent any repetition of the First World War, the

French began to insist that German territory on the left bank of the Rhine should be neutralized or annexed to France; and, since the French saw themselves as victims of German aggression, they began to insist on reparations from Germany as well.

Largely as a result of German unrestricted submarine warfare, the United States declared war on Germany on 6 April 1917. At first this made little difference to France, but during the course of 1918 the balance of power in financial, economic, military and diplomatic terms shifted from France (and, to a lesser extent, from Britain) to the United States. President Wilson of the United States had to convince the American Congress and American public opinion of the desirability of American military intervention on the Allied side in the First World War. This involved the formulation of a programme aiming to achieve the establishment of a new order in Europe, based on moral and democratic principles, rather than the satisfaction of the 'imperialist' ambitions of the Allied powers. With the publication of President Wilson's Fourteen Points, for the first time in history the United States was setting the agenda for European diplomacy and eclipsing the diplomatic importance of France, whereas the French had wanted the Americans simply to help them secure French war aims. For Clemenceau, the publication of the Fourteen Points constituted a most unwelcome development, however much he might mock ('The good Lord Himself required only ten points') (Sharp, 1991, p. 14): it demonstrated that President Wilson could take a major initiative without securing the agreement of, or even consulting with, his allies; it created a situation in which Wilson could appeal for support for his programme from political leaders and public opinion in Allied and belligerent states, over the heads of the other Allied governments; it represented a conscious American bid for occupation of the moral high ground (the American negotiator, Colonel House, observed to Wilson on 11 November 1917, 'unless the war is for some higher purpose it had better cease') (Wilson, vol. 45, 1984, p. 4); and the Fourteen Points did not take account of French demands for German colonial territory, the left bank of the Rhine and reparations, while the proposals for open diplomacy, the removal of trade barriers, disarmament and a League of Nations did not feature on France's diplomatic agenda.

The timing of the announcement of the Fourteen Points owed much to the situation in Russia. The Bolshevik seizure of power in Petrograd and Moscow during November 1917 was followed by the signing of an armistice between Russian and German delegates at Brest-Litovsk (5 December 1917) and the beginning of peace negotiations (21 December 1917). It was claimed that the Russian Provisional Government headed by Kerensky had lost the support of the Russian people due to the failure of the Allies to restate their war aims; and the head of the American Military Mission to Russia was warning Wilson by 14 November that that the crisis in Russia might put the country 'into anarchy and out of war' (Wilson, vol. 45, 1984, p. 104). Trotsky, the Bolshevik Commissar for Foreign Affairs, confirmed those fears by informing Allied ambassadors that the Bolsheviks proposed an immediate armistice on all fronts and the immediate opening of negotiations with a view to concluding peace on democratic principles. The Bolsheviks also published the secret treaties and agreements of the Allies, exposing their territorial ambitions, while in Britain Lord

Lansdowne's peace proposals in a letter to *The Daily Telegraph* (29 November 1917) received much publicity.

Wilson's Fourteen Points had an enormous influence on bringing the war to an end and on the subsequent peace settlement, but they failed to prevent Russia from making a separate peace with the Central Powers at the Treaty of Brest-Litovsk (3 March 1918), by which Russia ceded huge tracts of territory to Germany. This, in turn, led France to formulate a further war aim – the creation of a large and independent Polish state.

Document 6.2 The Paris Peace Conference

President Wilson. There is no nation more intelligent than the French nation. If you allow me to explain my point of view frankly to her, I have no fear of her judgement. Undoubtedly, if they saw that we were not applying the same principle everywhere, the French people would not accept a solution which appeared unfavourable to them; but if we show them we are doing our best to act justly everywhere similar problems arise, the sense of justice which is in the heart of French people will rise to answer me: 'You are right.' I have such an exalted idea of the spirit of the French nation that I believe she will always accept a principle founded on justice and applied with equity.

The annexation of these regions [the Landau and Saar regions] to France does not have a sufficient historical foundation. One part of these territories was French for only twenty-two years; the remainder has been separated from France for over one hundred years. I realize that the map of Europe is covered with ancient injustices which cannot all be redressed. What is just is to assure France the compensation which is due her for the loss of her coal mines and to give the entire Saar region the guarantees it needs for the utilization of its own coal. If we do that, we will do all that could reasonably be asked of us.

M. Clemenceau. I will keep in mind the words and excellent intentions of President Wilson. He eliminates sentiment and memory; it is here that I have a reservation about what has just been said. The President of the United States fails to recognize the basis of human nature. The fact of war cannot be forgotten. America did not see this war at a close distance for its first three years; during this time we lost a million and a half men. We have no more manpower. Our English friends, who lost less than we, but still enough to have suffered much, will understand me.

Our trials have created a profound feeling in this country about the reparation which is due us; and it isn't only a matter of material repairs: the need for moral redress is no less great. The doctrines just invoked, if they were interpreted in all their rigour, would allow refusing us even Alsace-Lorraine. In reality, the Saar and Landau are part of Lorraine and Alsace.

Our great enemies of 1815, against whom we fought for so many centuries – the English – insisted after the fall of Napoleon that Prussia should not take the Saar Basin. A generous gesture towards a people who suffered so much would not be in vain. It is a mistake to believe that the world is governed by abstract principles. These are accepted by certain parties, rejected by others – I do not speak of supernatural doctrines, about which I have nothing to say. But I believe there are no human dogmas; there are only rules of justice and common sense.

You seek to do justice to the Germans. Don't believe they will ever forgive us; they only seek the opportunity for revenge. Nothing will extinguish the rage of those who wanted to establish their domination over the world and who believed themselves so close to succeeding.

I will never forget that our American friends, like our English friends, came here to help us in a moment of supreme danger; and I'll tell you the argument I hold in reserve for the French, if I can't manage to convince you. I will say to them: 'Suppose the English and Americans had offered terms before coming to our help; would you have accepted them or not?' . . .

I won't change your opinion, I fear; you consider yourself bound by your word. I would observe nevertheless that these 350,000 men [inhabitants of the Landau and Saar regions], of whom at least 150,000 are French, do not constitute a nation. You don't want to make an exception to the principle [of national self-determination]? You will certainly be forced to do so by the facts. How will you tear the Germans of Karlsbad away from Bohemia without destroying Bohemia itself? Peoples who fought against each other for centuries have remained mingled as in a battle. In the Balkans, you won't be able to create a Greece which contains no Bulgarians, a Serbia which contains no Albanians.

Source: Conversations between President Wilson and MM. Clemenceau, Lloyd George, Orlando, and Tardieu, 28 March 1919; A.S. Link (ed. and trans.), The Deliberations of the Council of Four (24 March–28 June 1919): notes of the official interpreter, Paul Mantoux. Princeton: Princeton University Press. 1992, I, pp. 61–3

Once the tide had turned on the Western Front during the summer of 1918, the Allies became confident of winning the war some time in 1919. In fact, during the autumn of 1918 the Central Powers collapsed in rapid succession: Bulgaria submitted to an armistice on 29 September, Turkey on 30 October, Austria-Hungary on 3 November and Germany on 11 November. The German government had appealed to President Wilson to negotiate a peace settlement on the basis of his Fourteen Points on 4 October. Wilson had replied on 8 October, demanding, in addition to acceptance of the Fourteen Points, German evacuation of occupied territory and an assurance that the German government represented the German people and not just the German military élite. After Germany had accepted these and subsequent demands, including an end to the German policy of destruction in German-occupied territory and to German submarine warfare, Wilson recommended an armistice. The Germans thus thought that they had agreed to end the war on the basis of Wilson's Fourteen

Points, while Clemenceau and the British Prime Minister, Lloyd George, resented the exclusive and dominant role that Wilson had played in securing the armistice with Germany.

The peace conference was formally opened in Paris on 18 January 1919. Lloyd George had suggested meeting in a Swiss city but was overruled, so Paris hosted the most important international diplomatic gathering since 1815 (though English, as well as French, was recognized as an official language for the conference). Over a thousand diplomats and statesmen, representing over thirty countries, participated in negotiating a peace settlement on a global scale. The principal delegations came from the United States, France, Britain, Italy and Japan, and two representatives from each of these states formed the Council of Ten, the effective decision-making body of the conference until late March. Thereafter the key decisions were taken by a Council of Four consisting of Wilson (United States), Lloyd George (Britain), Clemenceau (France) and Orlando (Italy).

Wilson, a former academic from Princeton University, believed that the deficiencies in the old order had produced the war and that a new order should be constructed, based on moral principles, democracy and international co-operation. Lloyd George wanted to re-establish the balance of power in Europe and advance the interests of Britain and her empire. Clemenceau sought to redress the wrongs suffered by France in the Franco-Prussian War as well as in the First World War, to gain compensation for her terrible losses and to ensure her security in the future against Germany. Orlando's main objective was to gain as much territory as possible for Italy. These different goals inevitably led to disagreements, in which Clemenceau could find himself isolated.

With Germany's colonies all surrendered and her fleet interned, Britain and the British Empire seemed reasonably secure, so Lloyd George as well as Wilson did not share Clemenceau's obsession with Germany's future potential threat to European peace. Hence, when Clemenceau demanded not just the return of Alsace-Lorraine, Allied military occupation of the left bank of the Rhine and demilitarization of the right bank of the Rhine, but the cession to France of the Landau and Saar regions, he found himself isolated. Since the territories concerned had not been under French administration since 1815, and since their inhabitants overwhelmingly considered themselves to be German (the claim that at least 150,000 were French was unfounded), Clemenceau's isolation was unsurprising. However, in objecting to the universal application of the so-called principle of national self-determination, Clemenceau was on firmer ground. Wilson believed that, with the break-up of the Russian, German, Austro-Hungarian and Ottoman empires, the political map could be redrawn so that each 'nation' would have its own nation state, or, at the very least, its own 'right' to enjoy autonomous development recognized. But, as Clemenceau pointed out, national and ethnic groups were often intermingled, so that it was impossible to create a Czech state without ethnic Germans, a Greek state without ethnic Bulgarians, or a Serb state without ethnic Albanians. This problem was compounded by the need to make states viable, with appropriate frontiers and with access to the sea. Hence the new state of Poland acquired the Polish 'corridor', inhabited by an ethnic German majority, and Danzig became a free port under the League of Nations, although again the majority of the inhabitants were ethnic Germans.

Even Wilson did not always want to apply the principle of national self-determination, as when he opposed holding a plebiscite to determine where the German–Polish frontier should be drawn in Upper Silesia. The whole notion that 'nations' and nation states should be coterminous was arguably disastrous, since it failed to take account of ethnic diversity and national minorities within states and, in effect, encouraged governments to adopt 'ethnic cleansing', with Turkey, for example, massacring or expelling most of its Armenian and Greek minorities. Indeed, the peacemakers ought to have emphasized that states should be the guardians of human rights rather than the political expressions of single 'nations'.

With regard to the Saar, Clemenceau did not lose out completely. As compensation for the destruction of the coal mines in northern France, and as a partial payment of the reparations due to France from Germany, France was awarded the right to exploit the Saar coal mines, while the Saar region was placed under League of Nations administration, its eventual status to be determined by a plebiscite after fifteen years.

6.3 The Treaty of Versailles

Article 42
Germany is forbidden to maintain or construct any fortifications either on the left bank of the Rhine or on the right bank of the Rhine to the west of a line drawn 50 kilometres to the east of the Rhine.

Article 43
In the area defined above the maintenance and the assembly of armed forces, either permanently or temporarily, and military manoeuvres of any kind, as well as the upkeep of all permanent works of mobilization, are in the same way forbidden.

Article 51
The territories which were ceded to Germany in accordance with the Preliminaries of Peace signed at Versailles on February 26, 1871, and the Treaty of Frankfurt of May 10, 1871, are restored to French sovereignty as from the date of the Armistice of November 11, 1918.

Article 80
Germany acknowledges and will respect strictly the independence of Austria, within the frontiers which may be fixed in a treaty between that State and the Principal Allied and Associated Powers; she agrees that this independence shall be inalienable, except with the consent of the Council of the League of Nations.

Article 119
Germany renounces in favour of the Principal Allied and Associated Powers all her rights and titles over her overseas possessions.

Article 159

The German military forces shall be demobilized and reduced as prescribed hereinafter.

Article 160

By a date which must not be later than March 31, 1920, the German Army must not comprise more than seven divisions of infantry and three divisions of cavalry.

After that date the total number of effectives in the Army of the States constituting Germany must not exceed one hundred thousand men, including officers and establishments of depots. The Army shall be devoted exclusively to the maintenance of order within the territory and to the control of the frontiers.

The total effective strength of officers, including the personnel of staffs, whatever their composition, must not exceed four thousand.

Article 198

The armed forces of Germany must not include any military or naval air forces.

Article 227

The Allied and Associated Powers publicly arraign William II of Hohenzollern, formerly German Emperor, for a supreme offence against international morality and the sanctity of treaties.

Article 231

The Allied and Associated Governments affirm and Germany accepts the responsibility of Germany and her allies for causing all the loss and damage to which the Allied and Associated Governments and their nationals have been subjected as a consequence of the war imposed upon them by the aggression of Germany and her allies.

Article 245

Within six months after the coming into force of the present Treaty the German Government must restore to the French Government the trophies, archives, historical souvenirs or works of art carried away from France by the German authorities in the course of the war of 1870–1871 and during this last war, in accordance with a list which will be communicated to it by the French Government; particularly the French flags taken in the course of the war of 1870–1871 . . .

Article 428

As a guarantee for the execution of the present Treaty by Germany, the German territory situated to the west of the Rhine, together with the bridgeheads, will be occupied by Allied and Associated troops for a period of fifteen years from the coming into force of the present Treaty.

Source: The Treaty of Peace between the Allied and Associated Powers and Germany, signed at Versailles, June 28, 1919. *London: HMSO. 1925, pp. 29, 40, 51, 73, 82–3, 97, 106, 107, 127–8, 217*

The peace settlement after the end of the First World War took the form of a series of treaties, signed in former royal palaces around Paris, including the treaties of Versailles with Germany (28 June 1919), of St Germain-en-Laye with Austria (10 September 1919), of Neuilly with Bulgaria (27 November 1919), of Trianon with Hungary (4 June 1920), and of Sèvres with Turkey (10 August 1920). The Treaty of Versailles, which included the Covenant of the League of Nations and articles relating to a new International Labour Office and a new Permanent Court of International Justice, contained 440 articles. Of particular relevance to France were the acquisition from Germany of League of Nations mandates in Togoland and the Cameroons in West Africa (France also acquired from the former Ottoman Empire a League of Nations mandate in Syria), the return of Alsace and Lorraine, the demilitarization of the Rhineland, the Allied occupation of the left bank of the Rhine and certain strategic bridgeheads on the right bank for up to fifteen years, the right to exploit the coal mines of the Saar (which was placed under League of Nations administration for fifteen years), the reduction of the German army to 100,000 men, and the payment to France by Germany of reparations. The latter were to include financial payments over a thirty-year period from 1 May 1921, and payments in kind, notably millions of tons of coal as well as merchant ships, fishing boats, agricultural livestock and chemicals.

The principal French concern was for security against any possible future German aggression. Ideally, the French would have liked to have annexed all German territories on the left bank of the Rhine, or at least to have had an independent Rhineland state as a buffer between France and Germany, but they had to settle for less. The British government, on the other hand, believing that over-harsh treatment of Germany would be unwise, opposed the imposition of punitive reparations on Germany, did not want a prolonged Allied military occupation of the Rhineland, and favoured the early admission of Germany to the League of Nations. The influential British economist John Maynard Keynes went even further, and published a book highly critical of the Versailles Treaty and its framers, and of the reparations clauses.

In Germany, the Versailles Treaty was from the start deeply resented as an unjust settlement, dictated to a defenceless Germany. It was claimed that Germany had agreed to an armistice on the basis of Wilson's Fourteen Points, on the understanding that they would shape the peace settlement. The assumption of the 'war-guilt' clause (article 231), that the aggression of Germany and her allies had solely been responsible for the outbreak of the First World War, was totally rejected, as was the assertion that Germany was guilty of 'war crimes'. In addition, the surrender of all her colonies and most of her fleet, the loss of territory, particularly the Polish corridor and Danzig, the prohibition of any union with Austria, the disarmament stipulations, the obligation to pay reparations and the exclusion from the League of Nations were all regarded as unacceptably unfair. Only after the German government had resigned and the Allies had threatened to resume hostilities within twenty-four hours did the signing ceremony take place – on 28 June 1919 (the fifth anniversary of the Sarajevo assassinations) in the Hall of Mirrors of the Palace of Versailles (where the German Empire had been proclaimed on 18 January 1871).

The fairness and wisdom of the treatment of Germany in the Treaty of Versailles are always likely to be disputed. What is indisputable is that from the start Germans sought to evade the provisions of the treaty and that the treaty was unenforcible. The German fleet interned at Scapa Flow in the Orkney Islands was scuttled by the Germans on 21 June 1919. French flags captured in the war of 1870–1 were burnt rather than returned to France. The Netherlands refused to hand over the Kaiser for trial as a war criminal, and the Germans similarly refused to allow the extradition of other alleged war criminals. Restrictions imposed on Germany's armed forces were systematically ignored and evaded as official policy from 1919. Confronted by these violations, the Allies seemed powerless, just as they failed to enforce the Treaty of Sèvres, which had assigned territory in Thrace and around Smyrna in Asia Minor to Greece, granted an autonomous Kurdistan to the Kurds and restricted the Turkish army to 50,000 men. The Turkish parliament refused to ratify the treaty and the Turkish army defeated the Armenians and the Greeks. Allied military intervention was contemplated by Lloyd George, but he was not supported, so the Allies accepted the consequences of Turkey's military actions at the Treaty of Lausanne (24 July 1923). More immediately ominous for France was the refusal of the US Senate to ratify the Treaty of Versailles (19 March 1920). This began a period of American isolation from Europe, which fatally weakened the wartime alliance and the post-war settlement.

Document 6.4 The League of Nations

THE HIGH CONTRACTING PARTIES,

In order to promote international co-operation and to achieve international peace and security
by the acceptance of obligations not to resort to war,
by the prescription of open, just and honourable relations between nations,
by the firm establishment of the understandings of international law as the actual rule of conduct among Governments, and
by the maintenance of justice and a scrupulous respect for all treaty obligations in the dealings of organized peoples with one another,
Agree to this Covenant of the League of Nations.

Article 8
The members of the League recognize that the maintenance of peace requires the reduction of national armaments to the lowest point consistent with national safety and the enforcement by common action of international obligations.

Article 16
Should any member of the League resort to war in disregard of its covenants under Articles 12, 13 or 15 it shall *ipso facto* be deemed to have committed an act of war against all other Members of the League, which hereby undertake immediately to subject it to the severance of all trade or financial relations, the prohibition of all intercourse between their nationals and the nationals of the

covenant-breaking State, and the prevention of all financial, commercial or personal intercourse between the nationals of the covenant-breaking State and the nationals of any other State, whether a Member of the League or not.

It shall be the duty of the Council in such case to recommend to the several Governments concerned what effective military, naval or air force the Members of the League shall severally contribute to the armed forces to be used to protect the covenants of the League.

Source: The Treaty of Peace between the Allied and Associated Powers and Germany, signed at Versailles, June 28, 1919. *London: HMSO. 1925, pp. 7, 10, 15–17*

The concept of a supranational body to settle international disputes, which had a long history, was given a boost by the First World War and taken up by Lloyd George, President Wilson and many others. In January 1918 Lloyd George appointed a committtee to submit proposals for the organization and functions of a league of states. This committee suggested a league consisting initially of the wartime Allies, and possibly some neutrals, with a permanent base and with the role of settling international disputes, preferably by arbitration. If a state went to war before the established procedures had been exhausted, the member states of the league were to take collective financial, economic or even military action against the offending state. A French committee headed by Léon Bourgeois, a lawyer and politician with a long ministerial career, reported in somewhat similar terms on 8 June 1918. The French proposals envisaged an international council of heads of government meeting annually, and a smaller, permanent committee working throughout the year. An international tribunal would adjudicate on disputes which could be settled by law, with other disputes being referred to the international council. Bourgeois also wanted the league to have its own military forces, provided by contingents from member states, and to supervise the international control of armaments. President Wilson believed in compulsory and binding arbitration for all disputes that could not be settled through diplomacy, and he thought the government of each member state should send an ambassador to form the league's body of delegates.

The drafting of the Covenant or Constitution of what became the League of Nations reflected British and American rather than French proposals. For instance, the British Dominions (Australia, Canada, New Zealand and South Africa) and India were granted individual membership from the start, whereas the French idea of equipping the League with its own independent international army was rejected. Fears over the erosion of national sovereignty led to the exclusion of the internal domestic affairs of any member state from the competence of the League, while the obligation on member states to go to war in defence of the League's Covenant was abandoned. Geneva was selected as the headquarters of the League. A British diplomat, Sir Eric Drummond, became the League's Secretary General, and a Frenchman, Jean Monnet, his deputy.

The French had wanted the League to provide a perpetual guarantee for the Versailles Treaty and a perpetual defence against any future aggression by Germany.

The rejection of the French proposal for League military forces, the refusal of states to agree to any automatic commitment to go to war and the vote against the Versailles Treaty by the US Senate meant that from the start the League had very little power. Apart from the United States, a handful of states then of relatively minor significance (Arabia, Iceland, Mongolia and Tibet), and the colonies of the member states, all the states in the world eventually joined the League of Nations. It was therefore the most representative world political assembly to date, and it did much useful work. At first, though, the League seemed to be too much of a First World War victors' club. The Covenant of the League of Nations formed an integral part of the Versailles Treaty, which gave the League an administrative role in the Saar and Danzig and which sanctioned the appropriation of former German colonies, but which did not impose disarmament impartially and did not admit Germany to League membership until September 1926, Turkey until July 1932 and Russia (the Soviet Union) until September 1934. Above all, the League of Nations, like its successor the United Nations, always depended for its effectiveness on the co-operation of member states; and in the 1930s that co-operation was often not forthcoming.

Document 6.5 Depopulation and Birth Control

The doctor occupies an elevated position in society. (*Hear! Hear!*) He owes that not only to what his profession demands in terms of wide-ranging knowledge and scientific expertise, but above all in what it demands in terms of devotion, sympathy and high moral standards. (*Renewed exclamations of approval.*) The doctor heals when he can, and always comforts and consoles. You cannot turn him into a judge. This is not possible. When a doctor cares for someone who is ill, he is not concerned with whether or not the patient is guilty, he is concerned only with healing him. (*Hear! Hear!*) . . .

When a man wishes to have a family and create a household, he gives satisfaction to an instinct that every human being possesses, namely to be survived by one's descendants, thereby as it were prolonging one's life beyond the grave. But after a man has one or two children, the instinct is satisfied. To want a larger family, other considerations come into play. He wonders – and you cannot blame him for it – if he will be able to feed additional children, bring them up, keep them safe from misery, and enable them to develop physically and mentally.

As civilization progresses and as children become less and less able to earn their livings at an early age, they become for their families an ever greater responsibility for an increasing period of time. The legislation for which you have voted, legislation that you cannot abrogate and which you are even in the process of completing, such as legislation on child labour and compulsory education, helps to increase these difficulties. (*Hear! Hear!*)

The state needs children. It has more need of them than the individual. It must therefore take responsibility for surplus children. It should not restrict itself to granting derisory benefits to families with numerous children [*familles nombreuses*].

When you have done that, you will still not have solved the problem. It is not just the poor who do not have children. The rich have even fewer children, through egoism because they do not want their family wealth to be dispersed, because the wife dreads the pain and suffering of giving birth and fears that having children will give her premature wrinkles. What then will you do? Nothing.

Fathers and mothers want to live their lives without cares or worries. You are completely powerless, so attitudes must be changed. (*Hear! Hear!*)

Emile Goy in the Senate, 24 January 1919; Annales du Sénat, Débats parlementaires, *vol. 90, 1920, p. 27*

The First World War had a considerable impact on attitudes towards demography, women and sex in France. The terrible slaughter of the First World War and the shortage of young Frenchmen thereafter intensified longstanding concerns in France about the nation's relative demographic decline. Frenchwomen were therefore exhorted to have babies, not just to compensate for war losses and to close the demographic gap with Germany, but so as not to betray the millions of Frenchmen who had fought for their country, often at the cost of their lives.

The war had also popularized two contrasting images of women – the 'modern woman' and the 'mother'. The 'modern woman' was economically independent, probably single and certainly childless, and preoccupied with an essentially frivolous and pleasure-seeking lifestyle. This image of the 'modern woman' was based on the economic independence achieved by many working women in France during the First World War, and by widespread assumptions about the exploitation by women of opportunities created by the war for sexual promiscuity. After the war, this image was sustained by the popularity in the early 1920s of female fashions and lifestyles featuring short hair, loose and rather masculine clothes that tended to de-emphasize women's breasts and waists, and an active and elegant world of pleasure associated with tennis, cars, cocktails, jazz, dances such as the tango and the fox-trot, and smoking cigarettes through holders. The 'mother', on the other hand, was the sort of woman who during the war had looked after her family, nursed wounded soldiers, or 'adopted' a soldier at the front (writing letters and sending parcels to him as his 'godmother' or *marraine de guerre*), and who was now anxious to play the traditional caring roles of wife and mother. The war had also led to a greater diffusion of knowledge about contraception. To maintain morale among the troops, the French military authorities had often tolerated brothels, while at the same time issuing condoms to the troops, so that they would not become incapacitated by sexually transmitted diseases. Through this aspect of their war experience, therefore, many young Frenchmen were introduced to sex and contraception dissociated from love and procreation.

In this context pronatalist ideas flourished. Since 1896, the National Alliance against Depopulation had campaigned for repressive measures against abortion and contraception, family allowances, the introduction of a family vote and the teaching of demography in schools. Such proposals appealed to many parliamentarians. In the Chamber of Deputies, the parliamentary group for the protection of the birth rate and the family became the largest parliamentary lobby, including about half the total number of deputies in 1916 (Huss, 1990, p. 42). At the end of the war a bill was therefore introduced criminalizing abortion, the distribution of contraceptives and even the supplying of information about contraception. Abortionists were liable to a maximum of three years' imprisonment and a fine of 3,000 francs. Women who had abortions could be imprisoned. Those guilty of supplying contraceptives or 'neo-Malthusian propaganda' could be imprisoned for up to six months and fined a maximum of 3,000 francs. On 23 July 1920 the Chamber of Deputies voted by an overwhelming majority of 521 to 55 to accept the bill, which was approved by the Senate without discussion six days later. This anti-abortion and anti-contraception law, 'the most oppressive of its kind in Europe' (Roberts, 1994, p. 94), remained in force in France (with differing penalties) until 1967 and was not fully revoked until 1974. Its demographic impact, though, was limited. The French birth rate did rise slightly between 1920 and 1925, but then declined again to a record peacetime low in 1938.

Emile Goy, senator of the Haute-Savoie from 1910 to 1925, was a member of the Democratic Left and a medical doctor by training. After lawyers, doctors were the best-represented professional group in parliament, 358 medical doctors gaining election as deputies or senators between 1871 and 1914 (Ellis, 1990, p. 2). They were mostly left wing and inevitably took an interest in family matters. Goy is here arguing that it would be a betrayal of the Hippocratic Oath if doctors were to pass on medical information about their patients to the authorities in order to deter and punish those engaged in abortions (as had been suggested). While hostile to backstreet abortions, Goy was sceptical of the effectiveness of anti-abortion and anti-contraception legislation, instead stressing that family benefits should be more generous and that attitudes had to change. He also suggested that the French population should be rejuvenated by immigrants belonging to foreign ethnic groups, a suggestion which was not well received.

Document 6.6 *Familles Nombreuses*

After so many other 'days', a 'Day for the Mothers of *Familles Nombreuses*' has been announced for next Sunday. That is to say, on that day a certain number of well-intentioned people – principally young women and children, happy to play at being street vendors – will sell paper flowers and cardboard medals, for the benefit of unfortunate women whose youth is divided between childbirths and burials, and of the poor little brats who have been thrown into this world where there is no place for them . . .

I very much hope that, on this occasion, our 'repopulators' will receive some of the lessons which they deserve. I very much hope that, among the *familles nombreuses* mothers, there will be some with sufficient dignity and self-respect to throw the derisory and humiliating charitable gifts at the persons of those who offer them. I also hope, I hope above all, that there will be some supporters of 'responsible procreation' to give a categoric and determined 'no' to the appeals of the charity collectors.

We must not be led astray by a false sentimentality. The *familles nombreuses* mothers deserve our concern, that is clear. They deserve our concern because they suffer. Their children also, their children above all, deserve our concern, because they are not responsible for their births. They should therefore be helped. But the 'help' which is involved here is so insignificant that we can have no scruple in refusing it for them. And we will do them far more good in publicizing the reasons for our refusal.

It is unjust and immoral to make the wise pay for the foolish. It is unjust and immoral to ask from those who have had enough sense not to bring into this world more children than they can look after, their contribution, in whatever form, for the upbringing of the 'undesirable' progeny of those who have been unwilling or incapable of restraining their instincts. In our old overpopulated countries *familles nombreuses* – rich or poor – are never at any time 'desirable'. However, at a time when we lack bread, milk, coal, clothes, at a time when our weakened, exhausted and defiled race scarcely produces anything except pathetic scraps, at a time when we are threatened with famine, bankruptcy and degeneracy, *familles nombreuses 'are a social calamity, which we have the over-riding duty to discourage'*. And, if the 'encouragements' of our 'repopulators' turn out to be effective, if they encourage a significant increase in the birth rate . . ., the 'repopulators' will not just be imbeciles; they will have become criminals.

N. Roussel in La Voix des Femmes, *6 May 1920; N. Roussel,* Derniers combats. *Paris: L'Emancipatrice. 1932, pp. 106–8*

In addition to repressive measures, such as the anti-abortion and anti-contraception law of 31 July 1920 and another anti-abortion law of 27 March 1923, the French government in 1920 imposed a small surtax on the incomes of both male and female single persons over the age of thirty with no dependants. Couples married for two years and without dependants were also affected, apart from disabled war veterans and parents of those who had died during the war. At the same time, wives were given some positive encouragement to have babies. In 1920 Mother's Day (*Fête des Mères*) was instituted in France, setting aside a day for the celebration of mothers and the acknowledgement of their achievements. Families including five or more legitimate children, *familles nombreuses*, were in addition given their special day, when private charitable organizations raised money for such families, and when mayors in public ceremonies distributed bronze medals to mothers of five children, silver medals to mothers of eight children and gold medals to mothers of ten children. The government also set up in 1920 a National Birth Council (Conseil Supérieur de la Natalité), which co-ordinated a range of programmes: allowances and benefits to *familles nombreuses*, childbirth and post-natal care assistance, state-run maternity institutions and educational programmes.

Pro-natalist policies and propaganda were widely accepted in inter-war France and opposed only by a handful of socialists and by feminists such as Madeleine Pelletier and Nelly Roussel. A left-wing feminist who had become a pacifist during the First World War, Roussel was married and had two children, so she did not oppose maternity *per se*. However, she argued that national greatness depended not on the size of a nation's population, but on its quality. Therefore, the emphasis of parliamentary legislation and government policy should be on improving the physical, intellectual and moral standards of the population rather than on increasing its size. In a newspaper article published in December 1919, she mocked the old men comprising France's political élite who urged women to have babies without any consideration of the practical aspects of childbirth. She even suggested that women should go on a procreation strike (*grève des ventres*) unless certain conditions were met: serious guarantees of peace, so that babies would not become future cannon fodder; political rights for women, so that women could directly participate in public affairs; and recognition of the rights and needs of maternity, so that women could have their babies in safety and security.

In the article in *La Voix des Femmes*, reacting against the introduction of the special day for *familles nombreuses* in May 1920, Roussel attacked the charitable collections for *familles nombreuses* as inadequate and demeaning for the recipients and as unjust and immoral for the donors. She also argued that the whole concept of *familles nombreuses* was irresponsible, encouraging couples at a time of economic difficulty to have large numbers of children, irrespective of whether or not they could cope. In a subsequent article in *La Voix des Femmes* (3 June 1920) she recommended that the Medal of the French Family should be awarded, not to mothers of *familles nombreuses*, but to mothers of one or two healthy, strong and intelligent children, legitimate or illegitimate.

Large French families were not uncommon during the inter-war period, but most couples felt obliged to limit the size of their families for economic reasons. Parents were usually not in a financial position to support their adult daughters or give them dowries, so increasing numbers of women had to work; and the deaths of so many eligible men in the war made finding a suitable husband much more difficult. Moreover, child-rearing and household management became more demanding for middle- and upper-class wives and mothers as gradually fewer households employed domestic servants. The increasing threat from Fascist Italy and Nazi Germany, and the apparent success of their pro-natalist policies, nevertheless encouraged the Daladier government to introduce the laws of 12 November 1938 and 29 July 1939, known as the Family Code, which reorganized child allowances, granted extra benefits for *familles nombreuses*, imposed extra taxes on bachelors and childless couples, and renewed penalties for abortions (pornography was also targeted). The French birth rate did not start to rise, though, until 1941 under the Vichy regime, which also pursued pro-natalist policies.

Document 6.7 Women's Suffrage

M. Pierre-Etienne Flandin, committee spokesman. Gentlemen, to attempt
to demonstrate, to an Assembly composed exclusively of representatives of
the male sex, that the strict application of the democratic principles on which
the Republic is founded from now on requires the granting of political rights
to women might seem to be foolhardy. The fact is that our predecessors and
ourselves have demanded these democratic rights, which we even think our
public laws have incorporated, without our institutions until now granting any
voting rights to women. In France, demands for universal suffrage up to the
present have been limited to demands for male universal suffrage, and it seemed
to our predecessors that to have extended the right to vote to male electors,
even infirm and illiterate males, sufficed, and that there was no need to
enfranchise women . . .

Norway, Sweden, Denmark, the states of North America, Australia,
New Zealand, and Finland were the first countries to enfranchise women.
Subsequently, and particularly since the war has disrupted the peace of the
world, it has been the turn of nations closer to us, England, the new democratic
Germany, Russia, Austria, and most recently, Belgium . . .

May I suggest that, in my opinion, we cannot retain our conservative
attitude, which in France has always characterized the parties in power, except
under two conditions: if it can be demonstrated that these daring nations have
made a mistake and that the experience of female suffrage has not produced
happy results; or if it can be demonstrated that Frenchwomen do not possess
the same ability to exercise their political rights as Anglo-Saxon, Scandinavian,
Russian, German, or even French Canadian women.

M. Fernand Merlin. Women have a supremely important and admirable
role: to transmit life. Women should maintain the prestige of maternity,
which remains their highest function. Does that not constitute a pre-eminent
and powerful reason for not envying the role of men? To this philosophic
argumemt, more down-to-earth arguments can be added. I will summarize
them in a few words:

The Revolution proclaimed the rights of man, not the rights of women.
Women are not made for politics; their role consists in remaining at home and
looking after their children. The enfranchisement of women could compromise
the Republic and bring about the end of the regime.

Finally – last argument – women have no political education; they are
ignorant of everything concerned with public life.

Source: Debates in the Chamber of Deputies, 8 May 1919; Annales de la
Chambre des députés, débats parlementaires, *1920, pp. 1985 and 1995*

The First World War had a considerable impact on the position and role of women
in France. While the French government did not recruit women into the armed forces,
and even at first kept female nurses away from war zones, the military mobilization

of approximately 8,410,000 men, and the huge expansion of war industries and of the government bureaucracy, created unprecedented employment opportunities for women, which in turn meant that women played a crucial role in the national war effort. Far more women worked or had jobs than had been the case before the war, and the pattern of female employment changed, declining absolutely in domestic service and relatively in textiles and clothing while expanding dramatically in engineering and chemicals. The extent to which Frenchwomen can be considered to have benefited from the war is difficult to determine. On the one hand, many women, particularly those employed in luxury industries, lost their jobs at the beginning of the war; women subsequently employed in war industries often suffered long working hours, low rates of pay, strict disciplinary regimes and unhealthy and even dangerous working conditions; and women, of course, had to cope with inflation, shortages, separation from their menfolk and, in many cases, bereavement or incapacity within their circle of family and friends. On the other hand, many jobs previously reserved for men were opened up to women; labour shortages could mean relatively high wage rates for some women; and the overall contribution of women to France's war effort suggested to many that adult women should be regarded as citizens and not just as wives and mothers. The latter attitude gave a new impetus to the campaign for women's suffrage, and a bill was introduced in the Chamber of Deputies to give women the right to vote and to stand in all forms of election in the same way as men.

Pierre-Etienne Flandin, reporting on behalf of the parliamentary committee into women's suffrage, could point to the experience of many countries in which women's suffrage had successfully been introduced. To counter this argument, Fernand Merlin simply repeated traditional views about the role of women and their alleged incapacity for political and public life. Feminists such as Nelly Roussel confronted this argument head on, by maintaining that the maternal and caring roles of women qualified rather than disqualified them for the vote, and that it was ridiculous that women who brought up children successfully, who taught children in schools and who cared for the sick and the unfortunate should be deprived of the vote, while male imbeciles, alcoholics and illiterates could vote. Merlin's traditional views, though, accorded with a desire shared by many in 1919 to return to what might have seemed like the 'golden age' of pre-war France. Moreover, women were suffering something of a backlash as war jobs contracted, men regained jobs performed by women during the war, and attempts were made to reassert traditional values. Interestingly, Flandin was a conservative. He fought the November 1919 elections as a member of the conservative coalition known as the Bloc National, and he went on to hold a variety of ministerial posts in conservative coalition governments, including the premiership (November 1934–June 1935) and the Foreign Ministry (January–June 1936), before becoming head of the Vichy government under Pétain (December 1940–July 1941). In contrast, Fernand Merlin, the patriarchal traditionalist and opponent of women's suffrage, was one of the many left-wing medical doctors in the Chamber, and he fought the November 1919 elections on the list of the Bloc Républicain et Socialiste.

On 20 May 1919 the Chamber of Deputies approved the bill enfranchising women by 329 to 95 votes, though there was a significant number of abstentions, and some deputies may have voted for the bill knowing that the Senate would reject it, as indeed it eventually did, by the rather narrow margin of 156 votes to 134 (21 November 1922). This was not just due to conservatism, but because many senators feared, like Merlin, that women, under the influence of the Roman Catholic Church, would vote in a reactionary and clerical manner and thus undermine the Third Republic. Thereafter the women's suffrage campaign foundered on the continuing opposition of the Senate, the anti-clerical fears of Radicals and Radical-Socialists, the low priority given to the issue by the SFIO, and the élitist and marginal character of French feminism. Change did not occur until 21 April 1944, when the Committee of National Liberation at Algiers (France being still under German occupation) announced that women would vote in post-war elections. Frenchwomen first voted in the municipal elections of April–May 1945 and in the national referendum and parliamentary elections of 21 October 1945.

Document 6.8 The Sacred Union Condemned

The vanguard of the French proletariat will be entirely in agreement with us when we state that, during the four years of the imperialist war, nowhere, except in Germany, was socialism so despicably betrayed than in your country by the former majority of the Party.

The conduct since 4 August 1914 of the leaders of this former majority, Renaudel, Thomas and others, has been no better than the ignoble and treacherous conduct of Scheidemann and Noske in Germany. These leaders not only voted for war credits, but placed at the disposal of the imperialist bourgeoisie the entire newspaper press and political organization of the Party. These leaders of the French Socialist Party poisoned the soul of the soldier and of the worker. They helped the imperialist bourgeoisie to stir up throughout the country a polluted wave of abject chauvinism. They helped the bourgeoisie to establish a despotic regime in the workshops and factories and to suspend the most moderate legislation protecting labour. They assumed total responsibility for the imperialist slaughter. They took their places in the bourgeois government. They carried out the most contemptible commissions of the leaders of the Entente. When the Revolution broke out in Russia in February 1917, Albert Thomas, in the name of the French Socialist Party, was sent to us by the French imperialists to persuade Russian soldiers and workers of the necessity of continuing the imperialist slaughter. Thus, French socialists helped to prepare the struggle unleashed by the Russian White Guard against the class of workers and peasants. As for the former minority of your Party, it never waged against this abject majority the principled struggle, the clear and vigorous struggle, the revolutionary struggle, which it had the duty to wage. Having become the majority, it has continued until now to follow without clarity or energy an equivocal policy, which is sadly opportunistic.

Source: The Executive Committee of the Third International to all members of the SFIO and of the French Proletariat, Moscow, 26 July 1920; J.C.J. Girault, J.-L. Robert, D. Tartakowsky and C. Willard (eds), Le Congrès de Tours. *Paris: Editions sociales. 1980, pp. 113–14*

By the summer of 1915, the main French socialist party, the SFIO, was beginning to divide into the *majoritaires*, who supported the Sacred Union and the French war effort, and the *minoritaires*, who opposed the Sacred Union and who were prepared to offer, at most, only conditional support for the French war effort. The *majoritaires* and the *minoritaires* also disagreed over the resumption of international socialist contacts, with the *majoritaires* opposed to contacts with socialists from enemy countries, while the *minoritaires* supported such contacts in order to promote peace and (in the case of the extremists) revolution. Several small international socialist meetings were followed by an international socialist conference held in the Swiss village of Zimmerwald in September 1915. Albert Bourderon and Alphonse Merrheim attended as the French delegates, against the wishes of the *majoritaires* and of the CGT leadership, and voted for a manifesto drafted by Trotsky that blamed the war on the imperialist capitalist system, called for action for peace, and attacked the leadership of the various socialist parties for their chauvinism and for their participation in their countries' war efforts. Lenin, the Russian Bolshevik leader, urged a more radical programme: the conversion of the imperialist capitalist war into a revolutionary class struggle, and the replacement of the Second International with a new International. At the SFIO National Congress in December 1915, seventy-six delegates in effect voted against maintaining the Sacred Union, and at an SFIO National Council meeting in April 1916 over a third of the delegates voted to resume international socialist contacts. Yet at this stage even most *minoritaires* were reluctant to accept that France was not fighting a defensive war, as the French delegates to another international conference in Switzerland, held at Kienthal in April 1916, revealed. Nearly half the delegates at the SFIO National Congress of December 1916, though, while accepting the need to defend France, wanted peace initiatives to begin, international socialist contacts to be resumed, and socialist participation in government to end. Meanwhile, during 1917 and 1918, most of the *majoritaires* came round to backing the peace proposals of President Wilson.

The events of 1917 – the February Revolution in Russia, the failure of the Nivelle Offensive, the industrial strikes and army mutinies, the French government's refusal to allow French socialists to attend the projected Stockholm peace conference, the consequent ending of socialist participation in the French government, the return of Clemenceau to power and his vigorous conduct of the war – created a climate in which the Sacred Union effectively died. However, the Bolshevik seizure of power in Russia deepened the division within the SFIO between the *majoritaires* and the *minoritaires*. By publishing the texts of secret treaties negotiated by the Allied governments, the Bolsheviks exposed the imperialist war aims of the Allies, and by making peace with the Central Powers at Brest-Litovsk, the Bolsheviks unilaterally withdrew Russia from the war and enabled the Germans to launch a major offensive on the Western Front. At the same time, the Bolsheviks roundly condemned the Sacred Union as a betrayal of the proletariat and of international socialist ideals, and they presented the Bolshevik Revolution in Russia as a model for revolutionary action in other countries. Thus the Bolsheviks, and their decisions and policies, became central to the conflict between the *majoritaires* and the *minoritaires* within the French socialist and trade union movement.

At the extraordinary CGT Conference held at Clermont-Ferrand between 23 and 25 December 1917, a motion was unanimously passed condemning the Sacred Union and supporting the peace terms of President Wilson and the Bolshevik Revolution. The *majoritaires* just managed to remain in control of the SFIO until a National Council meeting on 28 July 1918, when a motion was passed condemning Allied military intervention in Russia against the Bolsheviks. The Allied victory in November 1918 might have ended the split between the *majoritaires* and the *minoritaires*, but the revolutionary movements in the former German and Austro-Hungarian empires, the slowness of demobilization, the acquittal of the assassin of Jaurès (March 1919), the 'imperialist' post-war treaty settlement, Allied military support for the Whites in the Russian Civil War, continuing economic and social difficulties and a huge expansion in CGT and SFIO memberships between 1918 and 1920 all helped to radicalize the French left.

Meanwhile, an international socialist congress held in Moscow between 2 and 19 March 1919 accepted Lenin's proposal that a new Third International should replace the Second International. In the following months a number of French socialists were drawn to Bolshevism; and when eleven SFIO deputies in July 1919 voted for military expenditure on demobilization, they were severely criticized, with four of them in effect eventually excluded from the SFIO. The unity of the SFIO was further undermined by the relatively poor performance of SFIO candidates in the general parliamentary elections of November 1919. The election results suggested to left-wing socialists that parliamentary democracy was just a bourgeois sham, and to their moderate opponents that the association of the SFIO with the Bolshevik Revolution was a vote-loser.

The advance of the Left continued at the SFIO National Congress held at Strasbourg between 25 and 29 February 1920, when it was agreed that the SFIO would leave the Second International and enter into negotiations with the Third International. In June 1920 two SFIO delegates, Marcel Cachin and Ludovic-Oscar Frossard, arrived in Moscow to discuss the SFIO's adherence to the Third International. It was made clear to them that the Bolshevik leadership demanded a total repudiation of the Sacred Union and of class collaboration, and an unqualified condemnation of Albert Thomas and Pierre Renaudel (prominent supporters of the Sacred Union and opponents of Bolshevism), whose conduct had allegedly been no better than that of Philip Scheidemann and Gustav Noske, respectively Chancellor and Minister of Defence in the German socialist coalition government responsible for the suppression of the Spartakist rising in Berlin and the deaths of Karl Liebknecht and Rosa Luxemburg (January 1919).

Document 6.9 The Third International

We make only one demand: namely that in your daily business, in the newspaper press, in the trade unions, in Parliament, in public meetings, you systematically and continually maintain a frank and honest propaganda in support of the ideas of the dictatorship of the proletariat and of Communism, that you clear the way for the proletarian revolution, and that you genuinely struggle against bourgeois reformist ideas.

The Conditions for Membership of the Third International

1   The French Socialist Party must radically change the character of its daily propaganda in the sense that we have indicated above.
2   On the question of colonies, it is necessary that the line of conduct of the parties of all the countries where the bourgeoisie dominates over colonial peoples should be very clear and totally unambiguous. The French Party must ruthlessly unmask the intrigues of French imperialists in the colonies and help not only by word but by deed every liberation movement. The following objectives must be adopted: the withdrawal of the imperialists from their colonies; the promotion of fraternal sentiments among the working-class masses of France towards colonial working-class populations; the conduct of a systematic campaign of propaganda in the French army against colonial oppression.
3   Reveal the duplicity and hypocrisy of social pacifism. Systematically demonstrate to the workers that without the revolutionary overthrow of capitalism no form of international arbitration and no system of international disarmament will save humanity from new imperialist wars.
4   The French Socialist Party must begin to organize revolutionary communist cells in the heart of the CGT, so as to struggle against the social traitors who lead the CGT.
5   The Socialist Party must secure, not just in words, but in deeds, the complete subordination of the parliamentary party.
6   The existing majority of the French Socialist Party must break completely with reformism and purge its ranks of those elements which do not wish to follow the new revolutionary path.
7   The French Party must also change its name and present itself before the whole world as the Communist Party of France.
8   Whenever the bourgeoisie imposes martial law on the workers and their leaders, the French comrades must recognize the necessity of combining legal action with illegal action.
9   The French Socialist Party, like all parties that want to join the Third International, must consider all the decisions of the Communist International as strictly binding. The Communist International will take full account of the different conditions in which the workers of different countries are obliged to struggle.

The Executive Committee of the Third International to all members of the

*SFIO and of the French Proletariat, Moscow, 26 July 1920; J. Charles, J.
Girault, J.-L. Robert, D. Tartakowsky and C. Willard (eds)*, Le Congrès de
Tours. *Paris: Editions Sociales. 1980, p. 119*

Cachin and Frossard were in Russia from 16 June to 29 July 1920, their stay extended
so that they could attend what was styled the Second World Congress of the
Comintern (19 July–7 August 1920). Speaking no Russian, and taken everywhere by
guides on official tours, Cachin, in particular, became an enthusiastic convert to
Bolshevism. Under pressure from their Soviet hosts, both Cachin and Frossard agreed
that the SFIO should adhere to the Third International. The Bolshevik leadership was
determined to impose the Leninist concept of centralized power in the hands of a
disciplined Communist Party and to ensure that all Communist Parties worldwide
adhered to an international organization known as the Comintern, which the Russian
Bolshevik leadership would control. Thus a French Communist Party could tolerate
no dissent within its ranks, would have to expel dissidents, and would have to take
its orders from Moscow. A French Communist Party would also have to be militantly
anti-colonial, have as its goal the revolutionary overthrow of capitalism and be
prepared to respond to repression with violence. Frossard, and even Cachin, disliked
these terms, but they had already publicly announced their conviction that the SFIO
should adhere to the Third International and they felt that, as socialists, they had to
rally to the Bolshevik Revolution. On 28 July Cachin and Frossard formally declared
their acceptance of the International's demands and undertook to work for a stronger,
more centralized and more revolutionary party.

After returning to Paris on 12 August, at a series of public meetings in Paris
and the provinces, and in articles published in *L'Humanité*, Cachin and Frossard
enthusiastically described Bolshevik achievements in Russia, defended Bolshevik
policies and urged the French proletariat to rally to their Russian comrades. Moderate
socialists such as Renaudel and Thomas, and even Jules Guesde, remained immune
to this propaganda, but many French socialists were won over. Disillusioned with the
Sacred Union and with War Socialism, disappointed by the November 1919 election
results and by the failure of a series of strikes called by the CGT in May 1920, alienated
by French military support for the Whites in the Russian Civil War and for the Poles
in their resistance against the Red Army, and attracted by the apparent vigour and
revolutionary purity of the Russian Bolsheviks, many French socialists began to regard
communism as their ideolgical home and the Soviet Union as their ideological
homeland.

The future of the French Left was decided at a special SFIO Congress held at
Tours between 25 and 30 December 1920. At the congress, moderate socialists,
such as Marcel Sembat, Léon Blum, Jean Longuet and Paul Faure, argued that
Bolshevism was a product of Russian conditions that did not prevail in France and that
French socialists should not abandon the democratic and reformist traditions of the
SFIO. However, by a majority of 3,208 to 1,022 the congress voted on 29 December
to join the Third International. The next day the SFIO split, with the majority forming
the French Communist Party (PCF) and retaining control of *L'Humanité*, while the
minority formed in effect a moderate socialist party under the old SFIO title.

Document 6.10 The Occupation of the Ruhr

ESSEN, INDUSTRIAL CAPITAL OF GERMANY, WILL TODAY BE UNDER ALLIED CONTROL

M. POINCARÉ WARNED THE REICH YESTERDAY AFTERNOON

FRANCE WILL KNOW HOW TO FOIL THE MANOEUVRES OF INTERNATIONAL FINANCE

Today, at 2.00 p.m., the first phase of the operation to establish control over the Ruhr will be an accomplished fact. Essen will be occupied.

For three years, different French governments have striven to maintain Allied unity for the execution of the terms of the Treaty of Versailles. Experience has revealed that unity was impossible on the execution of the most important of these terms, namely the measures required to make Germany pay reparations.

After having tried, in the course of more than twenty conferences, to find a common line between the opposing views of England and the other Allies, our negotiators have come to the decision that from now on a policy of fulfilment must be pursued, if necessary without England.

Today perhaps the British government will register a protest. It will have no validity against the clearly expressed views of France, Italy and Belgium. England is not going to help Germany. All it can do in the event of a French reverse is to say that it had foreseen the reverse.

Our situation, however, is excellent. With the methods advocated by the government of London, we were certain of gaining nothing, but with the methods which we have just put into action there are a great many opportunities for us. Supported by the Reparations Commission, faithful to the Treaty of Versailles, we can calmly view political manoeuvres such as the withdrawal of troops or delegates, and short-lived manoeuvres by banks.

After having exhausted all the resources of oratory in trying to persuade Germany, we are having recourse to a new form of argument. We are occupying the nerve centre of Germany. This centre is in the Ruhr and, while the Germans can remove their administration and their archives to somewhere else in Germany, they cannot remove their mines or factories.

In possession of this nerve centre, we will exercise the maximum pressure on those Germans whose wealth and credit are affected . . .

Once masters of the Ruhr, Belgium, France and Italy will be strong enough to withstand without weakening the threats of Wall Street and of the City of London.

Le Matin, 11 January 1923; O. Wieviorka and C. Prochasson (eds), La France du XXe siècle: documents d'histoire. *Paris: Editions du Seuil. 1994, pp. 260–2*

On the assumption that Germany and her allies had been responsible for the outbreak of the First World War, an assumption spelt out in the so-called war-guilt clause of the Treaty of Versailles (article 231), the Allies required Germany to pay reparations. The French were particularly concerned to extract reparations from Germany because French territory had been occupied and fought over by the Germans, because the economic and financial cost of the First World War had been so enormous for France and because France had contracted substantial wartime debts with Britain and the United States. The dismantling of inter-Allied economic co-operation after the armistice, and the ending of wartime exchange controls (March 1919), left France economically and financially vulnerable and reinforced French demands for reparations from Germany. Moreover, parliamentary elections in November 1919 produced the *Chambre bleu horizon*, or 'sky-blue Chamber' (after the colour of French army uniforms), a Chamber of Deputies whose many ex-servicemen and conservative majority were unwilling to conciliate Germany. The Allies, though, found it very difficult to agree on the amount Germany should and could pay, but eventually accepted the figure produced by the London Conference of the Reparations Committee (29 April–5 May 1921) – 132,000 million gold marks (£6,600 million). Germany agreed to pay this amount, having been threatened with military occupation of the Ruhr if it did not. However, in July 1922 the German government declared that it was unable to meet its reparations payments and requested a six-month moratorium. The losses and exhaustion due to the war, the disruption caused by the 'revolution' of 1918–19 and the ceding of territory of great economic significance all meant that Germany had a genuine case for non-compliance. Nevertheless, Poincaré (Prime Minister and Minister for Foreign Affairs since January 1922) refused to agree to any moratorium on reparations payments unless the Allies took over control of the mines of the Ruhr as a 'productive pledge'. After Germany had continued to default on reparations payments, at a conference in Paris on 2 January 1923 the French proposed an Allied military occupation of the Ruhr. Belgium and Italy, but not Britain, agreed, and the occupation of the Ruhr began on 11 January 1923 by French and Belgian troops, with a token contribution from Italy.

As the article in *Le Matin* suggested, the Franco-Belgian occupation of the Ruhr, without British participation, marked a watershed in Anglo-French relations. Unlike France, with the German surrender of all of her colonies and most of her fleet, Britain felt reasonably secure; and, again unlike France, with the transfer of 1,653,000 tons of German merchant shipping to her, Britain had already received substantial reparations payments from Germany. Also, German coal deliveries to France reduced British coal exports; and British public opinion had been strongly inflenced by J.M. Keynes's *The Economic Consequences of the Peace* (1919), a book by a young British economist who argued that the reparations demanded of Germany were excessive, unpayable and unjust. The French case would have been stronger, though, if France had not unilaterally undermined the Treaty of Sèvres, thereby helping to cause a crisis in British politics that resulted in the end of the coalition government and the fall of Lloyd George. Military differences between Britain and France had arisen during the war, with the French often complaining that Britain could have done more on the Western Front. The end of the war meant the resumption of imperial rivalries, particularly in the Middle East, but even in places such as Tangier, while the end of the Russian, German, Austro-Hungarian and Ottoman empires meant that an Anglo-French alliance no longer seemed so necessary. Now, the failure of France and Britain to enforce jointly the Treaty of Versailles, and to support the same policy towards Germany, was publicly demonstrated.

The Franco-Belgian occupation of the Ruhr had very serious consequences. The Germans responded with a general strike in the Ruhr as well as some sabotage and violent opposition. The French, in turn, resorted to coercion: some 180,000 Germans were expelled from their homes, 132 Germans were killed between January and September 1923, and there were also French and Belgian casualties. The general strike, and the German government's decision to print money to subsidize industry and pay wages to striking workers, caused such severe hyperinflation that by November 1923 the German mark was worthless.

Before then the German government had capitulated: on 26 September 1923 Gustav Stresemann, the new German Chancellor, ended the policy of passive resistance by calling off the general strike. Germany, though, had been fatally destabilized, with the savings of the middle classes wiped out and with the German people generally humiliated and alienated by high-handed and tactless French behaviour, including the deployment of coloured colonial troops in the Ruhr. The ground was thus prepared for separatist movements in the Rhineland and the Palatinate, communist revolution in Saxony, Thuringia and Hamburg, and right-wing revolts in Bavaria, including Adolf Hitler's Munich *putsch* of 8 November 1923.

France, too, suffered economically and financially, with a collapse of Franco-German trade, inflation, a state budget deficit, and a fall in the international value of the franc. Contrary to the hopes of *Le Matin*, the occupation of the Ruhr left France almost defenceless against Wall Street and the City of London. Meanwhile, the consolidation of fascist rule in Italy under Mussolini tended to discredit strong-arm 'fascist' tactics and to underline France's need for co-operation with Britain and the United States. The French government was thus reduced to accepting an American loan of $100 million on condition of tax increases and moves towards a balanced budget, and acceptance of the proposals of a committee chaired by an American banker for the rescheduling of German reparations payments, the Dawes Plan of April 1924. This, and the stabilization of the German currency, led to a period of financial stability and relative prosperity, but much damage had been done to Germany and France and to Franco-British relations.

Poincaré's personal responsibility for all this has been disputed. His critics have regarded him as a war-monger (*Poincaré-la-guerre*), while it has recently been argued that he was 'cornered into the occupation of the Ruhr' by pressure from public opinion and figures such as Alexandre Millerand (President of the Republic) and André Maginot (Minister of War), by Britain's reluctance to support France, and by Germany's determination to call Poincaré's bluff (Keiger, 1998, p. 60).

Document 6.11 Football

The first obstacle: parents. Apart from a very small number of the converted, how many parents twenty or thirty years ago would have tolerated their sons exhibiting themselves 'in an outfit as ridiculous and as indecent as that of a footballer'? 'You must be mad or a thug to play a violent game like that.' And, out of stupid humane concerns, sometimes out of fear, children were forbidden to play football by their father, or more often by their mother.

But if football is a sport, it is also a disease. I have known those who were – and still are – severely afflicted. What was then the importance of paternal opposition? Did the mother hide the modest football gear? There was no hiding-place sufficiently secure that it was not discovered. Did the father destroy the pair of shorts lovingly if inexpertly cut from an old pair of trousers? All such efforts were useless. The budding footballer always managed to get round obstacles with ingenuity, often with the complicity of a mother patiently and finally won over to the good cause . . . Sport! It was the death of academic study! The two could not be done at the same time. Football was certainly a game for the dunces and for the idle, etc. But footballers were a determined lot. Were ball games forbidden in the courtyard of the *lycée* or school? People played on the pavement opposite or in the nearest square. A boulevard, even a paved street, served as a training ground for future footballers. Sometimes there were accidents, and what accidents! Torn shorts, lacerated shoes, shins rainbow-coloured, and in the evening . . . paternal discipline. What attractions the sport had!

Source: Le Miroir des sports, *9 March 1922; A. Wahl (ed.)*, Les Archives du football: sport et société en France, 1880–1980. *Paris: Gallimard/Julliard. 1989, pp. 67–8*

Originally a British import, football was first played by members of British communities in cities such as Le Havre, Paris, Bordeaux, Dieppe, Lille and Amiens, and for decades club football remained largely confined to northern France and to the Bordeaux and Toulouse regions (rugby tended to be more popular in much of southern France, until football caught on in the Marseilles region). The ethos of French football was similarly British in origin, embracing concepts of amateurism, fair-play, playing the game and competing rather than winning, though (as in Britain) the ideal was often not attained. Despite the disapproval of members of the older generation, lack of facilities, the scarcity and expense of equipment (footballs were at first relatively expensive British imports), and some chauvinist opposition to 'English' sports, the game soon won a following in France, particularly from members of the urban middle class. As in Britain, it was widely assumed that sports, especially team sports, were character-forming, with their emphasis on physical fitness, courage, discipline, endurance, initiative and team spirit. The comradeship and social activities associated with football also helped to popularize the game.

By 1906 official football matches in France involved about 4,000 participants, who belonged to around 270 clubs (Wahl, 1989, p. 54), and football was acquiring national and international structures. A form of national championship was played from 1894, and various regional league competitions also developed. Matches between national teams followed after 1900, with the French national team playing against their counterparts from Belgium, Germany and Switzerland. On 21 May 1904 the Fédération Internationale de Football Association (FIFA) was founded, due to French rather than British initiative. England did not join FIFA until 1906, and the first international football match between England and France took place in November of that year at the Parc des Princes in Paris (England won 15–0). FIFA took the important decision of accepting professional footballers, and a split developed in French football between amateurs and professionals, though the split ended with all French football clubs in January 1913 recognizing the Comité Français Interfédéral pour la Propagation des Sports (CFI) as the common national governing body.

After the First World War, football in France became a mass-entertainment sport, as in many other countries. During the war, many ordinary French soldiers were introduced to football, with matches between teams from different units and divisions becoming commonplace. After 1919, the modest gains in affluence and leisure enjoyed by many French male workers, and increased attention given to football by popular newspapers, encouraged French football to lose its British and bourgeois character and to become essentially a male working-class sport. By the 1930s, the total number of football clubs in France had risen to over 5,000, and nearly 40,000 spectators might pay to watch an individual match (Holt, 1981, pp. 5 and 77). Football clubs and teams usually had a local focus (city, village), though they could also be institutional (university, school), religious (usually Catholic), political (usually socialist), or company (Société Générale, Peugeot).

During the inter-war period the principal city football teams, and the principal football competitions, acquired a modern character. New stadiums were constructed, with room for thousands of spectators and with facilities for players. In 1927 Gaston Doumergue, President of the Republic, established what almost became a presidential tradition by attending the final of the French national championship (known as the Coupe de France), though the Third Republic never adopted state sports programmes for the masses, like Fascist Italy or Nazi Germany. The Fédération Française de Football Association (FFFA), which had replaced the CFI as the governing body of French football in April 1919, drew up regulations for professional footballers and for their transfers between clubs in January 1932. This confirmed the professionalization and commercialization of football at league level (phenomena that became characteristic at this time of other sports, such as cycling and rugby). Prominent footballers became stars, though they were not particularly well paid (their salaries were limited to a maximum of 2,000 francs per month). Important football matches were covered by live radio commentaries. Foreigners, mostly Austrians, Czechs, Hungarians and Yugoslavs, were recruited to play in French teams. Wealthy businessmen and companies began to sponsor individual teams, and commercial advertisers began to target football. There were even some instances of football hooliganism. Altogether, an annual cycle of league and national competitions, as well as international matches (the first World Cup was staged in 1930, and Paris hosted the third World Cup in

1938), gave to many in France, especially to urban working-class men, a sense of identity and an interest, if not a passion.

Document 6.12 France's 'Civilizing Mission'

Social Conditions and Morality of the Natives

The moral and social development of the natives cannot, without the risk of provoking a crisis, be anything other than very slow. Therefore, in the course of a year, it is impossible to note any changes in the habits and customs of our protected peoples. Change is even less perceptible as it can be brought about only in accordance with the mentality appropriate for the peoples of this country. The role of the Mandatory Power is to effect change by guidance, rather than by confrontation under the pretext of accelerating change.

Also, from the social point of view, an attempt has been made to develop among the profoundly individualistic native population, apart from those influenced by Islam, the idea of solidarity, at least among members of the same tribe. This has been achieved through the establishment of agricultural co-operatives. These co-operatives fall into two categories: some are concerned with the common purchase of essential materials for the cultivation and preparation of agricultural products; others are concerned with the sale of agricultural products. The sale of agricultural products in large lots is much more satisfactory than their sale in small quantities. When these co-operatives were first established, most of the native population did not exhibit much enthusiasm. Little by little, though, the native population has begun to appreciate the advantages offered by co-operatives and has gradually freed itself of its prejudices against co-operatives.

Source: Rapport annuel adressé par le gouvernement français an Conseil de la Société des Nations, conformément à l'article 22 du Pacte, sur l'administration sous mandat du territoire du Cameroun pour l'année 1931, *1932, p. 65*

After the outbreak of the First World War, Entente forces attacked German colonies, including Togo (Togoland) and the Cameroons (Kamerun) in West Africa. Togo quickly fell to a Franco-British invasion, but German resistance in the Cameroons continued for nineteen months (resistance continued in German East Africa until November 1918). In accordance with an agreement between the French and British governments of 3–4 March 1916, Togo and the Cameroons were partitioned, the larger portions going to France with a strip of Togo being added to the Gold Coast and a strip of the Cameroons being added to Nigeria. However, President Wilson insisted that such colonial conquests should be League of Nations mandates, so on 24 July 1922 the League of Nations formally conferred on France mandates in her share of Togo and the Cameroons, as well as mandates in Syria and the Lebanon (which had the unintended consequence of the spread of Syrian and Lebanese communities in French West Africa). Whereas Syria and the Lebanon were classified as 'A' mandates, which committed France to 'facilitate their progressive development as independent states', Togo and the Cameroons were classified as 'B' mandates, their populations considered incapable of self-government 'under the strenuous conditions of the modern world'. One of the conditions of these mandates was the submission by France of an annual report to the League of Nations, and the 1931 report for the Cameroons included this mission statement.

It was widely believed in France that French civilization was superior to all other contemporary civilizations, that the values of French civilization were potentially universal and that the French had a special mission to spread their civilization throughout the world. The French 'civilizing mission' (*'mission civilisatrice'*) was thought to be particularly applicable to Africa, since the French, like other Europeans, tended to underestimate the cultural sophistication of traditional African societies. Yet the French generally were not enthusiastic imperialists, which allegedly led Jules Ferry to complain in 1889: 'All that interests the French public about the Empire is the belly dance' (Andrew and Kanya-Forstner, 1981, p. 17). The First World War diminished this indifference by demonstrating the potential value to France of its colonial empire as a source of manpower and raw materials. The election of a conservative-dominated Chamber of Deputies in November 1919, and the revival of traditional colonial rivalries with Britain, further fuelled the final bout of French colonial expansion at the end of the First World War.

In practice, France's 'civilizing mission' in her colonial empire did not often amount to very much during the inter-war period, partly through a lack of resources. There was usually some development of the infrastructure, such as the construction of roads, bridges, ports and railways (often using forced labour), the development (with the help of missionaries) of limited educational and health services, and the imposition of a French judicial system that helped to stamp out slavery.

A more radical interpretation of France's 'civilizing mission' was formulated by, among others, Blaise Diagne, a black African who represented Senegal in the French Chamber of Deputies from 1914 until his death in 1934. As a reward for military conscription during the First World War, which Diagne had helped to organize in French West Africa, Diagne argued that France's 'civilizing mission' should mean assimilation, including the extension of French education, French citizenship and French legal rights to France's colonial subjects. Instead, educational provision in the French colonial empire remained limited, French colonial subjects rarely gained French citizenship or were appointed to senior posts in the French colonial service, and French colonial rule in Africa favoured traditional authorities, such as tribal chiefs and councils of notables, rather than the new class of educated Africans.

In so far as French colonies had become part of the global economy, they suffered from the post-war slump of 1921–2 and from the Great Depression of the early 1930s, when world trade contracted and prices for colonial products fell. Partly to cope with the consequences of the Great Depression in their African colonies, the French promoted agricultural co-operatives or Sociétés Indigènes de Prévoyance (SIPs). Developed in Senegal before 1914, these co-operatives were designed to provide seed for planting the next year's crop, to store and market agricultural produce, and to assist with the provision of agricultural equipment. Such advantages made co-operatives attractive, but their introduction was often compulsory and they were usually run on autocratic lines. Also, agricultural co-operatives tended to disrupt traditional peasant agriculture by substituting cash-crop production, with export markets in view, for subsistence farming or production for local markets. From the French perspective, the transition to cash-crop production was welcome since it meant the export of raw materials and agricultural produce to France and the spread of the cash economy, which facilitated the collection of taxes. In this context plantations could be more efficient than agricultural co-operatives, but there tended to be restrictions on the European ownership of land in French West Africa.

The Cameroons were a relatively minor French colony. According to official figures, their population in 1931 comprised just 2,164 Europeans and 2,223,802 natives. Yet with the Great Depression and the accompanying erection of trade barriers, the French colonial empire as a whole became more important for France. By 1936 it accounted for 30 per cent of France's total trade, though the empire was more significant as a source of raw materials than as a market for French exports.

CHRONOLOGY

1919

18 January	Opening of Paris Peace Conference
2–19 March	Agreement to establish a Third International at Moscow Congress
19–21 April	Mutiny of French Black Sea fleet
23 April	Law introducing eight-hour working day
8 May	Introduction of women's suffrage bill in Chamber of Deputies
28 June	Signing of Versailles Treaty
11–14 September	SFIO Congress held in Paris
15–21 September	CGT Congress held in Lyons
16 November	Success of Bloc National in parliamentary elections

1920

25–9 February	Second International rejected by SFIO Conference
6 April–17 May	French military occupation of Frankfurt, Darmstadt and Hanau
1–28 May	Strikes called by CGT
16 June–29 July	Visit of Cachin and Frossard to Moscow
31 July	Anti-abortion and anti-contraception law
20–6 December	Congress of Tours

1921

8 March–30 September	French military occupation of Düsseldorf
11 March	Treaty between France and Turkey

1922

15 January	Poincaré appointed Prime Minister
12 July	German government request for moratorium on reparations
24 July	Mandates in Syria, Lebanon, Togo and the Cameroons conferred on France
13 September	Franco-Polish 10-year military convention
21 November	Rejection of women's suffrage bill by Senate

1923

11 January	Franco-Belgian occupation of the Ruhr
19 January	Policy of passive resistance in Ruhr ordered by Cuno government
27 March	Anti-abortion law
24 July	Treaty of Lausanne
26 September	Ending of passive resistance in the Ruhr by Stresemann government
12 October	Strike by PCF against Moroccan war

1924

25 January	Alliance between France and Czechoslovakia
25 March	Decree introducing *baccalauréat* programme into girls' schools
11 May	Success of Cartel des Gauches in parliamentary elections
1 June	Resignation of Poincaré
13 June	Gaston Doumergue elected President of the Republic
15 June	Edouard Herriot becomes Prime Minister
16 July	Acceptance of Dawes Plan
28 October	French recognition of the Soviet Union

BIBLIOGRAPHY

Adamthwaite, A., *Grandeur and Misery: France's bid for power in Europe, 1914–1940*. London: Arnold. 1995.

Andrew, C.M. and Kanya-Forstner, A.S., *France Overseas: the Great War and the climax of French imperial expansion*. London: Thames & Hudson. 1981.

Artaud, D., 'La Question des dettes interalliées et la reconstruction de l'Europe', *Revue Historique*, 261 (1979), 363–82.

Bard, C., *Les Filles de Marianne: histoire des féminismes, 1914–1940*. Paris: Fayard. 1995.

Bell, P.M.H., *France and Britain, 1900–1940: entente and estrangement*. London and New York: Longman. 1996.

Bennett, G.H., 'Britain's Relations with France after Versailles: the problem of Tangier, 1919–23', *European History Quarterly*, 24 (1994), 53–84.

Boemeke, M.F., Feldman, G.D. and Glaser, E. (eds), *The Treaty of Versailles: a reassessment after 75 years*. Cambridge: Cambridge University Press. 1998.

Boswell, L., *Rural Communism in France, 1920–1939*. Ithaca, NY, and London: Cornell University Press. 1998.

Clout, H., *After the Ruins: restoring the countryside of northern France after the Great War*. Exeter: Exeter University Press. 1996.

Conklin, A.L., *A Mission to Civilize: the republican idea of empire in France and West Africa, 1895–1930*. Stanford, Calif.: Stanford University Press. 1997.

Cross, G., 'The Quest for Leisure: reassessing the eight-hour day in France', *Journal of Social History*, 18 (1985), 195–216.

—— *A Quest for Time: the reduction of work in Britain and France, 1840–1940*. Berkeley, Los Angeles and London: University of California Press. 1989.

Crowder, M., *West Africa under Colonial Rule*. London: Hutchinson. 1968.

Darrow, M.H., 'French Volunteer Nursing and the Myth of War Experience in World War I', *American Historical Review*, 101 (1996), 80–106.

Ellis, J.D., *The Physician-Legislators of France: medicine and politics in the early Third Republic, 1870–1914*. Cambridge: Cambridge University Press. 1990.

Fuchs, R.G., 'Population and the State in the Third Republic', *French Historical Studies*, 19 (1996), 633–8.

Grayzel, S.R., 'Mothers, Marraines, and Prostitutes: morale and morality in First World War France', *International History Review*, 19 (1997), 66–82.

Guinn, P., 'On Throwing Ballast in Foreign Policy: Poincaré, the Entente and the Ruhr Occupation', *European History Quarterly*, 18 (1988), 427–37.

Hause, S.C. with Kenney, A.R., *Women's Suffrage and Social Politics in the French Third Republic*. Princeton, NJ: Princeton University Press. 1984.

Holt, R., *Sport and Society in Modern France*. London: Macmillan. 1981.

—— 'Sport, the French, and the Third Republic', *Modern and Contemporary France*, 6 (1998), 289–99.

Hughes, J.M., *To the Maginot Line: the politics of French military preparation in the 1920s*. Cambridge, Mass.: Harvard University Press. 1971.

Huss, M.-M., 'Pronatalism in the Inter-war Period in France', *Journal of Contemporary History*, 25 (1990), 39–68.

Jacobson, J., 'Strategies of French Foreign Policy after World War I', *Journal of Modern History*, 55 (1983), 78–95.

Keiger, J.F.V., *Raymond Poincaré*. Cambridge: Cambridge University Press. 1997.

—— 'Raymond Poincaré and the Ruhr Crisis', in R. Boyce (ed.), *French Foreign and Defence Policy, 1918–1940: the decline and fall of a great power*. London and New York: Routledge. 1998.

Kriegel, A., *Le Congrès de Tours*. Paris: Gallimard. 1975.

Maignien, C. and Sowerwine, C., *Madeleine Pelletier: une féministe dans l'arène politique*. Paris: Les Editions Ouvrières. 1992.

Margadant, J.B., *Madame le Professeur: women educators in the Third Republic*. Princeton, NJ: Princeton University Press. 1990.

McMillan, J.F., *Housewife or Harlot: the place of women in French society, 1870–1940*. Brighton: Harvester Press. 1981.

Prost, A., *In the Wake of War: anciens combattants and French society, 1914–1940*. Oxford: Berg. 1992.

Reynolds, S., *France between the Wars: gender and politics*. London and New York: Routledge. 1996.

Roberts, M.L., *Civilization without Sexes: reconstructing gender in postwar France, 1917–1927*. Chicago, Ill., and London: University of Chicago Press. 1994.

Sharp, A., *The Versailles Settlement: peacemaking in Paris, 1919*. London: Macmillan. 1991.

Sherman, D.J., 'Bodies and Names: the emergence of commemoration in interwar France', *American Historical Review*, 103 (1998), 443–66.

—— *The Construction of Memory in Interwar France*. Chicago, Ill.: University of Chicago Press. 1999.

Smith, P., *Feminism and the Third Republic: women's political and civil rights in France, 1918–1945*. Oxford: Clarendon Press. 1996.

—— 'Political Parties, Parliament and Women's Suffrage in France, 1919–1939', *French History*, 11 (1997), 338–58.

Stevenson, D., *French War Aims against Germany, 1914–1919*. Oxford: Clarendon Press. 1982.

—— 'France at the Paris Peace Conference: addressing the dilemmas of security', in R. Boyce (ed.), *French Foreign and Defence Policy, 1918–1940*. London and New York: Routledge. 1998.

Tomlinson, R., 'The "Disappearance" of France, 1896–1940: French politics and the birth rate', *Historical Journal*, 28 (1985), 405–15.

Trachtenberg, M., *Reparation in World Politics: France and European economic diplomacy, 1916–1923*. New York: University of Columbia Press. 1980.

Viennot, E. (ed.), *La Démocratie 'à la française' ou les femmes indésirables*. Paris: Publications de l'Université Paris 7 – Denis Diderot. 1996.

Wahl, A., *Les Archives du football: sport et société en France, 1880–1980*. Paris: Gallimard/Julliard. 1989.

Winter, J., *Sites of Memory, Sites of Mourning: the Great War in European cultural history*. Cambridge: Cambridge University Press. 1996.

Wohl, R., *French Communism in the Making*. Stanford, Calif.: Stanford University Press. 1966.

7 | The Popular Front

Like other countries in Europe during the 1930s, France was confronted by two major problems: how to cope with the economic and social consequences of the Great Depression and how to cope with the threat of fascism from both within France and abroad. Between 1936 and 1938 France's response to these problems was the Popular Front experiment, an attempt to form a broad-left coalition government that would introduce policies to combat the consequences of the depression and to confront the domestic and foreign fascist threats.

The French economy recovered remarkably well after the First World War and in the period between 1924 and 1929 experienced an average annual growth rate of 5 per cent. In those years agriculture generally flourished, while there was a rapid expansion of the motor-car and engineering industries, particularly around Paris, with new plants being constructed by Renault (at Boulogne-Billancourt) and Citroën (at the Quai Javel). A devaluation of the franc in 1928 helped French exports and the French tourist industry. However, the dramatic fall in share prices on the New York Stock Exchange of October 1929 (the Wall Street Crash), and the subsequent financial crises and sharp decline in overseas trade, inevitably hit France. The French economy was still fairly self-contained, so the crisis took longer to bite than in some other countries, notably Germany. Thus France did not really experience the consequences of the depression until 1931, although some of the French colonies, such as Indo-China, were affected sooner; and after 1931 the consequences in France were not as severe as in some other countries and their impact was delayed. Unemployment in France did not peak until 1935, when the official figure reached the comparatively modest level of 503,000 (though the real figure was probably around 1 million).

Nevertheless, for many French people the consequences of the depression were traumatic. French farmers suffered a dramatic fall in the prices of agricultural products. Between 1929 and 1935 the price of a quintal of wheat fell from 184 to 74 francs and of a hectolitre of wine from 154 to 64 francs. Overall agricultural incomes declined by approximately a third in the early 1930s. Yet the price of fertilizers and agricultural equipment remained fairly static, so rural France experienced a severe crisis. The monthly rate of bankruptcies in rural France increased by 77 per cent between 1929 and 1934. A general financial crisis struck the French banking industry – 118 banks closed in 1931. Overseas trade declined, a decline accentuated by the relative overvaluation of the French franc. All industrial production suffered, particularly in the metallurgical, engineering, electrical and construction industries. Unemployment rose steeply until the beginning of 1935 and did not begin to decline significantly until 1937.

For successive French governments, the depression created a very difficult situation. The decline in the economy and the increase in the number of unemployed on state benefits meant a fall in tax revenues and budget deficits. At the same time, the depression impacted on different sections of the population in different ways, making a consensus approach to the situation hard to achieve. Peasants and farmers wanted state intervention to raise agricultural prices. The unemployed wanted cheap food, improved benefits and the prospect of employment. Small businessmen and shopkeepers wanted government tax and spending cuts. The unions wanted higher wages and better working conditions for their members.

The fascist threat obviously existed before the early 1930s. Characteristics of fascist movements, such as anti-parliamentarianism, militaristic nationalism and anti-Semitism at times featured prominently in the history of the Third Republic prior to 1914; and Action Française, a proto-fascist organization, was founded as far back as 1898, while its more militant arm, the Camelots du Roi, dated from 1908. During the 1920s, while Mussolini established his Fascist regime in Italy and Hitler developed the Nazi Party in Germany, new extra-parliamentary fascist-style groups or leagues were founded in France: the Jeunesses Patriotes in 1924 and the Croix de Feu in 1927. Only after 1930, though, did the fascist threat from both abroad and within France seem really serious. Abroad, Hitler's Nazis emerged in the Reichstag elections of September 1930 as a major political party in Germany. Thereafter they achieved a series of spectacular electoral victories, Hitler became German Chancellor in January 1933 and Germany was transformed by anti-democratic, anti-Semitic and militaristic policies. With Germany's withdrawal from the League of Nations and the Disarmament Conference in Geneva (October 1933), the Non-Aggression Pact with Poland (January 1934), the attempted Nazi putsch in Vienna (July 1934) and the restoration of military conscription and open pursuit of rearmament, the threat to France was obvious. At the same time, Mussolini was known to covet various French territories and invaded Abyssinia in October 1935, a fascist movement was gaining ground in Spain and in Central Europe Hungary and Romania were succumbing to fascism. Meanwhile, within France, the impact of the depression, disillusionment with the apparent ineffectiveness of governments and with the alleged corruption of politicians, and intensified hostility towards communism, led to a resurgence of violent militancy on the part of the right-wing leagues.

Document 7.1 Communism and Colonialism

Comrade soldiers!
The cause that the Moroccans defend is also your cause. You are the enemies of French and Spanish capitalism, just as Abd el-Krim and his followers are. The defeat of Primo de Rivera is welcomed as much by the mutinous soldier of Malaga and the striking worker of Barcelona as by the victorious Moroccan.

The revolutionaries of France and Spain, the young communists who organized the fraternization in the Ruhr, tell you that your duty as a worker and as a peasant is to fraternize with the oppressed populations of Morocco.

In France, in Spain, our campaign for the evacuation of Morocco develops each day. Every moment, the pressure of the workers becomes stronger to halt this slaughter, which benefits only a few capitalist sharks.

The strength and unity of workers, peasants, soldiers and colonial peoples will force the capitalists of France and Spain to evacuate Morocco and other colonies.

Long live the evacuation of Morocco!

Long live the fraternization of French and Spanish soldiers with the Arabs!

Long live the total independence of Morocco!

Down with colonial wars!

The Action Committee of the Communist Youth of France and Spain

Paris, 30 September 1924

Source: J. Doriot, La Guerre du Rif: les impérialistes et le Maroc. *Paris: Librairie de l'Humanité. 1924, p. 54*

When the French Communist Party or PCF split from the SFIO on 30 December 1920 over the issue of recognition of the Third International, it enjoyed the support of a majority of the delegates attending the Congress of Tours. This majority position was soon lost. The delegates at Tours were probably more radical than most of those who voted SFIO, and they were certainly more radical than most SFIO deputies. In any case, the First World War, the erosion of support for the Sacred Union and the Second International, the revolutionary movements of 1918–19, and, above all, the success of the Bolshevik Revolution in Russia and the foundation of Lenin's Third International, created an exceptionally favourable climate for communism, which did not last. Also, the Bolshevik Revolution and Lenin's brand of communism were not fully understood in France. Many early French communists regarded the PCF as a purged and purified SFIO, rather than as a totally new party, completely subordinate to the Third International. They tended to retain some sympathy for the democratic and reformist traditions of Jean Jaurès, and to be reluctant to accept the iron discipline, rigid centralization and revolutionary commitment demanded by Lenin. Therefore, the early history of the PCF was partly one of purges, with moderates, Freemasons, alleged Trotskyists and even figures such as Frossard (January 1923), Pierre Monatte and Alfred Rosmer (December 1924) being expelled from the party.

At the same time, following the dictates of the Comintern, the PCF adopted extreme left-wing positions with regard to the Versailles Settlement, the Franco-Belgian occupation of the Ruhr and French colonialism. The PCF denounced the Versailles Settlement as imperialist, particularly the reparations payments demanded of Germany, the carve-up of former German colonies and Ottoman territories and the return of Alsace and Lorraine to France without a plebiscite. Anticipating the Franco-Belgian occupation of the Ruhr, the PCF formed on 22 December 1922 an anti-imperialist and anti-war committee that declared that any French occupation of

German territory constituted a crime against the French and German working classes. In response the government arrested leading PCF militants while the Chamber of Deputies on 18 January 1923 voted by a substantial majority to lift the parliamentary immunity of the PCF deputy Marcel Cachin, who was imprisoned. Most French electors regarded the PCF as extremist and anti-French, and did not oppose anti-communist harassment and repression. In the general parliamentary election of 11 May 1924, the PCF won just 16 seats in the Chamber of Deputies, whereas the number of SFIO deputies rose from 67 to 104.

The French colonial empire achieved its greatest extent as a result of the First World War, but the wartime demands imposed by France on its territories, and the experiences of French colonial troops who fought in France, encouraged new opposition to French colonial rule. Unrest in the French protectorate in Morocco was 'pacified' by Marshal Lyautey, but anti-European resistance under Abd el-Krim continued in the Spanish protectorate in northern Morocco. Concerned that the French protectorate might be threatened, in May 1924 Lyautey ordered French troops to participate in the campaign against Abd el-Krim. Since March 1924, *L'Humanité* had opposed such a move, in accordance with the anti-colonial position of the PCF. This opposition soon received a powerful boost from Jacques Doriot, whose election on 11 May 1924 as the PCF deputy for the Paris working-class suburb of Saint-Denis had secured his release from a prison sentence awarded for his activities against the occupation of the Ruhr.

Doriot, the son of a blacksmith, after distinguished service in the French infantry on the Western Front (he was awarded the Croix de Guerre), became a metalworker in Paris and joined the Communist Youth. He made an extended visit to the Soviet Union in 1921–2, was appointed Secretary to the Communist Youth in 1923, and soon gained prominence for his energetic and outspoken resistance to the occupation of the Ruhr, for which he was first imprisoned on 21 December 1923. His parliamentary election the following year at the age of twenty-five made him the youngest French deputy. On 10 September 1924, when it looked as though Abd el-Krim was going to triumph over the soldiers of the Spanish military dictator Primo de Rivera, Doriot and the Secretary of the PCF sent a public telegram to Abd el-Krim saluting the brilliant victory of the Moroccan people over the Spanish imperialists and expressing the hope that the struggle would continue until the whole of Morocco had been liberated from all imperialists, including the French. The manifesto of the Action Committee of the Communist Youth of France and Spain further stressed that French and Spanish workers and peasants shared a common interest in the overthrow of imperialism and capitalism and should form a common front to achieve that aim.

At the beginning of 1925 Lyautey launched an offensive against Abd el-Krim and Doriot's opposition to the Moroccan war intensified, earning him arrests, suspension from parliament and prison sentences. Undeterred, he broadened his anti-colonial attack to include French repression in Syria and Indo-China and, indeed, the whole system of European colonialism. He argued that European colonialism invariably impoverished the colonized while enriching the colonizers, provoked conflicts between the imperial powers, and temporarily strengthened capitalism and delayed the triumph of the proletariat. The solution was an anti-imperialist and anti-capitalist alliance of colonial peoples, the revolutionary proletariat of capitalist countries and the Soviet Union.

Document 7.2 Poincaré and the Communists

I am not unaware of the fact that there is now in France, as in all countries, a party that prides itself in receiving its orders from abroad and that on its membership cards reproduces as a form of command, to support its electoral campaign against both the bourgeoisie and social democracy, these words of Lenin: 'The task of the proletariat consists in breaking and destroying the governmental machine of the bourgeoisie, including the parliamentary institutions, whether they are republican or constitutional monarchist.' In fact, the Communists in recent months have vainly tried to disrupt the Chamber and to dishonour parliament. They have, at the same time, intensified their outrages against our gallant military commanders and have attempted, if not to incite immediately, at least to prepare, indiscipline in the barracks and the arsenals. MM. Barthou [Minister of Justice] and Sarraut [Minister of the Interior] have demonstrated to parliament, by facts, dates and statistics, that none of these criminal acts has remained unpunished, and these last days we have not willingly accepted that the only weapons that the law currently gives us to repress the Communists should be taken from us. We have similarly not accepted that parliamentary immunity should be diverted from its proper role and purpose so as to cover these attempts to cause disruption. We do not exaggerate the Communist danger. Soviet propaganda will never have a profound effect on a people such as ours, which has no need to seek in the East the lessons of progress, which has been tested by several revolutions, which has suppressed privileges, promulgated the Rights of Man and Citizen, proclaimed liberty and equality, and whose soil, lovingly cultivated, has long been divided among millions of property-owners. It is ridiculous that nevertheless a handful of so-called reformers wants to present as a model to twentieth-century France not an unexplored terrestrial paradise but a purgatory that is only too well known, where misery and unemployment reign, and where the appearance of calm is maintained only by prison and exile. French common sense will know how to judge these Muscovite utopias.

Source: Speech by Poincaré at Bordeaux, 25 March 1928; P. Milza (ed.), Sources de la France du XXe siècle. *Paris: Larousse. 1997, pp. 53–4*

Throughout the 1920s the ultimate aims of the PCF were the seizure of power, the destruction of the 'bourgeois' government system, and its replacement by a new government system realizing the dictatorship of the proletariat. Although the Second Congress of the Communist International (July 1920) had committed Communist Parties to the armed struggle for the overthrow of the 'bourgeois' international order, and although French Communists were prepared on occasion to resort to violence, they normally concentrated on such immediate objectives as the weeding out of alleged 'centrists' and the rejection of 'reformism', the denunciation of all members of the non-Communist Left as 'social patriots', opposition to the Versailles Settlement and the League of Nations, support for all anti-capitalist, anti-colonialist and anti-imperialist movements and a position of unqualified loyalty to the Soviet Union and unquestioning obedience to the Third International. The PCF's constant criticism of the Versailles Treaty, resistance to the Ruhr occupation, solidarity with opponents of French colonialism in Morocco and Syria, revolutionary agitation in the French army, endorsement of strikes and industrial militancy, and identification with the Soviet Union and international communism meant that French governments viewed the PCF and its members as unpatriotic and even as traitors. From January 1923 onwards, French governments periodically seized issues of *L'Humanité*, arrested PCF militants and lifted the parliamentary immunity of PCF deputies, who tended to behave as revolutionary agitators rather than as parliamentary legislators.

Raymond Poincaré, having presided over the occupation of the Ruhr in 1923, had resigned the premiership after the success of a left-wing coalition, the Cartel des Gauches, in the general parliamentary elections of 11 May 1924. However, a financial crisis persuaded President Gaston Doumergue to invite Poincaré to form a new government in July 1926. Poincaré's main priorities were the restoration of public finances on a firm footing and the re-establishment of confidence in the international value of the French franc. Through introducing additional taxes, public expenditure cuts, a new mechanism for the reduction of the international debt and a government-enforced devaluation of the franc, Poincaré was spectacularly successful; and he won the support of nearly all the political parties, with the notable exception of the PCF, which maintained a relentless assault against not just the Poincaré government, but the French state. The PCF thus confirmed its status as the enemy within, the target of vigorous denunciation by government ministers (Albert Sarraut, the Minister of the Interior, coined the phrase, *'Le communisme, voilà l'ennemi!'*) and of vigorous action by the police and the judicial system.

The most effective anti-Communist measure, however, was a change in the voting arrangements for parliamentary elections. Following a new electoral law of June 1927, the *arrondissement* rather than the department became the constituency, and, if no candidate gained an overall majority, a second ballot had to be held. Since the Communist vote tended to be concentrated in certain areas, such as the working-class districts of Paris, this law harmed the PCF so that, in the general parliamentary elections of 22 and 29 April 1928, the Communists won just fourteen seats in the Chamber of Deputies (as opposed to twenty-seven in the previous parliament), despite increased electoral support.

The excerpt from Poincaré's speech illustrates his oratorical skills, his patriotic republicanism, and his exasperation that the French Communists should look for inspiration and leadership to a foreign regime that was already guiding Russia towards disaster, while France possessed her own rich political traditions and remained in all respects a relatively successful country.

Document 7.3 French Fascism

As at the front [during the First World War], we combined together to fight against the common enemy, the invader, today we combine together to attempt to fight against these other common enemies: the wogs, the profiteers, the corrupt politicians, the politicians whose patriotism is dubious and who are almost certainly for sale, those who abandoned the struggle during the war and then profited from our victory . . . the promoters of disturbances and conflict, beneficiaries of a war even more terrible and tragic than the last war: civil war and revolution.

We are not fascists . . .

If 'fascists' means good and true Frenchmen as opposed to traitors and madmen who stab the country in the back . . . we are fascists; if 'fascists' means supporters of order and of freely accepted discipline . . . we are fascists. But if 'fascists' means supporters of brutal repression, violence in the service of particular interests, curtailment of the free expression of opinions . . . perpetual regimentation and militarization of the nation, we are not fascists . . .

We will mobilize on the streets, if necessary, to assist the army and the police to re-establish order by all means . . .

Our movement is in the interests of everybody because it is the movement of French courage and patriotism and because its doctrine is 'Honour and Fatherland'.

Source: Le Flambeau, *1 November 1929; J. Plumyène and R. Lasierra,* Les Fascismes français, 1923–1963. *Paris: Seuil. 1963, pp. 51–2*

French fascism had its roots in various radical right-wing political and intellectual movements that emerged in France during the decades leading up to the First World War. The development of mass politics, the introduction of compulsory military service, the dislocation caused by industrialization and urbanization and the alienation of significant sections of the population from liberal parliamentary democracy all helped to create a climate of opinion characterized by obsessive fears of national decadence, xenophobic prejudices, chauvinistic nationalism and a willingness to embrace a cult of violence. Intellectuals such as Georges Sorel, Charles Maurras and Maurice Barrès contributed to the development of a new radical right-wing political ideology, while the Dreyfus Affair spawned right-wing leagues that, like their fascist successors, were anti-parliamentarian, anti-Semitic, anti-liberal, anti-Marxist, fervently and militaristically nationalistic, and attracted to political violence.

Thereafter, Action Française became the main focus of the French radical right, but it was too monarchist, aristocratic and élitist to be genuinely fascist. Much closer to fascism was the Cercle Proudhon, founded in December 1911, which brought together both right-wing nationalists and members of the anti-democratic Left who hoped to eliminate class conflict and achieve national solidarity through a fusion of nationalism and socialism. Like Action Française, the Cercle Social envisaged some sort of monarchical restoration in France, which helped to ensure that it remained a small, marginal organization until its disruption by the First World War. That war, in France as elsewhere, exposed a generation of impressionable young men to military discipline and combat experience, to the comradeship of the trenches, and to officially inspired propaganda that stessed national unity, duty and sacrifice in the service of one's country, and heroic combat in a Darwinian-style struggle for national survival.

Nevertheless, during the 1920s fascism did not become a major political phenomenon in France, unlike in Italy and Germany, where the sense of frustrated nationalism, the financial and economic crises and the threat from the revolutionary Left were all much more severe. However, the débâcle of the Franco-Belgian occupation of the Ruhr in 1923, and the success of the left-wing Cartel des Gauches coalition in the national parliamentary election of 11 May 1924, stimulated the emergence of several groups with at least some fascist characteristics. In June 1924 a Catholic nationalist, General Noël de Castelnau, helped to found the Légion, which was anti-Left, anti-feminist, pro-Catholic, pro-nationalist and pro-imperialist. A year later the Légion was absorbed into the Jeunesses Patriotes, an offshoot of the Ligue des Patriotes. Under the leadership of another Catholic nationalist, Pierre Taittinger, the Jeunesses Patriotes recruited right-wingers, war veterans and students into a movement with over 100,000 members by 1929. They wore uniforms (blue shirts and Basque berets), were organized along hierarchical and militaristic lines, made a cult of athletic sports, openly espoused political violence, and subscribed to a programme that was anti-Masonic, anti-left, pro-Catholic and pro-social welfare. More ephemeral was the Faisceau, founded in November 1925 by Georges Valois, a former member of the Cercle Proudhon and of Action Française. He advocated fascist-style corporatism and attempted to exploit Joan of Arc as a nationalist icon. Finally, between September and November 1927 a small association of decorated war veterans was transformed by Maurice d'Hartoy and François Coty into a national organization that became known as the Croix de Feu.

At first, the Croix de Feu was a largely apolitical organization that lobbied the government on matters relating to the armed forces and that had a membership in June 1929 of around 3,000, most of whom were ex-servicemen (Nobécourt, 1996, p. 140). Gradually its membership increased and diversified, though it remained predominantly middle class, while its weekly newspaper, *Le Flambeau*, adopted a political programme. The programme published on 1 November 1929 characteristically recalls the national unity against the common enemy, the foreign aggressor, during the First World War. Now there were new enemies to fight – foreign immigrants, capitalist profiteers, corrupt politicians and left-wing agitators attempting to foment domestic conflict and even civil war and revolution. This list would have appealed to the xenophobic, anti-capitalist, anti-parliamentarian and anti-Left prejudices of the Croix de Feu membership, which also tended to believe that, while patriots had fought and died at the front during the First World War, traitors and war profiteers had simultaneously enriched themselves and stabbed their country in the back. The programme also included a clear threat of political violence, albeit in support of the 'forces of order', and an affirmation of support for order and discipline, of French nationalism and of patriotic values. Yet the programme claims that the Croix de Feu is not fascist.

Historians have debated the character of French fascism and even the extent to which genuine fascist movements existed in France before the Second World War. During the inter-war period, it has been suggested, fascism was a foreign rather than a French phenomenon, movements such as the Croix de Feu were really authoritarian and nationalist in the French Bonapartist tradition or at least not fundamentally fascist, and, in so far as fascist movements did exist in France, they were of marginal significance (Plumyène and Lasierra, 1963, Rémond, 1966, Burrin, *La Dérive*, 1986, and Milza, 1987). On the other hand, European fascism has been interpreted as originally a French phenomenon, drawing inspiration and support from both the Left and the Right. According to this interpretation, European fascism derives from a heady mixture of French Jacobinism, the left-wing and anti-Semitic ideas of French socialists such as Proudhon, and the ideology and tactics of the new radical right that developed in France at the time of Boulanger and Dreyfus (Sternhell, 1996). This interpretation has been criticized for exaggerating the left-wing element in French fascism and for underestimating the role of the First World War as the 'founder event' of European fascism. It has also been argued that movements with fascist characteristics gained a significant popular following in inter-war France and that their tactics and style, even if not all their policies, were distinctively fascist rather than conservative (Soucy, 1986).

However, the ambiguous, often contradictory, character of fascism, the gaps that often existed between fascist ideologies and fascist policies and the different forms that fascism took in Europe make fascism notoriously difficult to define. Certainly, ideas and political movements deriving their inspiration from both the Left and the Right and related to twentieth-century fascism can be found in France from the 1880s onwards. Between the First and Second World Wars fascism did not come to power in France, in contrast to the experience of several other European countries. Yet France did produce movements such as the Croix de Feu that for a time attracted mass followings and possessed at least some fascist characteristics, even if they were not as extreme, ruthless or violent as their Nazi counterparts.

Document 7.4 Hitler's Rise to Power in Germany

What impetus will Hitler give to the foreign policy of his country? On this matter his ideas fluctuate as they do on many others. If today and in recent months the National Socialist movement, preoccupied with Germany's domestic quarrels, appears to be somewhat disinterested in diplomatic problems, it should not be forgotten that between 1927 and 1931 all Hitler's propaganda was based above all on the hatred of France, on the abolition of reparations, and on the revision of the Versailles Settlement. However, there was a time, in 1921, when out of hatred of Bolshevism and respect for the principal military power on the European Continent, Hitler appealed to France and to her sense of European solidarity in the face of communism [in 1922 France gave military assistance to Poland when invaded by the Soviet Union]. At that time England was Hitler's pet hate [*bête noire*]. Now, the country of Lord Rothermere [a pro-fascist and pro-Nazi British press baron, whose newspapers included the *Daily Mail* and the *Evening News*] receives almost as many favours from the Führer as the Hungary of Admiral Horthy or the Italy of Mussolini. Above all, Hitler's foreign policy is Italophile. To draw closer to Italian Fascism, Hitler in 1923 did not hesitate to sacrifice the ethnic Germans of Southern Tyrol, under the pretext that Italian friendship was more important than the annexation by Rome of hundreds of thousands of ethnic Germans living south of the Brenner Pass. Today, the entente with Rome remains, it seems, the keystone of Hitler's diplomatic edifice.

Revival of Germany at home and abroad; destruction of all the 'chains' that the defeat of 1918, the German revolution and the mistakes and weaknesses of successive Weimar governments have imposed on Germany; defence against communism, Marxism and Social Materialism; purge of the public administration, reaction against 'intellectual bolshevism', return to traditional and Christian family values; struggle against the 'tyranny of international capitalism'; these are the essential articles in Hitler's creed. They have an evident verbal and oratorical attraction, but they are not capable of retaining popular support. They are a response to unconscious prejudices and obscure needs that Hitler has been able to perceive. It is important to remember that Hitler is not a man of the past, like Hugenberg [leader of the traditionalist German National People's Party], and that his objective is not, like Hugenberg's, the pure and simple restoration of the pre-1914 *status quo*. . . .

Hitler is a man of today; he loathes the German revolution of 1918 which, in his opinion, deprived Germany of the fruits of 'Victory' – but he never loses sight of the historical fact that this revolution constitutes, the stage it represents in the German destiny, and the sentiments it revealed in the popular masses. Certainly, the Third Reich . . . bears not the slightest resemblance to the state that the bourgeois socialism of Ebert and Hermann Müller [founders of the Weimar Republic] dreamt of; but it differs no less from the patrician regime, based on the willing submission of the popular classes, which Hugenberg and his supporters wanted to re-establish.

Source: André François-Poncet to Paul-Boncour, 8 February 1933;
Documents diplomatiques français, 1932–1939, *First Series, 1966, vol. 2, pp. 583–4*

Hitler's rise to power in Germany, and the character and policies of the Third Reich, had an enormous influence on France during the last years of the Third Republic. France's sense of national security was shattered by Hitler's open repudiation of the Versailles Settlement, commitment to rearmament, alignment with Mussolini and goal of territorial expansion. At the same time, the dynamism of the Nazi state, the apparent solution of Germany's economic and unemployment problems, the newfound unity, energy and discipline of the German people and Hitler's successive diplomatic triumphs proved fatally attractive to many in France. A France seemingly crippled by strikes, left-wing militancy and economic decline could be contrasted unfavourably with a resurgent Germany that was increasingly powerful and successful.

Thus, the new phenomenon of Nazi Germany profoundly affected French diplomacy, defence planning and domestic politics.

After military service in the First World War, André François-Poncet, a graduate in German of the élite Ecole Normale Supérieure, gained election as a deputy for the department of the Seine in 1924 and held various undersecretaryships between 1928 and 1931. In August 1931 he was appointed French ambassador at Berlin, where he remained until October 1938. Transferred at his own request to the French Embassy in Rome after the Munich Conference, which convinced him that Hitler was not interested in maintaining European peace, he then vainly attempted to detach Mussolini from the Axis alliance. An informed and perceptive observer of the Third Reich, François-Poncet while French ambassador at Berlin saw Hitler regularly and was one of the few foreign diplomats who conversed with the Führer without the aid of his interpreter. However, French governments did not seek out François-Poncet's advice, except in April 1936 (after the German reoccupation of the Rhineland), when he was summoned to Paris to confer with the Prime Minister and the Minister of Foreign Affairs and with his fellow ambassadors in Belgium, Britain and Italy.

In his first report to the French Foreign Minister after Hitler's appointment as German Chancellor, François-Poncet suggested that the presence in the Hitler cabinet of traditional conservatives, such as von Papen (Vice-Chancellor and Reich Commissioner for Prussia), von Neurath (Foreign Minister), von Krosigk (Finance Minister) and von Blomberg (Defence Minister), could have convinced President Hindenburg that he had surrounded himself with indispensable guarantees and that Hitler would find himself boxed in, which would have suited the President. However, François-Poncet does not seem to have been entirely convinced of this argument, and he described Hitler's appointment as an adventure and as a matter of concern (*Documents diplomatiques français*, 1966, vol. 2, pp. 542–3). Approximately a week later, in his dispatch of 8 February 1933, François-Poncet stressed the apparent fluctuations in Hitler's positions on foreign relations and diplomatic questions, the declared objectives of the Nazi Party, and that Hitler was a 'man of today', a different political species from the bourgeois socialists of the early Weimar Republic or the conservative Nationalists represented by Hugenberg, so that the Third Reich would be a new phenomenon. Although in the introduction to his account of his Berlin Embassy François-Poncet asserts that the Nazis aimed to overthrow the moral and intellectual foundations of Western civilization, in his dispatch of 8 February he did not emphasize the violence, contempt for parliamentary democracy or anti-Semitism that already characterized the Nazi movement, as his own memoirs recorded. Nevertheless, his diplomatic reports were sufficiently critical that, when they were read by the Nazis after the fall of France, they led to his condemnation as an enemy of the Third Reich and to his imprisonment in Austria from 1943 to 1945.

Document 7.5 Programme of the Croix de Feu (1 October 1933)

1   An immediate and rational reduction in the burden of taxation;
2   The defence of the national economy against all forms of unfair foreign competition, such as dumping, tariff wars, currency controls, etc;
3   An elimination of state ownership in sectors belonging to private capitalism (monopolies, agencies, more or less disguised nationalizations);
4   A relentless struggle: (a) against speculation; (b) against the excessive and unmerited pay awards crippling the general costs of businesses; (c) against corrupt manoeuvres on the stock markets and against fiscal fraud;
5   An effective guarantee of the rights of French workers, and the restriction and adaptation of foreign workers to the strict needs of French production;
6   The protection of the legitimate profits of saving and of family property.

Source: Le Flambeau, *1 October 1933; cited in S. Berstein (ed.),* Le 6 février 1934. *Paris: Collection Archives. 1975, p. 61*

France, partly because of its relative self-sufficiency, did not immediately suffer as severely as some other countries, such as the United States, Germany and Britain, from the consequences of the Depression. However, the international collapse in financial confidence, the effective suspension of German reparations payments in June 1931 the devaluation of the British pound in September 1931, and a two-thirds decline in the volume of world trade between early 1929 and mid-1932 inevitably had a financial and economic impact on France. Between February 1929 and November 1934 the French stock exchange index fell by 73 per cent, and between 1931 and 1935 nearly 400 bank failures occurred in France. Meanwhile, French agricultural prices in general nearly halved between 1929 and 1935, so that consumer spending by farmers and peasants declined drastically. Tourism declined similarly, as the international value of the franc rose until the devaluation of September 1936 and as foreign visitors stayed at home because of economic problems in their own countries. With exports as well as domestic consumer demand falling, manufacturers were compelled to cut production and lay off workers, so that industrial unemployment in France rose from approximately 3 per cent in the years 1928–30 to approximately 15 per cent by the middle of 1932. Confronted with this crisis and the consequent shortfall in tax revenues, and determined to avoid inflation and to maintain the franc's international value, French governments pursued deflationary and protectionist policies, which arguably only exacerbated the crisis. Certainly, French public opinion tended to blame the government, particularly for public-expenditure cuts, alleged economic mismanagement and the fall in value of stocks and shares. Foreigners, especially Americans, were also blamed, for the pre-October 1929 speculative frenzy, for the insistence on the payment of French war debts and for the imposition of tariffs and import restrictions.

Against the background of the Great Depression, the Croix de Feu acquired a new leader in Colonel François de La Rocque. A member of a minor aristocratic family, the de La Rocques de Sévérac, and the son of a Catholic and royalist general, La Rocque graduated from the Cavalry Academy at Saumur in 1908 and served as a cavalry officer in Algeria and Morocco. In January 1917 he joined an infantry regiment on the Western Front, and so distinguished himself that he received six citations for bravery, the Croix de Guerre with palms, and officer-rank in the Legion of Honour. He subsequently served with the French military mission that assisted the Poles against the Red Army and later in Morocco against the Abd el-Krim rebellion. Suffering from war wounds, discouraged by slow promotion and low pay, and reliant on Lyautey and Weygand as patrons rather than the increasingly powerful Pétain, La Rocque resigned from the army in August 1928 at the age of forty-one with the rank of lieutenant-colonel. Having joined the Croix de Feu in May 1929, he became a member of its executive committee in December 1929, its Vice-President in March 1930 and its President in February 1932.

La Rocque's assumption of the leadership, and the intensifying economic and social crisis in France, led to the Croix de Feu being transformed from a pressure group of decorated army veterans, which lobbied the government on matters relating to the armed forces, to a mass populist movement, which sought to force through fundamental changes in France. La Rocque and the Croix de Feu tended to blame France's problems on conspiracies – of corrupt politicians and political parties, of speculators and fraudsters, of Marxists and Freemasons united in an unholy alliance, of international capitalism based in London and New York. France needed a national renewal in which public morality would be restored by extending the military values of discipline and obedience throughout French society so that hedonism, materialism and decadence could be overcome. Specific demands were made for a strengthening of the powers of the President at the expense of parliament, a reform of the parliamentary system, including the introduction of proportional representation and a reduction in the number of deputies, an emasculation of the Left, particularly the Communists and the trade unions, so that they could not stir up conflict and disorder, and the promotion of economic nationalism through protectionist policies. The economic programme published in *Le Flambeau* was typically ambiguous. On the one hand, state taxes and the state's economic interventionist role should be reduced; on the other hand, the state should defend the French economy against unfair foreign competition, wage a relentless war against speculation, excessive profits and stock market and fiscal fraud, and protect the interests of French workers and the savings and property of French citizens.

French historians have portrayed La Rocque as basically a conservative and patriotic professional army officer (Nobécourt, 1996) and the Croix de Feu as an authoritarian movement in the French Bonapartist tradition (Rémond, 1966 and 1982), or at least as a movement that was not fundamentally fascist (Burrin, 1986, and Milza, 1987), while North American historians on the contrary have argued that the Croix de Feu was essentially fascist, sharing many characteristics with fascist movements elsewhere in Europe in the 1930s (Irvine, 1991, and Soucy, 1991 and 1995). La Rocque himself came from a traditional élite background (unlike Hitler or Mussolini), and he did not attempt to develop a fascist ideology (again unlike Hitler or Mussolini). Indeed, he professed loyalty to the Republic and acceptance of parliamentary democracy, and as a leader he was in the last resort cautious and law abiding rather than ruthless and charismatic. Nor was the Croix de Feu or its successor, the Parti Social Français or PSF, particularly anti-Semitic (except in Algeria) or anti-feminist. However, the Croix de Feu did become a mass movement, with an approximate membership of 30,000 in 1933 rising to possibly a million by April 1936, while the PSF may have had between 1.5 and 2 million members by September 1939 (Nobécourt, 1996, pp. 142, 375 and 386); it adopted as one of its slogans 'Work, Family, Fatherland' ('*Travail, Famille, Patrie*'), which became the motto of the Vichy regime; it went in for mass rallies and ritual annual commemorations – of the Marshals of France (22 April), Joan of Arc (13 May), the national holiday (14 July), the Battle of the Marne (22 September) and the First World War armistice (11 November); it formed paramilitary units composed of '*disponibles*' or '*dispos*', who disrupted political meetings and engaged in street violence, with Communists as the main targets; it recruited predominantly from among the middle classes; and it embraced populism, mass mobilization, a cult of violence, extreme nationalism and a hostility to parliamentary politics, liberalism and the Left. In all these respects, the Croix de Feu was characteristically fascist.

Perhaps the fairest conclusion is that the Croix de Feu 'operated on the boundary of the Fascist and non-Fascist (perhaps Bonapartist) radical Right, sometimes crossing to one side or the other' (Passmore, 'The Croix de Feu', 1995, p. 92). As for La Rocque, it is revealing that during the Vichy regime he accepted the authority of Pétain and supplied information to British Military Intelligence, so that he ended up being imprisoned by both the Nazis and the post-Liberation French government.

Document 7.6 The Stavisky Riots (6 February 1934)

The Republican Association of Army Veterans announces that it will participate in the demonstration planned by the National Union of Ex-Servicemen, but for its own reasons.

It intends to protest with the utmost energy against the regime of profit and scandal and at the same time against the mandate of the government of M. Daladier, author of the revision of pensions.

It intends to demonstrate its intense anger against this same government which, to intensify its imperialist war policy, claimed by way of sanction to give the post of Resident General of Morocco to Chiappe, the avowed accomplice and protector of Stavisky.

It intends to demand the arrest of Chiappe, together with that of Rossignol, President of the UNC [Union Nationale des Combattants or National Union of Ex-Servicemen] and compromised in the Stavisky Affair.

We do not want the ex-servicemen to act so as to play into the hands of swindlers and their accomplices.

The ex-servicemen of the UNC will be side by side with the ex-servicemen of the ARAC [Association Républicaine des Anciens Combattants or Republican Association of Ex-Servicemen] to defend the rights that they have acquired and to insist on the arrest of all those who are corrupt and dishonest. By shouting these slogans as loudly as possible, tens of thousands of ex-servicemen will achieve once more their common front:

Down with the revision of pensions!

Down with the sacrifices demanded from the survivors of the war!

Long live the inviolability of the pension rights acquired by the ex-servicemen!

Long live the revision of the rejection of pension applications!

Chiappe-Stavisky, Rossignol-Stavisky and all their accomplices, to prison!

Long live the ARAC! Down with fascism! Down with imperialist war!

Down with the government, stealer from the war-wounded and accomplice of swindlers!

Source: L'Humanité, *6 February 1934; cited in S. Berstein*, Le 6 février 1934. *Paris: Collection Archives. 1975, pp. 148–9*

The Stavisky Affair provoked one of the most important domestic political crises in France during the 1930s. Serge Stavisky, a Jew of Ukrainian origin, had been involved in financial malpractice connected with the municipal bank of Bayonne. Allegedly a number of people with government connections were also involved in this scandal, but before the truth could be established Stavisky was found dead by the police (8 January 1934). It was widely assumed that the police, acting on government orders, had murdered Stavisky.

From 9 January right-wing groups, including Action Française, the Camelots du Roi, the Jeunesses Patriotes and Solidarité Française, organized a series of protest meetings and (usually violent) demonstrations in Paris. Confronted by this mounting right-wing street violence, as well as by a virulent anti-government press campaign and revelations of yet another scandal, the government headed by Camille Chautemps resigned (27 January). Edouard Daladier, a Radical deputy with a ministerial career going back to 1924, formed a new government on 30 January. Like Chautemps, Daladier refused to hold an official inquiry into the Stavisky Affair, while one of his first actions was to secure the removal of Jean Chiappe, the Prefect of Police, who was thus apparently made the government's scapegoat. On 3 February 1934 Chiappe was offered the post of Resident General in Morocco, but he refused and resigned, together with the Prefect of the Seine. Two cabinet ministers also resigned in sympathy. Chiappe happened to be a popular figure with the French right, so his resignation, together with the others', further raised the political temperature. Right-wing municipal councillors of Paris issued appeals with the National Union of Ex-Servicemen for a massive popular demonstration outside the Chamber of Deputies on 6 February, the day the Daladier government was due to meet parliament for the first time.

The French Communist Party was at first uncertain how to respond to this crisis. On 3 February L'Humanité carried the headline 'No Panic'; and on 5 February the paper, refusing to distinguish between 'the cholera and the plague', called on its readers to demonstrate against both the 'fascist' right-wing leagues and the corrupt Daladier government. However, the following day *L'Humanité* ordered the Communist Ex-Servicemen's Union, the Republican Association of Army Veterans, to participate in the demonstrations planned for 6 February. This was to show solidarity with the National Union of Ex-Servicemen in their opposition to the Daladier government and its handling of the Stavisky Affair and to the erosion of veterans' pensions and allowances. Yet this did mean that Communists, by following instructions, participated in what were overwhelmingly right-wing demonstrations.

The Paris demonstrations of 6 February 1934, or Stavisky riots, were represented as an attempted right-wing *coup d'état* by the official parliamentary inquiry, and by Léon Blum and others, but there is no firm evidence to support such an interpretation (Beloff, 1959). However, right-wing fascist leagues were much in evidence, the riots occurred in front of the Chamber of Deputies and the casualty rate was high. On the side of the rioters, 14 were killed, 236 were taken to hospital and a further 419 were injured, while on the side of the police, 1 was killed, 92 were taken to hospital and a further 688 were injured. Altogether, the riots constituted the most serious street violence in Paris since the Paris Commune of 1871, and they led the following day to the resignation of the Daladier government.

French Communists and socialists reacted to these events rather differently. Both the extreme Right and the extreme Left had seized on the Stavisky scandal as an excuse and as an opportunity to demonstrate their contempt for parliamentary democracy and to bring down a centre–Right coalition government by violence. Yet on 9 February 1934 the Communists organized an anti-fascist demonstration in Paris. This was banned by the government but it nevertheless took place, resulting in nine deaths and several hundred wounded. The socialists responded with their own protest, a general strike and a peaceful demonstration in Paris on 12 February. The general strike was widely observed throughout France and there were also demonstrations in many provincial towns. Unofficially, many Communists supported the general strike and the demonstrations; and one prominent French Communist, Jacques Doriot, deputy and mayor of the Paris working-class suburb of Saint Denis, openly advocated united action with the socialists in a letter published on 11 April. This amounted to a challenge to the official PCF line and the party leadership; a challenge that the Communists could not ignore.

Popular support for the French Communists had declined, the threat of Nazi Germany loomed ever greater, the Republic seemed to be in danger from right-wing violence and a new movement for a united front against fascism, the Vigilance Committees of Anti-Fascist Intellectuals, was gathering momentum throughout France in 1934. The Communists resolved the situation by dropping Doriot while simultaneously adopting his policy. On 21 April 1934 Doriot and Maurice Thorez (the leader of the French Communist Party) were summoned to Moscow. Doriot declined to go. In his absence the Comintern confirmed Thorez as leader of the French Communist Party while at the same time a policy of support for a Popular Front against fascism was accepted. A French Communist Party conference in June duly expelled Doriot and endorsed the united front strategy. Negotiations between the Communists and the SFIO then ensued, culminating in an agreement signed on

27 July 1934. The two parties agreed to mobilize the working-class population against fascist organizations, to defend democratic liberties, and to oppose war preparations and the fascist terror in Germany and Austria (the Austrian Chancellor was murdered in an attempted Nazi *coup* in Vienna in July 1934). Each party also agreed to co-operate in joint action and not to attack the other, but each retained its autonomy. Thus the Stavisky riots had the paradoxical consequence of contributing to the formation of the broad-left alliance known as the Popular Front.

Document 7.7 The Formation of the Popular Front

We have worked for unity between urban and rural workers, between manual workers and intellectuals. We are happy to have campaigned for the idea of the Popular Front of work, liberty and peace, and to have loyally collaborated for a common programme with radicals, republicans and democrats. We have worked for the unity of the youth of France.

And now we are working for the unity of the French nation against the two hundred families and their mercenaries. We are working for a genuine reconciliation of the French people.

We hold out our hand to you, Catholic, worker, employee, artisan, peasant, we who are secular, because you are our brother, and because like us you are overwhelmed by the same anxieties.

We hold out our hand to you, national volunteer, ex-serviceman and member of the Croix de Feu, because you are a son of our people, because you suffer like us from the disorder and corruption, because you, like us, want to prevent the country from slipping into ruin and catastrophe.

We are the great Communist Party, composed of poor and dedicated militants, whose names have never been mixed up in any scandal and who cannot be tainted by any corruption. We are the supporters of the purest and noblest ideal that men can embrace.

We Communists, who have reconciled the Tricolour of our fathers with the Red Flag of our hopes, we appeal to you all, workers, peasants and intellectuals, young and old, men and women, all of you, people of France, to struggle with us and to declare on 26 April:

For prosperity, against misery.

For freedom, against slavery.

For peace, against war.

We appeal to you with confidence to vote Communist.

To vote for a strong, free and happy France, which is what the Communists want and which is what the Communists will achieve!

Source: Radio broadcast by Maurice Thorez, 17 April 1936; L. Bodin and J. Touchard, Front Populaire, 1936. *Paris: Colin.* 1961, pp. 52–3

The agreement reached between the French Communist Party and the SFIO on 27 July 1934 was first put to the test in the cantonal elections of October 1934. In

French elections only candidates who gained an overall majority were elected on the first ballot, so there was frequently a second ballot in which the candidate with the most votes was elected. The Communists and socialists arranged that in the event of a second ballot, whichever of their candidates had won the most votes in the first ballot would not be opposed by a candidate of the other party in the second ballot. This strategy worked well for both parties, with the Radical Party consequently suffering some losses. The co-operation continued into 1935. On 10 February that year about 100,000 people responded to a joint appeal by the two parties to attend a public commemoration of the victims of the 1934 riots in the Place de la République in Paris. The next local elections, for municipal councils, occurred on 5 and 12 May 1935, with the electoral pact still operating, resulting once more in gains for both parties and losses for Radicals.

The Radical Party had been suffering from a lack of effective leadership and a decline in electoral support since February 1934. Radicals opposed the violence associated with the right-wing leagues but at the same time opposed the Communists on a range of issues, including economic policy, France's colonial empire and French defence expenditure. However, Stalin, increasingly concerned about the threat to the Soviet Union posed by Nazi Germany (particularly after Hitler had restored military conscription and repudiated the disarmament clauses of the Treaty of Versailles on 16 March 1935), signed a Franco-Soviet pact on 2 May 1935 and subsequently publicly endorsed French rearmament. This prompted another U-turn by the French Communist Party, which obediently now withdrew its opposition to France's armed forces. This made it easier for the Radicals to join the Popular Front. They participated with the Communists and the socialists in spectacularly enthusiastic celebrations of France's national holiday on 14 July 1935. The following October a Radical Party conference endorsed the party's adhesion to the Popular Front.

Meanwhile, the conservative coalition government headed by Pierre Laval had earned much unpopularity with its deflationary economic policies and its abortive attempts to appease Mussolini over his invasion of Ethiopia; and the right-wing leagues disgraced themselves by an unprovoked physical assault on the SFIO leader, Léon Blum (13 February 1936). This prompted another huge demonstration in Paris in which hundreds of thousands marched from the Pantheon to the Place de la Bastille on 16 February. The Laval government was further weakened by the resignation of four Radical ministers, and Laval himself resigned on 22 February. A new government was formed under Albert Sarraut, but it lacked adequate parliamentary support and failed to respond effectively to Hitler's military occupation of the Rhineland (7 March 1936) in defiance of the Treaty of Versailles. A general parliamentary election was therefore held, with the first ballot on 26 April and the second on 3 May.

Maurice Thorez, from 1932 Communist deputy for Ivry-sur-Seine (a working-class town south-east of Paris) and from January 1936 General Secretary of the French Communist Party, had early showed signs of opposing the political isolation of his party. In 1927 he had criticized the Communist Party's 'class against class' stategy; in 1932 he had supported the Amsterdam–Pleyel Movement (a broad-left common front against fascism); and in 1933, after Hitler had come to power in Germany, he had made overtures to the SFIO leaders. On the other hand, as a party loyalist, Thorez had publicly advocated opposition to the SFIO at this time. At the Communist Party Congress in March 1932 he spoke for four hours, attacking the socialists as the most dangerous enemy, and as late as June 1934 he still displayed hostility towards them. Nevertheless, once the Comintern had decided on a united-front policy, Thorez embraced it enthusiastically. This did not, however, represent a conversion to democratic parliamentary consensus politics. Thorez saw a Popular Front government as a preparation for the seizure of power by the proletariat; and he was determined that no Communist should become a minister in a Popular Front government.

One of the most striking features of the electoral campaign of April 1936 was the exploitation of the radio by parliamentary candidates. Whereas in the general parliamentary election of April–May 1932 only the Prime Minister had made an election radio broadcast, in 1936 many of the candidates did, including Thorez. The text of his appeal of 17 April, part of a vigorous campaign launched by the Communists, was probably influenced by his close friend and collaborator Eugen Fried, a Communist intellectual of Czech origin. Fried may have been more committed to the concept of the Popular Front than Thorez and did not share the deep suspicion with which Thorez held the SFIO and its leaders. The broadcast obviously aimed to secure electoral support and to project the French Communist Party as a moderate party seeking goals that all reasonable French people would wish. Thus, Thorez mentions such goals as unity, work, liberty, peace, prosperity and freedom, and 'a strong, free and happy France'. Similarly, the Communist Party is presented as an opponent of 'disorder and corruption', 'ruin and catastrophe', misery, slavery and war, as well as of 'the two hundred families and their mercenaries'. The two hundred families had become a popular concept in the political rhetoric of 1936. The Bank of France was still private, with two hundred principal shareholders, and it was widely alleged that these shareholders, or families, could exercise enormous influence on France's financial and economic affairs. It was a concept that had considerable appeal, particularly for those who liked to believe in conspiracies perpetrated by the wealthy privileged few against the great mass of the French population, a notion that was very much part of the ideology of 1789.

The appeal made by Thorez attempted to be as comprehensive as possible. It embraced urban and rural workers, manual workers and intellectuals, radicals, republicans and democrats, young and old, men and women (even though the young and women did not have the vote). Given that the Communists traditionally derived most of their support from urban male workers, this represented a reaching out beyond their traditional heartland. Even more remarkable were the appeals directed to Catholics and to national volunteers, ex-servicemen and members of the Croix de Feu. The French Communist Party had inherited the anti-clerical traditions of the French Left, and the fate of Christian churches in the Soviet Union had further worsened relations between Communists and Catholics. National volunteers, ex-servicemen and members of the Croix de Feu were likely to be extremely right wing, if not fascist, and violently anti-Communist. However, many of them were also likely to be working class in social origin and, Thorez suggested, were likely to share the same suffering and the same hopes as Communists. Significantly, two groups not specifically mentioned in this appeal were supporters of the SFIO (whereas radicals, republicans and democrats were) and the bourgeoisie (other than intellectuals).

Thorez also associated the French Communist Party with morality and patriotism. Numerous scandals and cases of corruption had featured in French politics in this period. Since the French Communist Party had not been in government it could make a claim for moral purity. The reference to the Tricolour and Red Flag referred to the relationship between French Communism and French patriotism. The blue, white and red Tricolour became the emblem of the French Revolution in July 1789 and was adopted as the national flag of the French Republic in 1792. Thereafter it came to be universally accepted as the national flag of France (except during the Restoration Monarchy, 1814–30). An unsuccessful attempt had been made to have the Red Flag adopted as France's national flag after the revolution of February 1848; and a red flag, adorned with a gold hammer and sickle, was also, of course, the banner of communism. Because of the French Communist Party's apparent subservience to Moscow, and because of its past opposition to the Versailles Treaty, the occupation of the Ruhr and France's colonial empire and armed forces, it was widely perceived as unpatriotic. By claiming that Communists had reconciled the Tricolour with the Red Flag, Thorez was attempting to convince his listeners that the French Communist Party was a force for unity and reconciliation and that there was no conflict of loyalties between being a patriotic Frenchman and being a Communist militant.

Document 7.8 A Divided France

As we parked the car in the garage at Crécy, M. Marteau [the garage proprietor] came out to welcome us after our long absence. We generally closed the Villa des Tilleuls from November to March, and this was our first visit in the Spring of 1936. M. Marteau's face was very grave, and Edgar asked him how business was.

'Ah things are going very badly,' he said despondently. 'The countryside is mad, but *complètement fou* [completely mad].'

'Is it affecting you personally?' I asked.

He leaned forward to whisper. 'I'll tell you what's happening. I'm in a fix. One of these fascists came to me the other day . . . said I ought to join their party . . . a man I've done business with for years, mind you. I've no time for politics, I told him, I'm no party man. Now he no longer buys petrol from me but gets it in the *Revue Nationale*. Then another chap . . . a communist, tells me I should be with them . . . ought to realize my responsibilities. As if I had time for their nonsense. But he's left me too; took his motor-bike away and hasn't been near me since. I'm losing customers all around' . . .

'It's these Fascist rallies,' he [Marteau] explained; 'they are taking place, all over the country . . . twenty thousand of them at Meaux not so long ago . . . and at Bondy – regular motorized mobilizations. You should have seen them in their camions, with out-riders and flags. No one can stop them assembling if they are invited, you see.'

We strolled through the village and I went to the butcher to get something for lunch.

' . . . and discipline,' M. Vaudel [the butcher] was saying when I entered. 'We are patriots . . . and good Frenchmen.' . . . 'What we want is a clean, renovated France' . . .

There was certainly a new spirit in Crécy . . . I hardly recognized the little village which once had been so tranquil. Everyone arguing, everyone in a bad temper.

'What's come over the place?' we asked one evening of the hotel-keeper, with whom we often stopped to chat . . . The hotel-keeper opened his chubby arms wide. 'Crécy is like *that*,' he explained after greeting us effusively, 'Crécy is split wide open . . . but in two. Oh you should hear the rows . . . ' He hopped around in his excitement and dragged us into his bureau and began searching through a mass of papers. 'It's communist or fascist here all right . . . there are so many people who are fed up with the butcher, he's the chief fascist, that we've got a new chap selling meat now . . . he doesn't air his views quite so much . . . at least, not the same views . . . ' He winked elaborately. 'And the new coiffeur? Have you seen his place? Not far from you . . . calls it the "*Salon Populaire*" . . . people just stopped patronizing the coiffeur on the Marché . . . couldn't get their hair cut without having to listen to his twaddle . . . '

'And who heads the communists?' asked Edgar, highly amused at all the village *potins* [noise makers].

'Madame . . . the brunette . . . of the *Comptoirs Français*, of course.' A fitting figure certainly, this stout dame who ran the co-operative store . . .

'Ah here it is,' said our host, waving a newspaper clipping triumphantly. 'We have royalists too in town. *Figurez vou* [Imagine] . . . three months ago, on a Sunday . . . we woke to find *Vive le Roi* [Long live the King] painted in bright red letters on the white wall of the public urinal under the clock tower . . . Think of it!' he shouted, 'in Crécy! Well, we soon discovered the culprit . . . this silly chap used a leaking paint-pot . . . we traced him to his house . . . it was still quite early . . . but there was a crowd of us there, I can tell you. His wife came down to open the door . . . swore her husband had not been out all night . . . made a fine scene, too, declared *she* ought to know if he'd left her or not . . . and such *détails* . . . *la vache* [the cow] . . . but we found his paint-pot. Well that was a scandal! He was fined two hundred francs for defacing public property . . . and made to whitewash the urinal at his own expense. And that's not all. About five weeks ago, what with the rain, for it's been a wet winter this year, those words began showing through. There they were again, *Vive le Roi* as large as life. I tell you he was made to whitewash them again and the judge said he'd have to keep on doing it every time they appeared' . . .

Yet when our village, a dot in a wider constituency, finally found itself represented by a communist deputy, even the bolder spirits were staggered.

They had not intended to stand for any of the 'Hitler stuff', but after all, were not communists dreadful creatures too?

Source: L.T. Mowrer, Journalist's Wife. *London: William Heinemann. 1938, pp. 314–17*

The Popular Front alliance of Communists, SFIO and Radicals was meant to unite the French people against the fascist threat within and outside France and behind an agreed programme to tackle the country's economic and social problems. In fact, the Popular Front was very divisive, tending to polarize French public opinion between the Right and the Left and to politicize many aspects of French life. In addition, for many French people, the ordinary business of everyday living acquired a new edge, as people began to despair of the present and to be afraid of the future. The consequences for a provincial village community are illustrated by this text, which thus provides some insight into politics at the grass-roots level.

Lillian Mowrer was the English wife of an American journalist, Edgar Mowrer, whom she had married in 1916. After the First World War the Mowrers lived in Rome for eight years and then moved to Berlin, where Edgar became President of the Foreign Press Association. Quick to appreciate the evil character of the Nazis, Edgar wrote *Germany Puts the Clock Back* (1933 and several later editions), which won the prestigious Pulitzer Prize for the 'best correspondence from abroad' during 1932. After the Nazis came to power the Mowrers were virtually expelled from Germany, so they settled in Paris, arriving in time to witness the Stavisky riots from their hotel in the rue de Rivoli. While based in Paris they were able to use as a holiday and weekend retreat the Villa des Tilleuls, a house belonging to Edgar Mowrer's brother in Crécy-en-Brie, a village of around a thousand inhabitants between the towns of Meaux and Coulommiers in the department of Seine-et-Marne. Even this village in the depths of the French countryside was not immune to the tides of fascism and communism swirling over France in 1936; but by the time the Mowrers revisited Crécy-en-Brie the following spring, the *Salon Populaire* had closed down, the new *patron* [manager] of the co-operative store had 'no time for politics', M. Vaudel the butcher 'was not nearly so talkative', and 'the village was more like its old self' (Mowrer, 1938, p. 339).

Document 7.9 The Programme of the Popular Front

Gentlemen,
The government presents itself before you in the aftermath of a general election in which the verdict of manhood suffrage, the judge and master of us all, has been expressed with more clarity and authority than at any previous moment in the history of the Republic.

The French people have demonstrated their unshakeable determination to defend, against all attempts at subversion by violence or subterfuge, the democratic freedoms that they have achieved and which remain their property.

The French people have affirmed their resolution to seek in new ways the remedies for the crisis that overwhelms them, the means of relieving the agony and suffering which through their duration become ever more cruel, and the means of returning to an active, healthy and confident life.

Finally, the French people have proclaimed their desire for peace which completely animates them.

The task of the government that presents itself before you is therefore defined from the first moment of its existence.

The government does not have to find its majority or to rally a majority to it. It already has its majority. Its majority is the majority that the country wanted. It is the expression of that majority massed under the banner of the Popular Front. It possesses in advance the trust of that majority, and the only problem that confronts it will be to deserve and to retain that trust.

The government does not have to draw up a programme. Its programme is the common programme agreed to by all the parties that comprise the majority, and the only problem confronting the government will be to implement this programme.

The implementation of this programme will be rapid, because it is through the cumulative effect of its programme that the government expects to achieve the moral and material transformation demanded by the country.

From the beginning of next week, we will submit to the Chamber a collection of parliamentary bills that we ask the two chambers to pass before the end of the parliamentary session.

These parliamentary bills will be concerned with:

- The amnesty,
- The forty-hour week,
- Collective employment contracts,
- Paid holidays,
- A programme of major public works related to economic development and the infrastructure for health, science, sport and tourism,
- The nationalization of the arms industry,
- The Wheat Office, which will serve as a model for the promotion of other agricultural products such as wine, meat and milk,
- The raising of the school leaving age,
- A reform of the statutes of the Bank of France, guaranteeing that national interests will be paramount in its operations,
- A first revision of decrees – laws to benefit those public-sector workers and ex-servicemen who have been the most severely affected [by government expenditure cuts].

Source: Speech by Léon Blum to the Chamber of Deputies, 6 June 1936;
L. *Blum*, L'Exercice du pouvoir: discours prononcés de mai 1936 à janvier 1937. *Paris: Gallimard. 1937, pp. 66–8*

In the general parliamentary elections of 26 April and 3 May 1936 the SFIO won 149 seats in the Chamber of Deputies with 1,955,000 votes, the Radicals 109 seats with 1,423,000 votes, and the Communists 72 seats with 1,502,000 votes, giving a combined total of 330 seats. Since the centre–Right opposition coalition won only 222 seats, the Popular Front had a majority of 108 seats in the Chamber of Deputies. As Blum boasted in his address to the Chamber of Deputies on 6 June, this represented a massive electoral endorsement of the programme of the Popular Front and gave the Popular Front government an unprecedentedly large majority in the Chamber of Deputies.

However, Blum's position was not quite so strong as he suggested. A conservative majority remained in the upper house of the French parliament, the Senate. The Communists refused to allow any member of their party to serve as a minister in the Popular Front government, which meant that they could evade responsibility for government policies. Also, the Popular Front alliance had affected the electoral fortunes of the participating parties differently. In the previous general parliamentary elections of 1 and 8 May 1932, the Radicals had won 157 seats with 1,837,000 votes, the SFIO 129 seats with 1,964,000 votes, and the Communists 12 seats with 785,000 votes. In other words, comparing the results of the general parliamentary elections of 1936 with those of 1932, the SFIO vote had declined slightly, but paradoxically the SFIO had won 20 more seats, the Radicals had lost approximately 400,000 votes and 48 seats, while the Communists had won approximately 717,000 more votes and 60 more seats. This encouraged the Radicals to feel disenchanted with the Popular Front alliance, while many non-Communists reacted with concern, if not fear, to the dramatic improvement in the situation of the Communist Party. Moreover, the Popular Front did not come to power in favourable circumstances. Hitler had sent his troops into the Rhineland on 7 March 1936, a unilateral violation of the Treaty of Versailles to which France had made no effective military or diplomatic response; and in France the Popular Front electoral victory had helped to trigger a massive strike wave, which the outgoing Sarraut government failed to check and which therefore became the most pressing concern of the Blum government after its installation on 5 June 1936.

The implementation of the programme of the Popular Front was initially dominated by the settlement of the strikes. By June 1936 nearly 2 million French workers were on strike and 8,441 factories had been occupied, so that much of French manufacturing industry, especially where trade union membership was high, had become paralysed. While striking workers often created a carnival-style atmosphere in their occupied factories, and the Right fulminated against the infringement of property rights and denounced a Communist conspiracy, France's trade balance suffered, the international value of the franc fell, and private capital was moved out of the country. Blum managed to persuade representatives of the employers and the unions to meet and, after two days of intense negotiations at the official residence of the Prime Minister, the Hôtel Matignon, the so-called Matignon Agreements were signed on 7 June. These granted an amnesty to all strikers and introduced wage increases and the recognition of trade union rights, including collective bargaining. On 12 June the Blum government also introduced the right of all employees to enjoy two weeks' paid annual holiday and a maximum working week of forty hours. These measures strengthened the trade unions, increased the purchasing power of many workers (the wage settlements were often quite generous – the officially agreed maximum being 12.5 per cent), and enabled workers, in many cases for the first time in their working lives, to enjoy leisure and at least one proper holiday each year. On the other hand, the return to work was slow, France continued to suffer from a relatively high incidence of strikes, and the wage increases, paid annual holidays and a shorter working week all had to be paid for, particularly as there was no corresponding increase in productivity. By May 1938 cost-of-living increases equalled or even exceeded increases in wages, pensions and benefits. Nevertheless, the Popular Front programme did improve the lives of most workers, which arguably justified the price paid in terms of inconvenience (small shops and businesses closing down completely for two weeks during the summer), reduced profits, and the presence of holidaying workers and their families in what had previously been the exclusive resorts of the bourgeoisie.

Other aspects of the programme of the Popular Front were also rapidly introduced. On 18 June the right-wing leagues, which had been responsible for a significant amount of violence, were suppressed, though the Croix de Feu transformed itself into a political party, the Parti Socialiste de France. On 2 July the school-leaving age was extended to fourteen. On 24 July the Bank of France was reformed. An annual general meeting open to all shareholders replaced the previous annual general meetings restricted to the two hundred principal shareholders, and a board of twenty experts nominated by the National Economic Council and the government replaced the fifteen-member council of regents appointed by the old general meeting. The Bank of France nevertheless remained private – the Senate would have blocked any nationalization measure. On 11 August a law gave the government sweeping powers over the French arms industry. Eventually about a dozen factories were nationalized, principally in the aircraft industry, and other arms manufacturing plants and companies were brought under government control. On 15 August the National Wheat Office was established, against opposition from the Senate and agrarian interests. The National Wheat Office was given a monopoly of wheat imports and exports, was responsible for marketing wheat, and fixed the annual price. The experiment worked reasonably well, with the price of wheat being increased and encouragement being given to the creation of agricultural co-operatves, but the 'wheat barons' secured a curtailment of the powers of the National Wheat Office in 1939. Other measures improved the pay, pensions, allowances and tax obligations of public-sector workers and ex-servicemen; there was quite an ambitious public-works programme; and a new government department of Leisure and Sports promoted the construction of youth hostels and special holiday tickets on the railways.

The Popular Front programme and its rapid implementation were undoubtedly impressive, and the introduction of paid annual holidays has had a permanent and beneficial impact on French life. However, the social gains were achieved at some economic and financial cost. French production declined, the balance of trade deteriorated, the government deficit increased, inflation rose, capital continued to leave the country, and the unemployment figures did not improve significantly. The Blum government has been criticized for its failure to introduce exchange controls and for its delayed devaluation of the franc (27 September 1936), but it would have been very difficult to have successfully pursued policies that both created wealth and satisfied left-wing demands for social and economic reform, particularly at a time when France had not yet emerged from the Great Depression and when the international situation was so bleak.

Document 7.10 The Spanish Civil War: the French Communist Party

SOLIDARITY WITH SPAIN FOR THE SECURITY OF FRANCE

After the Nazi act of aggression of 7 March [the German occupation of the demilitarized Rhineland zone], directly threatening our eastern frontier, Hitler now pursues his warlike provocations on our frontier along the Pyrenees and in Morocco.

Methodically pursuing his plan to isolate and encircle France, the torturer of the German people has stirred up seditious rebellion that soaks Spain with blood.

For months and months, Nazi spies have made Spain and Morocco their sphere of activity, *giving orders and material assistance to the enemies of the [Spanish] Republic* and assuring them of the full support of Hitlerian Germany.

Thus Hitler aims not only to strangle freedom in Spain, but, pursuing the policies of William II in the Iberian peninsula and in Morocco, it is France that he wants to weaken.

Throughout Spain it is France that is targeted.

The government of the Spanish Republic, born of the popular will constitutionally expressed in the elections of last February, is being attacked by rebels, by some traitorous generals who do not hesitate to become the instruments of the policies of foreign powers.

These men, defeated in constitutional elections, having lost the confidence of the Spanish people, have unleashed civil war. With money from Berlin, they have armed mercenaries that they use against the Spanish people before they launch them against French Morocco.

Hitler and Mussolini have given vast sums of money to the Spanish rebels.

That is why these miserable rebels can still hold out, despite being opposed by all the Spanish people, *this magnificent people who struggle for their freedom, this people who are conscious of being the rampart of freedom and of peace, this people whose heroism and noble struggle all good Frenchmen can only salute.*

There is evidence that, besides giving the rebels money, Hitler is intervening directly in Spain. German aircraft have been supplied to the rebels, as have a certain number of Italian aircraft, *three of which have crashed in French territory in Morocco.* Mussolini, in supporting the rebels along with Hitler, reveals his objective of securing control of the Balearic Islands to assure for himself the mastery of the Mediterranean in opposition to both Britain and France.

Such a policy of intervention must concern all French people who are worried about the security of their own country, because if Hitler's men triumph in Spain, France will not only be threatened on the Rhine, but in the south and in the Mediterranean.

Source: L'Humanité, *3 August 1936*

On 17 July 1936 rebel soldiers seized control by force of towns in Spanish Morocco and on 18 July a military revolt broke out in mainland Spain. The rebellion was directed against a broad-left Popular Front government that had come to power through winning a general parliamentary election in the Spanish Republic on 16 February 1936. By the end of July the rebels had gained control of the whole of Spanish Morocco, and on the Spanish mainland of a broad swathe of territory from Algeciras and Cadiz to north of Seville, as well as all of north-western Spain, with the exception of the Basque Country.

General Franco, who on 28 September 1936 was to be chosen supreme military commander and head of state in what became known as Nationalist Spain, sent an emissary to Mussolini as early as 19 July with a request for twelve bombers and three fighter aircraft. On 22 July Franco also requested assistance from Germany in the form of ten transport aircraft. Besides being generally short of aircraft, the rebels needed transport aircraft to ferry troops from Spanish Morocco to mainland Spain, since most of the Spanish navy had remained loyal to the Popular Front government. On 25 July Mussolini decided to send twelve bombers to Spanish Morocco over the next few days, and on 26 July Hitler independently also agreed to help the rebels. Thirty Junkers-52 transport aircraft were immediately sent to Morocco, followed at the end of the month by six Heinkel fighters, to form what became known as the Condor Legion. Mussolini had long entertained grandiose ambitions for turning the Mediterranean into an 'Italian lake' and for recapturing the glories of the Roman Empire; he did not want to see a Communist state established in Spain; emboldened by his invasion of Abyssinia, he was seeking new foreign policy triumphs and new opportunities for exposing Italian servicemen to combat experience; and his Foreign Minister, Count Ciano, enthusiastically promoted intervention on the side of the rebels, particularly as the French were rumoured to be helping the Spanish Republic. Hitler saw a civil war in Spain as providing a useful distraction and a useful testing ground for his servicemen, for German military tactics and for German military equipment. He was also, of course, violently anti-Communist, and fully appreciated the strategic importance of Spain and its value as a supplier of iron and pyrite ore and other raw materials. The assistance provided by Mussolini and Hitler soon became public knowledge, particularly as on 30 July two Italian bombers *en route* from Sardinia to Morocco were forced to make a crash landing at Berkane in French Morocco, while a third Italian bomber crashed at Zaida in Algeria. The news of these incidents had reached the Paris press by 1 August.

The Comintern also reacted surprisingly promptly to the outbreak of the Spanish Civil War. On 26 July the Comintern decided to open a fund, to which Communist comrades in the Soviet Union and throughout the world could contribute, so as to give financial support to the Popular Front government in Spain. Maurice Thorez, the leader of the French Communist Party, was one of the chief directors of this fund. At the same time, French Communists on behalf of the Spanish Popular Front launched a massive propaganda campaign and an equally massive campaign to raise humanitarian aid. The latter was co-ordinated by the International Aid Committee for the Spanish People (Comité International de l'Aide au Peuple Espagnol), formed on 31 July.

The article on the Spanish Civil War in the official French Communist Party newspaper, *L'Humanité*, of 3 August 1936 is an early example of French Communist propaganda in support of the Spanish Republic. The article is trying to persuade French readers why they should identify with, and support, the Spanish Republic. Hence the stress on the threat to French national security posed by the assistance given to the rebels by Hitler and Mussolini. The Spanish Balearic Islands (principally Ibiza, Majorca and Minorca), off the eastern coast of Spain, were of particular concern to the French, since in 1926 Mussolini had negotiated a treaty with the Spanish dictator Primo de Rivera, whereby Italy was promised a military base in the Balearic Islands in the event of a war with France. Such a base would have threatened France's Mediterranean coast and her communications with French North Africa. The constitutional and democratic credentials of the Spanish Popular Front government are also stressed, as are the nobility and heroism of Spanish Republicans. Interestingly, the Spanish Communist Party and the Spanish proletariat are not specifically mentioned, presumably so as to appeal as widely as possible for French unity in support of the Spanish Republic. Nor at this point was there any suggestion of Communist military assistance or of Soviet military intervention.

Document 7.11 The Spanish Civil War: Léon Blum

I confirm what the Minister of Foreign Affairs has stated, there is for us in Spain only one legal government, or rather, only one government. The principles of what might be described as democratic law coincide in this instance with the undisputed rules of international law.

I acknowledge that the interests of France involve, and call for, the presence on Spanish soil of a government independent of other European influences. I admit without hesitation that the establishment in Spain of a military dictatorship bound by too exclusive ties of gratitude towards Germany and Italy would not only represent a blow to the international cause of democracy, but a concern – I do not want to say more – for French security and, consequently, a threat to peace . . .

I add – and I hope that nobody in the Chamber will do me the injury of being surprised – that I do not intend for a moment to repudiate the personal friendships that link me with Spanish Socialists and with many Spanish

Republicans and continue to attach me to them, despite the bitter deception that they feel and that they today express with regard to me.

I know all that. I know all that . . .

If really, in the name of international freedom, in the name of French security, we must at all costs prevent the victorious establishment of the rebellion on Spanish soil, then I declare that the conclusion of M. Gabriel Péri and of M. Thorez is not sufficient.

It is not sufficient to denounce the non-intervention agreement. It is not sufficient to re-establish the freedom of trade in military equipment between Spain and France.

Free trade in military equipment between Spain and France, this would not then be sufficient help, far from it.

No! To assure the success of Republican legality in Spain, it would be necessary to go much further, much further . . .

And yet, this is not proposed. And M. Maurice Thorez in this Chamber, just now, energetically denied proposing it.

Why? Precisely because, gentlemen, the dangers and risks that such a policy would involve are well understood, because it would add one more risk and one more danger to those that already weigh so heavily against the cause of peace. And conversely, the policy of non-intervention, despite the strains, despite the surprises, the disappointments, the divisions which it can cause, has at least diminished these risks and reduced these dangers.

Source: Léon Blum in the Chamber of Deputies, 5 December 1936; L. Blum, L'Exercice du pouvoir: discours prononcés de mai 1936 à janvier 1937. Paris: Gallimard. 1937, pp. 190–3

The outbreak of the Spanish Civil War created a very difficult situation for Léon Blum, the leader of the SFIO and head of the Popular Front government. The Prime Minister of the Spanish Republic sent a telegram to Blum during the evening of 19 July 1936, asking for immediate assistance in the form of arms and aircraft. The following day Blum held a meeting with Yvon Delbos, Minister for Foreign Affairs, and Edouard Daladier, Minister for War. They all agreed to help Republican Spain, even though both Delbos and Daladier were Radicals and therefore less likely to feel a bond of ideological sympathy with the Spanish Popular Front, which was more left wing than its French counterpart. Thus Blum assented to a formal request from the Spanish ambassador in Paris that France should send twenty bombers, together with a consignment of arms and ammunition, to Republican Spain.

There were several reasons why Blum initially agreed to give military assistance to the Spanish Republic. A Franco-Spanish treaty of 1935 already provided for the purchase of 20 million francs' worth of military equipment by Spain from France; and a law of 11 August 1936 was to bring the French arms industry under the ownership or control of the French government, making it easier for Blum to send arms to Spain. As a broad-left Popular Front coalition, the Spanish Republican government had an obvious ideological affinity with the French Popular Front, and, as Blum pointed out in his parliamentary speech, this affinity was reinforced by ties of personal friendship between him and Spanish Socialists and some Republicans (but not, significantly, any Spanish Communists). The civil war in Spain could also be presented as having parallels with the situation in France, in which right-wing leagues engaged in street violence with Communists and Socialists and there were fears of a right-wing or fascist *coup d'état*. In addition, the establishment of a fascist regime in Spain would threaten French national security, particularly if that regime were aligned with Hitler's Germany and Mussolini's Italy.

However, almost at once Blum began to change his mind. While at a pre-arranged meeting with representatives of the British government in London (23–4 July 1936), Blum learnt that the British did not welcome French military aid for Republican Spain but instead favoured non-intervention. The British wanted to avoid provoking a general European war: the catastrophic cost of the First World War for Britain was still very much a live issue; a relatively weak British economy and a rearmament programme that had scarcely begun offered inadequate security to a far-flung empire threatened by too many potential enemies (Germany, Italy, Japan and the Soviet Union); Britain had to protect significant investments in, and commercial relations with, Spain, as well as the fortress-colony of Gibraltar; and, while the Spanish Republic aroused much passionate support among intellectuals and the Left, conservatives, the official and business classes and Roman Catholics were generally hostile through their fears of revolutionary radicalism, Communism and violent anti-clericalism. When Blum returned from London he discovered that Nationalist sympathizers in the Spanish Embassy in Paris were leaking to right-wing Paris newspapers details of the French secret arms sales to the Spanish Republic. The media sensation this caused led Daladier and Delbos to withdraw their approval for arms sales to Spain and alarmed many prominent Radicals, including President Albert Lebrun and Edouard Herriot (President of the Chamber of Deputies). The Blum government proceeded to deny publicly the arms sales, while Pierre Cot (Air Minister) hastened the delivery of aircraft to Republican Spain and the adoption of an official policy of non-intervention began to be considered. On 31 July Britain declared its neutrality over the Spanish Civil War and imposed an arms embargo on both sides. Since Britain was France's only significant ally, Blum felt obliged to follow suit and on 8 August issued a similar unilateral arms embargo. The British and French governments then persuaded the Soviet Union (23 August), Germany (24 August) and Italy (28 August) to adhere to a Non-Intervention Agreement, which was supposedly implemented by a Non-Intervention Committee, meeting in London from 6 September.

As early as 6 August Maurice Thorez publicly condemned the proposed international arms embargo on Spain, a line adopted not just by the French Communist Party but by much of the French Left, including the main trade union organization, the Confédération Générale du Travail (21 August). During 1934 and 1935 Stalin, to contain the Nazi and other fascist threats to Communist Parties and the Soviet Union, had adopted a policy of supporting the League of Nations, collective security and broad-left coalitions to keep fascists out of power. Hence in August 1936 he sanctioned Soviet financial aid to the Spanish Republic and in September the direct delivery of significant quantities of military equipment, including tanks and aircraft, in return for the gold reserves of the Bank of Spain. The Communists also helped to recruit thousands of volunteers, mainly from Europe and North America, to join the International Brigade to fight for the Spanish Republic; and in France the French Communist Party campaigned for arms and assistance for Republican Spain and against the arms embargo and the policy of non-intervention. At the same time, the Germans increased their military commitment to the Nationalists to approximately 5,000, while the Italians from 27 August occupied Majorca (though Minorca remained in Republican hands) and began to make an even more substantial commitment of troops. Responding to accusations from Gabriel Péri (militant Communist deputy for Seine-et-Oise) and Maurice Thorez that non-intervention and the arms embargo represented a betrayal of the proletariat and a capitulation to fascism, and to the refusal of all Communist deputies to support the Blum government by abstaining in a parliamentary vote on foreign policy on 4 December 1936, Blum in his parliamentary speech of 5 December maintained that only French military intervention in Spain could guarantee a victory for the Republic, but that any such intervention would risk a general European war. Given France's military and diplomatic situation, and the division within France between a Left generally passionately pro-Republican and, as in Britain, Conservatives (as well as many Radicals and even some Socialists), the official and business classes and Roman Catholics who tended to be at least non-interventionist, non-intervention was almost certainly the only feasible policy for France (though a considerable amount of unofficial French aid for Republican Spain continued). It was, however, an unheroic and hypocritical policy, which even Blum could not defend with much conviction, which soured France's relations with Italy, which split the SFIO, and which alienated the PCF, the leadership of the CGT and much of French intellectual left-wing opinion.

Document 7.12 The Parti Populaire Français

The Parti Populaire Français is the only political formation which, in complete conformity with its ideology and its objectives, has, within a few days, placed two wreaths, one at the foot of the statue of Joan of Arc and the other at the 'mur des Fédérés'.

This did not represent either a complicated tactical move or a publicity stunt, but simply a faithful expression of the fundamental principle of Jacques Doriot and of the PPF: the uniting of the social and the national . . .

Joan of Arc is not only the country's saint and heroine; she is a symbol.

The symbol of the France of the early fifteenth century, essentially provincial and peasant, but already preoccupied with a secret and tenacious desire for unity.

Our ancestors, the artisans and peasants of those days, proud of the rights that they had acquired with much difficulty, solid on their feet and with their feet firmly planted in their native soil, could not tolerate the foreign invasion and its collaborators, the enemies within.

Whether one was a bishop, a lord, a bourgeois or a simple man-at-arms, if you served the English you were completely driven out.

The love of their native soil, of their freedom and of their country combined into the same condemnation of the foreigner and his collaborators.

The national rising of that time coincided with a peasant revolt and the consciousness that the village community had collective social interests, together with a growing consciousness of the French identity.

Four centuries later the Commune in many respects provides, in a different context and among new social classes, evidence of similar sentiments. The Paris National Guard – in other words the textile workers, the artisans and the shopkeepers – rejected the defeatists of Versailles who had submitted to the Prussians.

A great dream of liberation and of renewal was then closely associated with this popular explosion and the concept of a federation of French communes and of a social Republic, allied with the intense Parisian anger directed against defeatist rural notables. Thus Joan of Arc and the Commune are two stages in our national history, which we should understand and reconcile, not oppose.

Source: Paul Marion in L'Emancipation nationale, *5 June 1937; J. Plumyène and R. Lasierra,* Les Fascismes français, 1923–1963. *Paris: Seuil. 1963, pp. 127–8; and P. Milza (ed.),* Sources de la France du XIXe siècle. *Paris: Larousse. 1997, pp. 75–6*

On 11 February 1934 Jacques Doriot proposed the formation of an anti-fascist vigilance committee to a meeting in his constituency, the working-class Paris suburb of Saint Denis. The meeting included representatives of all the political organizations in Saint Denis involved in the anti-fascist protests, demonstrations and strikes of 9 and 12 February 1934, following the Stavisky riots. An anti-fascist vigilance committee was duly formed in Saint Denis, headed by eight Communists and five socialists, at a time when Communists still officially regarded socialists as 'social fascists'. For this independent initiative and premature attempt to form a broad-left anti-fascist front, Doriot was condemned by his party and summoned to Moscow. He declined to go and was eventually expelled from the PCF on 27 June 1934, on the grounds that he had attempted to split the party. Doriot decided to remain in politics, initially as head of a political group called the Unité Ouvrière. He resigned as mayor of Saint Denis and on 6 May 1934 was re-elected, unopposed by a Communist candidate. However, the formation of the Popular Front coincided with a surge in popularity for the PCF, and in the general parliamentary elections of 26 April and 3 May 1936 Doriot was re-elected, though only on the second ballot and with a narrow majority over the PCF candidate, Fernand Grenier (11,585 votes to 10,887). Moreover, in the second ballot the SFIO, in accordance with the national agreement, backed Grenier, and Doriot was able to win only with centrist and conservative support. During the electoral campaign Doriot even appealed to the Croix de Feu for help in his re-election.

Shortly after the 1936 elections, Doriot was encouraged by Gabriel Leroy-Ladurie, director of the Banque Worms, to form a new political party. With financial backing from Leroy-Ladurie and his friends, and together with a small group including Victor Arrighi, Henri Barbé and Paul Marion, Doriot proceeded on 28 June 1936 to found his own political party, the Parti Populaire Français or PPF, and to transform a local newspaper, *L'Emancipation de Saint-Denis*, into his own weekly newspaper, *L'Emancipation nationale*. Like Doriot, Arrighi, Barbé and Marion were all ex-Communists, yet they created a party that was 'authentically fascist' (Plumyène and Lasierra, 1963, p. 124), with its leader (*chef*), flag, salute, anthem, loyalty oath and mass meetings.

The founders of the PPF claimed that they were united in refusing to accept a 'decadent' France, characterized by a low birth rate, an enfeebled economy, a neglected colonial empire, a Marxist-dominated working class, a poor national standard in sport, an invasion of foreign immigrants, an inadequate protection of the institution of the family, and a decadent national culture (for instance, they accused the French film industry of producing stupid films). They were also united both in their opposition to communism, the Soviet Union and the Franco-Soviet Mutual Assistance Pact of 2 May 1935, and in their determination to reconstruct France (*refaire la France*) so as to create a new political, economic, social and spiritual order. Specific proposals included: the creation of a customs union for France and her colonial empire to protect French agriculture and French industry from foreign competition; restrictions on the investment of French capital abroad and the promotion of French domestic investment to stimulate the economy; compulsory retirement for all at the age of sixty to help reduce unemployment; the encouragement of small and medium-sized businesses and industries so that they could compete with large-scale capitalist enterprises; the reform of inheritance laws to enable family farms to survive; the provision of welfare, sporting and cultural services and facilities in rural villages as well as in urban areas; the improvement of state allowances and benefits to help mothers, particularly single mothers bringing up large numbers of children; the offering of low-interest loans to young married couples to encourage young people to marry and start families; the reform of the constitution to strengthen the executive, weaken parliament and provide for referenda; and the realignment of France's diplomatic relations by ending the Franco-Soviet Pact, improving relations with Italy and Germany, and formally recognizing the Nationalist regime in Spain. This programme combined a left-wing suspicion of large-scale capitalism and concern for the well-being of the working class with a right-wing authoritarianism, nationalism and anti-communism. Like most fascist movements, therefore, the PPF combined both the Left and the Right, but it differed from the Nazi movement in Germany and the Fascist movement in Italy. Apart from a xenophobic hostility to foreign immigrants, the PPF was not originally particularly racist, though Doriot did make a number of anti-Semitic statements; and territorial expansion through military conquest was never part of the PPF programme.

The annual ritual of the PPF included wreath-laying ceremonies at the statue of Joan of Arc in the Place des Pyramides in Paris and at the 'mur des Fédérés', a wall in the Père Lachaise Cemetery where Communards had been executed at the end of the Paris Commune of 1871. Action Française had made Joan of Arc an icon of the Right, representing the Maid of Orleans as a royalist, patriot and Catholic who personified the 'true France', while the 'mur des Fédérés' had become a traditional pilgrimage shrine for the Left. By honouring both sites and both memories the PPF was symbolically embracing both the Right and the Left, and stressing that a common nationalism and resistance to defeatism united Joan of Arc and the Communards.

The PPF attracted support from among both the proletariat, particularly the unemployed, and the middle classes, especially during the Popular Front era (1936–8), as well as from right-wing intellectuals such as Drieu La Rochelle and Bertrand de Jouvenel. PPF membership reached 130,000 on 1 March 1937 (Plumyène and Lasierra, 1963, p. 126). However, in contrast to Italy and Germany, members of the French élite did not associate with the party. Doriot himself was defeated in the election for the post of mayor of Saint Denis by the Communist Grenier in June 1937, and he shortly afterwards resigned his parliamentary seat (29 June 1937). As the 'danger' of the Popular Front receded in 1938, so the PPF lost popular support and most of its prominent members. The fall of France and the Vichy regime temporarily rescued Doriot from increasing political irrelevance: he inspired the creation of a military unit consisting of Frenchmen who volunteered to fight with the Germans against the Soviets, the Légion des Volontaires Français contre le Bolchévisme. Thus, in ironic contrast to Joan of Arc and the Communards, Doriot ended up working and fighting for a foreign invader and occupier before his death in an air attack on 22 February 1945.

CHRONOLOGY

1925

7–14 January	Paris conference on inter-Allied debts
10 April	Fall of Herriot government
17 April	Formation of Painlevé government with Briand (Foreign Affairs) and Caillaux (Finance)
11 November	Foundation by Georges Valois of the Faisceau
28 November	Formation of Briand government

1926

26 May	End of Moroccan revolt with submission of Abd el-Krim
23 July	Formation of Poincaré government

1927

12 July	Electoral law re-establishes *scrutin d'arrondissement* and introduces two-ballot elections

1928

22 and 29 April	Right-wing gains in general parliamentary elections
25 June	France returns to the gold standard

1929

31 May	Signing of Young Plan for German reparations

27 July	Resignation of Poincaré; succeeded by Briand (29 July)
25 October	Wall Street stock market crash
1 November	First issue of *Le Flambeau* (newspaper of the Croix de Feu)
3 November	Tardieu heads government with Briand at Foreign Affairs

1930

21 February	Formation of Chautemps government

1931

27 January	Formation of Laval government
13 May	Doumer elected President of the Republic
21 September	Devaluation of pound sterling

1932

14 February	La Rocque elected President of the Croix de Feu
21 February	Formation of Tardieu government
6 May	Assassination of President Doumer
1 and 8 May	Left make gains in general parliamentary elections
10 May	Lebrun elected President of the Republic
3 June	Formation of Herriot government
18 December	Formation of Paul-Boncour government

1933

28 January	Fall of Paul-Boncour government
30 January	Appointment of Hitler as German Chancellor
31 January	Formation of Daladier government
24 October	Fall of Daladier government; succeeded by Sarraut government
26 November	Formation of Chautemps government

1934

8 January	Death of Stavisky
27 January	Resignation of Chautemps government
30 January	Formation of Daladier government; succeeded by Doumergue government (9 February)
3 February	Resignation of Chiappe as Prefect of Police
6 February	Stavisky riots in Paris
7 February	Resignation of Daladier government
9 February	PCF anti-fascist demonstrations
12 February	SFIO anti-fascist strikes and demonstrations
27 June	Doriot expelled from PCF
27 July	PCF–SFIO electoral pact
9 October	Assassination of Barthou (Minister of Foreign Affairs)
8 November	Resignation of Doumergue government; succeeded by Flandin government

1935

2 May	Franco-Soviet Mutual Assistance Pact

| 5 and 12 May | Left-wing gains in municipal elections |
| 7 June | Formation of Laval government |

1936

22 January	Resignation of Laval government; succeeded by Sarraut government
13 February	Blum injured by Camelots du Roi
14 February	Dissolution of Action Française
7 March	German military reoccupation of the Rhineland
26 April and 3 May	Popular Front victory in general parliamentary elections
26 May	Beginning of factory occupations
6 June	Formation of Blum government
8 June	Matignon Agreements
18 June	Decree dissolving right-wing leagues
20 June	Law introducing two-week annual paid holidays
21 June	Law introducing forty-hour week
24 June	Law on collective agreements
28 June	Parti Populaire Français (PPF) founded by Doriot
17–18 July	Outbreak of Spanish Civil War
24 July	Reform of the Bank of France
1 August	Policy of non-intervention in Spain proposed by Blum
11 August	Compulsory school-leaving age raised from 13 to 14; law on arms industries
15 August	Establishment of National Wheat Office
27 September	Devaluation of the French franc
18 November	Suicide of Salengro (Minister of the Interior)

1937

13 February	Blum announces 'pause'
16 March	Clichy riots
24 May	Inauguration of Universal Exhibition in Paris
21 June	Resignation of Blum
22 June	Chautemps heads government, Blum Vice-President of the Council
30 June	Further devaluation of the French franc
31 August	Creation of the SNCF (state-owned French national railways)

1938

19 January	Formation of Chautemps government without SFIO
14 March	Formation of Blum's second Popular Front government
8 April	Senate rejects Blum's financial policies
9 April	Resignation of Blum, who is succeeded by Daladier (13 April)

BIBLIOGRAPHY

Allardyce, G.D., 'The Political Transition of Jacques Doriot', *Journal of Contemporary History*, 1 (1966), 56–74.

Anderson, M., 'The Myth of the Two Hundred Families', *Political Studies*, 13 (1965), 162–78.

Beloff, M., 'The Sixth of February', in J. Joll (ed.), *The Decline of the Third Republic*. London: Chatto & Windus. 1959.

Bernard, P. and Dubief, H., *The Decline of the Third Republic, 1914–1938*. Cambridge: Cambridge University Press. 1985.

Berstein, S., *Histoire du Parti Radical*, vol. 2, *Crise du radicalisme*. Paris: Presses de la Fondation Nationale des Sciences Politiques. 1982.

Bodin, L. and Touchard, J., *Front Populaire, 1936*. Paris: Colin. 1972.

Bourdé, G., *La Défaite du Front Populaire*. Paris: Editions du Seuil. 1977.

Brower, D.R., *The New Jacobins: the French Communist Party and the Popular Front*. Ithaca, NY: Cornell University Press. 1968.

Brunet, J.-P., *Jacques Doriot*. Paris: Balland. 1986.

Burrin, P., *La Dérive fasciste: Doriot, Déat, Bergery, 1933–1945*. Paris: Editions du Seuil. 1986.

—— 'Diplomatie soviétique, Internationale communiste et PCF au tournant du Front Populaire (1934–1935)', *Relations Internationales*, 45 (1986), 19–34.

Caron, V. 'The Antisemitic Revival in France in the 1930s: the socioeconomic dimension reconsidered', *Journal of Modern History*, 70 (1998), 24–73.

—— *Uneasy Asylum: France and the Jewish refugee crisis, 1933–1942*. Stanford, Calif.: Stanford University Press. 1999.

Chafer, T. and Sackur, A., *French Colonial Empire and the Popular Front: hope and disillusion*. Basingstoke: Macmillan, and New York: St Martin's Press. 1999.

Cohen, W.B., 'The Colonial Policy of the Popular Front', *French Historical Studies*, 7 (1972), 368–93.

Cross, G., *A Quest for Time: the reduction of work in Britain and France, 1840–1940*. Berkeley, Los Angeles and London: University of California Press. 1989.

Dutter, G., 'Doing Business with the Fascists: French economic relations with Italy under the Popular Front', *French History*, 4 (1990), 174–98.

—— 'Doing Business with the Nazis: French economic relations with Germany under the Popular Front', *Journal of Modern History*, 63 (1991), 296–326.

Fauvet, J., *Histoire du Parti Communiste Français*, vol. 1, *De la Guerre à la guerre, 1917–1939*. Paris: Fayard. 1964.

Greene, N., *Crisis and Decline: the French Socialist Party in the Popular Front Era*. Ithaca, NY: Cornell University Press. 1969.

Haslam, J., 'The Comintern and the Origins of the Popular Front', *Historical Journal*, 22 (1979), 673–91.

Irvine, W.D., 'French Conservatives and the "New Right" during the 1930s', *French Historical Studies*, 8 (1974), 534–62.

—— *French Conservatism in Crisis: the republican federation of France in the 1930s*. Baton Rouge: Louisiana State University Press. 1979.

—— 'Fascism in France: the strange case of the Croix de Feu', *Journal of Modern History*, 63 (1991), 271–95.

Jackson, J., *The Politics of Depression in France, 1932–1936*. Cambridge: Cambridge University Press. 1985.

—— *The Popular Front in France: defending democracy, 1934–1938*. Cambridge: Cambridge University Press. 1990.

Johnson, H.C., *Gold, France, and the Great Depression, 1919–1932*. New Haven, Conn. and London: Yale University Press. 1997.

Joll, J., 'The Making of the Popular Front', in J. Joll (ed.), *The Decline of the Third Republic*. London: Chatto & Windus. 1959.

—— 'The Front Populaire – after Thirty Years', *Journal of Contemporary History*, 1 (1966), 27–42.

Kergoat, J., *La France du Front Populaire*. Paris: La Découverte. 1986.

Lacouture, J., *Léon Blum*. New York and London: Holmes & Meier. 1982.

Larmour, P.J., *The French Radical Party in the 1930s*. Stanford, Calif.: Stanford University Press. 1964.

Lefranc, G., *Histoire du Front Populaire*. Paris: Payot. 1974.

Levey, J., 'Georges Valois and the Faisceau: the making and breaking of a fascist', *French Historical Studies*, 8 (1973), 279–304.

Milza, P., *Fascisme français: passé et présent*. Paris: Flammarion. 1987.

Mitzman, A., 'The French Working Class and the Blum Government (1936–7)', in J.C. Cairns (ed.), *Contemporary France: illusion, conflict, and regeneration*. New York and London: New Viewpoints. 1978.

Monnet, F., *Refaire la République: André Tardieu, une dérive réactionnaire, 1976–1945*. Paris: Fayard. 1993.

Mouré, K., 'Undervaluing the Franc Poincaré', *Economic History Review*, 49 (1996), 137–53.

Mowrer, L.T., *Journalist's Wife*. London: William Heinemann. 1938.

Nobécourt, J., *Le Colonel de La Rocque, 1885–1946, ou les pièges du nationalisme chrétien*. Paris: Fayard. 1996.

Ory, P., *La Belle Illusion: culture et politique sous le signe du Front Populaire, 1935–1938*. Paris: Plon. 1994.

Passmore, K., 'The French Third Republic: stalemate society or cradle of fascism?', *French History*, 7 (1993), 417–49.

—— 'The Croix de Feu: Bonapartism, national populism or fascism?', *French History*, 9 (1995), 67–92.

—— 'Business, Corporatism and the Crisis of the French Third Republic. The example of the silk industry in Lyon, 1928–1935', *Historical Journal*, 38 (1995), 959–87.

—— 'Boy Scoutism for Grown-ups? Paramilitarism in the Croix de Feu and the Parti Social Français', *French Historical Studies*, 19 (1995), 527–57.

—— *From Liberalism to Fascism: the Right in a French province, 1928–1939*. Cambridge: Cambridge University Press. 1997.

Paxton, R.O., *French Peasant Fascism: Henry Dorgères's Greenshirts and the crises of French agriculture, 1929–1939*. New York and Oxford: Oxford University Press. 1997.

—— 'The Five Stages of Fascism', *Journal of Modern History*, 70 (1998), 1–23.

Pinto, A.C., 'Fascist Ideology Revisited: Zeev Sternhell and his critics', *European History Quarterly*, 16 (1986), 465–83.

Plumyène, J. and Lasierra, R., *Les Fascismes français, 1923–1963*. Paris: Seuil. 1963.

Réau, Elizabeth du, *Edouard Daladier, 1884–1970*. Paris: Fayard. 1993.

Rémond, R., *The Right Wing in France from 1815 to de Gaulle*. Philadelphia: University of Pennsylvania Press. 1966.

—— *Les Droites en France*. Paris: Aubier-Montaigne. 1982.

Reynolds, S., 'Women and the Popular Front in France: the case of the three women ministers', *French History*, 8 (1994), 196–224.

Robrieux, P., *Maurice Thorez: vie secrète et vie publique*. Paris: Fayard. 1975.

Rossiter, A., 'Popular Front Economic Policy and the Matignon Negotiations', *Historical Journal*, 30 (1987), 663–84.

Santore, J., 'The Comintern's United Front Initiative of May 1934: French or Soviet inspiration?', *Canadian Journal of History*, 16 (1981), 405–21.

Sauvy, A., 'The Economic Crisis of the 1930s in France', *Journal of Contemporary History*, 4 (1969), 21–35.

Seidman, M., 'The Birth of the Weekend and the Revolts against Work: the workers of the Paris region during the Popular Front (1936–38)', *French Historical Studies*, 12 (1987), 249–76.

Sherwood, J.M., 'Rationalization and Railway Workers in France: Raoul Dautry and Les Chemins de Fer de l'Etat, 1928–1937', *Journal of Contemporary History*, 15 (1980), 443–74.

Soucy, R., 'The Nature of Fascism in France', *Journal of Contemporary History*, 1 (1966), 27–55.

—— *French Fascism: the first wave, 1924–1933*. New Haven, Conn., and London: Yale University Press. 1986.

—— 'French Fascism and the Croix de Feu: a dissenting interpretation', *Journal of Contemporary History*, 26 (1991), 159–88.

—— *French Fascism: the second wave, 1933–1939*. New Haven, Conn., and London: Yale University Press. 1995.

Sternhell, Z., *Neither Right nor Left: fascist ideology in France*. Princeton, NJ: Princeton University Press. 1996.

Sweets, J.F., 'Hold that Pendulum! Redefining fascism, collaborationism and resistance in France', *French Historical Studies*, 15 (1988), 731–58.

Turner, A., 'Anglo-French Financial Relations in the 1920s', *European History Quarterly*, 26 (1996), 31–55.

Wall, I.W., 'French Socialism and the Popular Front', *Journal of Contemporary History*, 5 (1970), 3–20.

—— 'The Resignation of the First Popular Front Government of Léon Blum, June 1937', *French Historical Studies*, 6 (1970), 538–54.

Weber, E., 'Nationalism, Socialism, and Nationalism-Socialism in France', *French Historical Studies*, 2 (1962), 273–307.

—— *The Hollow Years: France in the 1930s*. London: Sinclair-Stevenson. 1995.

Whitney, S.B., 'Embracing the Status Quo: French Communists, young women and the Popular Front', *Journal of Social History*, 30 (1996), 29–53.

Wohl, R., 'French Fascism, both Right and Left: reflections on the Sternhell controversy', *Journal of Modern History*, 63 (1991), 91–8.

Woolman, D.S., *Rebels in the Rif: Abd-el-Krim and the Rif rebellion*. Stanford, Calif.: Stanford University Press. 1969.

The fall of France (June 1940) | **8**

The fall of France in June 1940 has been described as 'one of the defining events in twentieth-century world politics' (Adamthwaite, 1995, p. vi). It has also been claimed that 'No event in contemporary history has caused greater shock and consternation than the fall of France in June 1940', since it was so sudden, so unexpected and so complete (Boyce, 1998, p. 1). To the distinguished French historian Marc Bloch, 'It was the most terrible collapse in all the long story of our national life' (Shirer, 1970, p. 4). A nation state, which had been one of the Great Powers of Europe for centuries and controlled one of the most extensive European colonial empires, was over-whelmed in a military campaign that lasted forty-four days (10 May–22 June 1940); and the defeat was so devastating that, according to the terms of the armistice, France accepted the neutralization of her armed forces, the loss (once again) of Alsace-Lorraine, German occupation of northern France and of a broad swathe of territory down her Atlantic coastline to the Spanish frontier, and the conversion of what remained of France into a vassal state of the Third Reich. Moreover, the fall of France in June 1940 was more than just a military defeat. To a considerable extent, national morale and confidence in the Third Republic collapsed: hence the millions of civilian refugees who joined a mass exodus in front of the advancing Germans, the unwillingness of civilians to resist in any way the German invasion, the widespread relief with which the news of the armistice was greeted, the large parliamentary majority in favour of transferring full constitutional powers to Marshal Pétain, and the initial official and popular acceptance of the Vichy regime.

Traditionally, explanations of this catastrophe for France have emphasized long-term factors and causes. A well-known exponent of this view is the contemporary observer and bestselling American historian William Shirer. He has emphasized the unfavourable origins of the Third Republic – humiliating defeat in the Franco-Prussian War, the Paris Commune of 1871, the royalist majority in the National Assembly elected in 1871 and the establishment of the Third Republic almost by default, because of the divisions among the royalists and because it was the regime that divided Frenchmen least. Thereafter the Third Republic was plagued by divisions, conflicts and scandals, by a corrupt élite, by an alienated working class, by both right-wing and left-wing political extremism, and by a rapid succession of short-lived governments. France did, indeed, emerge on the winning side at the end of the First World War, but only just, only with the help of her allies, and only at a terrible cost. Moreover, the Treaty of Versailles failed to guarantee France's national security, the Germans failed to pay the reparations they owed and the Great Depression hit France from the early 1930s. Also, from about 1925 the Third Republic allegedly went downhill – 'its strength gradually sapped by dissension and division, by an incomprehensible blindness in foreign, domestic and military policy, by the ineptness of its leaders, the corruption of its Press and by a feeling of growing confusion, hopelessness and cynicism in its people' (Shirer, 1970, pp. xiii–xiv). On every level – social, economic, political, diplomatic, military, psychological – France was not in a condition to withstand a German attack in 1940. Thus the French defeat was virtually inevitable, as was the almost complete breakdown of French society – 'a collapse of the army, of government, of the morale of the people . . . too tremendous to believe' (ibid., 1970, p. 4).

This apocalyptic vision has been challenged. The Paris Commune was arguably the product of very special circumstances, and gained little significant provincial support. The monarchist majority in the 1871 National Assembly was an aberration, as subsequent elections rapidly demonstrated, and after 1871 the overwhelming majority of the French electorate firmly turned their backs on any form of monarchical restoration. Conflicts such as those surrounding the Dreyfus Affair 'attracted only marginal interest' from the French peasantry (Burns, 1984, p. 171), still the single most numerous social group in the country, who were being turned into patriotic and republican Frenchmen by a combination of manhood suffrage, compulsory primary education and compulsory military service, improved road and rail communications, the development of a national economy, increasing seasonal and more permanent migration, the waning of the local power of traditional élites, and the breakdown of regional identities and local cultures (Weber, 1977). Scandals and corruption certainly featured prominently in the political life of the Third Republic, but probably no more so than in other parliamentary regimes, then and since. Short-lived governments were another feature, but they could amount to little more than a reshuffling of the pack of seasoned politicians, who often had long ministerial careers in a series of different administrations. France had her extremes of Right and Left, as well as working-class alienation, but these were Europe-wide phenomena, by no means unique or specially pronounced in France. All in all, France's performance in the First World War was a magnificent tribute to the endurance of French citizens and of their loyalty to the Republic. After 1918, France admittedly suffered a series of setbacks, but she remained one of Europe's Great Powers; her economy made a remarkable post-war recovery, particularly in the late 1920s; she weathered the storms of communism, fascism and the depression much more successfully than many other European states; and the Popular Front, with its introduction of workers' rights, forty-hour working week and annual paid holidays not only kept French fascism at bay, but gave French workers reasons for identifying with the French state.

The diplomatic and military situation did increasingly deteriorate for France after Hitler's appointment as German Chancellor in January 1933. However, arguably the situation for France was not completely hopeless. There were diplomatic options available to France other than those pursued, just as different military plans and strategies could have been adopted. Luck or chance played a bigger role in events than has sometimes been acknowledged, as, for example, regarding Hitler's change of invasion plans in January 1940. Even as late as May 1940 the balance of military strength between France and her allies on the one hand and Germany on the other was not as unequal as has sometimes been suggested. In other words, the fall of France in June 1940 was not so much the final and inevitable culmination of a long-term process begun in 1870, 'not one long slide to disaster' (Adamthwaite, 1995, p. viii), but more the short-term consequence of inadequate policies, inadequate leadership and inadequate decision-making.

Document 8.1 Decadence

Today, as formerly, Europe has its 'sick man'. Formerly, it was the Ottoman Empire; today, despite certain probably ephemeral appearances to the contrary, it is France.

The causes of this sickness are the same. In both cases, a disproportion between declining strength (of which population is the index for France) and an overextended territory, which by a kind of senile megalomania still tends to be increased. Above all, in both cases, a decline in the spiritual force that constituted the power of the state; religious spirit in the case of Turkey, cult of individual liberty in the case of France.

The symptoms are also the same. The discussions on international debt settlements, the tariff wars, etc., have revealed the same process of economic and financial colonization for France in 1931 as for pre-war Turkey; with this difference, that France's colonial power is the United States whereas Turkey was colonized by the nations of Europe. At the same time, the nation's sovereignty is removed bit by bit across frontiers and seas, just as historic buildings are carried off stone by stone . . .

France is respected like a classified historic monument. Since Italy has become fascist and gained another image, France remains the supreme example of the heritage country [*pays-musée*]. Having been obliged to admire the stones of the streets of Paris, the castles of the Loire, the Côte d'Azur, and the portraits of Napoleon, people go into raptures over the Paris luxury product, the French female office worker or sales assistant, the disinterested and scruffy French intellectual, the poor but honest French artisan, the French critic, and various other remarkable objects that join the spinning wheel of our grandmothers or the first motor car in the exhibition stand of bygone treasures.

Source: R. Aron and A. Dandieu, Décadence de la nation française. Paris: Editions Rieder. 1931, pp. 12–13 and 27–8

A view widely shared, particularly among French intellectuals, was that France by the 1930s had become 'decadent'. It is not immediately clear why this should have been so, since France in those years was not conspicuously scandal-prone, immoral, unstable or self-indulgent. However, the First World War had undermined confidence in the old certainties, values and authorities. During the 1920s France became the world's leading host country to immigrants, ahead of the United States, so that by 1931 foreign immigrants numbered nearly 3 million, almost 7 per cent of the national population and 9.2 per cent of the population of Paris (Weber, 1995, pp. 87–8). The almost doubling of France's immigrant population in ten years was all the more marked given the low birth rate of the native French, seen as both a cause and a symptom of national decadence. From 1930 the depression made life even more uncertain, deepened the gulf between rich and poor, sharpened hostility towards foreigners who 'stole' French jobs, and created seemingly insoluble problems. Meanwhile, the vigour, dynamism, unity and success associated with Fascist Italy, and later with Nazi Germany, contrasted unfavourably with the corresponding weakness, decline, division and failure associated with France. For those alienated from the Third Republic, the whole system and values of a hated and despised regime could be conveniently dismissed as 'decadent'. The charge of 'decadence' could also explain French failures, provide an excuse for rejecting many of the modern aspects of French life and supply the grounds for claiming some sort of moral superiority.

The increasing dependence of France on the 'Anglo-Saxons' (Britain, the British Empire, the Dominions and the United States) during the First World War, the failure of France to achieve her war aims at the Versailles Peace Conference, the demonstration of French weakness and American strength over inter-Allied war debts and reparations and the ever-more formidable challenge to France of the economic and cultural imperialism of the United States convinced Robert Aron, Arnaud Dandieu and many others that France had become a second-rate country compared to the United States and even Britain, a *'petit seigneur suivant les grands seigneurs'* (Aron and Dandieu, 1931, p. 114). France still had a large colonial empire, but there were problems in Morocco, Syria and elsewhere, and France did not have sufficient resources to defend or develop her empire effectively. At the same time, France's inheritance from the past – her historic buildings, her artistic treasures, her traditional crafts and industries, her revolutionary tradition – suffocated the country, which tourists and foreigners now admired only as a heritage theme park. France was also losing her national sovereignty, her financial independence, her economic strength and her cultural heritage and identity, principally to the United States. Major international decisions affecting France were now being determined by the United States and, to a lesser extent, Britain. American-inspired plans named after the American bankers Dawes and Young scaled down German reparations payments, until they were effectively ended by the Hoover Moratorium of 1931, while the Americans still insisted on the repayment of French war debts to the United States. Prohibition laws and import tariffs drastically cut French exports to the United States. The Great Depression was frequently seen as originally an American phenomenon, caused by the Wall Street stock market crash. American millionaires bought up French artistic treasures and heritage items, even removing historic buildings stone by stone across the Atlantic. The popularity of American films harmed not only France's trade balance but allegedly undermined her cultural values, as did other American imports such as jazz, advertising and mass-production techniques. It was feared that French individualism, even the French national genius, would be smothered by internationalism and by the soulless and regimented culture of the United States.

A belief that France had become decadent was often associated with a general xenophobia, a specific dislike of the 'Anglo-Saxons', anti-Semitism and an attraction to fascism. Aron and Dandieu complained that, when an ethnic Arab from Algeria won one of France's few medals at the previous Olympic Games, the French press had rejoiced over 'a French victory' (Aron and Dandieu, 1931, p. 42). These two writers also collaborated on a book more specifically attacking the United States, *Le Cancer américain* (1931), and on another book recommending an authoritarian regime run by technocrats, *La Révolution nécessaire* (1933). Aron on his own even went on to write *Victoire à Waterloo* (1937), which maintained that Napoleon had won the Battle of Waterloo. Anti-Semitism came to be linked with a preoccupation with decadence, since Jews were often identified with supposed elements of decadence, such as materialism, rationalism, liberalism, internationalism and all forms of corruption. French fascists tended to believe that they were engaged in a revolt against decadence, which embraced Marxism, liberalism, secularism and feminism, as well as physical and moral failings such as hedonism, cowardice and self-indulgence.

Document 8.2 The Next War

War will break out in five years. France and Germany will pounce on each other. If France is on her own, she will be beaten, even more certainly than in 1914: for several years there will be one young Frenchman against two young rearmed Germans. Thus, other countries must intervene. All the other countries. They will all be needed.

The English and the Italians know very well that they will be needed. The English know very well that, in order to maintain an insular entity that no longer exists, it is not sufficient to reject the proposal to construct a tunnel under the Channel. They also know very well that the British Empire as a political and economic unit is just a still-born utopia and that consequently they cannot shrug off German victories on the Continent by relying on their power outside Europe. Australia, Canada and South Africa are far away and will have other fish to fry. The three dominions will be hit by the Japanese explosion in the Pacific and by the revolt in India, which will then occur, and they will draw closer to the United States. They will align with the only major white state on the Pacific rim, like them directly threatened by Asiatic subversion. Besides, the brutal expansion of Japan will probably provoke the world war, which will be a world war in which the European conflict will be just a counter-blow.

Italy knows very well that if she marches with Germany she will find herself in a position of absolute inferiority with respect to her wartime ally as soon as victory has been achieved . . .

What will Russia do? Although in potential conflict with Japan, Russia will go to war with Germany. The reason for this is that Germany (whether Hitlerian or not) is more dangerous for Russia than any other state . . .

Whether Poland sides with Germany or not, *Russia will invade her*. This is what will give the new world war its special character. As a friend or as an enemy, Russia will invade Poland and all the new Slav states on her borders, as well as the Baltic states. Russia will invade Romania, Poland and Estonia. In all these states, soviets will be proclaimed – whether Moscow wants this or not.

Source: P. Drieu La Rochelle, 'La Prochaine Guerre', *in* Socialisme fasciste. *Paris: Gallimard. 1934, pp. 162–4*

Pierre Drieu La Rochelle was one of the most intelligent and influential right-wing intellectuals in France from the end of the First World War until his suicide on 15 March 1945. Born into a middle-class, politically conservative, Catholic family, he early became obsessed with the notion that France was decadent and in decline. Like many young men of his generation, he was profoundly influenced by the First World War, in which he served with distinction. He came to believe in virility, violence and the empowerment of the human will, while at the same time associating decadence with democracy, liberalism and Marxism, together with the hedonistic, materialistic and egalitarian values that they supposedly promoted. In 1917 he published a collection of war poems, and he went on to publish plays, war memoirs, political studies, numerous articles in newspapers and journals, and a succession of bestselling novels. Impressed by the 'virility' of the participants in the Stavisky riots, in 1934 he converted to fascism and between 1936 and 1938 he was one of the leading writers for Jacques Doriot's PPF.

As an analyst and commentator on foreign affars, Drieu La Rochelle was remarkably perceptive and far-sighted. In a number of publications he developed ideas about a united Europe, at a time when that concept seemed utopian and was a minority interest. His book *Socialisme fasciste* (1934) is principally concerned with exposing the 'myths' of Marxism, but it also contains astonishingly accurate predictions about the Second World War. He accurately predicts the year of its outbreak in Europe, the struggle between France and Germany, and the defeat of France if not effectively supported by allies, given France's demographic inferiority to Germany. The British might wish to isolate themselves from Europe, as their long opposition to early Channel Tunnel projects indicated, but they knew that a German-dominated Europe was not in their national interests, and that the British Empire could not compensate for a victorious Germany controlling the European Continent. As he correctly pointed out, Australia, Canada and South Africa were far away and had their own national interests to defend, interests that were not identical with those of Britain, while India was likely to be subverted by political unrest. Unlike most French observers at this time, Drieu La Rochelle appreciated the importance of the threat posed by Japan, which had begun the invasion of Manchuria in September 1931 and was openly pursuing policies of aggressive territorial expansion in defiance of the League of Nations. Drieu La Rochelle was equally perceptive in appreciating that Australia would look to the United States for protection against Japanese expansionism, and that the conflict in the Pacific would turn the next war into a world war. Italy in 1934 was not yet aligned with Nazi Germany. Indeed, in July 1934 Mussolini strongly objected to an attempted Nazi coup in Austria. Also, in any alliance between Italy and Germany, Italy would always be the junior partner. This was, of course, true, but in the end was not sufficient to deter Mussolini from forming an alliance with Hitler in November 1937 and from joining Hitler in the war against Britain and France in June 1940. As Drieu La Rochelle indicates, the role of the Soviet Union would be crucial. He correctly foresaw that Stalin would be more concerned with Nazi Germany than with Japan, and that Stalin would invade Poland, Romania and the Baltic states. Understandably, he did not foresee the Nazi–Soviet Pact of 23 August 1939, but he did predict the spread of communism in Eastern Europe, thus in effect foreseeing the Cold War as well as the Second World War.

For Drieu La Rochelle in 1934, the danger confronting France was that the country would succumb either to communism or to Nazi Germany. He hoped that France, Britain and Italy could form a 'third party', which would resist both Moscow and Berlin. However, with the Italian invasion of Ethiopia and the military support given by both Italy and Germany to Franco in Spain, Mussolini drifted into Hitler's embrace; and the Franco-British alliance was unable to check the German invasion of France in May–June 1940. The German military victories enormously impressed Drieu La Rochelle, who decided to collaborate with the Nazis and to become the intellectual advocate of a Continental Europe united on the basis of German hegemony. Germany, Drieu La Rochelle now argued, was the natural leader of a united Europe, and only a united Europe could stand up to the world's other major power blocs, the United States, the Soviet Union and Asia.

Document 8.3 The Maginot Line

I regret that you are installing precisely at this moment garrisons in the new fortifications of your frontier. I appreciate that this represents a redeployment of your forces and not an increase in the number of your troops. But this redeployment is attracting the attention of our public and provides our newspapers with an opportunity to publish editorials that are not always timely. Also, I personally consider that you are making a mistake in constructing these fortifications. Huge sums of money will be uselessly swallowed up in these projects. But that is your business! At least I see in this the sign that French military thinking has turned towards the defensive, which cannot displease me!

Source: François-Poncet to Paul-Boncour, reporting General von Schleicher, 7 January 1933; Documents diplomatiques français, 1932–1939, *First Series, vol. 2, 1966, p. 373*

The Maginot Line has become a symbol of all that was wrong with French defence planning and military thinking between the two world wars. The concept of a 'Maginot Line mentality' has even taken root, suggesting a fatal attraction to obsolete defensive strategies, a futile diversion of enormous resources to useless projects and an obstinate refusal to take account of new technological developments and their potential applications. The decision to construct the Maginot Line, and the consequences of that decision, have been held at least partly responsible for the fall of France in June 1940. The construction of hugely expensive fortifications starved the French armed forces of money; the fortifications had to be garrisoned by large numbers of troops, who were effectively neutralized; and, since the fortifications stretched from just the Swiss to the Luxembourg frontier, an invading German army had simply to bypass them by going through Belgium and Luxembourg, which was precisely what happened in May 1940.

For centuries, the French had attempted to guard their frontiers with forts and fortifications. After defeat in the Franco-Prussian War, the French constructed or modernized eighty-nine forts and twenty smaller defensive works along the frontier between the Pas de Calais and Switzerland; and some of these forts and fortifications, particularly those around Verdun, played a valuable role in the First World War. With the development of the Russian alliance, the French army felt able to develop an offensive strategy, but the experience of the First World War seemed to demonstrate the primacy of defence over offence. Also, the memory of the invasions of 1814, 1815, 1870 and 1914, France's demographic weakness, the vulnerability of France in a war situation before reserves had been mobilized and concentrated, the reduction of the term of compulsory military service from three years to eighteen months (April 1923) and then to twelve months (April 1927) and the location of much of France's coal and iron deposits and industrial capacity within striking distance of the Franco-German frontier all reinforced the attractiveness of a defensive strategy. General Eugène Debeney (Chief of the French General Staff, 1923–30) and Marshal Philippe Pétain (Vice-President of the Senior War Council, or Conseil Supérieur de la Guerre, and Inspector-General of the Army, 1922–31) were particularly important in pressing for the construction of the fortifications that became known as the Maginot Line. The experience of the First World War, in which he had commanded the troops defending Verdun in 1916, convinced Pétain of the destructiveness of modern fire-power ('*le feu tue*', or fire-power kills, became one of his favourite maxims) and of the effectiveness of underground fortifications (which played a successful role in the defence of Verdun). After eight years of discussion and planning, on 14 January 1930, when the French government budget was untypically in surplus, a parliamentary vote finally allocated 3.7 billion francs for the construction of the Maginot Line, named after André Maginot, Minister of War from November 1929 until his premature death in January 1932. The fortifications, which did not really constitute a 'line', were built between 1930 and 1937.

Much of the criticism levelled at the Maginot Line is not fully justified. As General von Schleicher (German Chancellor, December 1932–January 1933) pointed out, the fortifications were expensive. On the other hand, the project enjoyed widespread public support, which probably would not have been forthcoming for a programme of offensive rearmament; the project served as a much-needed labour-intensive job-creation scheme; and, if the money had not been spent in this way, there is no certainty that it would have been spent on national defence or the armed forces. Only the Franco-German frontier was heavily fortified. However, to have extended the fortifications to the Channel coast would have been prohibitively expensive; the terrain near France's frontiers with Luxembourg and Belgium is generally flat and liable to flooding, which renders it unsuitable for underground fortifications (though fortifications were constructed near Valenciennes and Maubeuge); and the French did not want to treat neutral Luxembourg or their ally Belgium as potential enemies or as countries France would not defend. The fortifications did assume a static war of defence, but they were planned in the 1920s long before Germany had acquired significant numbers of tanks and aircraft. Moreover, not a single major fortress of the Maginot Line fell to the Germans before the armistice came into effect on 25 June 1940; and during October and November 1944 the Maginot Line, now defended by the Germans, delayed the advance of General Patton's US Third Army. In the 1970s and 1980s the deep and air-conditioned ammunition magazines of the Maginot Line even provided ideal storage space for French nuclear warheads. It could, then, be said that there was nothing intrinsically wrong with the Maginot Line, though it could promote an unwarranted complacency, an unjustified sense of security and a tendency to think and plan purely in defensive terms.

Document 8.4 Armoured Warfare

In the future the professional army will operate entirely with tracked vehicles. Every combatant and service element will advance over the terrain in appropriate vehicles. Not a single soldier, not a single gun, not a single shell, not a single loaf of bread should thus be unable to get down to the job. A large military unit, raising camp at dawn, will have travelled fifty leagues by the evening. It will require only one hour for a large military unit to travel fifteen kilometres to engage the enemy with its combat forces, or, by breaking contact, to disappear out of range of enemy fire . . .

A heavily armoured brigade, travelling across fields as quickly as a galloping horse, equipped with 150 medium guns, 400 smaller guns, 600 machine-guns, crossing ditches three metres wide, surmounting embankments ten metres high, toppling forty-year-old trees, demolishing walls with the thickness of twelve bricks, crushing all gates, fences and barriers, that is what industry can equip every professional army division with . . .

A group of observation aircraft, co-ordinated of course with the force, designed not to operate on an episodic basis for unknown units, but to keep a particular general constantly informed, to escort always the same comrades into battle, to direct the fire of familiar artillery batteries, this group of aircraft will provide the eyes of the force . . .

Six divisions grouping together army units, all up to strength and on a permanent footing, will be the backbone of the professional army. One hundred thousand young and selected volunteers, operating with great rapidity, thanks to mechanization, extremely powerful weapons, will form the substance.

Source: C. de Gaulle, Vers L'Armée de métier. *Paris: Berger-Levrault. 1934, pp. 109–112, 114 and 139–40*

Charles de Gaulle did not become a major political figure until the very end of the Third Republic, but during the 1930s he gained a reputation in French military circles as a controversial theoretician on military matters. The son of a patriotic Catholic schoolmaster, who had fought in the Franco-Prussian War and been wounded in the siege of Paris, de Gaulle entered the Military Academy of Saint Cyr in 1910 at the age of nineteen. He graduated in 1912 and was commissioned into the 33rd Infantry Regiment, commanded by Colonel Philippe Pétain, with whom he early established a somewhat fraught relationship. After the outbreak of the First World War, the regiment was almost immediately engaged in action in which de Gaulle was wounded. In March 1916 he was wounded for the third time and captured in fierce fighting near Fort Douaumont, one of the forts guarding Verdun, and he spent the rest of the war in captivity. As a prisoner, besides making five unsuccessful escape attempts, de Gaulle improved his German, gave lectures on history and strategy to his fellow prisoners, and reflected critically on the First World War and on why Germany was eventually defeated, which became the subject of his first book, *La Discorde chez l'ennemi* (1924).

After release from captivity following the armistice, de Gaulle served in Poland (1919–20), as a lecturer at Saint Cyr (1921–2), as a student at the Ecole de Guerre (1922–4), as a member of the staff of the Army of the Rhine (1924–5), as a member of Pétain's personal staff (1925–7), as commander of a battalion of light infantry in the German Rhineland (1927–9), as a member of the French military intelligence staff in Syria and the Lebanon (1929–31), and as a member of the General Secretariat of National Defence (1931–7). This amounted to a varied career, combining combat experience, overseas service and unusually long periods devoted to the teaching, research and planning of modern warfare.

Whereas Pétain believed in the decisiveness of fire-power and in the virtues of static defensive strategies, during the 1920s de Gaulle became convinced that the future would principally see wars of movement. De Gaulle respected Pétain as a national hero, the defender of Verdun and the queller of the French army mutinies of 1917, and he accepted Pétain's invitation in April 1925 to join a team researching and writing a study of the lessons of the last war and a more general study of the French army in recent history. Pétain, for his part, admired de Gaulle as an intelligent junior officer, with an original mind and a good literary style, and he personally intervened to raise de Gaulle's marks at the Ecole de Guerre in 1924 and to arrange for de Gaulle to lecture there in 1927. However, de Gaulle was too independent of mind to allow respect and gratitude to influence his judgements. As early as December 1925, in an article published in the *Revue Militaire Française*, while accepting France's need for frontier fortifications, he opposed seeking security in a continuous defensive line and emphasized the importance of the French army's ability to manoeuvre; in 1930 he produced for Pétain a eulogy of Marshal Foch that Pétain rejected as too uncritical of his former rival; in 1932 he published a number of reworked lectures and articles, mainly on the theme of military leadership, in *Le Fil de l'Epée* (*The Edge of the Sword*), which included veiled criticisms of France's current military leadership and of Pétain himself; and in 1933 he outlined his concept of an all-professional army in an article in the *Revue Politique et Parlementaire*. Above all, de Gaulle was determined to become nobody's protégé, to publish his own work under his own name and to challenge publicly France's military orthodoxies and military hierarchy.

The development of self-propelled vehicles, from motor-cycles to tanks, together with the development of aircraft, transformed the possibilities of modern warfare. After the British first used tanks in 1916, the French enthusiastically adopted this new weapon and with considerable success. At Villers-Cotterêts in July 1918 300 French tanks achieved a deep penetration of the German front, and by November 1918 the French army possessed some 4,000 tanks (Doughty, 1985, p. 136). However, the defensive strategy adopted by the French army in the inter-war period meant that the tank came to be viewed as an infantry-support weapon, and priority was given to the production of light tanks that would accompany the infantry in battle.

Confronted with the need to ensure the security of French national territory, with an exposed north-eastern frontier, and with army conscripts who generally disliked military service, served for too short a period (eighteen months after April 1923 and twelve months after April 1928), and were consequently inadequately trained and ill-prepared to use modern, sophisticated equipment, de Gaulle proposed in *Vers L'Armée de métier* (1934) the creation of a highly trained, well-equipped professional army, with its core component consisting of 100,000 carefully selected young men manning six fully mechanized and self-sufficient armoured divisions. This vision of 'the army of the future' (the title of the 1940 translation of de Gaulle's book) fundamentally challenged the French military orthodoxies of the time. Nearly all French military units, except the Foreign Legion, consisted of a mixture of professional and conscript soldiers. This followed French military traditions going back to the revolutionary armies of the 1790s, accorded with the republican concept of the army as the nation in arms, and met the French army establishment's concern over manpower strengths, particularly in view of France's demographic weakness in comparison with Germany and the defence requirements of France's colonial empire.

De Gaulle's concept of an all-professional army alarmed the Left, with the spectre of an army that might become the instrument of a right-wing *coup d'état* and with the prospect that young Frenchmen would no longer be exposed to the social discipline and republican values supposedly inculcated by military service. The army establishment was equally alarmed by the possible loss of conscript soldiers, the fear that an all-professional army would encounter recruitment and financial problems, and the public challenge to its orthodoxies by a relatively junior officer (de Gaulle was promoted major in September 1927, lieutenant-colonel in December 1932 and colonel in December 1937). As for de Gaulle's concept of armoured divisions, this apparently clashed with the orthodox defensive strategy and might not permit the protection of all the national territory from enemy invasion. Thus, de Gaulle's book had little immediate impact on French military policies and planning, but it was read with interest in Germany by members of the Nazi and military élite and in the Soviet Union by Marshal Tukhachevsky, Chief of Staff of the Red Army.

The astonishing successes achieved by German panzer divisions and blitzkrieg tactics are well known. In contrast, in May–June 1940 almost half of France's tanks were employed in an infantry-support role, with less than a quarter in armoured divisions, two of which were formed in January 1940, one in April and the third after 10 May. It has therefore been suggested that de Gaulle was right and that France fell in

May–June 1940 because the French military hierarchy had ignored his ideas. The truth, though, seems to be more complex. De Gaulle was not the only French military expert to advocate the creation of fully mechanized armoured divisions and their use in a mobile and offensive manner. Such ideas were advanced by others, notably General Estienne during the 1920s. De Gaulle's manner and tactics may have been counter-productive: he was widely considered within the French military hierarchy to have been aloof, arrogant and insubordinate; the publication of his ideas under his own name alone by commercial publishers alienated Pétain particularly, and his cultivation of relations with sympathetic politicians such as Paul Reynaud and with influential newspapers such as *L'Echo de Paris* was judged by many to be unprofessional conduct for a career army officer. Also, de Gaulle, in assigning simply an observation and reconnaissance role to aircraft, failed to appreciate their offensive potential until he had absorbed the lessons of the Polish campaign of September 1939. When it came to the Battle of France in May–June 1940, the Maginot Line and French fortifications along the Franco-Italian frontier performed very much better than France's armoured divisions. Well-constructed, well-sited and determinedly defended fortifications could still be effective, while slow-moving armoured divisions, inadequately supplied with fuel and ammunition, lacking air, artillery and infantry support, good radio communications and a decentralized system of command, could still be ineffective.

Document 8.5 Appeasement and the Italian Invasion of Ethiopia

Italy has in a manner tied its fate to that of Germany. But the countrymen of Machiavelli know perfectly well how to untie what they have tied up. Mussolini is too intelligent to have abandoned the entire destinies of his country to Hitler. He has, since the signature of his pact [the Rome–Berlin Axis, proclaimed on 1 November 1936], made some discordant notes which proved that harmony between the two governments has not been established completely.

What concerns us is what divides us from Italy, the Ethiopian affair. I maintain that the Ethiopian affair cannot divide France and Italy, whatever judgement may be passed on Italian colonization, for the following reasons: a colonial power such as France cannot contest the right of our wartime ally and neighbour also to possess colonies. A legal reason even confirms that we should never have contested this right. It is exactly fifty years since Italy should have been mistress of Ethiopia. If it had had the military capability, half a century ago, to acquire what France and Britain had granted it in the treaty dividing Ethiopia, we would certainly now not be confronted with the problem.

Are we going to reproach Italy for having taken fifty years to achieve this conquest? I do not think so. And even if there had not been the legal arguments, even if there had not been the Franco-British commitment – a commitment partially qualified by Ethiopia's admission to the League of Nations, but that is another matter – there exist other reasons, of an economic nature, which ought to encourage us to be more circumspect in our relations with Italy over this matter.

There is the fact that a million Italians are leaving for Ethiopia, and that will to some extent relieve Italy's demographic and economic difficulties. It is certain that a half-satisfied people is a much less dangerous people than Italy was a few years ago, when Italy was still seeking satisfaction.

Source: J. Doriot, La France avec nous! *Paris: Flammarion. 1937, pp. 68–9*

During the inter-war period France sought security through diplomacy as well as through military defence. French diplomacy attempted to create a network of alliances with European states comparable to the alliance system constructed by Bismarck after 1871. A variety of military agreements, friendship treaties and diplomatic alliances were negotiated by France with Belgium (1920), Poland (1921), Czechoslovakia (1924), Romania (1926) and Yugoslavia (1927). Besides increasing French security, the aim of this policy was to form Czechoslovakia, Romania and Yugoslavia into a 'Little Entente' bloc that would check the expansion of both Germany and the Soviet Union. However, France did not have sufficient economic, financial or military resources to provide the assistance these states needed to compensate for their weaknesses, whether economic, military, political or diplomatic. Belgium and Czechoslovakia were relatively prosperous, but the other states suffered from varying degrees of economic backwardness; separatist movements divided Czechoslovakia and Yugoslavia; and all the states were involved in regional conflicts and frontier disputes – Belgium with Germany, Poland with the Soviet Union and Germany, Czechoslovakia with Poland and Germany, Romania with Hungary, and Yugoslavia with Austria, Italy and Albania. Thus, French support for Poland was likely to alienate the Soviet Union, while French support for Yugoslavia was likely to alienate Italy. Under Aristide Briand, Foreign Minister from April 1925 to January 1932, French foreign policy also attempted to achieve a *rapprochement* with Germany and to become more idealistic, with Franco-German recognition of existing frontiers at the Locarno Conference (October 1925), French agreement to reductions in German reparation payments and an early withdrawal of Allied troops from the Rhineland, the denunciation of war as an instrument of national policy in the Kellogg–Briand Pact (August 1928), the proposal for the creation of a federal European union (September 1929), and the proposal for the establishment of an international police force (February 1932).

Apart from Turkey, the first state to challenge the post-First World War settlement was Italy. Denied territory promised by the Allies in 1915 and after October 1922 under the leadership of Mussolini, who believed in the invigorating effects of war and harboured ambitions to recreate a Roman Empire, Italy occupied the Greek island of Corfu in 1923 on the pretext that an Italian general had been assassinated. Corfu was eventually evacuated by Mussolini, who concentrated instead on 'pacifying' Libya. When that task had been completed, he turned to Ethiopia. A late nineteenth-century Italian attempt to conquer Ethiopia had failed in a series of humiliating defeats, climaxing with the Battle of Adowa (March 1896), in which 5,000 Italian soldiers were killed and nearly 2,000 taken prisoner. To revenge this disaster and to expand Italy's

African empire, Mussolini launched a massive invasion of Ethiopia on 3 October 1935. The deployment of over half a million Italian troops, together with aircraft that sprayed resisting Ethiopians with mustard gas, ensured an Italian victory by May 1936.

The Italian invasion of Ethiopia was a flagrant breach of the charter of the League of Nations. The League's Council rapidly branded Italy as an aggressor and on 19 October imposed sanctions. The British and French governments, though, were very reluctant to alienate Mussolini. Hitler's appointment as German Chancellor (January 1933), and his withdrawal of Germany from the League of Nations and the Geneva Disarmament Conference (October 1933), his non-aggression pact with Poland (January 1934), and his restoration of military conscription and repudiation of the disarmament clauses of the Treaty of Versailles (March 1935), had alarmed the British and French governments and convinced them of the need to secure the co-operation of Mussolini. At a conference held at Stresa in April 1935, Britain, France and Italy agreed to establish a common front against Germany. Mussolini's invasion of Ethiopia thus posed a difficult problem for the British and French governments. On the one hand, they wanted to uphold, or at least appear to uphold, the League of Nations; on the other hand, they wanted to maintain co-operation between themselves and with Mussolini. Hence a compromise policy was pursued: Britain and France agreed to sanctions against Italy, but they also agreed that sanctions should exclude steel, coal and oil, that the Suez Canal should not be closed to Italian shipping, and that there should be no Anglo-French naval blockade of Italy. In December 1935 Pierre Laval (French Foreign Minister, October 1934–January 1936) and Sir Samuel Hoare (British Foreign Secretary, June–December 1935) negotiated a pact whereby Italy was to be allowed to retain all the territory she had conquered, about two-thirds of Ethiopia, and to be offered the possibility of additional cessions of territory by Britain and France. These proposals had been hastily put together, without consulting the Emperor of Ethiopia or other members of the League of Nations; and when the details were leaked, the public outcry was such that Hoare and Laval rapidly had to resign.

Anglo-French policy ultimately failed completely: Mussolini, in defiance of international disapproval, completed the conquest of Ethiopia; the reputation of the League and the effectiveness of its sanctions were undermined; sanctions harmed, and alienated, other countries, particularly Yugoslavia; and Mussolini was encouraged to underestimate Britain and France and to be drawn into Hitler's embrace, leaving the Stresa Front in January 1936 in return for German support over Ethiopia, a process which led, following the unopposed German military reoccupation of the Rhineland (March 1936) and the outbreak of the Spanish Civil War (July 1936), to the formal announcement of the Rome–Berlin Axis on 1 November 1936.

Given the many similarities between Hitler and Mussolini and their respective regimes, their common opposition to the Versailles Settlement and their common pursuit of aggressive and expansionist foreign policies, the announcement of the Rome–Berlin Axis may well seem to have been an inevitable development. Observers at the time, though, did not necessarily think so. As Jacques Doriot pointed out, harmony between the leaders of Nazi Germany and Fascist Italy was not achieved –

there were too many personality clashes and too many policy differences. Doriot also had a valid point in stressing that Britain and France, as major colonial powers, were not well placed to oppose an Italian conquest in Africa that might have occurred in the 1890s. He might also have indicated that Mussolini had acted forcefully over Austria, protesting against a projected Austro-German customs union in March 1931 and moving troops to the Brenner Pass after the failed Nazi coup in Vienna of July 1934, and that the ethnic German population of the Italian South Tyrol was always a sensitive issue for Mussolini. Yet Doriot was wrong in suggesting that Ethiopia alone divided Italy from France and that Mussolini's conquest of it would satisfy his territorial ambitions. Italy competed with France (and Britain) in the Mediterranean and North Africa, and Mussolini coveted French territories such as Nice, Savoy, Corsica and Tunisia. Doriot was also wrong in underestimating the opposition of British and French public opinion to Mussolini's unprovoked aggression against a relatively defenceless African state, and to the brutal conquest and occupation of a country that had been a member of the League of Nations since September 1923. However, at the same time there was no public enthusiasm in Britain or France for war with Italy over Ethiopia. The British and French governments had little room in which to manoeuvre. They could not afford to condone Mussolini's actions, or to go to war with Mussolini, or to drive Mussolini into Hitler's arms. Ultimately, the Italian invasion of Ethiopia illustrated the problems and dilemmas of appeasement, as well as in itself marking an important milestone on the road to the Second World War.

Document 8.6 Marshal Pétain

Without seeking a clone of Mussolini or Hitler, and without returning to the Napoleons, the least that one has the right to demand is the substitution of an authoritarian Republic, with a professional basis in which political factions will have no role and no place, for the parliamentary Republic, based on the existence of political factions.

An authoritarian Republic? In other words, the head of state exercises full legislative and executive powers; he governs by decree laws, assisted by a vice-president chosen by him and by ministers responsible to him alone; he administers the country through prefects and mayors, all appointed by him; to give him an indisputable authority, he is elected by plebiscite for ten years and is eligible for re-election, with all adult French men and women being eligible to vote, and with heads of families having as many supplementary votes as they have children under the voting age; he presents his successor for election in a plebiscite; . . .

In place of today's sovereign parliament, elected by the political parties, there will be a Council of State, representing the professional organizations of agriculture, industry, commerce and the major public services . . .

We have it, the illustrious, prestigious and popular name; we have it, the Man of Providence [*l'homme providentiel*] that France always finds in its hours of extreme peril.

Who?

Pétain, the great soldier of Verdun, the most illustrious of the survivors of the Great War, since Clemenceau, Joffre and Foch have departed from us.

He is too old?

Certainly, it would have been preferable if he had been younger. But, when at one of the most desperate moments of the Great War Clemenceau took the reins of power, he was almost as old as Pétain is today, and history recounts that Clemenceau was not exactly lacking in energy . . .

Besides, do we know of another man, young or old, more capable than Pétain of rallying the nation and of restoring French unity, broken by the factions?

Any known political figure who could be chosen, long corrupted by parliamentary life and worn out by past and present conflicts of party and faction, would appear, in comparison with Pétain, lacking in prestige and moral authority . . .

With Pétain, nothing like that: he is above politics; he does not owe his reputation and his prestige to politics. It is for this reason that President Doumergue invited him to serve as Minister of War in a government that Doumergue intended to be a government of national unity, of national reassurance and of national reconciliation.

Source: G. Hervé, C'est Pétain qu'il nous faut! *Paris: Editions de la Victoire. 1936, pp. 26–7 and 34–8*

Marshal Pétain was the key figure in the political demise of the Third Republic and the head of state with full executive and legislative powers in the Vichy regime that followed. The First World War rescued him from obscurity and made possible his remarkable career. A colonel, aged fifty-eight and close to retirement in 1914, he ended the war as a marshal of France, having won the status of national hero as the successful defender of Verdun in 1916 and the humane queller of the army mutinies of 1917. From May 1917 Pétain was Commander-in-Chief of all French forces on the Western Front, so in the French public imagination he shared only with Prime Minister Clemenceau and his fellow marshals Joffre and Foch the personal glory for the victory of 1918. Between 1920 and 1931 Pétain served on all the most important military committees, and after retirement from active military service he retained his membership of the Conseil Supérieur de la Guerre and of the Conseil Supérieur de la Défense Nationale. He assumed a more political role from February to November 1934 as Minister of War in Doumergue's government, formed after the Stavisky riots; and in March 1939 he was sent to Spain as France's first ambassador to the Franco regime.

By 1935 Pétain was France's only surviving marshal, apart from the much less well-known Franchet d'Esperey, who survived until 1942 but had been severely injured in a car accident in 1933. As such, Pétain began to attract a cult following from sections of the press, various right-wing organizations and some politicians. Comparisons were made between Pétain and Joan of Arc as symbols of national unity and potential saviours of their country. After a popular Paris newspaper, *Le Petit Journal*, had conducted a poll of its readers as to who would be the most suitable French dictator, Pétain was announced on 11 January 1935 as the clear winner. A Pétain-to-power campaign was subsequently launched by Gustave Hervé, a teacher turned journalist who had gained notoriety before the First World War for his extreme anti-militarism. However, with the First World War his newspaper, *La Victoire*, became an organ of patriotic nationalism and in 1916 he was expelled from the SFIO. After 1919 he preached Franco-German reconciliation and campaigned for the revision of the Versailles Treaty, for a United States of Europe and for an authoritarian republic in France. In the run-up to the Popular Front elections of April–May 1936 he contributed to *La Victoire* a series of pro-Pétain articles, which were later republished in book form.

In rejecting the parliamentary system of the Third Republic as corrupt, inefficient and faction-ridden, in urging the establishment of an authoritarian republic with a head of state exercising virtually dictatorial powers, checked only by the need to be elected every ten years, and in seeing in Marshal Pétain the Man of Providence who would rally the nation and restore national unity, Hervé was articulating the views of a number of French right-wing newspapers at this time, including *Action Française*, *L'Ami du Peuple*, *Le Jour*, *Le National* and *La Voix du Combattant*. The campaign, though, did not attract a wider following, and the cautious and constitutionally minded Pétain distanced himself from it. Nevertheless, despite Pétain's age attracting some negative comment, the campaign helped to nurture Pétain's political ambitions and helped to prepare the ground for future events.

Document 8.7 Upper-class French Attitudes

A few days after this visit to Chartwell I was in France with my car. Being convinced we should be at war in a few weeks and that this was likely to be my last holiday for years, I crossed the Channel on the day after the House [of Commons] adjourned for the recess.

The French friends I stayed with were of the sort, so I thought at the time, that nothing could alter. They were hospitable and kind as always, but I found a perceptible change amongst their friends and relations. These belonged to the class known in France as *gens du monde*. The shadow of war hung over the land, and they hated and resented it. They made no attempt to conceal their belief that England was bent on using France as a shield in a war she was seeking against Hitler's Germany. I could sense hostility amongst people I had known quite well, and it was very unpleasant.

French people can change quickly and are adept at conveying the fact by *nuances* of manner and tone. I was made to feel I was a member of a race against whom latent prejudice always exists in France. Here was perfidious Albion at it again. I argued with myself that these people represented no one but themselves, but I was saddened that they should adopt an attitude that took so little account of what we deemed to be not only a matter of national honour to both our countries, but one which involved their continued independence.

Self-appointed guardians of the good taste if not of the culture of their race, these people hated the *Front Populaire* and all that it stood for. They pointed to the setback in orderly progress that upheaval had brought about, which was true, but failed to take into account that the very violence of the Socialist reaction was due to the selfish, the merciless attitude of the property-owning, in particular of the industrial, classes, the *Patrons*. With the pleasant, mundane, rich people I met on this occasion there could be no argument. They thought, and did not hesitate to say, that anything, absolutely anything, was better than the re-emergence of the Popular Front and of its leader, the man they hated above all others, Léon Blum. That war would place power in the hands of the Left made it doubly hateful. It was all nonsense anyway, argued these self-assured men and superbly-dressed women, the latter a little shrill, with an output of words per minute comparable only to the trills of an electric bell: France was too weak even to defend herself, let alone launch forth into adventures at the other end of Europe. The Czechs, upstart successors of a Great Power, were of but little interest, and the Poles? – some of them were agreeable no doubt, but they were for ever in trouble. It would be demented to allow their ill-planned and ill-constructed country to lead us all into war. Hitler was no doubt odious, but he hated communism, and at least stood for order. The high-pitched voices of the ladies invited no reply.

Source: Major-General Sir E. Spears, Assignment to Catastrophe, vol. 1, Prelude to Dunkirk, July 1939–May 1940. London: Willliam Heinemann. 1954, pp. 3–4

Appeasement characterized the foreign policies of Britain and France towards Italy and Germany from 1935 until the spring of 1939. After failing to oppose effectively the Italian invasion and occupation of Ethiopia, the British and French governments neither intervened in the Spanish Civil War nor responded to Italian and German intervention in Spain. Similarly, they failed to act when Germany occupied Austria in March 1938, and at the Munich Conference of September 1938 they forced Czechoslovakia to surrender the Sudetenland to the Third Reich. Having claimed that the Sudetenland would be his last territorial demand in Europe, on 15 March 1939 Hitler occupied the remainder of Czechoslovakia. He rapidly followed this flagrant act of aggression by demanding that Poland should return Danzig and the Polish corridor to Germany (21 March), by occupying the Lithuanian territory of Memel (23 March), and by denouncing Germany's Non-Aggression Pact with Poland (28 March). These developments at last convinced political and public opinion in Britain, and to a lesser extent in France, that appeasing Hitler did not secure peace but simply whetted his appetite for further territorial expansion. On 31 March the British and French governments formally guaranteed to support Poland if its independence should be threatened. Similar guarantees were made to Greece and Romania on 13 April after Italy had invaded Albania on 7 April. The diplomatic tension was heightened by preparations for war, with Britain introducing military conscription on 27 April.

Conscious of the huge costs of the last war with Germany, fearful that the costs of a new war with Germany would be even greater, and deeply divided socially and politically as a result of the economic crisis and the Popular Front experiment, the French nation desperately hoped for peace. Thus the Munich Agreements dismembering Czechoslovakia were generally welcomed in France, the only significant opposition coming from Communist members of the Chamber of Deputies. French foreign policy changed in March 1939, but French public opinion, particularly in right-wing circles, registered much less of a change. It was felt that French foreign policy was led by Britain, which, protected by the Channel, the Royal Navy and the RAF, and with only a small army available for European operations, would happily sacrifice France in any future war. Czechoslovakia and Poland were seen as recent and artificial creations, rather than as historic and genuine nation states, and the status of the Sudetenland, Danzig and the Polish corridor as of little concern to France, and for which it would be a criminal absurdity to fight a war with Germany. The direction of French foreign policy had allegedly been captured by a conspiracy of Englishmen, Jews and Communists, who for their own reasons wanted to drag France into a war with Nazi Germany, contrary to the national interests of France, which should alone determine French foreign policy. There was also the belief that France's real enemies were not the Italian Fascists or the German Nazis but the Soviet Communists and their French Communist allies, who threatened France with Bolshevik-style upheaval and revolution.

These views were encountered by Edward Spears at the beginning of August 1939. Born and educated in France with an English father of German-Jewish ancestry, Spears had used his fluency in French and his knowledge of France with great success during the First World War. As a junior officer in 1914 his liaison work had prevented a rift between British and French commanders, and subsequently as a brigadier he had headed the British military mission in Paris from 1917 to 1920. After retiring from the army, he was elected a Conservative MP for Loughborough (1922–4) and Carlisle (1931–45), becoming known in the House of Commons as 'the member for Paris' for his outspoken Francophile views. He was also a friend of Winston Churchill, with whose criticisms of the appeasement policies of the Chamberlain government he agreed. His visit to Normandy in August 1939 was sandwiched between lunch at Chartwell, Churchill's country home in Kent, and a short tour with Churchill of the Maginot Line.

The problem with Spears was that he believed in an idealized image of France and of the French, the product of happy childhood memories, his First World War experiences and his regular visits to his wealthy French friends in the inter-war period. Unfortunately, this image did not correspond with the reality, at least in 1939 and 1940, when French people on the whole could not understand why they should make enormous sacrifices and endure terrible suffering for the sake of other countries, and who distrusted British arguments based on the defence of national honour and of shared values and principles. On 24 May 1940 Churchill, who had succeeded Chamberlain as British Prime Minister on 10 May, appointed Spears as his personal liaison officer with Paul Reynaud, the head of the French government from 21 March to 16 June 1940. With increasing desperation and lack of success, Spears attempted to stiffen French resistance to the German invasion, but he did manage to spirit de Gaulle out of France on 17 June. The end of the special relationship between Spears and France, and more particularly between Spears and de Gaulle, finally came with his appointment in July 1941 as head of a mission to Syria and the Lebanon, which he had to take over from Vichy and French control.

Document 8.8 The Nazi–Soviet Pact (23 August 1939)

The Soviet Union's action in concluding the non-aggression pact with Germany will contribute towards a reinforcement of the general peace. It throws disarray into the fascist camp and happily transforms the situation in the Far East. It is now up to Paris and London to conclude an agreement with the USSR to organize common resistance against the aggressor . . .

Declaration of the French Communist Party

At the moment when the Soviet Union brings a new and invaluable contribution to the maintenance of peace, which is constantly jeopardized by the fascist warmongers, the French Communist Party addresses to the socialist motherland, to its Party and to its great leader Stalin a hearty salute.

For twenty-two years, the power of the workers has demonstrated to the peoples of the world that *socialism is peace* [*le socialisme, c'est la paix*].

The first act of government of the soviets, on 8 November 1917, was an appeal in favour of peace, and it was addressed particularly to '*the most politically conscious workers of the three most advanced nations of humanity: England, France and Germany*'.

Since then, on every occasion, the Union of Soviet Socialist Republics has held high the banner of the great peace of humanity.

Source: L'Humanité, *25 August 1939, p. 1*

The Nazi–Soviet Pact of 23 August 1939 represented a diplomatic revolution and led almost immediately to the outbreak of the Second World War. Stalin had responded to the establishment of the Nazi regime in Germany by supporting Popular Front governments in France and Spain. The end of the Popular Front experiment in France with the resignation of the second Blum government (8 April 1938), and the victory of Franco in the Spanish Civil War (1 April 1939), seemed to demonstrate the failure of this policy. Stalin's parallel policy of support for the League of Nations and for the principle of collective security had seemingly been equally unsuccessful. The Soviet Union had joined the League of Nations on 18 September 1934, but the League had failed to halt Italian aggression in Ethiopia and had thereafter been sidelined by the British and French governments and by their appeasement policies. British and French inaction over the reoccupation of the Rhineland, the Spanish Civil War and the German annexation of Austria apparently demonstrated that they would never resist Hitler or Mussolini. This assumption seemed to be confirmed by the Munich

Agreements of 30 September 1938. Admittedly, the French armed forces were partially mobilized on 25 September and the Royal Navy was mobilized the following day, but at Munich the British and French conceded to Hitler virtually all his demands, which involved transferring the Sudetenland from Czechoslovakia to the Third Reich without the consent of the Czechs.

The Soviet Union was not invited to the Munich Conference, and Poland and Romania had formally declared on 11 September that Soviet forces would not be allowed passage through their territory to help the Czechs. Feeling diplomatically isolated and betrayed by Britain and France (which had agreed a pact of mutual assistance with the Soviet Union on 2 May 1935), as well as threatened by the possibility of joint German and Japanese aggression implicit in their Anti-Comintern Pact (25 November 1936), Stalin began to consider coming to an agreement with Hitler. The subsequent German occupation of the remainder of Czechoslovakia in March 1939 and Hitler's new threats against Poland led to the abandonment of appeasement policies by Britain and France, but Stalin did not fully appreciate this, perhaps understandably, given Anglo-French inaction over the Italian invasion of Albania. Stalin distrusted the Anglo-French guarantee to Poland, which for historic and ideological reasons was profoundly anti-Soviet, and he continued to contemplate reaching an agreement with Germany. On 3 May 1939 Litvinov was dismissed as Commissar for Foreign Affairs and replaced by Molotov, who did not share Litvinov's commitment to a policy of collective security against Nazi Germany. The British and French, for their part, underestimated the Red Army (whose officer corps had recently been purged), were anxious not to alienate Poland and remained deeply suspicious of Stalin and of the Soviet Union. The fundamental problem, though, was that the states bordering the western frontiers of the Soviet Union – Finland, Estonia, Latvia, Poland and Romania – refused to co-operate with the Soviet Union in any anti-Nazi pact.

Nevertheless, by May 1939 French foreign policy, directed by Daladier (Prime Minister), Bonnet (Foreign Minister) and Alexis St Léger (head of the Ministry of Foreign Affairs), favoured an alliance with the Soviet Union and helped to persuade a reluctant Chamberlain to send a joint Anglo-French military mission to Moscow. Arriving in Moscow on 11 August, the Anglo-French military mission could achieve nothing since the Poles continued to reject any military co-operation with the Soviet Union. Stalin therefore turned to Hitler and on 23 August Molotov signed with Ribbentrop, Hitler's Foreign Minister who had flown to Moscow, the Nazi–Soviet Pact.

Ostensibly a ten-year non-aggression pact, the Nazi–Soviet Pact provided for a joint Nazi–Soviet invasion and partition of Poland, and additional secret agreements provided for Soviet control of Finland, Estonia, Latvia and the Romanian province of Bessarabia. This meant that Hitler could now risk a war with Britain and France over Poland, even if Italy remained neutral, since he had a guarantee of the neutrality of the Soviet Union. While making war in Europe almost inevitable, the Nazi–Soviet Pact paradoxically made war in the Far East, at least for a time, less likely. Japanese aggression in China had continued since 1931, and in August 1939 Japanese forces even engaged in serious fighting with units of the Red Army in Mongolia. Since joining the Anti-Comintern Pact, Japan had considered Germany to be her ally, only to find the latter now allied with her enemy, the Soviet Union. In a climate of national betrayal, the Japanese government fell and relations between Tokyo and Berlin were delivered a serious blow.

It was not just the Japanese who felt betrayed by the Nazi–Soviet Pact, but communists throughout Western Europe who had come to see communism as the antithesis of fascism and the Soviet Union as the most reliable bulwark against Nazi and Fascist aggression. With the failure of the Popular Front experiment in France, the PCF had retreated into political isolation, criticizing French government policies for alleged economic failures, for the Munich Agreements of September 1938 and for the defeat of the Republicans in the Spanish Civil War. The PCF thus cut themselves off from the SFIO and left-wing Radicals, and from the mainstream of the French nation. The Nazi–Soviet Pact took the PCF leadership by surprise, but *L'Humanité* on 24 August 1939 proclaimed that the Soviet Union was 'at the head of the defence of peace' and urged Britain and France to follow Germany's example by negotiating a non-aggression pact with the Soviet Union. The French government, however, now considered *L'Humanité* to be the propaganda sheet of a regime that had become an ally of Nazi Germany, with which France might soon be at war. The newspaper was therefore banned on 25 August and did not legally reappear until 1944.

Despite claiming that they would support the national defence of France against Nazi aggression, the PCF were now regarded with enormous suspicion, which intensified after the German invasion of Poland on 1 September and the French declaration of war against Germany on 3 September. PCF deputies did vote for war credits on 2 September, but the PCF Central Committee saluted the Soviet Union's invasion of Poland on 17 September as the liberation of the Ukraine and Belarus and demanded that the French parliament should be recalled to examine the Soviet Union's peace proposals. In response, the French government dissolved the PCF and its affiliated organizations on 26 September. On 4 October the leader of the PCF, Maurice Thorez, deserted from the army unit into which he had been called up and slipped into Belgium, to re-emerge in the Soviet Union during the summer of 1940. On 8 October forty other PCF deputies were arrested, while members of the PCF were excluded and suspended from posts in local government, if not arrested as well. The attack launched on 30 November by the Soviet Union against Finland further confirmed the pariah status of the PCF in France. Its newspapers banned, its party and affiliated organizations suppressed, its leader in exile, its parliamentary deputies arrested, its local government office-holders disqualified, its party membership divided, demoralized and drastically reduced in numbers, and its ideological line now a muddled combination of opposition to Hitler and fascism but also opposition to the 'imperialist' war waged by Paris and London against Germany, the PCF entered the Second World War in a shattered state.

Document 8.9 The Proposal for Anglo-French Union (16 June 1940)

At this most fateful moment in the history of the modern world the Governments of the United Kingdom and the French Republic make this declaration of indissoluble union and unyielding resolution in their common defence of justice and freedom against subjection to a system which reduces mankind to a life of robots and slaves.

The two Governments declare that France and Great Britain shall no longer be two nations, but one Franco-British Union.

The constitution of the Union will provide for joint organs of defence, foreign, financial and economic policies.

Every citizen of France will enjoy immediately citizenship of Great Britain, every British subject will become a citizen of France.

Both countries will share responsibility for the repair of the devastation of war, wherever it occurs in their territories, and the resources of both shall be equally, and as one, applied to that purpose.

During the war there shall be a single War Cabinet, and all the forces of Britain and France, whether on land, sea, or in the air, will be placed under its direction. It will govern from wherever best it can. The two Parliaments will be formally associated. The nations of the British Empire are already forming new armies. France will keep her available forces in the field, on the sea, and in the air. The Union appeals to the United States to fortify the economic resources of the Allies, and to bring her powerful material aid to the common cause.

The Union will concentrate its whole energy against the power of the enemy, no matter where the battle may be.

And thus we shall conquer.

Source: W.S. Churchill, The Second World War, *vol. 2,* Their Finest Hour. *London: Cassell & Co. 1949, pp. 183–4*

The Second World War in Europe began with the German invasion of Poland on I September 1939. German blitzkrieg tactics and the Soviet invasion of 17 September achieved the total defeat of Poland by 6 October. Britain and France declared war against Germany on 3 September, but took no effective action to interfere with Germany's Polish campaign. The need for the German army to re-equip and regroup after the Polish campaign, and the onset of winter, led to a pause in the land war. The virtual stand-off known as the phoney war or *drôle de guerre* was shattered by the German invasions of Denmark and Norway on 9 April 1940. Denmark capitulated the following day, but the Norwegians fought on, and British and French troops were landed in Norway between 14 and 17 April. There were some Allied naval successes, and the Allies removed Norway's stock of heavy water, essential for the production of atomic bombs. However, too many strategic points were already in German hands, and Allied air cover was too ineffective, to make a reconquest of Norway possible.

In any case, events in France precipitated the evacuation of Allied troops from Norway by 8 June, and two days later Norway capitulated.

Avoiding the Maginot Line, the Germans invaded The Netherlands, Belgium and Luxembourg on 10 May. Luxembourg was rapidly overrun and the Dutch signed an armistice on 15 May. Meanwhile, German panzer divisions raced through the Ardennes region of Belgium and by 13 May German artillery and dive bombers were pounding French positions on the Franco-Belgian frontier near Sedan. After a three-day battle, the Germans burst through the French lines and raced to the Channel ports via Cambrai and Arras, so as to cut off the British and French forces in Belgium. Thanks to the Dunkirk evacuation (28 May–4 June), approximately 200,000 British troops and 139,000 French were extricated, but the Germans were now able to launch a new offensive deep into French territory. On 14 June German troops entered Paris, which was declared an 'open city' and was not defended by the French.

The rapid and unexpected crumbling of France's military defence, and the mass exodus of millions of civilians fleeing the German advance and clogging up French roads, enveloped the French administration in crisis. The Daladier government had fallen over France's failure to help Finland rather than Poland: on 12 March 1940 the Finns felt obliged to accept an armistice that involved surrendering a considerable amount of Finnish territory to the Soviet Union. This provoked an upsurge of anti-Soviet feeling among French deputies and senators, who began to abstain in crucial parliamentary votes, leading to Daladier's resignation on 20 March and to the formation of a new government under Paul Reynaud two days later. An opponent of appeasement and a friend of de Gaulle and Churchill, Reynaud was reputed to favour a vigorous prosecution of the war. His aim was an all-party coalition government, and he made an unusually large number of appointments (there were twenty-two ministers and eleven under-secretaries). Reynaud himself, though, belonged to the Alliance des Républicains de Gauche, or Alliance of Left-Republicans, a small, moderate conservative party, over half of whose deputies failed to support him. Therefore, he depended upon the SFIO and Radicals. Although Reynaud excluded Léon Blum from his government so as not to alienate conservatives, six members of the SFIO received posts and the party emerged as the one most loyal to the Third Republic. The Radical Party was much less reliable, despite eleven posts going to its members, including Daladier, Chautemps and Sarraut. Daladier, the Radical leader, resented being replaced by Reynaud, insisted on becoming Minister of War and National Defence (a post he had held six times previously) rather than Minister of Foreign Affairs, and successfully opposed de Gaulle's appointment as Secretary of a smaller war cabinet (the future Pétainist, Paul Baudouin, was appointed instead). In the vote approving the Reynaud government, 33 Radical deputies voted for, 10 against and no less than 70 abstained. Overall, 268 deputies voted for, 156 against and 111 abstained, most of the opposition coming from the Right, the centre and a substantial section of the Radical Party. Thus, from the start, Reynaud enjoyed only a slender majority in the Chamber of Deputies, and he had many influential parliamentary opponents such as Georges Bonnet, Pierre-Etienne Flandin and Pierre Laval.

The politically weak Reynaud government was ill-equipped to cope with the disasters overwhelming France. After the initial German breakthrough, on 18 May Reynaud tried to strengthen his government by moving Daladier from War and National Defence to Foreign Affairs and Georges Mandel from Colonies to Interior, and by appointing Pétain as an additional Deputy Prime Minister. The next day Reynaud replaced General Gamelin with General Maxime Weygand, who became Commander-in-Chief of France's armed forces in all theatres of operations. The German advance meanwhile continued relentlessly, so from 10 June politicians and officials fled Paris, first to various châteaux in the Loire and then from 15 June to Bordeaux. By 12 June Weygand was insisting on an armistice, in order to save the French army from total destruction and to prevent any left-wing revolutionary movement from breaking out in Paris or anywhere else in France. A pro-armistice faction quickly emerged, including, besides Weygand, Pétain, Paul Baudouin (since 5 June Under-Secretary of State for Foreign Affairs), Yves Bouthillier (since 5 June Minister of Finance), Admiral Darlan (Minister for the Navy), Jean Prouvost (since 5 June Minister of Information), Colonel Paul de Villelume (head of Reynaud's military staff) and Jean Ybarnegaray (since 10 May Minister of State), who faced only a handful of opponents, notably Mandel, de Gaulle (since 25 May an acting brigadier-general and since 6 June Under-Secretary at the Ministry of War and National Defence) and Roland de Margerie (head of Reynaud's diplomatic staff).

The British government was anxious to stiffen French resistance to the Germans in France, to encourage the French to evacuate forces to French North Africa and continue the war from there, and to prevent the French fleet from falling into German hands. Between 11 and 13 June a series of meetings was held between Churchill and some of his closest advisers and the key members of the Reynaud government. British talk of guerrilla resistance, a Breton redoubt and withdrawal to North Africa was countered by Weygand's complaints about the inadequacy of the British military commitment to France and the failure to devote the entire resources of the RAF to the defence of France. On 13 June Reynaud told Churchill that Weygand wanted to sue for an armistice, possibly in order to shock the British into giving France more aid. Meanwhile, in London Jean Monnet (Chairman of the Anglo-French Co-ordinating Committee) and René Pleven (member of the French Economic Mission in London), together with some British officials, had drawn up a plan for an Anglo-French union. De Gaulle, who had flown to London, presented the plan to Churchill, who accepted it and won over the British cabinet. On 16 June the plan was communicated by Reynaud to twenty-four French government ministers, who rejected it outright. Weygand, informed in advance through the tapping of Reynaud's telephone lines, had energetically campaigned against the proposal before the meeting (Reynaud, 1963, p. 430). At the meeting itself, Pétain allegedly claimed that union with Britain would be like 'fusion with a corpse', while Ybarnegaray argued that it would be better for France to become a Nazi province than a British dominion (Churchill, vol. 2, 1949, p. 187; Spears, vol. 1, 1954, p. 298). Instead, the French government accepted a proposal from Chautemps to explore the terms of a Franco-German armistice. Reynaud then resigned and President Lebrun invited Pétain to form a government. The next day the new government was announced: Chautemps (Deputy Prime Minister), Laval (Foreign Affairs), Weygand (Defence), Darlan (Navy), Bouthillier (Finances), Ybarnegaray (Veterans and the Family) – all leading supporters of an immediate armistice. This government at once began to initiate armistice negotiations.

The proposal for an Anglo-French union was a remarkable document. It envisaged a fusion of the two countries and a pooling of their respective national sovereignties, thus going far further than any previous wartime alliance between two states. If it had been presented earlier, before France's military situation had become so desperate and before the pro-armistice faction had become so powerful, it might have been accepted. But in mid-June 1940 it was dismissed by its French critics as a sinister ploy to turn France into a vassal state of Britain, as a means whereby Britain could take over France's colonial empire, and as a desperate attempt by Britain to keep France in the war. 'If the union proposal had been accepted, the exiled governments of Poland, Czechoslovakia, Belgium, The Netherlands, Luxembourg and Norway might have joined an Anglo-French union, and a European union including Britain might have rapidly developed after the end of the Second World War' (Shlaim, 1974, p. 59). Instead, Jean Monnet and others constructed after 1945 a very different European union, based on a Franco-German partnership and not including Britain until 1973. The French rejection of the Anglo-French union proposal also meant, besides the resignation of Reynaud, the formation of the Pétain government and the negotiation of the Franco-German armistice, the end of an era in Anglo-French relations. Since 1904 the maintenance of the Anglo-French *entente cordiale* had been the cornerstone of the foreign policies of Britain and France. After 16 June 1940, Britain drifted into dependence on the United States, while France turned to collaboration with Germany.

Document 8.10 Pétain's Appeal to the French (17 June 1940)

Frenchmen, at the invitation of the President of the Republic, I am assuming from today the direction of the government of France. Confident in the affection of our admirable army that struggles with a heroism worthy of its long military traditions against an enemy superior in numbers and in arms, confident that by its magnificent resistance it has fulfilled its duties towards our allies, confident in the support of army veterans whom I had the honour to command, I offer to France the gift of my person to lighten her misfortunes.

At this time of sorrow I think of the unfortunate refugees who, in a state of extreme destitution, are on our roads. I express to them my compassion and my concern. It is with a broken heart that I say to you today that we must end the fighting.

I have tonight contacted the adversary to ask him if he is ready to search with us, soldier to soldier, after the struggle and in an honourable way, the means whereby hostilities may be brought to an end. May all Frenchmen fall in behind the government over which I preside during these hard ordeals and keep their anguish silent in order to hear only their faith in the destiny of their country.

Source: M. Ferro, Pétain. *Paris: Fayard. 1987, pp. 85–6*

At the time of the Popular Front, Pierre Laval and others had looked to Marshal Pétain as a potential head of a right-wing government, but Pétain was suspicious of Laval and determined not to act in an unconstitutional manner. However, Pétain once again became an active public figure when on 2 March 1939 he accepted his appointment as French ambassador to the newly victorious Franco regime in Spain. Although lacking any diplomatic training or experience, Pétain was well suited for this post, because of his military prestige, his (nominal) Catholicism and his role in the suppression of the Rif rebellion in Morocco during 1925–6, for which he had been decorated by the Spanish government. While establishing good relations with Franco, Pétain continued to nurture political ambitions, particularly after the outbreak of the Second World War, though he declined to join the goverment of Daladier (11 September 1939). However, on 18 May 1940 Pétain accepted Reynaud's offer that he should become Deputy Prime Minister. From 25 May, overcoming personal rivalries dating back to the First World War, Pétain began to co-operate with Weygand in pressing upon Reynaud the thesis that the Battle for France was lost. At a cabinet meeting on 9 June, just before the government left Paris, Pétain read out a memorandum arguing that the government should now seek an armistice on honourable terms. At subsequent cabinet meetings Pétain persisted with this pro-armistice line, presenting another memorandum on 13 June. This dismissed the proposal of a national redoubt as impractical, insisted that the government should remain on French soil and maintained that an armistice was the essential precondition for the survival of 'eternal France'. In this way Pétain undermined Reynaud and the Reynaud government's will to resist, while at the same time preparing the ground for President Lebrun's invitation to him on 16 June to form a government.

By midnight of 16 June a request had been submitted to the Germans, via the Spanish ambassador (in whom Pétain had confided since the end of May, despite Spain's close ties with Germany), for a cessation of hostilities and for the terms of a Franco-German armistice. Before a German response had been received, and without consulting his government colleagues (apart from Camille Chautemps), Pétain made his radio broadcast at midday on 17 June. His message was a remarkable exercise in spin-doctoring. Addressing just Frenchmen, he began by stressing the 'heroism' and 'magnificent resistance' of 'our admirable army', when in fact the French army was experiencing its greatest military disaster in modern times. He also suggested that the defeat had been inflicted by an enemy superior in numbers and weaponry, and that France's obligations to her ally Britain had been fulfilled. Modern calculations suggest that, in the campaign of May–June 1940, 114 German divisions confronted 94 French, 22 Belgian, 10 British and 9 Dutch divisions, and that the disparities in weaponry between the opposing sides were not very significant, apart from aircraft. As for Britain, on 28 March 1940 the British and French governments had publicly declared that they would not negotiate or conclude an armistice or peace treaty except by common agreement. The phrase about presenting France with the gift of his person suggested an act of disinterested and patriotic personal sacrifice on Pétain's part, while the concerns he expressed for the refugees were an obvious ploy to win popular support and claim the moral high ground. The announcement that fighting should cease and that armistice negotiations had been initiated clearly compromised the French position, since no cease-fire or armistice had yet been agreed by the Germans. Fortunately for Pétain, Hitler was anxious to discourage any further French resistance, to achieve the rapid isolation of Britain, and to check the ambitions of Mussolini, who wanted to advance the Italian frontier to the Rhône and to secure an Italian occupation of Corsica and Tunisia.

On 20 June a French delegation left Bordeaux and met the German negotiators and Hitler the next day in Foch's railway carriage at Rethondes in the forest of Compiègne, thus symbolically re-enacting in reverse the armistice of 11 November 1918. On 22 June the armistice agreement was signed: hostilities ceased on 25 June (when the armistice came into force), the French army was disarmed and demobilized (except for colonial units and a force of 100,000 men subsequently permitted to the French state), the French navy was interned (except for ships guarding France's colonial empire), German prisoners of war and German civilians in French custody were handed over to the German army, German refugees in France and in French-controlled territories were also handed over if wanted by the Germans, French prisoners of war were to remain in captivity until the conclusion of peace, and northern France and a broad swathe of territory down the Atlantic coast to the Spanish frontier came under German occupation, while the remainder of French territory, the non-occupied zone or 'zone nono', became the French state or Etat Français under the Vichy regime of Marshal Pétain.

After negotiating an armistice with Italy on 24 June, by which France accepted a small Italian occupation zone, Pétain made another radio broadcast on 25 June. He again attributed the defeat to Germany's crushing military superiority; he claimed that French honour had been saved; he asserted that to continue the war in France's colonies would mean the sacrifice of French blood in the pursuit of a dream; and he promised a 'new order' based on the 'honest' soil of France ('*la terre, elle, ne ment pas*'), the youth of France and an intellectual and moral recovery. Underlying all this was the assumption that there was no practical alternative to the armistice and to collaboration with Germany, since Germany had won the war and Britain would soon 'have her neck wrung like a chicken' (Churchill, vol. 2, 1949, p. 187). Yet no other government of a European state defeated and occupied by the Third Reich had thrown itself so abjectly into a policy of collaboration with the enemy; and on 18 June de Gaulle presented a very different analysis of France's defeat and a very different response to that defeat.

Document 8.11 De Gaulle's Appeal to the French (18 June 1940)

The leaders who, for many years, have been at the head of the French armies, have formed a goverment.

This government, excusing the defeat of our armies, has established contact with the enemy to end the fighting.

Certainly, we have been, and we are, submerged by the enemy's mechanized force on land and in the air.

To a much greater extent than their numbers, it has been the tanks, the aircraft and the tactics of the Germans that have made us retreat. It has been the tanks, the aircraft and the tactics of the Germans that have surprised our leaders to the extent of bringing them to the position in which they are today.

But has the last word been spoken? Should hope disappear? Is the defeat final? No!

Believe me, speaking to you in the full knowledge of the situation, I tell you that France has not lost everything. The same means that have conquered us can one day be made to win victory.

France is not alone! She is not alone! She has a vast empire behind her. She can form a common front with the British Empire, which commands the seas and continues the struggle. She can, like England, use without limits the immense industrial resources of the United States.

This war is not limited to the unfortunate territory of our country. This war has not been concluded by the Battle of France. This war is a world war. All the mistakes, all the delays, all the suffering do not remove the fact that there are in the world all the necessary means for eventually crushing our enemies. Today overwhelmed by mechanized force, we can conquer in the future by a superior mechanized force. The destiny of the world lies there.

I, General de Gaulle, currently in London, invite all French officers and soldiers who find themselves on British territory or who manage to reach British territory, with or without their arms, as well as engineers and specialist workers in arms industries who find themselves on British territory or who manage to reach British territory, to establish contact with me.

Whatever happens, the flame of French resistance should not be extinguished and will not be extinguished.

Tomorrow, like today, I will broadcast on Radio London.

Source: C. de Gaulle, Discours et messages. *Paris: Plon. 1970, I, pp. 3–4*

De Gaulle's appointment as Under-Secretary of State at the Ministry of War and National Defence on 6 June 1940 was due to his reputation as a military theorist, his close relations with Reynaud, and his achievement (at considerable cost) of minor successes near Laon (17 May) and Abbeville (28 May) as commander of the French Fourth Armoured Division. His appointment displeased Pétain, who thought de Gaulle to be vain and ungrateful, and who nursed a number of personal grudges against him, notably over the publication of a book, *La France et son armée* (1938), which de Gaulle had published as his own work without, in Pétain's opinion, adequately acknowledging Pétain's contribution. Weygand was also hostile to de Gaulle, regarding him as jumped-up, insubordinate, and more of a journalist than an officer, and dismissing his forty-nine-year-old government colleague to Reynaud as 'a child' (Reynaud, 1963, p. 387; Spears, vol. 2, 1954, pp. 85 and 177). These animosities intensified as Pétain and Weygand argued with increasing persistence for an end to hostilities and an armistice, while de Gaulle wanted to fight on, to create a redoubt or defensive position in Brittany, and to evacuate French forces to North Africa so as to carry on the war from there. After the resignation of Reynaud on 16 June, de Gaulle feared his own arrest would be ordered by Weygand and asked Spears and the British ambassador to France for help in escaping to England. With Churchill's permission, during the morning of 17 June Spears and de Gaulle flew in a British plane from Bordeaux to London. That afternoon de Gaulle met Churchill at Downing Street and asked if he could make a radio broadcast, using the facilities of the BBC.

Since their first meeting in London on 9 June, Churchill and de Gaulle had developed a mutual regard, each recognizing in the other a resolute determination to continue the war. De Gaulle had subsequently helped to transport the Norwegian heavy water from France to Britain, supported the proposal for an Anglo-French union, and diverted a ship carrying American military equipment from France to a British port, all of which must have raised him in Churchill's esteem. De Gaulle communicated the draft text of his address to the British war cabinet the next day. Anxious not to destroy what little remained of the Anglo-French alliance, the members of the war cabinet at first considered the proposed broadcast to be undesirable, but Spears persuaded them to change their minds. Therefore, at 10 p.m. that evening, after the briefest of voice-tests (de Gaulle just uttered two words, '*la France*') (Lacouture, 1990, p. 224), de Gaulle made the most famous of what were to be many wartime broadcasts on the BBC.

De Gaulle claimed that France had been overwhelmed, not by German numerical superiority (as Pétain had said), but by German tanks, aircraft and military tactics. It has been calculated that in May 1940 France's north-eastern frontiers were defended by 2,285 French tanks, not counting the tanks of her allies, while the Germans had 2,547 tanks in ten panzer divisions (Doughty, 1985, p. 183). German tanks were generally superior to Allied tanks (in May–June 1940 British light tanks and Bren gun carriers were of little use), and German tank crews were better trained and more experienced than their Allied counterparts. Also, almost half the French tanks were employed in infantry-support roles, while fewer than a quarter were grouped in armoured divisions, two of which were formed in January 1940, the third in April and the fourth (commanded by de Gaulle) in May. Yet German tactics had evolved quite recently, especially in response to the lessons of the Polish campaign of September 1939. 'Although the first three panzer divisions were authorized on 15 October 1935, as late as September 1939 only 1,251 of Germany's 3,195 tanks and nine of her thirty-three tank battalions were in armoured divisions rather than in infantry-support roles' (Kiesling, 1996, p. 158). Statistics on aircraft do not seem to be so readily available, but the Germans certainly established air superiority in the Battle of France with their Messerschmitt fighters and Stuka dive bombers, and through the effective use of radio communications they brilliantly co-ordinated land and air operations. De Gaulle tended to regard Weygand as *le grand coupable*, the man principally responsible for France's military defeat, but that responsibility really lies with General Maurice Gamelin, Weygand's successor as head of the French army's General Staff (9 February 1931), Vice-President of the Superior War Council (21 January 1935), head of the National Defence Staff (21 January 1938), and Commander-in-Chief of Allied forces in France from September 1939 until 19 May 1940. Besides failing to form armoured divisions that could match German panzer divisions, General Gamelin made crucial strategic mistakes in assigning half his army to guard the Maginot Line, which could have been manned effectively with far fewer troops, in allowing France's frontiers with Luxembourg and Belgium to be inadequately defended, and in committing the Allied strategic reserve to an advance into Belgium to the River Dyle, with some French units even reaching Breda in The Netherlands on 11 May. On the other hand, the French were unlucky in that Hitler changed his invasion plans after a German aircraft carrying secret documents had crash-landed in Belgium on 10 January 1940. According to the original German invasion plan, the main thrust of the attack would have been through Belgium north of the Ardennes, a move that Gamelin had predicted. Only after January 1940 was a new invasion plan developed, concentrating on an attack by seven panzer divisions through the Ardennes forest, considered by the French to be unsuitable terrain for tanks. Also, Gamelin was not helped by the unco-operative attitudes of the Belgians and Dutch, who vainly hoped that strict neutrality would preserve their countries from invasion.

France's military defeat, though, was not due just to German tanks, aircraft and military tactics. German army commanders tended to be younger and more flexible than their French counterparts, much more willing to lead from the front, and with much better radio communications at their disposal. Similarly, German soldiers were generally fitter and better trained than their French (and British) opponents. Also, the Allies lacked or failed to use effectively anti-aircraft guns, anti-tank mines and anti-tank weapons to counter German blitzkrieg warfare. There were, in addition, fundamental problems, such as a shortage of skilled men, who were desperately needed both by the armed forces and by the arms industries. The state of French morale is difficult to gauge. Opinion polls suggest a stiffening of French resolve between September 1938 and the summer of 1939: 57 per cent indicated they supported the Munich Agreements, but only 17 per cent opposed a French resort to force to prevent Germany from seizing Danzig (Irvine, 1998, p. 95). Once the war had begun, pacifism had few supporters, yet after the German breakthrough in May 1940 the behaviour of many French servicemen and the exodus of millions of civilian refugees do indicate at least a partial collapse of national morale.

De Gaulle was on firmer ground in his appreciation that the Battle of France was not 'the last word' but rather a serious reverse in what would become a global conflict, and that France could fight on, supported by her own colonial empire, by Britain, the dominions and British colonial territories, and by the immense industrial resources of the United States. He was also correct in predicting that the Germans had no monopoly in the effective use of tanks and air power, and that Germany could be defeated by the same means that had defeated France.

The appeal to French servicemen, engineers and specialist workers in arms industries, who were on or might reach British soil, to rally to de Gaulle represented a crucial step from analysis to action. De Gaulle was just a temporary brigadier-general (and on 25 May 1940 the Pétain government demoted him to the rank of colonel and put him on the retired list), he had served as a junior government minister for just ten days (6–16 June 1940), and he had no government, parliamentary, legal or constitutional authority for making his appeal. Although the Pétain government and the armistice were not sanctioned by any popular vote in France, they seem to have been overwhelmingly accepted by French public opinion, by senior office-holders in all branches of French government service, and by the rump of the French parliament, which voted on 10 July 1940 by a massive majority (468 in favour, 80 against and 20 abstentions) to transfer full executive powers to Marshal Pétain.

De Gaulle claimed to represent the honour and independence of France, but it was an unsubstantiated claim. Significantly, de Gaulle did not emphasize the evil character of the Nazi regime or the need to defend democracy and human rights. In fact, to a considerable extent, de Gaulle, Pétain and Weygand shared the same discourse of honour and independence, though of course they interpreted and applied it very differently. The concluding statement that he would give another radio broadcast the next day demonstrated de Gaulle's own independence of action, for he had not received any prior consent from the British government or the BBC.

Few French listeners heard de Gaulle's appeal on 18 June, and hardly any French newspapers printed extracts from his text. Similarly, by the end of July 1940 only about 7,000 men and a handful of senior officers had rallied to de Gaulle (Shennan, 1993, p. 13), while France's colonial empire remained loyal to Vichy with the exception of some minor Pacific and African territories (including the New Hebrides, the Cameroons, Tahiti, New Caledonia, Gabon). Nevertheless, de Gaulle's appeal of 18 June is one of the most important texts of twentieth-century French history. It planted the only standard of French resistance outside of France. On 21 June about thirty deputies, including Daladier, Mandel and Pierre Mendès-France, embarked on the steamship *Massilia* for Casablanca in French Morocco, but General Noguès, Resident-General of French Morocco, rebuffed proposals from de Gaulle and the British to establish a centre of French resistance in Morocco, detained the *Massilia* passengers and arrested Mandel. The British government therefore recognized de Gaulle on 28 June as 'the head of the Free French': his adventure as 'the man of destiny' had begun.

Document 8.12 The Dunkirk Evacuation and Anglo-French Relations: a French View

France unfortunately carries the heavy responsibility of having in the end followed Great Britain [in declaring war on Germany on 3 September 1939], though not without resistance. But it was England that had the desire for war. It was England that wanted the war, that declared war first, that systematically dismissed all the possibilities of peace – without considering or studying what might be the fate of France in this conflict. The outbreak of war was essentially because London had made the decision. And the defeat of our armies was not due only to the mistakes of our leaders and to the lack of preparation in terms of training and morale of our troops. It was due to the devastating inadequacy of Britain's military assistance. In a word, the defeat and occupation of our country is above all England's fault.

To demonstrate the truth of my assertion, I can easily refer to the evidence of the statements and communications of the government of Marshal Pétain, which have been published in the weeks following the armistice. The glorious soldier of Verdun and his spokesmen, notably M. Baudouin, have informed France how poor in quality and how deficient in quantity was the assistance on land and even in the air provided by England to our country during the war (let us remind ourselves of the statistics: ten British divisions instead of eighty-five in May 1918!). They have said how miserly Britain was in terms of men and equipment, and with what dramatic speed these men and this equipment were re-embarked for England as soon as the military situation became unfavourable. Those of our soldiers who, having carried out the magnificent retreat to Dunkirk, were saved and repatriated have in their turn related appalling examples of English egoism. But all this is current in the French memory. Wherever one turns, one finds the proof of Britain's determination to think only of English interests and to sacrifice our blood, our flesh and our soil to the exclusive profit of the imperialism of London. That was true yesterday as the day before yesterday, as during the entire nineteenth century, and as during previous centuries.

Source: J. Luchaire, Les Anglais et nous: l'action britannique contre la France jusqu'au 13 décembre 1940. *Paris: Éditions du Livre Moderne. 1941, pp. 59–60*

As the impact of the Great Depression, the increasing threat from Nazi Germany and Mussolini's expanding ambitions imposed new strains on Anglo-French relations, so more critical attitudes towards Britain gained currency in France. The French press presented the Anglo-German Naval Agreement of 18 June 1935 as an example of typical British perfidy and hypocrisy, while British policy towards Mussolini's invasion of Ethiopia was interpreted as an attempt to advance British imperial interests in Africa by luring France into a war with Italy. London, many in France believed, dictated French foreign policy over the Spanish Civil War and Czechoslovakia, and was also responsible for France's gradual abandonment of appeasement in 1939. The successful British royal visit to Paris in July 1938, with its emphasis on the sacrifice and unity of the First World War and on shared cultural and moral values, and the participation of the Grenadier Guards and the RAF in the Bastille Parade of 14 July 1939, failed to inject much genuine warmth into Anglo-French relations. When war came on

3 September, significantly the British ultimatum expired at 11 a.m., whereas the French ultimatum expired at 5 p.m., reinforcing the widely held assumption that Britain had dragged France into a war against Germany, contrary to France's national interests. Britain's military commitment to France was then criticized for its alleged inadequacy; and, after the German breakthrough on 13 May 1940, the British government was condemned for withholding the full resources of the RAF, while the Dunkirk evacuation was portrayed as an ignominious betrayal rather than as a miraculous escape.

Such views were given publicity and a historical context by Jean Luchaire. Having begun his career as a journalist with the mass-circulation Paris newspaper *Le Matin*, he became the founder and editor of *Notre Temps*, a review that appeared spasmodically, and at times with French Foreign Ministry subsidies, between June 1927 and July 1939. *Notre Temps*, like several other French publications in the late 1920s such as *L'Europe Nouvelle* and *L'Européen*, supported the League of Nations, European unity and the policies of Aristide Briand. Luchaire at this time also published two pamphlets advocating the creation of a united federal Europe, *Vers L'Union fédérale européenne* (1929) and *De L'Union fédérale européenne à la réforme de l'état français* (1931). During the 1930s Luchaire became more right wing. He developed personal friendships with Pierre Laval and Otto Abetz, a German enthusiast for Franco-German reconciliation who involved Luchaire in the Comité France–Allemagne and subsidized his journal; and he recruited Marcel Déat and Paul Marion (both government ministers under Vichy) as contributors to *Notre Temps*.

After the armistice Luchaire returned to *Le Matin*. Having become anti-Communist, hostile to the Popular Front and critical of the Daladier government, and on foreign affairs anti-Soviet and supportive of Mussolini, Hitler, Franco and Japan, *Le Matin* effortlessly assumed the role of a collaborationist newspaper. With the assistance of Abetz (ambassador of the Third Reich in Paris, August 1940–August 1944), Luchaire in November 1940 launched a Paris evening newspaper, *Les Nouveaux Temps*, which advocated French collaboration with the Nazis and the integration of France into Hitler's new European order. In June 1941 he created an organization representing the French collaborationist press in the occupied northern zone, the Corporation Nationale de la Presse Française, and he also became the director of the Office des Papiers de Presse, which controlled the distribution of newsprint to French newspapers.

The aim of *Les Anglais et nous* was to portray England as the eternal opponent of European unity and as the hereditary enemy of France. Taking a long-term historical perspective, perhaps because his grandfather, Achille Luchaire, had been a distinguished historian of medieval France, Jean Luchaire argued that England or Britain had consistently opposed European unification since the empire of Charlemagne and had been the enemy of France since the Hundred Years War. England/Britain was accused of supporting the French Protestants against Richelieu, stripping France of her principal colonies in the eighteenth century, contributing through her agents to the outbreak of the French Revolution of 1789, fighting against French attempts to unify Europe during the Revolutionary and Napoleonic eras, attempting to thwart French and Italian colonial ambitions in Africa and helping to provoke the First World War. After the First World War, Britain, afflicted with permanent economic and financial decline and increasingly surpassed by the United States, should have worked for the formation of a United States of Europe. Instead, the British clung to their empire and blocked Germany's perfectly justified aim of annexing Danzig and the Polish corridor. Aided by Polish obduracy and the machinations of an immense international Jewish conspiracy, Britain thus sabotaged French efforts to preserve European peace. Once the war had begun, Britain then betrayed France by the feebleness of her military assistance and by the withdrawal of her troops from Dunkirk. In June 1940 the British proposed that the French government should surrender itself by choosing exile in Britain, while the British offer of an Anglo-French union was designed to exploit French weakness so as to make off with her colonial empire.

The British Expeditionary Force in France certainly comprised only ten divisions in May 1940, and those divisions were inadequately equipped. On the other hand, Britain had a large navy, and, without a peacetime conscript army, it took time to form, train and equip a mass army. In May 1940 the BEF staged a fighting retreat to Dunkirk. In the circumstances, this was the only feasible option, though on 25 May the British military commander, Lord Gort, had to order a retreat on his own initiative, without reference to Weygand. The evacuation obviously meant the withdrawal of most British troops from France, but the alternative to evacuation was capture, the fate of the 51st Highland Division. At Dunkirk the French did form the rearguard, most of whom were eventually captured by the Germans. However, of the 338,226 troops evacuated, 139,097 were French, and the British troops evacuated from Dunkirk went on to form new Allied armies, whereas nearly all the French opted for repatriation to France.

As regards the RAF, Churchill did deliberately withhold twenty-five fighter squadrons for the defence of the British Isles; and, particularly after RAF bases in France had been bombed or overrun, many RAF planes had to operate at long range from Britain, which limited their effectiveness. Nevertheless, the RAF lost 931 aircraft in the Battle of France, including 477 fighters, the RAF covered the Dunkirk evacuation quite well and every RAF fighter was soon to be needed in the Battle of Britain. Thus, Luchaire's strictures on Britain's contribution to the Battle of France are unfair, particularly in view of the French initiative in seeking an armistice with Germany. This contravened the Anglo-French mutual commitment not to negotiate or conclude any armistice or peace treaty except by common agreement (28 March 1940) and contrasted with French government condemnation of the capitulation of Leopold III, King of the Belgians, on 28 May 1940.

Yet Luchaire's judgement of and hostility towards Britain were widely shared among his compatriots. For instance, by the end of May 1940 the French were often refusing food to retreating British troops and even to British nurses (Spears, 1954, vol. 1, p. 288, and vol. 2, p. 320). On European unity, an echo of Luchaire's views can be found in the declaration of the National Assembly of 7 July 1940, three days before the deputies voted to bury the Third Republic by voting the transfer of full executive powers to Marshal Pétain: 'We propose to you to reconstruct with enthusiasm a

France integrated into the new Europe' ('*Nous vous proposons de reconstruire dans l'ardeur une France intégrée à la nouvelle Europe*') (Milza, 1997, p. 202). Luchaire personally discredited himself by becoming such a prominent pro-Vichy and pro-Nazi propagandist, by his authority over the French collaborationist newspaper press and by his acceptance of subsidies and favours from the Germans (which earned him the nickname 'Louche Herr'). Following the Liberation, he joined other senior collaborators and Vichy officials in the German castle of Sigmaringen, where he was eventually captured. He was tried for his collaborationist activities, condemned to death and executed (22 February 1946). However, much of what Luchaire stood for – hatred of Britain, enthusiasm for European unity and willingness to collaborate with Germany – remained powerful forces in French politics.

CHRONOLOGY

1924
25 January	Alliance between France and Czechoslovakia
2 October	Adoption by League of Nations of Geneva Protocol for peaceful settlement of international disputes
28 October	French recognition of the Soviet Union

1925
5–16 October	Locarno Conference

1926
10 June	Treaty between France and Romania
2 September	Treaty between Italy and the Yemen

1927
11 November	Franco-Yugoslav Friendship Treaty

1928
28 March	French military service reduced to 12 months
2 August	Italian–Ethiopian Friendship treaty
27 August	Briand–Kellogg Pact renouncing war
14 September	Creation of the French Air Ministry

1929
5 September	Briand proposal at the League of Nations for a United States of Europe
29 December	Funds for construction of Maginot Line voted by parliament

1930
31 March	Outbreak of revolt in Ethiopia

1932
February	French proposal for international police force at Geneva Disarmament Conference

1933

30 January	Hitler appointed German Chancellor
14 October	Withdrawal of Germany from the Disarmament Conference
16 October	Withdrawal of Germany from the League of Nations

1934

26 January	Ten-year non-aggression pact between Germany and Poland
16–17 March	Rome Protocols signed between Italy, Austria and Hungary to form Danubian bloc against the Little Entente (Czechoslovakia, Romania and Yugoslavia)
25 July	Murder of Chancellor Dollfuss in Nazi *putsch* in Vienna
9 October	Assassination of King Alexander of Yugoslavia and Louis Barthou (French Minister of Foreign Affairs) in Marseilles

1935

7 January	Franco-Italian agreement signed by Laval and Mussolini
16 March	Military conscription restored in Germany and disarmament clauses of Treaty of Versailles repudiated
11–14 April	Stresa Conference involving Britain, France and Italy
2 May	Franco-Soviet Mutual Assistance Pact
18 June	Anglo-German Naval Agreement
2 October	Italian invasion of Ethiopia
19 October	Imposition of League of Nations sanctions against Italy
9 December	Hoare–Laval Pact

1936

7 March	German military reoccupation of the Rhineland
9 May	Italian annexation of Ethiopia
17–18 July	Outbreak of the Spanish Civil War
14 October	Ending by Belgium of military alliance with France
31 October	Creation of PSF by Colonel de La Rocque
25 November	Anti-Comintern Pact signed by Germany and Japan

1937

7 July	Outbreak of war between China and Japan
6 November	Anti-Comintern Pact joined by Italy

1938

11–13 March	German annexation of Austria
19–21 July	Visit of King George VI to Paris
27 September	Publication of de Gaulle's *La France et son armée*
28–30 September	Munich Conference on Czechoslovakia
17 December	Franco-Italian Agreement of Marseilles (1935) denounced by Italy

1939

27 February	French recognition of Franco regime in Spain

15–16 March	German occupation of Bohemia, Moravia and Slovakia
21–4 March	Official visit of President Lebrun to London
28 March	German–Polish Non-Aggression Pact (1934) ended by Hitler
31 March	Anglo-French guarantee to Poland
5 April	Lebrun re-elected President of the French Republic
7 April	Italian invasion of Albania
13 April	Britain and France guarantee independence of Romania and Greece
17 May	Military agreement between France and Poland
22 May	Pact of Steel signed by Hitler and Mussolini
23 June	Mutual assistance agreement between France and Turkey
12–21 August	Failure of British and French military missions to Moscow
23 August	Nazi–Soviet Non-Aggression Pact
25 August	Seizure of *L'Humanité*
1 September	German invasion of Poland; general mobilization in France
2 September	Emergency war expenditure voted by French parliament
3 September	Declaration of war by Britain and France on Germany
17 September	Soviet invasion of Poland
26 September	Decree dissolving the PCF and its affiliated organizations
5–10 October	Arrest of PCF deputies
30 November	Soviet invasion of Finland

1940

12 March	Soviet–Finnish armistice
20 March	Resignation of Daladier and formation of Reynaud government
28 March	Franco-British agreement not to negotiate a separate peace or armistice
9 April	German invasion of Denmark and Norway
19 April	Landing of French troops in Norway
10 May	German invasions of The Netherlands, Luxembourg and Belgium
14 May	Capitulation of the Dutch army
18 May	Pétain appointed Deputy Prime Minister
19 May	Weygand appointed Commander-in-Chief in place of Gamelin
28 May	Capitulation of Belgium
28 May–4 June	Dunkirk evacuation
5 June	De Gaulle appointed to government
10 June	Departure of French government from Paris; Italian declaration of war on France and Britain
14 June	Entry of German troops into Paris
16 June	Reynaud replaced by Pétain as head of French government
18 June	De Gaulle's first radio broadcast on the BBC
21 June	Departure of the *Massilia* for Casablanca
22 June	Franco-German armistice
24 June	Franco-Italian armistice
28 June	De Gaulle recognized by British government as the head of the Free French

29 June   Departure of French government from Bordeaux for Vichy
2 July   Convocation of the National Assembly in Vichy
10 July   Vote by National Assembly to transfer full executive powers to Pétain
11 July   Promulgation of the first constitutional acts of the French state; end of the
          Third Republic

BIBLIOGRAPHY

Adamthwaite, A., *Grandeur and Misery: France's bid for power in Europe, 1914–1940*. London: Arnold. 1995.

Alexander, D.W., 'Repercussions of the Breda Variant', *French Historical Studies*, 8 (1974), 459–88.

Alexander, M.S., *The Republic in Danger: General Maurice Gamelin and the politics of French defence, 1933–1940*. Cambridge: Cambridge University Press. 1992.

Aron, R. and Dandieu, A. *Décadence de la nation française*. Paris: Editions Rieder. 1931.

Atkin, N., *Pétain*. London and New York: Longman. 1998.

Bankwitz, P.C.F., *Maxime Weygand and Civil–Military Relations in Modern France*. Cambridge, Mass.: Harvard University Press. 1967.

Bell, P.M.H., *France and Britain, 1900–1940: entente and estrangement*. London and New York: Longman. 1996.

Blatt, J. (ed.), *The French Defeat of 1940: reassessments*. Providence, RI, and Oxford: Berghahn Books. 1998.

Bond, B. and Alexander, M., 'Liddell Hart and de Gaulle: the doctrine of limited liability and mobile defence', in P. Paret (ed.), *Makers of Modern Strategy from Machiavelli to the Nuclear Age*. Princeton, NJ: Princeton University Press. 1986.

Boyce, R. (ed.), *French Foreign and Defence Policy, 1918–1940: the decline and fall of a great power*. London and New York: Routledge. 1998.

Burns, M., *Rural Society and French Politics: Boulangism and the Dreyfus Affair, 1886–1900*. Princeton, NJ: Princeton University Press. 1984.

Cairns, J.C., 'Some Recent Historians and the "Strange Defeat" of 1940', *Journal of Modern History*, 46 (1974), 60–85.

Churchill, W.S., *The Second World War*, vol. 2, *Their Finest Hour*. London: Cassell & Co. 1949.

Doughty, R.A., *The Seeds of Disaster: the development of French army doctrine, 1919–1939*. Hamden, Conn.: Archon Books. 1985.

—— *The Breaking Point: Sedan and the fall of France, 1940*. Hamden, Conn.: Archon Books. 1990.

Dutton, D. (ed.), *Statecraft and Diplomacy in the Twentieth Century: essays presented to P.M.H. Bell*. Liverpool: Liverpool University Press. 1995.

Fauvet, J., *Histoire du Parti Communiste Français*. 2 vols. Paris: Fayard. 1964 and 1965.

Ferro, M., *Pétain*. Paris: Fayard. 1987.

Gaulle, C. de, *Mémoires de guerre*, vol. 1, *L'Appel, 1940–1942*. Paris: Plon. 1954.

Hughes, J.M., *To the Maginot Line: the politics of French military preparation in the 1920s*. Cambridge, Mass.: Harvard University Press. 1971.

Irvine, W.D., 'Domestic Politics and the Fall of France in 1940', in J. Blatt (ed.), *The French Defeat of 1940*. Providence, RI, and Oxford: Berghahn Books. 1998.

Joll, J. (ed.), *The Decline of the Third Republic*. London: Chatto & Windus. 1959.

Jordan, N., *The Popular Front and Central Europe: the dilemmas of French impotence, 1918–1940*. Cambridge: Cambridge University Press. 1992.

Kaufmann, J.E. and Kaufmann, H.W., *The Maginot Line: none shall pass*. Westport, Conn., and London: Praeger. 1997.

Kiesling, E.C., *Arming against Hitler: France and the limits of military planning*. Lawrence: University of Kansas Press. 1996.

Koos, C.A., 'Fascism, Fatherhood, and the Family in Interwar France: the case of Antoine Rédier and the Légion', *Journal of Family History*, 24 (1999), 317–29.

Lacouture, J., *De Gaulle: the rebel, 1890–1944*. London: Collins Harvill. 1990.

Milza, P., *Sources de la France du XIXe siècle*. Paris: Larousse. 1997.

Nobécourt, J., *Le Colonel de La Rocque, 1885–1946, ou les pièges du nationalisme chrétien*. Paris: Fayard. 1996.

Parker, R.A.C., 'Great Britain, France and the Ethiopian Crisis, 1935–1936', *English Historical Review*, 89 (1974), 293–332.

Reynaud, P., *Mémoires*, vol. 2, *Envers et contre nous*. Paris: Flammarion. 1963.

Salerno, R.M., 'The French Navy and the Appeasement of Italy, 1937–9', *English Historical Review*, 112 (1997), 66–104.

Schuker, S.A., 'France and the Remilitarization of the Rhineland, 1936', *French Historical Studies*, 14 (1986), 299–338.

Shennan, A., *De Gaulle*. London and New York: Longman. 1993.

Sherwood, J.M., *Georges Mandel and the Third Republic*. Stanford, Calif.: Stanford University Press. 1970.

Shirer, W.L., *The Collapse of the Third Republic: an enquiry into the fall of France in 1940*. London: The Literary Guild. 1970.

Shlaim, A., 'Prelude to Downfall: the British offer of union to France, June 1940', *Journal of Contempoary History*, 9 (1974), 27–63.

Shore, Z., 'Hitler, Intelligence and the Decision to Remilitarize the Rhine', *Journal of Contemporary History*, 34 (1999), 5–18.

Soucy, R., 'Romanticism and Realism in the Fascism of Drieu La Rochelle', *Journal of the History of Ideas*, 31 (1970), 69–90.

—— 'French Fascist Intellectuals in the 1930s: an old new Left?', *French Historical Studies*, 8 (1974), 445–58.

—— *Fascist Intellectual: Drieu La Rochelle*. Berkeley and Los Angeles: University of California Press. 1979.

—— *French Fascism: the second wave, 1933–1939*. New Haven, Conn., and London: Yale University Press. 1995.

Spears, Major-General Sir E., *Assignment to Catastrophe*. 2 vols. London: William Heinemann Ltd. 1954.

Stone, G., *Anglo-French Relations in the Twentieth Century*. London: Routledge. 1999.

Szaluta, J., 'Marshal Pétain's Ambassadorship to Spain: conspiratorial or providential rise toward power?', *French Historical Studies*, 8 (1974), 511–33.

Thomas, M., 'At the Heart of Things? French imperial defense planning in the late 1930s', *French Historical Studies*, 21 (1998), 325–61.

Thomson, D., *The Proposal for Anglo-French Union in 1940*. Oxford: Clarendon Press. 1966.

Warner, G., *Pierre Laval and the Eclipse of France*. London: Eyre & Spottiswoode. 1968.

Watt, D.C., *How War Came: the immediate origins of the Second World War, 1938–1939*. London: Heinemann. 1989.

Weber, E., *Peasants into Frenchmen: the modernization of rural France, 1870–1914*. London: Chatto & Windus. 1977.

—— *The Hollow Years: France in the 1930s*. London: Sinclair-Stevenson. 1995.

Young, R.J., 'The Aftermath of Munich: the course of French diplomacy, October 1938 to March 1939', *French Historical Studies*, 8 (1973), 305–22.

—— 'The Strategic Dream: French air doctrine in the inter-war period, 1919–39', *Journal of Contemporary History*, 9 (1974), 57–76.

—— *In Command of France: French foreign policy and military planning, 1933–1940*. Cambridge, Mass., and London: Harvard University Press. 1978.

—— *France and the Origins of the Second World War*. London: Macmillan. 1996.

General bibliography

Agulhon, M., *The French Republic, 1879–1992*. Oxford and Cambridge, Mass.: Blackwell. 1993.

Alexander, M.S. (ed.), *French History since Napoleon*. London: Arnold. 1999.

Anderson, R.D., *France, 1870–1914: politics and society*. London, Henley and Boston: Routledge and Kegan Paul. 1977.

Atkin, N. and Tallett, F. (eds), *The Right in France, 1789–1997*. London and New York: I.B. Tauris. 1998.

Azéma, J.-P., *From Munich to the Liberation, 1938–1944*. Cambridge: Cambridge University Press. 1984.

Bellanger, C., *et al.*, *Histoire générale de la presse française*, vol. 3. Paris: Presses Universitaires de France. 1972.

Bernard, P. and Dubief, H., *The Decline of the Third Republic, 1914–1938*. Cambridge: Cambridge University Press. 1985.

Brogan, Sir D., *The Development of Modern France, 1870–1939*. London: Hamish Hamilton. 1967.

Cobban, A., *A History of Modern France*, vol. 3, *1871–1962*. Harmondsworth, Penguin. 1965.

Gildea, R., *France, 1870–1914*. London and New York: Longman. 1996.

Larkin, M., *France since the Popular Front: government and people, 1936–1996*. Oxford: Clarendon Press. 1997.

Magraw, R., *France, 1815–1914*. Oxford: Fontana. 1983.

Mayeur, J.-M. and Rebérioux, M., *The Third Republic from its Origins to the Great War, 1871–1914*. Cambridge: Cambridge University Press. 1984.

McMillan, J.F., *Twentieth-century France: politics and society, 1898–1991*. London: Edward Arnold. 1992.

Thomson, D., *France: Empire and Republic, 1850–1940. Historical documents*. London and Melbourne: Macmillan. 1968.

—— *Democracy in France since 1870*. Oxford: Oxford University Press. 1977.

Tombs, R., *France, 1814–1914*. London and New York: Longman. 1996.

Vinen, R., *France, 1934–1970*. Basingstoke: Macmillan. 1996.

Wieviorka, O. and Prochasson, C. (eds.), *La France du XXe siècle: documents d'histoire*. Paris: Editions du Seuil. 1994.

Zeldin, T., *France, 1848–1945*. 2 vols. Oxford: Clarendon Press. 1973 and 1977.

Index